The Music Trade in Regional Britain, 1650–1800

Music in Britain, 1600–2000

ISSN 2053-3217

Series Editors:
BYRON ADAMS, RACHEL COWGILL AND PETER HOLMAN

This series provides a forum for the best new work in the field of British music studies, placing music from the early seventeenth to the late twentieth centuries in its social, cultural, and historical contexts. Its approach is deliberately inclusive, covering immigrants and emigrants as well as native musicians, and explores Britain's musical links both within and beyond Europe. The series celebrates the vitality and diversity of music-making across Britain in whatever form it took and wherever it was found, exploring its aesthetic dimensions alongside its meaning for contemporaries, its place in the global market, and its use in the promotion of political and social agendas.

Proposals or queries should be sent in the first instance to Professors Byron Adams, Rachel Cowgill, Peter Holman or Boydell & Brewer at the addresses shown below. All submissions will receive prompt and informed consideration.

Professor Byron Adams,
10760 Missouri Avenue, Unit 103
Los Angeles, CA 90025-7625
email: byron.adams@ucr.edu

Professor Rachel Cowgill MBE,
School of Arts & Creative Technologies
Humanities Research Centre, University of York
York, YO10 5DD
email: rachel.cowgill@york.ac.uk

Emeritus Professor Peter Holman MBE,
119 Maldon Road, Colchester, Essex, CO3 3AX
email: peter@parley.org.uk

Boydell & Brewer, PO Box 9, Woodbridge, Suffolk, IP12 3DF
email: editorial@boydell.co.uk

*Previously published volumes in this series
are listed at the back of this volume.*

The Music Trade in Regional Britain, 1650–1800

Edited by
Stephanie Carter and Simon D.I. Fleming

THE BOYDELL PRESS

© Contributors 2025

All rights reserved. Except as permitted under current legislation
no part of this work may be photocopied, stored in a retrieval system,
published, performed in public, adapted, broadcast
transmitted, recorded or reproduced in any form or by any means,
without the prior permission of the copyright owner

First published 2025
The Boydell Press, Woodbridge

ISBN 978 1 78327 794 0

The Boydell Press is an imprint of Boydell & Brewer Ltd
PO Box 9, Woodbridge, Suffolk IP12 3DF, UK
and of Boydell & Brewer Inc.
668 Mt Hope Avenue, Rochester, NY 14620–2731, USA
website: www.boydellandbrewer.com

Our Authorised Representative for product safety in the EU is Easy Access
System Europe – Mustamäe tee 50, 10621 Tallinn,
Estonia, gpsr.requests@easproject.com

The publisher has no responsibility for the continued existence or accuracy of URLs for
external or third-party internet websites referred to in this book, and does not guarantee
that any content on such websites is, or will remain, accurate or appropriate

A CIP catalogue record for this book is available
from the British Library

❧ Contents

	List of Illustrations	vii
	List of Contributors	ix
	Acknowledgements	xii
	List of Abbreviations	xiii
1	London and Beyond: Rethinking a Nation's Trade in Music *Stephanie Carter and Simon D.I. Fleming*	1
2	*Musick's Hand-maid* in Westmorland: A Story of the Music Trade in Early Modern England *Stephanie Carter*	18
3	'Rul'd paper for Musick': How long was the reach of the Playfords? *Robert Thompson*	34
4	The Music Trade in York, 1650–1800: Proprietors and Purchasers *David Griffiths*	49
5	Joseph Barber of Newcastle upon Tyne and William Flackton of Canterbury: Booksellers, Music Publishing and the Subscription Market in Eighteenth-Century Britain *Simon D.I. Fleming*	75
6	Distributing Irish Reprints in England: The Activities of Liverpool's John Bridge Pye *Nancy A. Mace*	99
7	Edward Miller of Doncaster: The Composer and the Music Trade *Christopher Roberts*	129
8	Thomas Underwood and his Successors: The Music Shops of Eighteenth-Century Bath *Matthew Spring*	148
9	Thomas Bewick's Dealings with North-Eastern Musicians, 1770–1800 *Roz Southey*	168

10   Makers, Repairers, Teachers, Dealers and Printers: The Music
     Trade Network in Late Eighteenth-Century West Midlands   190
     Martin Perkins

11   'Quacks in the Musical … Science'? The Curious Case of
     Stephen Moore, Piano Maker, and the Organ of St Paul's Chapel,
     Aberdeen   207
     Simon D.I. Fleming

     Select Bibliography   225
     Index   231

Illustrations

❧ Plates

4.1	A single manual harpsichord with pedal by Thomas Haxby. Image courtesy of York Museums Trust, used with permission, https://yorkmuseumstrust.org.uk/Public Domain.	70
5.1	Charles Avison's *Six Concertos in Seven Parts*, op 2 (1740), Title-page. Image courtesy of the Newcastle Literary and Philosophical Society, used with permission.	79
6.1	Edward Harwood, *Kind God of Sleep … Printed by J.B. Pye* (Liverpool, [*c.*1787]). Reproduced from the original print in Simon D.I. Fleming's collection, GB-DRu Fleming 584.	104
8.1	Lintern's Royal Appointment, *Bath Chronicle*, 24 November 1796. Image courtesy of Bath Record Office, reproduced with permission.	162
8.2	Advertisement for James Mathews' concert, 'The Day: Or, the Camp of Pleasure', *Bath Herald*, 24 March 1792. Image courtesy of Bath Record Office, reproduced with permission.	165
9.1	A concert ticket in the Bewick Collection. Image courtesy of Newcastle City Library, used with permission.	177

❧ Tables

4.1	Music Books in John Hildyard's 1751 catalogue.	53
5.1	Musical works to which John Walsh snr and John Walsh jnr subscribed.	80
5.2	Subscribers of the published works of William Flackton known to have been involved with music or the book trade.	97
6.1	Works published by John Bridge Pye.	106
6.2	Song collections and musical entertainments mentioned in the lawsuit against John Bridge Pye by Anne Bland and Edward Weller.	118

6.3	Individual songs mentioned in the lawsuit against John Bridge Pye by Anne Bland and Edward Weller.	121
7.1	The published music of Edward Miller.	130
7.2	Sellers identified in the subscription list of Edward Miller's *Psalms of David* (1790).	138
8.1	Timeline of Bath music shops, 1740–1800.	150
9.1	Musicians listed in Bewick's records.	170
9.2	Tickets purchased by Matthias Hawdon, and Adam and Alexander Kinlock.	184

The editors, contributors and publisher are grateful to all the institutions and persons listed for permission to reproduce the materials in which they hold copyright. Every effort has been made to trace the copyright holders; apologies are offered for any omission, and the publisher will be pleased to add any necessary acknowledgement in subsequent editions.

Contributors

Stephanie Carter is a Research Associate at Newcastle University, UK, County Editor for the Northamptonshire Victoria County History Trust and Archivist at Carlisle Cathedral. She completed her doctoral thesis at the University of Manchester on late seventeenth-century English music print culture, and has published on music ownership and circulation, the role of the publisher as music editor, and the sale of printed music outside London in *Early Music History*, *The Library* and other publications. Most recently, she has co-edited (with Kirsten Gibson and Roz Southey) *Music in North-East England, 1500–1800* (2020), and contributed an essay on the subscribers of Thomas Mace's *Musick's Monument* (1676) in *Music by Subscription: Composers and their Networks in the British Music-Publishing Trade, 1676–1820*, edited by Simon D.I. Fleming and Martin Perkins (Routledge, 2022). Her present research focuses on the archives at Alnwick Castle, the Sharp Library at Durham Cathedral, the movement of musical goods as recorded in the Exchequer port books (thanks to funding from the Bibliographical Society) and the music trade in early modern England.

Simon D.I. Fleming is a Durham-based musicologist whose research focuses on music in the British provinces during the long eighteenth century. He has recently completed his first monograph: *The Musical World of Charles Avison: Melodic Charm and the Powers of Harmony* (Routledge, 2025). He has been involved in establishing the online *Dataset of Subscribers to Eighteenth-Century Music Publications in Britain and Ireland* and co-edited a multi-author book, *Music by Subscription: Composers and their Networks in the British Music-Publishing Trade, 1676–1820* (Routledge, 2022). Furthermore, he has contributed essays to *Women and Music in the Age of Austen* (Bucknell, 2024), *Data Visualization in Enlightenment Literature and Culture* (Palgrave Macmillan, 2021) and *Music in North-East England, 1500–1800* (Boydell, 2020). His current research involves the establishment of a dataset of music ownership, indexing publications issued in the anglophile world before *c.*1820. Simon's extensive collection of early music prints and manuscripts is held by Durham University Library.

David Griffiths read music at the University of Leeds and librarianship at the University of Sheffield, taking the degrees of BA and MA, respectively. At the University of York his doctoral thesis was written on the subject of institutional music-making in York between *c.*1550 and 1950. He is also a former organist and continuo player, with the A.R.C.O. diploma. David has compiled catalogues of the early printed and music in York Minster Library; written on various aspects of the musical history of York Minster between 1700 and 1860; and has latterly transcribed and edited music by York composers, now published by the York Early Music Press.

Nancy A. Mace is Professor of English, Emerita from the US Naval Academy. She is the author of *Henry Fielding's Novels and the Classical Tradition* (1996) and articles on the eighteenth- and early nineteenth-century British music trade, music copyright and eighteenth-century theatre, which have appeared in the *Papers of the Bibliographical Society of America*, *The Library, Music & Letters, Journal of the Royal Musical Association, Book History, Theatre Survey* and *Philological Quarterly*. She has also contributed essays on eighteenth-century music copyright to *The Research Handbook on the History of Copyright Law* (Elgar, 2016) and on music, copyright and the Stationers' Company Archives for the Adams Matthew digital Stationers' Company Archive database. She is currently working on a history of British music copyright in the late eighteenth and early nineteenth centuries.

Martin Perkins is a scholar, performer and educator with a particular interest in music of the seventeenth and eighteenth centuries. He gained BMus and MA degrees in performance from Royal Birmingham Conservatoire and embarked on a career specialising in early keyboards and continuo. He subsequently gained an MPhil in critical editing from the University of Birmingham and has since published the first modern editions of music by Giovanni Battista Vitali, Barnabas Gunn, John Valentine, Jacchini and Graun. As a director Martin has performed operas by Handel, Lampe, Mozart and Purcell, and has overseen projects to reconstruct passion oratorios by Keiser and Telemann. With his ensemble, the Musical & Amicable Society, he has directed over 70 concerts, many of them featuring first performances of music relating to his research. Their recordings, informed by his research into late eighteenth-century music-making in Britain, led to a dedicated programme as part of BBC Radio 3's *Early Music Show*. More recently he completed a PhD in music-making in the English country house, 1750–1820. Martin is the Head of Historical Performance and Instrument Curator at Royal Birmingham Conservatoire. His organology research has included work on the Historical Instrument Collection of seventeenth- to nineteenth-century wind, brass and keyboard instruments, and digitisation projects.

Christopher Roberts is Head of Music at Benslow Music and has previously held positions at Cambridge Early Music, the National Centre for Early Music in York and the Historically-Informed Summer School. His PhD thesis, awarded by the University of Leeds, explored the musical interests, activities and networks of members of the provincial population in eighteenth-century Yorkshire. He has recently contributed an essay on the Doncaster composer Edward Miller (1735–1807) in *Music in North-East England 1500–1800*, edited by Stephanie Carter, Kirsten Gibson and Roz Southey (Boydell, 2020). In his spare time Chris enjoys composing and playing the harpsichord and cello. His music has been performed by Fretwork on BBC Radio 3, The Clothworkers Consort of Leeds and Leeds Baroque Choir and Orchestra.

Roz Southey is a research associate at Newcastle University. She is the author of *Music-Making in North-East England during the Eighteenth Century* (Ashgate, 2006) and *The Ingenious Mr Avison: Making Money and Music in Eighteenth-Century Newcastle* – a biography of Charles Avison (Tynebridge, 2009). She also co-edited (with Eric Cross) *Charles Avison in Context* (Ashgate, 2018) and (with Stephanie Carter and Kirsten Gibson) *Music in North-East England, 1500–1800* (Boydell, 2020). She has also published articles in *The Consort* and *Early Music* and has given papers at a number of musical and historical conferences; she appeared in *Rule Britannia: Music, Mischief and Morals* (BBC4), and on BBC Radio 3 with Lucie Skeaping in a programme on music in eighteenth-century Newcastle. She is also the author of several novels, including *The Charles Patterson Mysteries* – a crime series featuring a musician-detective in eighteenth-century Newcastle – and a volume of articles on local history in the Lake District, as well as several short stories.

Matthew Spring gained a first-class music BA from Keele University, an MMus in Ethnomusicology from Goldsmith's College London University, and a PhD from Magdalen College, Oxford. Matthew studied lute with Diana Poulton and Jacob Lindberg at the RCM and has published both on lute music and British provincial music. He was a Reader in Music at Bath Spa University and is now Visiting Fellow. He has made over 50 recordings and his recent recording of Scottish lute music from the Balcarres Lute Book is the culmination of a long study of the book and the production of a scholarly edition for the Music of Scotland series. Matthew's solo authored books include: *The Balcarres Manuscript* (2010 AHRC grant) and *The Lute in Britain* (OUP, 2001). Recent book chapters were included in *The Musicians of Bath and Beyond* (Boydell, 2016) and *The Lute in the Netherlands in the Seventeenth Century* (Newcastle, 2015).

Robert Thompson taught at Colfe's School, Lee, London from 1981 until his retirement in December 2014. A member of the Purcell Society committee, he was curator of 'The Glory of the Temple and the Stage', the British Library's 1995 exhibition commemorating the tercentenary of the composer's death, and in 2000, jointly with Robert Shay, published *Purcell Manuscripts: the Principal Musical Sources* (Cambridge, 2000). His edition of Purcell's continuo anthems forms Purcell Society vols. 28 (2020) and 29 (2011).

Acknowledgements

The editors would like to thank Michael Middeke and Crispin Peet of Boydell & Brewer for their patience and support from the beginning. We are also indebted to the two anonymous readers who provided encouraging comments on the project. We are grateful to our contributing authors for writing such varied essays for this collection and for the staff working in the institutions cited in the individual essays for their help in making available resources for this book. We are most grateful to our families for their love and encouragement throughout the project and for putting up with us working through nights, weekends and holidays. Their support enabled us to bring this volume to completion.

Abbreviations

This collection adopts RISM library sigla, as listed here:

GB-A	Aberdeen, University Library
GB-CA	Canterbury, Cathedral Library
GB-Cfm	Cambridge, Fitzwilliam Museum
GB-Ckc	Cambridge, King's College Rowe Music Library
GB-DRc	Durham, Cathedral Library
GB-DRu	Durham, University Library
GB-En	Edinburgh, National Library of Scotland
GB-Enr	Edinburgh, National Records of Scotland
GB-GL	Gloucester, Cathedral Library
GB-Gu	Glasgow, University Library
GB-KENac	Cumbria Archives, Kendal
GB-Lbl	London, British Library
GB-Lna	London, National Archives
GB-Mch	Manchester, Chetham's Library
GB-NWr	Norwich, Record Office
GB-Ob	Oxford, Bodleian Library
GB-Och	Oxford, Christ Church Library and Archive
GB-Y	York, Minster Library

1

London and Beyond: Rethinking a Nation's Trade in Music

Stephanie Carter and Simon D.I. Fleming

Thomas Busby, in his *A Complete Dictionary of Music* (1801), described a music seller as 'not only … dealing in printed music, but likewise all kinds of musical instruments[. It is] an extensive, complex, and mysterious trade, and requires a capital, and a stock of information and experience'.[1] The 'extensive, complex, and mysterious' nature of Britain's commercial music trade is adeptly described in an advertisement by Newcastle-based stationer and music dealer John Atkinson in 1777 as incorporating:

> Stationary Goods of all Kinds; Books of different Sorts … Music, Operas, Songs, Sonatas, Duetts, Solos, Symphonies, Minuets, Country Dances, Single Songs, Books of Instruction for most Instruments, ruled Paper and Books for Music, of various Sorts; All new Music, Songs, &. as soon as published: musical Instruments, &c. viz. Violins, Violoncello, Guittars, French Horns, Trumpets, Hautboys, Clarinets, German Flutes, Common Flutes, Fifes, Pitch Pipes, Mouth Pieces for the easy sounding of German Flutes; best Roman Strings, Violin, Bass and Tenor Bows, Bridges, Mutes, Pegs, Rosin Boxes, Music Desks, Tuning Forks, Hammer for tuning Harpsichords, Wire for ditto, of all Kinds Hautboy and Bassoon Reeds, and every other Article in the musical Way.[2]

Eighty years earlier, music publisher and instrument seller John Carr had advertised 'all sorts of Musical Instruments and Strings, all sorted of Ruled Paper, Ruled Books of all sizes, and all sets of MUSICK, and Single SONGS and TUNES fairly Prick'd'.[3] Throughout the period of this study – 1650–1800 – commercial music traders dealt in a broad range of goods, services and activities to supply Britain's music-making. To the above lists, we can add the sale of manuscript music, binding of music books, trade in preowned musical scores, printing and sale of concert tickets, securing of teachers, soliciting and managing book subscriptions, advertising musical events and the sale of other music-related ephemera. The commercial trade in musical goods and services has continued to underpin the nation's music-making for centuries, and music traders and their retail outlets became part-and-parcel of the high street by the

---

[1] Thomas Busby, *A Complete Dictionary of Music* (London, [1801]).
[2] *Newcastle Chronicle*, 22 June 1771.
[3] *The Banquet of Music* (London, 1692), sig. A1v.

nineteenth century. The likes of Banks of York (which traded between 1756 and 2023), along with numerous retailers in market towns and cities across Britain, were instrumental in serving and supplying customers until the popularity of internet shopping by the 2020s and the ease of downloading music scores online saw an abrupt diminution of their presence. This continuing departure from the high street removes localised hubs where musical knowledge and expertise are shared and exchanged, and risks the loss of accessible points of entry for music learners and lovers, the disappearance of an experienced, skilled workforce and the demise of a central pillar in Britain's cultural history: that of the commercial trading activities, networks and people that have supported the dissemination, circulation and consumption of music across Britain. The essays in this collection set out to shed light upon this aspect of our economic and cultural history, to bring our domestic commercial trade in music to the forefront of national narratives of our musical culture and heritage by shining a spotlight on the people, places and processes that made up its activities and operations.

The mid-sixteenth century to the turn of the nineteenth century witnessed significant changes in mass-market printing technologies, instrument design and invention, legislation, transport links and musical practice. Provincial printing and news media flourished, the culture of public concerts and music clubs arose, the desire for and consumption of music grew and music shops and warehouses opened across the country. The commercial music trade resourced the demand for music and equally encouraged further demand. However, the history of the music trade has long privileged the profession of the musician and the often-multifarious nature of musicians' careers, balancing performance, composition and tuition to varying degrees.[4] Other studies of the trade have tended to investigate individual aspects of its activities separately, such as print production, publishing and instrument-making, with a focus on London and the university towns of Oxford and Cambridge and the largest and most important sellers.[5] Important bibliographical studies provide evidence from newspapers, sales catalogues and advertisements alongside relics of the trade itself in surviving books, manuscripts and instruments.[6] However, there

---

[4] See, for example, Stephen Rose, 'Music in the market-place', in Tim Carter and John Butt (eds), *The Cambridge History of Seventeenth-Century Music* (Cambridge, 2005), 55–87.

[5] Examples include D.W. Krummel, *English Music Printing, 1553–1700* (London, 1975); Jeremy Smith, *Thomas East and Music Publishing in Renaissance England* (Oxford, 2003); Christopher Marsh, *Music and Society in Early Modern England* (Cambridge, 2010); Michael Kassler (ed.), *The Music Trade in Georgian England* (Farnham, 2011); Tessa Murray, *Thomas Morley: Elizabethan Music Publisher* (Woodbridge, 2014); Michael Fleming and John Bryan, *Early English Viols: Instruments, Makers and Music* (London, 2016).

[6] Examples include Cyrus Lawrence Day and Eleanore Boswell Murrie, *English Song-Books 1651–1702* (London, 1940); Charles Humphries and William C. Smith, *A Bibliography of the Musical Works Published by the Firm of John Walsh During the Years 1721–1766* (London, 1968); William C. Smith and Charles Humphries,

is yet in the history of music a study that includes a collective narrative for the commercial trade in musical goods and services. This collection begins to explore what this collective narrative may look like, concentrating on the trading community rather than the consumers, on supply rather than demand, on accessibility, availability and distribution of musical goods and services across the country. It has been made possible by the collaboration of the respective expertise of the editors and contributors across a broad spectrum of research on the music trade. As a mark of this collaboration towards a collective narrative of the trade, the respective contributions of this introductory chapter reflect the different areas of expertise of the editors.

There are a number of reasons why the national scale of commercial trading in musical goods and services has been underestimated, or worse overlooked – including the lack of detailed evidence available for the operations and stock of music sellers and provincial booksellers and the often-multifarious occupations of those working in the trade as (for example) carpenters and mercers. The difficulties in identifying and locating the workforce of the commercial music trade, let alone elaborating on the networks and exchanges of the trade, has justifiably limited the ability of musicologists to recreate a topography of the trade in musical goods in early modern England. However, the purchase of musical goods – instruments, accessories, books, paper – and the availability of associated services (including tuning and copying) were – and still are – a necessary and regular practice connected to the act of making music. As such, the trade in these goods and services has to be included in our narrative around musical practice and consumption in early modern England.

❧ The Music Trade in London

It is no surprise that evidence, however sketchy, for the earliest known traders in musical goods is to be found in London, as the capital had been prominent as a leading European commercial city for centuries. London offered the best supply of resources (skilled craftspeople and the importation of raw materials), customers and regulatory powers and consequently attracted skilled workers from abroad, including Dutch virginal makers, William Treasorer and Lodeuyke Tyves, recorded in 1568.[7] Musical instruments were both exported and imported between London and the Continent, with a trade substantial enough by 1545 for musical goods to be listed in a custom rates book: 'Clarycordes the payre

---

Handel: A Descriptive Catalogue of the Early Editions (2nd edn, Oxford, 1970); Charles Humphries and William C. Smith, *Music Publishing in the British Isles from the beginning until the end of the nineteenth century: second edition with supplement* (Oxford, 1970); Michael Tilmouth, 'A Calendar of References to Music in Newspapers Published in London and the Provinces (1660–1719)', *Royal Musical Association Research Chronicle*, 1 (1961); 2 (1962), 1–15; *RISM Online*, at rism.online; Clifford Bevan (ed.), *Musical Instrument Collections in the British Isles* (Winchester, 1990).

[7] R.E.G. Kirk, *Returns of Aliens in the City and Suburbs of London 1598-1625* (Huguenot Society, 1907), x/iii, 344 and 435.

ii*s*', 'Harp strynges the boxe x*s*.', 'Leute stringes called mynikins the groce xxii*d*.', 'Orgons to playe on the payre ut sint in valore', 'Virginales the payre iii*s*. iiii*d*.' and 'Wyer for clarycordes the pound iiii*d*'.[8] Early music copying and stationery services were available in the 1570s when Nicholas Strogers, a London-based parish clerk, was paid for 'Rulyng of songe bookes'.[9] Only a handful of printed musical items are known to have been printed in London before 1540, although the early use of the technology of printing polyphony from single-impression moveable type demonstrated in Britain in this early period was to revolutionise the printing of music for mass production.[10] It was during this early period that the sale of music paper – that is, sheets of paper with blank printed staves – is first recorded.[11] John Rastell (*c*.1475–1536) is one of the earliest known printers of music in England, and one who demonstrates how music was just one part of a broad, multi-faceted career that went far beyond the realms of printing and publishing – a theme that runs throughout this volume. Rastell operated close to the capital's focal location for the general book trade – St Paul's Cathedral – as did the psalm-book printer John Day from the *c*.1560s and music printer Thomas East in 1588 in Aldersgate Street.[12] The majority of music produced in this first half of the sixteenth century was intended for the local market. As John Milsom observed:

> the limited activities of [London music] printers are of particular interest because their products were apparently created for use by the community, not for export. … those produced by John Rastell and his contemporaries may never have circulated beyond the few square miles of the City of London and its environs. Certainly their use of the English language must have limited their potential usefulness as export items, since English was barely read or spoken beyond Britain's shores.[13]

Despite the limited evidence from Tudor England, the successful request from two royal composers – William Byrd and Thomas Tallis – for exclusive control over printed music paper and music importation suggests that by 1575 there was not only a significant trade in music paper and books but also a distinction between these two areas of the trade.[14] However, financial success from the monopoly on music books was not forthcoming as it was reported in 1582 that the '*paper* is somewhat beneficiall, as for the *musick bookes*, I would not provide

---

[8] *The rates of the custome house bothe inwarde and outwarde* (London, 1545), [13, 22, 27, 32, 45–6].

[9] Lynn Mary Hulse, 'Musical Patronage of the English Aristocracy' (PhD dissertation, University of London, 2013), 325.

[10] John Milsom, 'Songs and Society in Early Tudor London', *Early Music History*, 16 (1997), 235–93, at 237–8.

[11] Iain Fenlon and John Milsom, '"Ruled Paper Imprinted": Music Paper and Patents in Sixteenth-Century England', *Journal of the American Musicological Society*, 37 (1984), 139–63, at 142.

[12] Smith, *Thomas East*, 17; Fenlon and Milsom, '"Ruled Paper Imprinted"', 139.

[13] Milsom, 'Songs and Society in Early Tudor London', 237.

[14] Smith, *Thomas East*, 34.

necessarie furniture to haue them'.[15] By 1598, the later patent-holder Thomas Morley declared the abundance of hand-ruled paper as having undermined the market for printing ruled music paper.[16] The rise of the entrepreneurial music publisher and seller John Playford in the 1650s brought a new approach to the publishing of music aimed at the amateur market no longer controlled by patent holders or master printers. Sitting alongside the general book trade within the area of Fleet Street and St Paul's Churchyard, the shops of John Playford and John Carr at the Temple are some of the earliest known music shops, with Samuel Scott setting up 'at the Miter by Temple-Barr' in the late 1680s and John Hudgebut in Chancery Lane by 1679.[17] A contemporary account provides a lively description of such shops:

> We ... came amongst the music-shops, in one of which were so many dancing masters' 'prentices fiddling and ping bores and minuets, that the crowd at the door could no more forbear dancing into the shop, than the merry stones of Thebes could refuse capering into the walls, when conjur'd from confusion into order by the power of Amphion's harmony. Amongst 'em stood a little red-fac'd blade, beating time upon his counter, as if a Bartholomew Fair consort, with the assistance of a jack-pudding, had been ridiculing an Italian sonetta, and he was prodigally pert in giving his instructions to the rest as a young pedagogue tutoring a discipline in the hearing of his father.[18]

Playford and Carr not only sold printed music books but also offered 'all sorts of Rul'd Paper, and Rul'd Paper Books ready bound up', 'very good Black Ink for Pricking of Musical Lessons', stationery ware and manuscript-copying services as illustrated in Robert Thompson's chapter in this collection.[19] Carr's shop included 'a secretary's office ... for wrighting the theatricall tunes, to accommodate learners and country fiddlers'.[20] Both Playford and Carr published together and must have had a strong working relationship as the former left his business not only to his son but also the latter's son, Robert Carr.[21] Clearly, Playford and Carr's businesses operated in a spirit of co-operation and collaboration alongside competition. Playford advertised 'Choice Violins and other

---

[15] Christopher Barker, Upper Warden of the Stationer's Company, to Sir Robert Cecil. British Library, MS Lansdowne 48, fols 189–94.
[16] Fenlon and Milson, '"Ruled Paper Imprinted", 141.
[17] John Carr, *Vinculum Societatis, Or The Tie of Good Company ... The First Book* (London, 1687), title page; John Hudgebut, *A Vade Mecum* (London, 1679), title page.
[18] Ned Ward, *The London Spy, 1703* (ed.), Kenneth Fenwick (London, 1955), Part I, 15.
[19] John Playford, *Musick's Recreation* (London, 1661); John Playford, *Musick's Delight n the Cithren* (London, 1666); John Carr, *Tripla Concordia* (London, 1675); John Playford, *Choice Ayres and Songs ... The Third Book* (London, 1681); Robert Thompson, 'Manuscript Music in Purcell's London', *Early Music*, 23 (1995), 605–18.
[20] J. Wilson, *Roger North on Music: Being a Selection from his Essays Written during the Years c.1695–1728* (London, 1959), 29.
[21] John Playford, *Choice Ayres, Songs and Dialogues ... The Fifth Book* (London, 1684), 'To All Lovers and Understanders of Musick', sig. A2.

Instruments, also good Strings, are Sold by Mr. Carr, at his Shop',[22] and acted as a broker between customers and traders by providing names of instrument sellers and teachers in London.[23]

Both Playford and Carr demonstrate a theme of increased specialism in the trade during this period, offering music shops as cultural hubs within the capital from which to buy, exchange or loan music, exchange musical knowledge and skills and discover a broad range of music-related services. Further collaboration between members of the commercial music trade can be seen towards the end of the seventeenth century, with instrument-makers and music publishers working in partnership, including Henry Playford and Richard Meares, and John Hare and Barak Norman. The flourishing of a commercially successful music publishing trade in the second half of the seventeenth century, coupled with an increase in the cheaper method of printing by engraved plates that reduced the dependence on a few printers who owned specialist moveable type, saw not only a rise in publishers of music from the late 1680s but also a proactive advertising campaign by instrument-makers as they expanded their range of musical goods for sale.[24] For example, by 1679 John Hudgebut sold:

> all sort of Instruments; as Lutes, Viols, Violins, Harps, Guittars, and Strings of all sorts for the same Instruments: Rechorders, Hoe-boys of all sorts, Flagellets and Castinets; All sorts of Rul'd Paper, and Books for the same Instruments; with new Set of Ayrs for One, Two, Three or Four Parts, and all new Songs whatsoever.[25]

Likewise, Richard Meares was selling 'all sorts of Musical Instruments, Books & songs, with Tunes Rul'd Paper &c.' and Alexander Livingstone stocked 'all sorts of Musical Instruments, Books and Songs, with Tunes String Rul'd Paper &c.' in London by the close of the seventeenth century.[26]

These early music shops were not the sole specialist outlets that we may encounter today and a growing body of evidence suggests that the selling of musical goods was not viable as a single occupation during this early period. The Playfords published and sold non-music books and goods from political and religious tracts to chapbooks and poetry, and from art to 'sympathetical powder'.[27] Similarly, early instrument-makers also worked as carpenters, joiners and tanners, making identification of such individuals particularly

---

[22] John Playford, *The Dancing Master ... The Fourth Edition* (London, 1670), 'Advertisement'.
[23] John Playford, *Introduction to the Skill of Musick* (London, 1664 and 1672); *The Dancing Master* (London, 1670); *A Musicall Banquet* (London, 1651).
[24] Frank Kidson, 'Handel's Publisher, John Walsh, His Successors, and Contemporaries', *The Musical Quarterly*, 6/3 (1920), 430–50.
[25] John Hudgebut, *A Vade Mecum* (London, 1679).
[26] Benjamin Hebbert, 'Three Generations of the Meares Family in the London Music Trade 1638–1749' (MMus dissertation, University of Leeds, 2001), 28–9.
[27] John Playford, *Select Ayres and Dialogues ... The Second Book* (London, 1669); *The Dancing Master* (London, 1670); *Choice Songs and Ayres* (London, 1673).

difficult.[28] Chapters by Stephanie Carter and Simon D.I. Fleming demonstrate how music printers likewise did not restrict themselves solely to music. Most London booksellers engaged in publishing to some degree so it is not surprising that some tried their luck with the market for music notation.[29] The literary-anthology specialist Humphrey Moseley published music books by Henry Lawes and John Gamble in the 1640s and 1650s,[30] and anti-Parliamentarian publisher Henry Brome was the principal publisher for viol-player and theorist Christopher Simpson. Even booksellers who did not try their hand at publishing music notation dealt in musical goods from an early date. London bookseller Henry Bynneman had a large stock of music paper available in his shop in 1583,[31] and two years later both printed and manuscript music were recorded in the Shrewsbury shop stock of London-based trader Roger Ward.[32] Others may have bought and sold music stock: in 1600 an inventory of William Barley's goods included '16 quires of Ruled paper'.[33]

With music books and paper available in general bookshops and the establishment of seemingly specialist music shops in the capital by the mid-seventeenth century onwards, these more formal retail outlets still only represent some of the multitude of ways to sell musical goods and services. Playford used his own home as a point of retail as well as space for private musical gatherings, as did many professional musicians who sought to balance a performance career alongside composing and teaching throughout the period covered by this book. The advent of newspaper advertisements from the late seventeenth century onwards provides a wealth of examples of musicians promoting their multifaceted businesses, offering tuning and repairing of instruments alongside teaching, inviting subscriptions and announcing the publication of their latest printed lessons. Chapters by David Griffiths, Martin Perkins, Christopher Roberts, Carter and Fleming offer multiple examples of the diversification of music traders' portfolios throughout this period. Chapters by Fleming, Griffiths, Perkins and Thompson all demonstrate the additional work particularly carried out by cathedral singing men during the period, including music copying, teaching, tuning instruments, sourcing paper and collecting subscriptions.

---

[28] Christopher Marsh, *Music and Society in Early Modern England* (Cambridge, 2010), 137.
[29] Michael Treadwell, 'London Trade Publishers 1675–1750', *The Library*, 4 (1982), 99–134, at 99.
[30] See, for example, Henry Lawes, *Choice Psalmes* (London, 1648) and John Gamble, *Ayres and Dialogues* (London, 1657).
[31] Mark Eccles, 'Bynneman's Books', *The Library*, 12 (1957), 81–92, at 87.
[32] Items include: '42 singinge psalmes alone', 'i pomand[er] with singinge sphalmes', and 'i Singinge sphalmes gylte' as well as 'i lutinge booke' (possibly an edition of one of Adrian Le Roy's publications), 'i Sitherne booke ruled' (almost certainly a blank ruled manuscript book), and six copies of 'Sorofull songes for sinful sowles' (Hunnis's *Seven Sobs*). Alexander Roger, 'Roger Ward's Shrewsbury Stock', *The Library*, 13 (1958), 247–68; transcribed inventory given at 250–62.
[33] Gerald D. Johnson, 'William Barley, "Publisher & Seller of Bookes", 1591–1614', *The Library*, 11 (1989), 10–46, at 16.

The late seventeenth-century also witnessed an increase in second-hand book sales and auctions, with the former library collections of clergy, academics and gentlemen containing books of music theory and singing psalms.[34] The second-hand market continued as an important element in the trade into the eighteenth-century; for example, Charles Avison bought an 'old Music Book' from Martin Bryson in 1747.[35] Second-hand musical instruments were also available at this time, with John Carr advertising in 1677 chests of viols dating back to 1598 and 1633, respectively. Chapters by Carter, Fleming and Griffiths demonstrate different aspects of the formal and informal second-hand market for music books and instruments, the extent of which has yet to be examined. By the eighteenth century, music teachers were selling new or second-hand instruments, often from their own homes.[36] Whitehaven-based William Howgill even took advantage of his trips to London to secure musical material on behalf of interested clients with orders taken in advance.[37]

At the turn of the century, John Walsh emerged to fill the void left by John Playford at the same time as music printing became dominated by engraving technology and the use of pewter plates with punches.[38] The eighteenth century witnessed an exponential growth in music traders and instrument manufactures with music shops and warehouses across the capital, with London holding an international reputation for the quality of its instruments and the high specialisation and innovation of its makers. The manufacture and sale of instruments was spread across eighteenth-century London.[39] Larger firms developed during this later period with multiple outlets, including Longman and Broderip, who dominated the music trade in the last quarter of the century.[40] Longman and Broderip were major manufacturers of musical instruments;

---

[34] See examples given in Stephanie Carter and Kirsten Gibson, 'Printed Music in the Provinces: Musical Circulation in Seventeenth-Century England and the Case of Newcastle upon Tyne Bookseller William London', *The Library*, 18 (2017), 428–73, at 434–5.

[35] *Newcastle Courant*, 25 April 1747.

[36] Roz Southey, *Music-Making in North-East England during the Eighteenth Century* (Aldershot, 2006), 179.

[37] Simon D.I. Fleming, 'The Howgill Family: A Dynasty of Musicians from Georgian Whitehaven', *Nineteenth-Century Music Review*, 10 (2013), 57–100, at 66.

[38] David Hunter, 'The Printing of Opera and Song Books in England, 1703–1726', *Notes*, 46 (1989), 328–51, at 328; Richard Hardie, '"All Fairly Engraven"?: Punches in England, 1695 to 1706', *Notes*, 61 (2005), 617–33; Michael Tilmouth, 'A Note on the Cost of Music Printing in London in 1702', *Brio*, 8 (1971), 1–3; David Hunter, '"A Note on the Cost of Music Printing in London in 1702" Revisited', *Brio*, 26 (1989), 71–72; Peter Ward Jones and Kelly Domoney, 'The Earliest Surviving Engraved Musical Plates?', in Peter Lynan and Julian Rushton (eds), *British Musicians and Institutions c.1630–1800: Essays in Honour of Harry Diack Johnstone* (Woodbridge, 2021), 240–62, at 240–1.

[39] Jim Bennett, 'Shopping for instruments in Paris and London', in Pamela Smith and Paula Findlen (eds), *Merchants and Marvels* (London, 2002), 370–95, at 372.

[40] Nancy A. Mace, 'The Market for Music in the Late Eighteenth Century and the Entry Books of the Stationers' Company', *The Library*, 10 (2009), 157–87, at 162–3. This

one advertisement, indicating London's importance in the trade in musical instruments, reported that 'LONDON has become as famous for every species of musical instrument, as CREMONA has been for exceeding in *violins*'.[41] Such large businesses continued to offer a broad range of musical goods and services, with Longman and Broderip selling concert tickets alongside their publishing and manufacturing operations.[42]

Other major players during the second half of the eighteenth century include Robert Birchall, Joseph Dale, John Johnson, John Preston and Peter Welcker,[43] operating alongside a plethora of smaller businesses that traded in music alongside non-music goods. For instance, in c.1794 London-based 'Dealer in Music' William Gawler advertised 'Stationary, Stamps &c.' alongside music books and instruments.[44] This later period also witnessed the formation of music circulating libraries, often managed by music publishers and retailers. One of the earliest was established by London music seller and publisher Samuel Babb in c.1770; in 1778, it was claimed to consist of approaching 20,000 music books.[45] By 1786, Babb's stock and circulating library had passed to Joseph Dale when it was reported to have comprised over 100,000 books.[46]

❧ *The Music Trade Beyond London*

There is a growing body of evidence coming to light to indicate that the commercial music trade was far more geographically dispersed, economically significant, culturally broad and available outside London much earlier than has been previously acknowledged. John Bryan and Michael Fleming have demonstrated a trade in musical instruments from the sixteenth century in cultural hubs including Bristol, Chester, Maidstone, Norwich, Salisbury and York[47] and, as early as 1338, one 'Adam of Darlington' was contracted to build an organ at York Minster.[48] To this, we can add sixteenth-century virginal maker Andrew Marsam in Leicester and seventeenth-century organ builders John Loosemore and Thomas Thamar in Exeter and Peterborough, respectively.[49] Many regional

---

figure includes publications issued by Longman and Broderip's successor, Longman, Clementi & Co.

[41] *The Times*, 31 January 1778. Quoted from Jenny Nex, 'Longman & Broderip', in Kassler (ed.), *The Music Trade in Georgian England*, 9–93, at 10.
[42] See, for example, *Oxford Journal*, 27 November 1787.
[43] D.W. Krummel and Stanley Sadie, *Music Printing and Publishing* (New York, 1990), 101–2.
[44] See GB-DRu, Fleming 416.
[45] Humphries and Smith, *Music Publishing*, 58; Alec Hyatt King, 'Music Circulating Libraries in Britain', *The Musical Times* 119/1620 (1978), 134–38, at 134.
[46] Ibid.
[47] Fleming and Bryan, *Early English Viols*.
[48] Stephen Bicknell, *The History of the English Organ* (Cambridge, 1996, rpt 2001), 26.
[49] Donald H. Boalch, *Makers of the Harpsichord and Clavichord 1440–1840* (Oxford, 1974), 107, 111 and 178.

instrument-makers had trade links with those residing in London during this period: the violin-making family of Pamphilons, for instance, were active in rural Essex but their instruments were for sale on London Bridge in the c.1680s.[50] Conversely, London-based traders worked with those outside of the capital: Henry Playford listed a 'Mr. *Dolliff* Bookbinder in *Oxford*' as a supplier of his 1690 sale catalogue,[51] and in c.1695 Playford advertised the sale of all the books contained in his *A General Catalogue of all the Choicest Music-Books in English, Latin, Italian and French, both Vocal and Instrumental* as available for sale 'at his Shop in the Temple Change, Fleetstreet' and also 'in most of the Cities and Publick Places in England, Ireland, and Scotland'.[52]

Chapters by Matthew Spring, Carter, Fleming, Perkins, Roberts and Thompson highlight the important theme of this collection: that of the trading networks and two-way flow of music and musical goods between London and the regions throughout the timespan covered by this book. Thompson also outlines the development of ruled music paper being produced outside London towards 1700 and is joined by Perkins and Spring in identifying the availability of music-copying services in the regions in the eighteenth century. Likewise, Stephanie Carter and Kirsten Gibson have highlighted the sale of printed music in sixteenth-century York and seventeenth-century Newcastle upon Tyne.[53] Their analysis of a sample of surviving inventories of provincial booksellers from the sixteenth and seventeenth centuries reveals the stocking of books containing music notation in smaller market towns by at least the 1580s onwards.[54] Chapters by Carter, Roberts and Thompson further highlight modes of dissemination and distribution of musical goods across the country in the seventeenth and eighteenth centuries. Provincial booksellers and bookbinders were vital components in the dissemination of printed music across the country throughout the period in question but also in the binding and mending of music books and the provision of ruled paper.[55] The York stationer Anthony Foster was paid for binding paper into books ready for 'prickings of songs for the quere' in the 1580s.[56] Chapters by Carter, Fleming, Griffiths, Roberts, Spring and Thompson offer further evidence of regional booksellers trading in music-related goods and the regional printing and publishing of music (some of which was to find its way to London thanks to metropolitan-based music sellers subscribing to these books).

---

[50] John Dilworth, 'Pamphilon, Edward', *Grove Music Online*.
[51] GB-Lbl Harl. MS 5936/419–420.
[52] Henry Playford, *A General Catalogue of all the Choicest Music-Books in English, Latin, Italian and French, both Vocal and Instrumental* ([London: Henry Playford, ?1695]).
[53] Carter and Gibson, 'Printed Music in the Provinces', 428–73.
[54] Ibid., 445 and 448–51; see also, Stephanie Carter's contribution in this volume.
[55] See, for example, the numerous references in surviving trade bills and receipts belonging to the Dean and Chapter of Durham Cathedral. D. Pearson, *Book Trade Bills and Vouchers from Durham Cathedral Library 1634–1740* (Wylam, 1986), [8–12].
[56] Cited in Barnard and Bell, 'Early Seventeenth-Century York Book Trade', [31]7. Original source: York Minster Library, Fabric Rolls, E.3/57–58, fol. 50r.

Outside of London, Oxford and Cambridge during this early period, the printing of books (including music) was limited by the prohibition and control of the Stationers' Company from the mid-sixteenth century onwards. Within the capital itself, the Stationers' Company tried to prevent non-members from printing and selling music books: in April 1687 Humphrey Salter, who had published *The Genteel Companion* (1683) with the instrument seller Richard Hunt, was summoned to explain his printing and selling of music books in St Paul's Churchyard without authority.[57] The Licensing Act (1662) permitted the printing under licence in York until the lapse of this act in 1695 removed restrictions and regional printing began to flourish. Such restrictions to printing did not apply in Scotland, and London-based traders are known to have had business connections extending north. Thomas Vautrollier – printer of William Byrd and Thomas Tallis's inaugural publication *Cantiones sacrae* (1575) – was supplying books to Edinburgh stationers from the 1570s.[58] The 1577 inventory of Edinburgh stationer Thomas Bassadyne includes English psalm books and 'tua Lute bukes'.[59] The earliest known example of music publishing in Scotland is Robert Lekprevik's metrical psalms, issued at Edinburgh in 1564; John Forbes's [*Cantus*] *Songs and Fancies* was printed in Aberdeen in 1662.[60]

In England, there are few examples of music printed outside London and the university towns prior to 1695 – largely due to the legal restrictions but also the limitations in the availability of the specialist music type and the financial risks balancing with commercial success. Following the Licensing Act, Abraham Barber, bookseller and musician in Wakefield, published 'A Book, of Psalmes Tunes in four Parts … with some few directions how to name your notes' in York in 1687.[61] A year earlier, Newcastle-based bookseller John Story had partnered with London counterpart Benjamin Tooke to publish George Stuart's *A Joco-Serious Discourse* including music notation for four songs.[62] These examples suggest that booksellers and musicians outside London considered there to be a large enough audience of musically-literate local customers to ensure a viable return on their financial investment.

More specialist music shops began to emerge outside London towards the close of the seventeenth century, such as Francis Hildyard's shop at the 'Sign of the Bible' in York from 1682 and William Prior's shop at 'the sign of the

---

[57] Donald McKenzie and Maureen Bell, *A Chronology and Calendar of Documents Relating to the London Book Trade 1641–1700*, 3 vols (Oxford, 2005), iii: *1686–1700*, 26.
[58] F.S. Ferguson, 'Relations between London and Edinburgh Printers and Stationers (–1640)', *The Library*, 8 (1927), 146–98.
[59] W. Scott, D. Laing and T. Thomson (eds), *The Bannatyne Miscellany*, 3 vols (Edinburgh, 1836), ii, 191–204, at 199.
[60] David Johnson, 'Music', in Stephen W. Brown and Warren McDougall (eds), *The Edinburgh History of the Book in Scotland, Volume 2: Enlightenment and Expansion 1707–1800* (Edinburgh, 2012), 585–94; Anne Dhu McLucas, 'Forbes' *Cantus, Songs and Fancies* revisited', in James Porter (ed.), *Defining Strains: The Musical Life of Scots in the Seventeenth Century* (Bern, 2007), 269–98.
[61] Humphries and Smith, *Music Publishing in the British Isles*, 63.
[62] George Stuart, *A Joco-Serious Discourse in two Dialogues* (London, 1686).

Musical instruments' in Newcastle from at least 1699.[63] Prior sold music books, instruments and accessories with a sideline in mathematical instruments and artificial teeth.[64] Others, despite being of a different trade, saw opportunity in expanding their activities into the sale of musical wares, such as Newcastle-based clock and watch-maker John Hawthorn whose 1763 advertisement is dominated by music-related goods, including the sale or hire of musical instruments.[65]

Chapters by Griffiths, Perkins, Roberts and Spring demonstrate the growth in music shops as cultural hubs across Britain from the late seventeenth century onwards, with larger music warehouses and music circulating libraries appearing by the second half of the eighteenth century alongside a broader range of retail settings offering musical goods for sale linked with increased conspicuous consumption, including toyshops and early department stores. Some London-based sellers, such as Longman and Broderip, set up temporary shops to profit from this regional trade; in 1789 they established shops for the sale of musical instruments in Brighton and Margate to capitalise on the 'watering season'.[66] Other Londoners moved into the regions to benefit from the growing trade there. Ralph Agutter described himself as a 'Musical-Instrument Maker of London' when in Newcastle in 1712,[67] and a Mr Fairbridge, 'Musical Instrument Regulator … from London' was active in Reading in the 1780s and 1790s.[68] In other places, they developed a close two-way relationship with an existing business, with local sellers becoming agents for London-made instruments, just as metropolitan-based sellers stocked instruments and books created in the regions. The Salisbury-based violin maker Benjamin Banks reputedly sold his instruments in Longman and Broderip's shop;[69] as Fleming notes, Avison had most of his early works printed in Newcastle and made available to consumers in the capital through an agent.[70]

General traders diversified into music to gain a growing share of the market as much as music sellers diversified into other areas to offer customers as much enticement to spend as possible. Traders in music had to work in a spirit of co-operation and collaboration as well as competition, epitomized by the threat of cheap illegal imprints to undercut their profits or quackery in the trade to undermine the specialist skills required. Chapters by Nancy A. Mace

---

[63] Southey, *Music-Making in North-East England*, 220.

[64] *Newcastle Courant*, 1 February 1724.

[65] *Newcastle Courant*, 11 June 1763. For more on Hawthorn, see Roz Southey, 'John Hawthorn's shop at the Head of the Side, near the Post Office', in Colin Coleman and Katharine Hogg (eds), *A Handbook for Studies in 18th-Century English Music*, 24 (2020), 1–44.

[66] Humphries and Smith, *Music Publishing*, 216.

[67] See, for example, *Newcastle Courant*, 7 June 1712.

[68] See, for example, *Reading Mercury*, 12 September 1785.

[69] Jennifer Susan Nex, 'The Business of Musical-Instrument Making in Early Industrial London' (PhD dissertation, University of London, 2013), 88.

[70] Simon D.I. Fleming, *The Musical World of Charles Avison: Melodic Charm and the Powers of Harmony* (Abingdon, 2025), 53.

and Fleming illustrate these types of conflicts within the trading community with dishonest traders seeking to make a profit. Other attempts to monopolise the trade include John Abell's failed attempt following the death of John Playford to revive the patent on music printing from the early decades of the seventeenth century, petitioning the king 'for letters patent for the solo printing and publishing of vocal and instrumental music books'.[71] Roz Southey's chapter offers an additional level to our understanding of the commercial music trade with a North-East case-study examining a trade in goods to service musicians in their trade.

Growth and Expansion

The progression of the music trade in Britain and its growth throughout the period here examined is heavily linked with changes in British society and the improvement of the country's infrastructure. Since the dawn of the music trade, well-established trading routes were used to convey musical goods around the country, but one of the most important developments in the seventeenth and eighteenth centuries was the turnpike system of roads. They made it easier, faster and safer to transport both people and goods across Britain.[72] Road improvements led to a faster and more reliable postal service.[73] Sheet music could be folded and sent as a letter,[74] but it was cheaper and more practical to send musical material in larger quantities. Since there were limits as to the volume of goods that could be sent by a stagecoach, port towns witnessed continual growth as important centres for the consignment of 'bulk carriage' to other parts in Britain and beyond.[75] One of the foremost *entrepôts* was Liverpool, which, by 1800, was coming to challenge London's dominance.[76]

The growth of English-speaking regions outside Britain also helped boost trade in the home country. While the shipping of musical goods abroad is beyond the confines of this collection of essays, the burgeoning global trade in British-made musical goods should be noted as an important element to the commercial trade in the later eighteenth century. One of the largest markets for exported musical wares was North America, where there was a desire to emulate and even match European triumphs.[77] There was also significant

---

[71] McKenzie and Bell, *A Chronology and Calendar of Documents*, iii, 34.
[72] William Albert, 'The turnpike trusts', in Derek Aldcroft and Michael Freeman (eds), *Transport in the Industrial Revolution* (Manchester, 1983), 31–63, at 55.
[73] Susan E. Whyman, *The Pen and the People: English Letter Writers 1660–1800* (Oxford, 2009), 57–8.
[74] Simon D.I. Fleming, 'Sammelband Books of Music: Five Case Studies from the Eighteenth and Early Nineteenth Centuries', forthcoming.
[75] John Feather, *The Provincial Book Trade in Eighteenth-Century England* (Cambridge, 1985), 63.
[76] Gordon Jackson 'Ports 1700–1840', in Peter Clark (ed.), *The Cambridge Urban History of Britain, Volume II: 1540–1840* (Cambridge, 2000), 705–31, at 709.
[77] Nicholas Temperley, *Bound for America: Three British Composers* (Illinois, 2003), 4–5.

trade with British colonies such as the West Indies and India.[78] Exports were not limited to English-speaking regions either, with British pianos heavily marketed in both Germany and Austria.[79] In 1774 John Broadwood exported instruments to Russia, Denmark, Portugal, Italy and France.[80] Businesses also set up relationships with similar enterprises abroad. Walsh cultivated a link with Estienne Roger of Amsterdam, importing the Dutchman's editions and occasionally reusing Roger's plates;[81] Longman and Broderip was in effect the London-based agent of the Viennese music publisher Artaria.[82] Artaria, in return, sold instruments manufactured in Longman and Broderip's workshop.[83]

While the growth in external trading links did help develop the music trade in Britain, much of the growth was fuelled domestically by increases in population size and average wealth.[84] Many, now elevated into the new middle class, had the means and the time to indulge in leisurely pursuits and that included the development of an appreciation of music and the cultivation of some musical skill.[85] This, in turn, led to an increased demand for music, met by a growth in music retail opportunities across the country. Largely unchallenged, other regional towns and cities grew in significance as their populations burgeoned, which, in turn, drew a small but increasing amount of business away from the capital. Chapters by Carter, Fleming, Griffiths, Mace, Perkins, Roberts and Spring demonstrate how important music retailers were to the local and regional consumption of music throughout the period covered by this collection.

By 1800, Edinburgh had become Britain's second centre for the purchase of music-related goods; in third place was the spa town of Bath. The Scottish capital was naturally going to be a major hub, due to the presence of a well-heeled society, which, after the 1707 Act of Union, sought to emulate the musical trends south of the border. Despite the publishing activities of the previous centuries, Scottish music publishing was slow at first but, from the 1720s there developed a growing fashion for Italian music and Scots songs.[86] Many early editions were engraved and printed by Richard Cooper, a Londoner by birth,

---

[78] Ian Woodfield, *Music of the Raj: A Social and Economic History of Music in Late Eighteenth-Century Anglo-Indian Society* (Oxford, 2000), 29–30.
[79] David Rowland, 'Pianos and pianists *c*.1770–*c*.1825', in David Rowland (ed.), *The Cambridge Companion to the Piano* (Cambridge, 1998), 22–39, at 32.
[80] John Broadwood & Sons, www.broadwood.co.uk.
[81] Krummel and Sadie, *Music Printing and Publishing*, 466.
[82] David Wyn Jones, 'From Artaria to Longman & Broderip: Mozart's Music on Sale in London', in Otto Biba and David Wyn Jones (eds), *Studies in Music History presented to H.C. Robbins Landon on his seventieth birthday* (London, 1996), 105–14, at 107–8.
[83] Nex, 'The Business of Musical-Instrument Making', 95.
[84] Peter Razzell, 'The Growth of Population in Eighteenth-Century England: A Critical Reappraisal', *The Journal of Economic History*, 53 (1993), 743–71, at 768–9.
[85] Simon D.I. Fleming, 'The Gender of Subscribers to Eighteenth-Century Music Publications', *Royal Musical Association Research Chronicle*, 50/1 (2019), 94–152, at 104–5.
[86] Johnson, 'Music', 586.

who 'cornered the market' for music publishing for almost half a century.[87] Subsequently Robert Bremner and Domenico Corri, having established themselves in Edinburgh, carved a slice out of the London trade by relocating to the British capital. Both men, however, sought to maintain their place in the Scottish trade; Bremner for instance employed a manager, John Brysson, to manage his Edinburgh shop.[88]

Bath's prominence in the trade was largely due to its popularity as a fashionable resort for health, leisure and recreational diversions, and that included the participation and patronisation of musical activities. Other towns across Britain witnessed growth in the trade as merchants sought to provide music materials for their local markets. Many places still had to rely on the stock of non-specialist booksellers and traders in other fields, but others had enough business to support a specialist shop, in some cases several. An inherent danger was that some towns were not large enough to support multiple competing businesses and so, as Perkins reveals in his contribution to this collection, insolvency could be a real prospect. In a highly competitive market, music sellers became increasingly entrepreneurial in their attempts to stay in profit, evident from Spring's discussion of the spectacle that was Bath's spa season.

The Music Trade in Regional Britain

The chapters contained within this collection deal with various aspects of the commercial trade as it grew and transformed over the period 1650–1800 to underpin the production, consumption and reception of music across Britain. Several chapters focus on regional centres with their own distinct trading characteristics and musical cultures, and as hubs in wider national patterns of circulation and consumption. Griffith's chapter seeks to reconstruct the trade in York in the long eighteenth century, positioning the city's music shops alongside the importance of the local trade in organ building and indicating the importance of the northern cathedral city as a regional hub for music-making activities. Chapters by Perkins and Spring similarly situate the music trade within the context of its locality. Spring's chapter focuses on trading activities in the eighteenth-century spa town of Bath and its uniqueness for its seasonal customer base that encouraged traders to be entrepreneurial in their approach towards the growing commercialisation of leisure with temporary hiring of instruments and teachers and a bespoke manuscript copying service to supply the latest tunes heard by Bath audiences. Perkin's chapter compares the trading activities between the ancient cathedral city of Worcester and the new industrial town of Birmingham, and how diverse trades were within the region of the West Midlands.

A similar thread running throughout the volume is the importance of regional music and non-music retailers for the circulation of music and the

---

[87] Joe Rock, 'Richard Cooper Sr and Scottish Book Illustration', in Brown and McDougall (eds), *The Edinburgh History of the Book in Scotland*, 81–90, at 81 and 85.
[88] Johnson, 'Music', 587.

trading networks by which that circulation was facilitated. Chapters by Carter and Thompson explore the networks and processes by which musical material moved across the country to reach customers far removed from the metropolis. Carter's chapter reconstructs the life of a single copy of John Playford's keyboard tutor book, *Musick's Hand-maid*, through its manufacture and production in London to its distribution for sale in Westmorland in the 1680s. Thompson's chapter examines a wealth of surviving sources to explore the production and distribution of ruled manuscript paper across late seventeenth-century England. Chapters by Fleming and Roberts demonstrate the crucial role of regional retailers in circulating music as agents for book subscriptions. Fleming's chapter places the careers of geographically diverse booksellers – Joseph Barber of Newcastle and William Flackton of Canterbury – within the broader context of contemporaneous subscription lists to reveal the important networks underpinning circulation of printed music books. Roberts' chapter focuses on the subscription list of Doncaster-based composer Edward Miller's *The Psalms of David* (1790) as a means to examine the vital role of the trading community in disseminating music books across Britain. Southey's chapter further explores music retailers through the unusual lens of traders servicing the music trade, with particular focus on the Newcastle-based engraver Thomas Bewick's transactions with North-East musicians. Southey provides a detailed insight into the support Bewick's business gave to the trading in music, from the printing of concert tickets and visiting cards to the production of seals for letters and engraved door plates.

The growth and diversification of the trade in musical goods between 1650 and 1800 undoubtedly brought competition as well as collaboration for traders, whether they were primarily music-specialist retailers and manufacturers or non-specialists seeking to gain a profitable share of the market. Chapters by Fleming and Mace demonstrate the types of misdemeanours of business within this context. Fleming's chapter explores the misleading claims and ultimately damaging work of piano maker Stephen Moore in Aberdeen. Mace's chapter examines the involvement of Liverpool's John Bridge Pye in the importation of unauthorised Irish reprints for resale in late eighteenth-century England and how London-based publishers worked to combat illegal reprints.

The chapters collected in *The Music Trade in Regional Britain, 1650–1800* offer new insights into aspects of the nation's commercial music trade during a time of great technological innovation, development in infrastructure and legislation, escalation in the commercialisation of leisure and the growing desire for and consumption of music. Each essay in this collection begins to map and understand a trade in musical goods and services that made it possible for the dissemination and distribution of musical goods across the country and that underpinned local, regional and national music-making. The growth of leisure and conspicuous consumption is directly linked with the opening of music shops and warehouses across the country during this period. Towards the close of the seventeenth century, we begin to see a merging of two principal aspects of the trade, with instrument-sellers becoming music publishers, undoubtedly largely thanks to the financial viability of engraving technology and the growing vitality of the market.

However, this period is also characterised, on the one hand, by the unerring presence of the general bookselling workforce offering music books and products as part of their broader trade, and, on the other hand, sellers offering non-music books and products alongside their primary trade in music. Just as Aberdeen bookseller Alexander Angus imported prints, drawing books and stationery from London in 1767 alongside printed songs from the capital's last season, music tutor books and 'An Assortment of German Flutes',[89] so Newcastle music dealer Joseph Atkinson sold prints, frames, optical and mathematical instruments and riding canes beside his extensive collection of music.[90] Noting the presence of musical goods and services sitting alongside other trading goods and services encourages us to embed the commercial trade in music into the broader context of the history of a nation's commerce and trade, and the changing circumstances of society in general. By doing so, we not only identify the importance in the commercial trade in music for underpinning the circulation, consumption and practice of music during this period but also understand that this specialist trade was not divorced from other areas of a nation's domestic economy. Taken as a whole, the chapters in this book offer starting points for further research into the people, places and processes involved in the commercial trade of music to contribute to a burgeoning national historiography of British musical life.

---

[89] *Aberdeen Press and Journal*, 5 October 1767.
[90] *Newcastle Chronicle*, 22 June 1771.

2

Musick's Hand-maid in Westmorland: A Story of the Music Trade in Early Modern England

Stephanie Carter

The Lake District, or more specifically Westmorland, was famously described by Daniel Defoe during his tour of Great Britain in the early eighteenth century as:

> a country eminent only for being the wildest, most barren and frightful of any that I have passed over in England, or even in Wales itself.[1]

While this seems a harsh description of today's tourist hotspots of the Lake District and Eden Valley, the topographical contrasts and stark climate of the area must have prevented easy cross-county communication in the seventeenth century.[2] Such a description does not suggest an obvious location for literate, amateur music-making during the early modern period, let alone the sale of printed music. However, 2.5 miles north of Windermere beyond the village of Ambleside stands Rydal Hall, the home of magistrate and bibliophile Sir Daniel Fleming (1633–1701) and his family. Fleming's library, believed to contain *c*.1500 books,[3] was dispersed during the twentieth century.[4] However, the survival of an extensive archive, including his personally compiled library catalogue, book

---

[1] Daniel Defoe, *A Tour Through the Whole Island of Great Britain* (London, 1724; Penguin edition (ed.), Pat Rogers, 1971), 550.

[2] For example, politician Sir Philip Musgrave was absent from London on 31 October 1664 due to 'deep snow' on 'the terrible mountain Stainmore'; he dared not to 'venture on horseback'. *Calendar of State Papers Domestic: Charles II, 1664–5* (London, 1863), 49. See also G. Manley, 'Sir Daniel Fleming's meteorological observations at Rydal, 1689–93', *Transactions of the Cumberland & Westmorland Antiquarian & Archaeological Society*, 77 (1977), 121–26.

[3] 'Sir Daniel Fleming 1633–1701', *Book Owners Online*, at www.bookowners.online.

[4] Nicolas Barker, 'Sir Daniel Fleming, 1633–1701: Magistrate, Antiquary and Book-Collector', *The Library*, 23/2 (2022), 191–205. Further notable scholarship on Fleming includes J.R. Magrath, *The Flemings in Oxford*, 3 vols (Oxford, 1902–24); Scott Sowerby and Noah McCormack (eds), *The Memoirs of Sir Daniel Fleming of Rydal Hall from 1633 to 1688* (Carlisle, 2021); Blake Tyson (ed.), *The Estate and Household Accounts of Sir Daniel Fleming of Rydal Hall, Westmorland* (Carlisle, 2001).

bills and receipts, letters and household accounts,[5] provides not only spectacular insight into the reading and collecting habits of a northern gentleman during the seventeenth century but also rich evidence of multigenerational, familial music-making. Within Fleming's archive is a bookseller's bill from 1679 that details his purchase of *Musick's Hand-maid*, a printed keyboard tutor book published by John Playford. This bill allows an interrogation of the people, places and processes that made it possible for a London-produced music book to be available for sale to a customer in North-West England. By exploring England's domestic commerce in musical goods, the networks underlying such trade and its different components – through manufacturing and production to distribution and retail – it is possible to begin not only to recreate England's topography of the trade in musical goods but to describe the human involvement in music trade activities in early modern England.[6]

The very survival of early modern books and instruments, and references to these objects in archives and sale catalogues, hint at what are now largely invisible trading exchanges of a mostly over-looked economic activity; one that functioned as the essential link between the manufacture of musical goods and the consumption of music. The lack of scholarship in this area to date is undoubtedly due to the dearth of surviving sources concerning the nature of the trade and its workforce.[7] The music trade naturally encompassed a multitude of commercial processes, goods and services including, but not limited to, the manufacture of musical instruments, the printing and publishing of music, the copying of music in manuscript, the distribution networks and sale of goods including instruments and related paraphernal, and the maintenance of instruments and books. Previous studies of the seventeenth-century English music trade have tended to concentrate on the multifarious activities of professional musicians and the role of individual instrument-makers, printers and publishers, with an understandable focus on London as the country's unrivalled centre for the trade.[8] Studies have centred almost exclusively on

---

[5] GB-KENac WDRY/4.
[6] For the trade in continental music goods in England during this period, see D. Krummel, 'Venetian Baroque Music in a London Bookshop: The Robert Martin Catalogues, 1633–50', in O. Neighbour (ed.), *Music and Bibliography: Essays in Honour of Alex Hyatt King* (New York, 1980), 1–27.
[7] For example, only two known pieces of evidence survive relating to the printing and publishing businesses of the wider Playford family, as explored in Frank Kidson, 'The Petition of Eleanor Playford', *The Library*, 7 (1916), 346–52; and Cyrus Lawrence Day and Eleanore Boswell Murrie, 'Playford *versus* Pearson', *The Library*, 17 (1937), 427–47.
[8] See, for example, Stephen Rose, 'Music in the market-place', in Tim Carter and John Butt (eds), *The Cambridge History of Seventeenth-Century Music* (Cambridge, 2008), 55–87; Michael Fleming and John Bryan, *Early English Viols: Instruments, Makers and Music* (London, 2016); D.W. Krummel, *English Music Printing, 1553–1700* (London, 1975); Andrew R. Walkling, 'The Ups and Downs of Louise Grabu', *Royal Musical Association Research Chronicle*, 48/1 (2017), 1–64, especially 49–53; Richard Luckett, 'The Playfords and the Purcells', in Robin Myers, Michael Harris and Giles Mandelbrote (eds), *Music and the Book Trade from the Sixteenth to the*

manuscripts, exploring the identification of music copyists, provenance issues and modes of transmission and circulation.[9] More recently, scholars have begun to explore the ownership and distribution of printed music books.[10] However, little attention has yet been paid to the commercial trade in musical goods that underpinned the circulation, consumption and practice of music during this period. Unusually, though fortuitously for this case-study, not only does the bookseller's bill for Daniel Fleming's music book survive but the very book itself is now held at Glasgow University Library.[11] By tracing the life cycle of Fleming's copy of *Musick's Hand-maid*, this chapter helps to demonstrate the nature of the commercial music trade and its operations – how people

---

Twentieth Century (London, 2008), 45–67; Alon Schab, 'Distress'd Sources? A Critical Consideration of the Authority of Purcell's *Ayres for the Theatre*', *Early Music*, 37 (2009), 633–45; Alon Schab, 'Revisiting the Known and Unknown Misprints in Purcell's *Dioclesian*', *Music & Letters*, 91 (2010), 343–56; Rebecca Herissone, 'Playford, Purcell and the Functions of Music Publishing in Restoration England', *Journal of the American Musicological Society*, 63 (2010), 243–90; Stephanie Carter, 'Music Publishing and Compositional Activity in England, 1650–1700' (PhD dissertation, University of Manchester, 2011); Kirsten Gibson, 'Author, Musician, Composer: Creator? Figuring Musical Creativity in Print at the Turn of the Seventeenth Century', in Rebecca Herissone and Alan Howard (eds), *Concepts of Creativity in Seventeenth-Century England* (Woodbridge, 2013), 63–86; Stephanie Carter, 'Published Musical Variants and Creativity: An Overview of John Playford's Role of Editor', in *Concepts of Creativity*, 87–104; Robert Thompson, 'The Elusive Identity of John Playford', in John Cunningham and Bryan White (eds), *Musical Exchange Between Britain and Europe, 1500–1800* (Woodbridge, 2020), 344–56; Simon D.I. Fleming and Martin Perkins (eds), *Music by Subscription: Composers and their Networks in the British Music-Publishing Trade, 1676–1820* (Abingdon, 2022).

[9] See, for example, Rebecca Herissone, *Musical Creativity in Restoration England* (Cambridge, 2013); Robert Shay and Robert Thompson, *Purcell Manuscripts: The Principal Musical Sources* (Cambridge, 2006).

[10] Andrew Woolley, 'Manuscript Additions to a Copy of John Playford's *Select Musicall Ayres and Dialogues* in the Dolmetsch Library: A Little-known Source of 17th-century English Music', *The Consort*, 66 (2010), 35–53; David Greer, 'Manuscript Additions in Early Printed Music', *Music & Letters*, 72 (1991), 523–35; David Greer, 'Manuscript Additions in "Parthenia" and other Early English Printed Music in America', *Music & Letters*, 77 (1996), 169–82; David Greer, *Manuscript Inscriptions in Early English Printed Music* (Farnham, 2015); Robert Thompson, 'Sources and Transmission', in Rebecca Herissone (ed.), *The Ashgate Research Companion to Henry Purcell* (Farnham, 2012), 13–64; Stephanie Carter, '"yong beginners, who live in the Countrey": John Playford and the Printed Music Market in Seventeenth-Century England', *Early Music History*, 35 (2016), 95–129; Stephanie Carter and Kirsten Gibson, 'Printed Music in the Provinces: Musical Circulation in Seventeenth-Century England and the Case of Newcastle upon Tyne Bookseller William London', *The Library*, 18 (2017), 428–73; Stephanie Carter and Kirsten Gibson, 'Amateur Music Making Amongst the Mercantile Community of Newcastle upon Tyne from the 1690s to the 1750s', in Stephanie Carter, Kirsten Gibson and Roz Southey (eds), *Music in North-East England, 1500–1800* (Woodbridge, 2020), 192–215.

[11] GB-Gu Sp Coll Q.c.88, John Playford, *Musick's Hand-maid* (London, 1678).

and places fit together – to support music-making activities in seventeenth-century England, even in the 'wildest, most barren' corners of the country.

🎵 *Producing Music Books*

In 1663, London music publisher John Playford published the first edition of his printed keyboard tutor book, *Musick's Hand-maid*.[12] Aimed at amateurs, *Musick's Hand-maid* comprises simplified arrangements and 'catchy' tunes; it includes a canon of popular tunes that appeared across Playford's series of beginner instrumental tutor books which Playford undoubtedly had a hand in reworking and rearranging for different instruments.[13] There was clearly interest in the book (known purchasers include Samuel Pepys)[14] and a reprint was advertised in 1673; at least one other edition was published in 1678 and *The Second Part of Musick's Hand-maid* appeared in 1689.[15] Daniel Fleming's book is the second edition issued in 1678, which included instructions 'to play by book', for:

> Many of those that bought of the former Impressions of *Musicks Hand-maid*, were not well satisfied, (especially such who dwelt in the Country remote from an able Master) because she brought not with her some Rules and Directions for playing those Lessons contained therein … For the satisfaction of the aforesaid persons, and likewise for the ease of such Teachers, who account it too much pains to write down all that is necessary for their Scholars, I have in this new Edition adventured to publish the following Instructions.[16]

However, Playford continues to advise the supervision of a teacher: 'having briefly set down these plain and useful Instructions … I doubt not but by putting them in practice, and a little assistance from an able Master, they may in a short time learn to play all these Lessons by Book'.[17] The publisher had personal dealings with individual composers and undoubtedly obtained musical texts from a network of theatre copyists, text authors, orchestral musicians, friends and associates, not to mention musicians and apprentices acting as middlemen providing and assisting with the preparation of musical texts.[18] Such networks

---

[12] Playford had been advertising it as 'shortly to come forth' since 1659. See John Playford, *Select Ayres and Dialogues* (London, 1659), 'A Catalogue of Musick Books'.

[13] Carter, 'Published Musical Variants and Creativity', 87–104.

[14] Carter, '"yong beginners, who live in the Countrey"', 115–16.

[15] In *The Musical Companion* (1673), Playford advertised '*Musicks Handmaid*, presenting choice Lessons for the *Virginals*, newly reprinted in Quarto, with Additions, price stitch'd 2s. 6d.' By 1675, it was priced at 2s. (*The Dancing Master* (London, 1675)).

[16] John Playford, *Musick's Hand-maid* (London, 1678), 'The Preface'. For an initial discussion of Playford's customers, see Carter, '"yong beginners, who live in the Countrey"', 95–129.

[17] Ibid.

[18] Thurston Dart has suggested that London-based virginals teacher Ben Sandley was involved in assembling the contents of *Musick's Hand-maid*. Thurston Dart (ed.), *Musick's Hand-maid* (London, 1969), 'Notes' (unpaginated); Andrew Woolley, 'English

were at the core of the compilation of the contents of Playford's books, but the very construction of the printed book required a much wider network of trade personnel – not all specialising in music. Of course, Playford himself also published non-music books and sold non-musical goods: the production of music, although a small and specialist trade aimed at a niche market, was not divorced from other areas of the nation's trade in goods. A particularly rich example of the secondary trade in goods to support the service of music copying is provided in the court records: a bill in 1675 included 'the prickers dyet … the prickers chamber rent, fire, candle, ruled paper, Inke and pens'.[19]

Production of *Musick's Hand-maid* was probably supervised by Playford in partnership with his chief printer William Godbid, although the printer is not named on the title pages. Little is known of the business dealings between music publisher and printer, including the cost of setting the music type or etching the engraved plates, or of course the cost of printing title pages and preliminaries; nor do we know much about the trade deals for the paper required although Robert Thompson has clearly shown that the cost of paper was paid for by the publisher;[20] presumably the printer paid for the other raw materials: the ink and, in the case of the music pages of *Musick's Hand-maid*, the production of the engraved plates. The printing of music was a specialist skill requiring unique equipment during the type-set era, and the music type itself circulated among a small network of printers: from Thomas East in the 1580s to Thomas Harper in the 1650s, who intermixed leftovers of three different types dating back to the late sixteenth century, and so on to William Godbid and then his widow Anne and John Playford jnr from 1679.[21] The majority of the music pages in *Musick's Hand-maid* are, of course, engraved rather than printed from type (although there are type-set psalm tunes at the end); the engraved plates were probably made of copper at this time – as indicated by the 1689 title page. Although it is not clear who engraved the music pages, the books' frontispiece at least was engraved by one 'Gui:Vaughan', active from at least 1663 and known to have made engravings of animals.[22]

Music printing, either using type or engraving, was not the sole occupation of the printer until later in the century: Godbid, described elsewhere as a 'versatile printer', was also well-known for printing mathematical books and traders' technical books, as his predecessor Harper had done.[23] Equipment in

---

Keyboard Sources and their Contexts, c.1660–1720' (PhD dissertation, University of Leeds, 2008), 27.

[19] Andrew Ashbee, *Records of English Court Music*, 9 vols (Snodland, 1986–96), i, 155.

[20] Robert Thompson, 'Manuscript Music in Purcell's London', *Early Music*, 23 (1995), 605–18, at 608. For a broader study of the trade in paper in early modern Europe, see Daniel Bellingradt and Anna Reynolds (eds), *The Paper Trade in Early Modern Europe: Practices, Materials, Networks* (Leiden, 2021).

[21] Donald W. Krummel, *English Music Printing, 1553–1700* (London, 1975), 61.

[22] London, British Museum, no. 1983, 1001.8.25.

[23] Katherine Hunt, 'Convenient Characters: Numerical Tables in William Godbid's Printed Books', *Journal of the Northern Renaissance*, 6 (2014), at northernrenaissance.org/convenient-characters-numerical-tables-in-william-godbids-printed-books.

his successor John Playford jnr's shop was described in 1686 as 'ready fitted and accommodated with good presses and all manner of letter [sic] for choice works of Musick, Mathematicks, Navigation and all Greek and Latin books'.[24] Music printing was also not isolated from other areas of the general book trade; the supply of raw materials to produce *Musick's Hand-maid* was part of the greater and older trade in paper and stationery wares being imported into London, with such goods made, moved and sold by a large international community including merchants, sailors, papermakers, mould-makers and ink producers across the English Channel.[25] And, as a part of the broader national economic landscape, the music trade was likewise constrained by the multiple variables that affected material productivity ranging from military conflicts through to resource availability, formal rules imposed by political authorities and environmental factors (such as harsh winters). The significant involvement of an interconnected community of traders and distributors of raw materials did not necessitate the detachment of the production of the printed music book from either the broader trade in musical goods and services or the general book trade. Bringing attention to the trade in the materials and services required for the manufacturing of musical goods enriches our understanding of the broader implications of the interconnected economic activities and practices that the consumption and practice of music ultimately relied upon.

✣ *Distributing Music Books*

Most finished products emerging from the printing house or workshop were ultimately destined for a commercial venue, such as the music shops of Playford and John Carr in London. Other bookshops in the capital must have at least been willing to source a music book if they were not a stockist to satisfy the desires of a customer. However, a metropolitan shop was not the only sale point for music books; in fact, the processes and practices for the distribution of musical goods were multifarious within the diverse networks of communication and travel in early modern England. Recent studies have begun to explore the modes of dissemination that enabled consumers to access manuscript and printed music, indicating a broader geographical and social spread of literate

---

[24] Frank Kidson, 'John Playford, and 17th-Century Music Publishing', *The Musical Quarterly*, 4/4 (1918), 516–34, at 533.

[25] Robert Thompson has traced the supply of paper for seventeenth-century music manuscripts in England from France and then Holland. High-quality paper was necessary for music manuscripts, just as for accounts books, drawings, etc. No equivalent study of the paper trade for printed music has been undertaken, although Thompson has explored the paper types for Purcell's *Sonnata's of III Parts* and *The Vocal and Instrumental Musick of the Prophetess* in 'Sources and Transmission', 53–62. See also Robert Thompson, 'English Music Manuscripts and the Fine Paper Trade, 1648–1688', 2 vols (PhD dissertation, King's College, London, 1988); Robert Thompson, 'Paper in English Music Manuscripts: 1620–1645', in Andrew Ashbee (ed.), *William Lawes (1602–1645): Essays on his Life, Times and Work* (London, 1998), 143–54.

music artefacts than has been previously acknowledged.[26] Informal networks of family members, friends, former employees, agents or business contacts, either based in London (ready to oblige a request for purchasing and dispatching a book) or who were visiting London for pleasure or business (and could therefore procure and carry the goods back to the intended recipient), were undoubtedly important in the dissemination of music out from the capital. For example, agents of the Cavendish family located instruments and music books during London visits between 1601 and 1606.[27] Samuel Pepys was asked by his uncle, who lived in Brampton *c*.20 miles north-west of Cambridge, to supply an instrument in 1661:

> Today I received a letter from my Uncle to beg an old fiddle of me for my Cosen Perkin the Miller, whose mill the wind hath lately broken down and now he hath nothing to live but by fiddling – and he must needs have it against Whitsuntide to play to the country girls. But it vexed me to see how my Uncle writes to me, as if he were not able to buy him one. But I entend tomorrow to send him one.[28]

Such networks may have involved music teachers or musicians, supplying instruments or printed music (particularly copies of their own compilations). Bass viol player and teacher John Moss (*d*.1707) self-published his *Lessons for the basse-viol* (1671) in which he addressed his scholars that the book would 'ease myself of so many tedious Transcripts'.[29] Lutenist and Cambridge singing-man Thomas Mace listed names of family members and friends from whom one could obtain a copy of his *Musick's Monument* (1676).[30] Itinerant traders such as chapmen and pedlars spread goods across the country, not just to fairs and markets but to individual households; the singing and selling of ballads is well-known but the sale of printed music, including song books, and manuscript music may well have been among the trade of some street-sellers.[31]

---

[26] Thompson, 'Sources and Transmission'; Carter, '"yong beginners, who live in the Countrey"'; Carter and Gibson, 'Printed Music in the Provinces'.

[27] David C. Price, *Patrons and Musicians of the English Renaissance* (Cambridge, 1981), 18–19.

[28] Robert Latham and William Matthews (eds), *The Diary of Samuel Pepys*, 11 vols (London, 1970–83), ii, 96.

[29] J. Moss, *Lessons for the basse-viol* (London, 1671), 'To his Present and Quondam Scholars'. See Carter, '"yong beginners, who live in the Countrey"', 102–03.

[30] Thomas Mace, *Profit, Conveniency, and Pleasure, to the whole Nation* ([London], 1675), 26. Mace's *Musick's Monument* is the earliest known music book to be published with a subscription list. See Stephanie Carter, 'Thomas Mace and Music in Seventeenth-Century Cambridge', *Journal of Seventeenth-Century Music*, 28/1 (2022), at www.sscm-jscm.org ; 'Thomas Mace's *Musick's Monument* (1676) and his Subscribers in Late Seventeenth-Century England', in Simon D.I. Fleming and Martin Perkins (eds), *Music by Subscription: Composers and their Networks in the British Music-Publishing Trade* (Abingdon, 2022), 21–38.

[31] Although recorded much later in the nineteenth century, four street-sellers were recorded in London selling manuscript music in 1861 with average weekly takings of 4*s*. and 1*s*. 6*d*. average value of stock. Henry Mayhew, *London Labour and the London Poor* (London, 1861), i, 305–09. Mayhew described how this 'piratical' trade '*used to be*

The dissemination of printed music books outside of London was also part of the wider general book trade networks, highlighted by the growing evidence bringing to light the music stocked in provincial bookshops across the country.

There were two options for the transportation of goods during this period: water and road, although in reality domestic transport was an interconnected system of road and water with the latter comprising river navigation and coastal shipping.[32] Water transport was cheap; although slow, it was arguably more reliable particularly for larger consignments, and head ports were centres of collection and distribution serving large inland regions via smaller ports, rivers and land carriage. For example, a 'payer virginalles' was shipped from London to King's Lynn in December 1575, possibly bound for Cambridge.[33] In Hull in the early 1630s, 'one payre of Virginalls' was among various goods onboard a ship bound for London tailor Richard Norris from an Ambrose Losse of York.[34] The shipment of musical wares did not necessitate passage through London, of course: the Earl of Lauderdale (1616–1682) shipped virginals (along with chairs, tables and a billiard table) between his private residences of Ham (Kent) and Edinburgh in 1672.[35] Unfortunately, declared consignments at ports did not include details such as book titles or subjects. For example, between 1673 and 1679, 67 consignments of paper, 29 of books (both bound and unbound), 21 of stationer's wares, five of pasteboard and one of bookbinder's tools were imported into Newcastle upon Tyne from London.[36] However, the two shipments of virginals to Newcastle in the 1670s along with evidence of music stocked in the town's bookshops during this period hint at the transportation of music books by water.[37] Carlisle bookseller, Richard Scott, who was active in the 1650s and 1660s, used ships bound for Newcastle from London followed by

---

more extensively carried on in the streets than it is at present'. Ibid., 305. My emphasis. For ballads, see Christopher Marsh, *Music and Society in Early Modern England* (Cambridge, 2010), 225–87; for itinerant distribution networks, see Jeroen Salman, *Pedlars and the Popular Press: Itinerant Distribution Networks in England and the Netherlands 1600–1850* (Leiden, 2014), 97–165.

[32] T.S. Willan, *The English Coasting Trade 1600–1750* (Manchester, 1938), xi; N.J. Williams, *The Maritime Trade of the East Anglian Ports 1550–1590* (Oxford, 1988), 139. One example of the transportation of an instrument via river and road can be found in 1620 when the Earl of Cumberland paid for an organ to be moved from Lincolnshire to Yorkshire, 'via the Rivers Trent and Ouse and overland'. Lynn Mary Hulse, 'The Musical Patronage of the English Aristocracy, c. 1590–1640' (PhD dissertation, King's College, London, 1992), 114.

[33] Williams, *The Maritime Trade of the East Anglian Ports*, 180.

[34] GB-Lna HCA 13/50, f. 30r. Thanks to Colin Greenstreet for this reference.

[35] Sebastian Pryke, 'The Eighteenth Century Furniture Trade in Edinburgh: A Study based on Documentary Sources' (PhD dissertation, University of St Andrews, 1995), 82. Furthermore, Michael Fleming and John Bryan have demonstrated imports of virginals and viols from the Continent in the 1570s. Fleming and Bryan, *Early English Viols*, 3.

[36] GB-Lna E 190/196/1 and E 190/198/3.

[37] Carter and Gibson, 'Printed Music in the Provinces'.

pack-horse to Carlisle for his book orders, sometimes travelling to Newcastle himself to collect them.[38]

However, book historian James Raven states that 'the most direct means of supplying provincial retailers and customers was by common London pack-horse drivers and wagoners',[39] despite the slow speed of road transport for larger book and paper consignments, and the state of seventeenth-century roads. Certainly, there were areas of the country where the transportation of books by water does not appear to have been viable. The ports on the Cumberland coast, for instance, were not well established at the time, which undoubtedly made Newcastle a more attractive option for Scott in Carlisle. Westmorland's sole port was Milnthorpe, eight miles south of Kendal, but little is known of its imports before the eighteenth century beyond a description by Fleming in 1671 as: 'Here are wines and other commodities brought from beyond the sea, and brought in small vessels'.[40] For Fleming's copy of *Musick's Handmaid*, it is possible that its journey (following a stay in Playford's shop, home or warehouse prior to conveyance north) involved a combination of water and road transport, either via Newcastle or possibly Milnthorpe, particularly as the roads around Kendal were described in 1634 as 'nothing but a most confus'd mixture of Rockes and Boggs'.[41] Similarly, Celia Fiennes described the road from Lancaster to Kendal in 1698 as comprising 'steepe stony hills all like rocks … far worse than the Peake in Darbyshire'.[42] Despite the state of the roads, Kendal bookseller James Cocke preferred the movement of books by land, charging his customers 2*d*. per pound for carriage between London and Kendal.[43] However the book made its way out of London, provincial booksellers certainly had to establish relationships with at least one London bookseller or agent and carrier to negotiate terms and credit to satisfy their northern clientele.

Selling Music Books

The bill dated 19 April 1679 and addressed to Daniel Fleming from Kendal bookseller, James Cocke, included the following item:

> 20th [March 1677/8] 1 Musick's Hand=maid - - 00: 02: 02.[44]

---

[38] Christine Churches, 'Daniel Fleming, Richard Scott and James Cocke: The Making of a 17th Century English Provincial Library' (Honours dissertation, University of Adelaide, 1984), 19.

[39] James Raven, *The Business of Books: Booksellers and the English Book Trade* (New Haven, 2007), 61. Also see Robert Thompson's contribution to this volume.

[40] Quoted in W.T. McIntire, 'The Port of Milnthorpe', *Transactions of the Cumberland & Westmorland Antiquarian & Archaeological Society*, 36 (1936), 34–60, at 34.

[41] GB-Lbl Add. MS 34754, pp. 19–20, quoted in John F. Curwen (ed.), *Records Relating to the Barony of Kendale* (Kendal, 1926), iii, 1–20.

[42] Christopher Morris (ed.), *The Journeys of Celia Fiennes* (London, 1949), 190 and 192.

[43] Churches, 'Daniel Fleming, Richard Scott and James Cocke', 42.

[44] GB-KENac WDRY/4/8/2/3–4, 'Letters and Bills of James Cocke of Kendal, 1666–1700', separate sheet, 'A Note of particules for Daniel Ffleming Esqe As ffolloweth'.

It is not clear whether Cocke stocked music by a matter of course or if the music book was obtained specifically for Fleming, but we can imagine that *Musick's Hand-maid* at least passed through Cocke's bookshop on receipt of the carrier.[45] This information adds to the growing evidence of the importance of provincial booksellers in the trade of musical goods, and the presence of more specialist books, including those with music notation, in the distribution networks between London and regional booksellers in line with the general book trade. The number of music books on a provincial bookseller's shelf was undoubtedly small – the largest contemporary examples are the twelve book titles in William London's Newcastle shop in the 1650s and the eleven book titles in John Foster's York shop in the 1600s – but music books were certainly there.[46]

The sale of printed music and ruled paper in early modern university and cathedral centres and regional cultural hubs such as York, Newcastle, Exeter, Norwich, Durham, Lincoln, Oxford and Cambridge is not unexpected, with the concentration of musicians and clergy forming a ready market.[47] What is perhaps surprising is the availability of printed music in smaller urban centres: Kendal, but also Shrewsbury where Roger Ward was selling both printed and manuscript music in 1585;[48] and possibly even Warrington where Robert Booth stocked 'Ruled paper' in 1648.[49] In Exeter in 1608, a (presumably local) bookbinder was paid 'for bindinge of 12 bookes of Anthemes' for the cathedral there.[50] Such localised booksellers and bookbinders were an important stage in the supply chain of music books and stationery, and hints at a larger provincial commercial trade in musical goods that was not only available in market towns across England but a trade that was much older than we tend to give credit for.[51] Not only were members of the book trade important to the sale of music, but

---

[45] Unfortunately, Cocke's probate inventory of 1685/6 does not include his shop stock. Kendal Library, 'Probate records of the Deanery of Kendal, 1660–1700', microfilm.

[46] For both William London and John Foster, see Carter and Gibson, 'Printed Music in the Provinces'.

[47] Ibid.; Ian Maxted, 'A Common Culture?: The Inventory of Michael Harte, Bookseller of Exeter, 1615', in Todd Gray (ed.), *Devon Documents in Honour of Margery Rowe* (Tiverton, 1996), 119–28; Jennifer Winters, 'The English Provincial Book Trade: Booksellers Stock-lists, c.1520–1640', 2 vols (PhD dissertation, University of St Andrews, 2012), i, 40–7; David Pearson, *Book Trade Bills and Vouchers from Durham Cathedral Library 1634-1740* (Wylam, 1986), [4–11]; Andrew Clark (ed.), *The Life and Times of Anthony Wood*, 5 vols (Oxford, 1891), i, 211 and 237.

[48] Alexander Roger, 'Roger Ward's Shrewsbury Stock', *The Library*, 13 (1958), 247–68.

[49] W.H. Rylands, 'Booksellers and Stationers in Warrington, 1639 to 1657, with the Full List of the Contents of a Stationer's Shop There in 1647', *Transactions of the Historic Society of Lancashire and Cheshire*, 37 (1888), 67–115.

[50] Ian Payne, *The Provision and Practice of Sacred Music at Cambridge Colleges and Selected Cathedrals c.1547–c.1646* (New York, 1993), 74; Exeter Cathedral Archives D&C 3553 (10 Sept. 1608).

[51] This trade also included musical instruments. For example, a sackbut was bought at Clitheroe (Lancashire) in 1612. David George (ed.), *Records of Early English Drama: Lancashire* (Toronto, 1991), 172; Lancashire Record Office DDKs 18/8 p. 155.

other non-specialist traders dealt with musical goods as well. For example, the Durham mercer, alderman and virginal-owner John Farbeck (*d*.1597) stocked 'virginall wyer' among psalm books, paper and 'best parchment' in his shop.[52] Further examples hint at the trade networks between provincial and metropolitan counterparts: Newcastle bookseller William Corbett, whose shop inventory included 'psalmes in foure p[art]es' in 1626 was in debt to 'John Wright', 'John Maigaite' and 'John Grisman[d]' of London at his death.[53] Richard Scott of Carlisle ordered books from 'his friend' in London and gave orders for directing post to certain booksellers in London when he was there.[54]

What is also worthy of note is the relationship between individual customers and booksellers. Fleming collected books on divinity, law, education, history and antiquarian scholarship alongside more unusual books on science, technology and contemporary poetry and fiction. Between 1656 and 1665, Fleming bought books from Carlisle bookseller Richard Scott, during which time he not only expected Scott to anticipate his wishes but knew titles that had been published before the bookseller: 'As to what you write concerning Hugh's *Grant Abridgement*, the third part, and *The Epitome of all the New Acts* since his Majesties Restoration, tho' they bee not yet extant, yet I know this terme will produce them, which made mee write for them to have them with your first'.[55] News spread between London and those living in the regions through informal networks of communication, ensuring that those residing in the country were not intellectually isolated.[56] Printed book catalogues were also important sources for new titles: Fleming used Newcastle-based William London's *Catalogue of the Most Vendible Books* when compiling a list of books worth buying.[57] Scott and Fleming's relationship was delicate,

---

[52] William Greenwell (ed.), 'Wills and Inventories from the Registry of Durham, Part II', *Surtees Society*, 38 (1860), 281–3.

[53] GB-DRu DPR/I/1/1626/C7/1. See also *William Corbett's Bookshop*, at www.corbettsbookshop.omeka.net. John Grisman (or Gridmond) was a London bookseller, printer and type-founder between 1618 and 1638, and John Wight snr was an active bookseller in London between 1605 and 1658. See R.B. McKerrow (ed.), *A Dictionary of Printers and Booksellers in England and Ireland and of Foreign Printers of English Books, 1557–1640* (London, 1910), 118; Henry R. Plomer, *A Dictionary of Booksellers and Printers who were at Work in England, Scotland and Irland from 1641 to 1667* (London, 1907), 197.

[54] Churches, 'Daniel Fleming, Richard Scott and James Cocke', 15.

[55] Letter quoted in Ibid., 7.

[56] F.J. Levy, 'How information spread among the gentry, 1550–1640', *Journal of British Studies*, 21/2 (1982), 11–34, at 18.

[57] William London, *A Catalogue of the Most Vendible Books in England* (London, 1657). Photograph of first page of Fleming's 'Books worth buying' provided between pages 8 and 9 of Churches, 'Daniel Fleming, Richard Scott and James Cocke'. For more on London's catalogue, see Carter and Gibson, 'Printed Music in the Provinces' and Margaret Schotte, '"Books for the Use of the Learning and Studious": William London's *Catalogue of Most Vendible Books*', *Book History*, 11 (2008), 33–57.

with Fleming suspicious from the beginning of Scott inflating his prices due to a lack of clarity in the latter's bills; Scott repeatedly tried to explain his 1d. per shilling profit margin to cover shipping charges, box costs and porter hire.[58] Scott extended credit to Fleming, supplied shoes, gloves and groceries alongside books and stationery, and sent his client unordered books with the hope of a purchase. On the other hand, Fleming returned books he had specifically ordered, requested credit for such returns and reduced prices for imperfect books.[59] From 1665 Fleming changed his allegiance to James Cocke, bookseller in Kendal, whose bills are itemised with the individual book titles alongside carriage and 1d. per shilling profit margin. The Cocke family sold stationery, cloth and medicines alongside books, and acted as an agent for local subscriptions to prospective London publications.[60]

The price of 2s. 2d. for Fleming's copy of *Musick's Hand-maid* is 4d. lower than all of Playford's advertisements for this book between 1679 and 1690, suggesting that Cocke sold *Musick's Hand-maid* to Fleming at the wholesale price available to the bookseller.[61] Cocke gave costings of binding and carriage separate to the books themselves.[62] Fleming's copy survives as a stitched, uncut copy in a worn, contemporary marbled paper wrapper. This appears to be the original condition of the book with no evidence for the more substantial calf binding typical of Fleming's books[63] – suggesting that this was the typical condition of music books emerging from the printer's workshop ready for customers' individual binding requirements. Certainly, it is probable that Fleming bought a new copy of *Musick's Hand-maid*; however, it is worth noting the existence – and importance – of the second-hand market within the commercial trade of musical goods. Numerous sales catalogues of private libraries, where book collections were to be sold at auction, have survived from the Restoration onwards and include listings of printed and manuscript music.[64] In London, John Playford was known for exchanging and loaning books, and John Carr appears to have dealt in second-hand instruments; such dealings were familiar aspects of the wider bookshop trade.[65] Evidence for such dealings outside London is rare; although Fleming helpfully obliges us with a few details pertaining to what appears to be the procurement of two second-hand keyboard instruments:

---

[58] Magrath, *The Flemings in Oxford*, i, 102.
[59] Churches, 'Daniel Fleming, Richard Scott and James Cocke', 17 and 23–33.
[60] Ibid., 34–40.
[61] Between 1679 and 1691 (from 1689 described as 'the First Part') Playford advertised the 1678 edition for sale at 2s. 6d. For further contemporary pricing, see fn 15.
[62] Churches, 'Daniel Fleming, Richrd Scott and James Cocke', 42.
[63] 'Sir Daniel Fleming 1633–1701', *Book Owners Online*.
[64] See examples in Carter and Gibson, 'Printed Music in the Provinces, 434–5.
[65] Carter, 'Music Publishing and Compositional Activity in England, 1650–1700', 45. For the general book trade, see Robert D. Hume, 'The Economics of Culture in London, 1660–1740', *Huntington Library Quarterly*, 69 (2006), 487–533, at 500.

1668 … Oct. 10. Paid to Mrs. Carlile for my Lady Mary, beeing for Ketty's many-cords £1 6s. 0d.

…

[1670] Mar. 18. Item, Spent in goeing to Warcupp for the harpsicalls 1s. 6d.[66]

Fleming's daughters Katherine ('Ketty') and Alice were taught both 'the harpsicalls and manicords'.[67] The former owner of the 'many-cords' (clavichord) appears to be Lady Mary Fletcher, the sister-in-law of Fleming's wife, demonstrating the less formal commercial trade in second-hand musical instruments within wider family circles. It is possible that the harpsichord was also obtained through family connections. Warcop, now a sleepy village between Appleby and Kirkby Stephen, was important for its medieval bridge over the River Eden and had a large cattle fair and horse fair in the seventeenth century.[68] There is no evidence for the manufacture or sale of instruments at Warcop, and Fleming's accounts suggest only the cost of moving the instrument was paid. Exploring the history of Warcop itself, it seems more likely that Fleming received the instrument, perhaps as a gift, from a member of his extended family: Warcop Hall had been owned by the second sons of Ambleside's Braithwaite family since 1590, and the contemporary owner Richard Braithwaite and Daniel Fleming were cousins. Fleming was a godfather to Braithwaite's third son in 1666 and both were named as supervisors in the will dated 1674 of Thomas Braithwaite of Ambleside.[69]

Fleming's accounts indicate that the purchasing of an instrument or musical wares, whether new or previously owned, was not the only route to becoming an owner; gifts and inheritance would have undoubtedly played a significant part in procuring musical goods. However, even such gifts involved additional outlay – such as carriage – and are subsequently part of a much broader understanding of the commercial trade in music. Such a trade included not only bookshop personnel but merchants and other non-specialist traders. By at least the eighteenth century, music teachers were also part of the trade in musical goods, including the sale of new and second-hand instruments.[70]

---

[66] Historical Manuscripts Commission, *The Manuscripts of S.H. Le Fleming, Esq., of Rydal Hall* (London, 1890), 378 and 380. 'Lady Mary' may refer to Mary Fletcher, who was married to Fleming's brother-in-law, George Fletcher.
[67] Ibid., 381.
[68] Cumbria County History Trust, 'Warcop', at www.cumbriacountyhistory.org.uk.
[69] Magrath, *The Flemings in Oxford*, i, 428. GB-KENac WD TE/UB 104. A letter survives, written at Warcop by Richard Braithwaite to Daniel Fleming dated 5 May 1695 concerning the horse militia. GB-KENac WDRY/5/4807.
[70] Roz Southey, *Music-Making in North-East England during the Eighteenth Century* (Aldershot, 2006), 179.

❦ *Consuming Music Books*

The delivery of *Musick's Hand-maid* from Cocke to Fleming sees the completion of the journey of the printed music book from production, distribution and sale to a customer but not the full extent of its life cycle which includes consumption. At Rydal Hall, the music book would have been used alongside other musical goods and services that formed the broader commercial music trade that underpinned the musical activities of both amateurs and professionals in early modern England. As such, it seems sensible to place the narrative of Fleming's *Musick's Hand-maid* within the broader context in which it found itself: the multi-generational music-making activities of the Fleming family.

Alongside the acquisition of keyboard instruments in 1668 and 1670, a 'William Hutchinson' features regularly in the account books from 1670 onwards described as a music master and 'Virginal-master', teaching Fleming's daughters Katherine, Alice, Barbara and Mary.[71] By 1678, on the arrival of the keyboard book, Hutchinson was teaching the three younger daughters.[72] *Musick's Hand-maid* thus appears to have been used for how Playford originally intended it: as a complement to lessons with a music teacher. Unfortunately, there are no annotations or signs of use on Fleming's copy beyond the signature 'Dan[iel]: Fleming' on the title-page and typical library catalogue markings – including a 'P' on the titlepage – found in Fleming's books.[73] The book certainly did not replace the teacher: Hutchinson remained a frequent visitor to Rydal for twenty years, with references in the accounts from 1685 including payments to Hutchinson for 'Tuneing yᵉ Virginals'.[74]

Hutchinson's move from teacher to tuner demonstrates a diversification by musicians during this period to safeguard their employment beyond the years teaching the daughters of a household. Music teachers sat alongside instrument-makers and joiners employed to mend, tune and even alter instruments, just as local booksellers and binders were engaged to finish books to the customer's particular requirements or to mend, re-bind or add paper. For example, local booksellers and binders were employed by the Dean and Chapter of Durham Cathedral for 'mending and putting paper' into anthem books, binding 'four books for the organ and quire' and supplying 'large ruled paper' in the 1690s.[75] At Norwich in 1591/2, 5s. was paid 'for makyng a new Trumpet of old peces'.[76] In contrast, by 1648, scientist and philosopher William Petty encouraged the education of children to include 'some gentile Manufacture'

---

[71] GB-KENac WDRY/4/7/8.
[72] Historical Manuscripts Commission, *The Manuscripts of S. H. Le Fleming*, 392.
[73] J. McL. Emmerson, 'Dan Fleming and John Evelyn: Two Seventeenth Century Book Collectors', *Bibliographical Society of Australia and New Zealand Bulletin*, 27 (2003), 48–61.
[74] See, for example, GB-KENac WDRY/4/7/8, f. 220.
[75] Pearson, *Book Trade Bills and Vouchers from Durham Cathedral Library*, [8–12].
[76] Norfolk Record Office, Norwich Chamberlain's Accounts 18.a, fol. 110v.

including 'Making Musicall Instruments'.[77] In 1676 Thomas Mace likewise suggested lute repairs could be undertaken 'by your self, or by your own Directions to any Country Work-man'.[78]

The Fleming family's engagement with music extended beyond the typical education expected of a gentleman's daughters. Fleming's wife, Barbara (d.1675), had been a pupil of Edward Lowe in Oxford in the late 1640s: a lost manuscript book included a letter dated 25 March 1652 from Lowe to his pupil requesting she:

> play thes [sic] Lessons in the Order sett downe Constantly once a day, if you have health and leasure. Play not, without turning the Lesson in your Booke before you & keepe your eye (as much as you can) in your Booke. If you Chance to miss goe not from the Lesson, till you have perfected it. Above all, Play not too fast. Thes few rules observed you will gaine your selfe much Honnour & some Creditt to your master.[79]

Music also extended beyond the women of the family: Fleming sent his son Henry to Oxford in 1678 with a collection of books including 'The Reading & singing Psalmes, &c'.[80] Fleming's extensive catalogue of books written in his own hand includes 'A singing of Psalms', 'Psalter ... But, with notes how to sing them ... sung by Turns ... Divided into 5. Books' and 'A Psalter in Verse, (very ancient)'.[81] As for Daniel Fleming himself, evidence of his own engagement with music is provided in his commonplace book, dated 1650–1661, where he recorded song texts including the ballad 'We'll go no more to the old Exchange'.[82] Other lyrics written in his hand give a sense of the young man's humour, including a mock-song by John Wilson dedicated to the privy that begins 'Let other buttockes have ye power'.[83] Fleming appears to have been an archetypal law student during his short stay at Gray's Inn, London, in 1653.[84] There we can imagine Fleming wandering down Chancery Lane to frequent John Playford's music shop by the Temple Church; Fleming bought two copies of the 'English-Dancing-Maister' between February and June 1653.[85] In August, he recorded visiting the 'Musicke-house', presumably referring to the music house at the Mitre, near St Paul's.[86]

---

[77] W[illiam] P[etty], *The Advice of W.P. to Mr. Samuel Hartlib For The Advancement of some particular Parts of Learning* (London, 1647), 6.

[78] Thomas Mace, *Musick's Monument* (London, 1676), 55–61.

[79] Magrath, *The Flemings in Oxford*, i, 541; Mary Chan, 'Edward Lowe's Manuscript British Library Add. MS 29396: The Case for Redating', *Music & Letters*, 59/4 (1978), 440–54, at 440–1.

[80] GB-KENac WDRY/5/2035.

[81] Ibid., WDRY/4/8/2/9.

[82] Ibid., WDRY/4/1/2, f. 123. For further song texts, see ff. 36v, 133v–134r and 140.

[83] Ibid., f. 37.

[84] C.B. Philips, 'Fleming, Sir Daniel', *Oxford Dictionary of National Biography*.

[85] Magrath, *The Flemings in Oxford*, i, 46 and 57. Fleming's accounts presumably refer to John Playford's *The English Dancing Master* (London, 1650–).

[86] Magrath, *The Flemings in Oxford*, i, 62.

❧ Conclusion

Fleming's copy of *Musick's Hand-maid* and accompanying bookseller's bill allows us to tease out a thread in the complex ecology of the commercial trade in musical goods in early modern England. It suggests a specialist trade whose community did not operate cohesively but rather relied on complex networks of related trades interconnecting at different points of the product's journey, operating in a spirit of co-operation and collaboration as well as competition, and existing at local, regional, national and international levels. Trading in musical goods at whatever level does not appear to have been viable as a sole occupation during this period – even the central figure of John Playford published and sold non-music books and products. Local booksellers continued their important role as conduits of music books supporting amateur music-making activities well into the eighteenth century. For customers in Kendal in the 1730s, for instance, bookseller and publisher of the *Kendal Weekly Courant* Thomas Cotton advertised the sale of 'Paper, Ink, and other Stationary Ware, Song Books and Ballads'.[87] The distribution network of printed music appears to have been largely dependent upon the preferences of the bookseller and their customers rather than the presence of cohesive music trade networks undoubtedly due to the small, specialist trade and market demand.

By tracing the journey of Fleming's copy of *Musick's Hand-maid*, this case-study hints at a cultural and intellectual vibrancy to northern and regional England in the early modern period which was far from the caricatured view we have inherited from Daniel Defoe and others. This chapter demonstrates not only that amateur music-making was happening in remote corners of northern England but that there were complex, economically viable commercial trade networks that underpinned literate music-making activities across early modern England.

---

[87] GB-KENac WDY/657.

3

'Rul'd paper for Musick': How long was the reach of the Playfords?

Robert Thompson

Hand-made and hand-ruled manuscript paper sometimes offers useful evidence about the music written upon it as well as the context in which sources were created.[1] In seventeenth-century England, the availability of commercially produced manuscript paper contributed to a cultural change apparent both in the success of instruction books such as Playford's *Introduction to the Skill of Music* and in the variety of material created for and by amateur as well as professional musicians.[2]

English manuscript sources of the later seventeenth century normally display a remarkable degree of standardisation.[3] Their paper is sourced from specific areas, and stave ruling is normally applied by practised hands using multi-stave compound rastra.[4] Formats are usually confined to folio, in which a single complete sheet of paper creates two leaves of a book, oblong quarto,

---

[1] The development of this aspect of source studies is summarised in J.K. and E.K. Wolf, 'Rastrology and its Use in Eighteenth-Century Manuscript Studies', in E.K. Wolf and E.H. Roesner (eds), *Studies in Musical Sources and Style: Essays in Honor of Jan LaRue* (Madison, WI, 1990), 232–92, at 267–87. See also Robert Thompson, 'Sources and Transmission', in Rebecca Herissone (ed.), *The Ashgate Research Companion to Henry Purcell* (Farnham, 2012), 13–63, at 17–21.

[2] See Stephanie Carter, 'Music Publishing and Compositional Activity in England, 1650–1700' (PhD dissertation, University of Manchester, 2011), especially 24–37.

[3] For fuller details of the production and supply of paper for music, see Robert Thompson, 'English Music Manuscripts and the Fine Paper Trade, 1648–1688', 2 vols (PhD dissertation, King's College, London, 1988), i, 17–85. Details of a wide range of seventeenth-century stave-rulings are given in C.J. Miserandino-Gaherty, 'The Rastrology of English Music Manuscripts, c.1575–c.1642' (PhD dissertation, University of Oxford, 1999); Jonathan Wainwright, *Musical Patronage in Seventeenth-Century England: Christopher, First Baron Hatton (1605–1670)* (Aldershot, 1997), 215–[422]; Robert Shay and Robert Thompson, *Purcell Manuscripts* (Cambridge, 2000; hereinafter *PM*), 334–7; Andrew Ashbee, Robert Thompson and Jonathan Wainwright (compilers), *The Viola da Gamba Society Index of Manuscripts Containing Consort Music* (hereinafter *VdGSIM*), 2 vols (Aldershot, 2001–8), i, pp. xiii–xiv and ii, pp. xii–xiii.

[4] The characteristics of each compound rastrum – its overall span, and the widths of individual staves and spaces – provide potentially valuable evidence in assessing

in which the sheet is also folded and cut horizontally to produce four folios, and oblong sexto, with two horizontal folds making six folios; oblong formats were preferred to their upright equivalents because they preserve the original width of the paper, thus allowing for longer staves and fewer line-ends. Such consistency in paper, format and ruling is highly unlikely to have arisen by chance or through a common understanding of what was needed, suggesting, on the contrary, a well-informed and highly centralised controlling commercial interest. The Playfords, who dominated the market in printed music during the later seventeenth century and regularly advertised 'Rul'd paper for Musick' in their publications,[5] undoubtedly played a pivotal role in this aspect of the music trade, and GB-Lbl Add. MS 31430, a set of manuscript partbooks demonstrably linked to John Playford, may be taken as representative of the kind of material he supplied as blank volumes or scribal copies.[6]

While John Playford developed a commercially viable music trade to a hitherto unprecedented extent, earlier English manuscripts had also used compound rastra, and household and institutional accounts indicate that the practice of buying manuscript paper from a specialist supplier rather than ruling one's own was of much longer standing. 'Ruled paper' is frequently listed as a purchased commodity,[7] and context, or a more specific description such as 'singing paper', sometimes confirm beyond doubt that the reference is to music manuscript paper rather than paper ruled for other purposes. Pre-Playford sources, however, show a greater variety in paper type; they occasionally use paper inadequate for the task, and for that reason are copied on one side only or have adjacent pages pasted together, and are sometimes made of larger-sized, heavier and more expensive paper in upright quarto format to produce a book similar in size to a folio volume made of cheaper paper. This format is rare between c.1650 and c.1690 but reappears when trade embargoes brought about by the Nine Years' War (1688–1697) interrupted the supply of high-quality paper from south-western France. In terms of stave ruling, the consistently high quality of the 'Playford period' disappears quite early in the eighteenth century

---

relationships between different sources, or, more often, establishing the internal history of material now bound within the same covers.

[5] For an example, from *Select Ayres and Dialogues* (London, 1659), see Robert Thompson, 'Manuscript Music in Purcell's London', *Early Music*, 23 (1995), 605–18, at 612.

[6] Illustrated in Thompson, 'Manuscript Music in Purcell's London', 607 and 616, and Alan Howard, 'Manuscript Publishing in the Commonwealth Period: A Neglected Source of Consort Music by Golding and Locke', *Music & Letters*, 90 (2009), 35–67, at 43–4.

[7] See, for example, *PM*, 197–9; J.E. Thorold Rogers, *A History of Agriculture and Prices in England*, 7 vols (Oxford, 1866–1902), vi, 566; Thompson, 'Manuscript Music in Purcell's London', 606–7; Lynn Mary Hulse, 'The Musical Patronage of the English Aristocracy, c.1590–1640' (PhD dissertation, King's College, London, 1992); Philip Riden (ed.), *The Household Accounts of William Cavendish, Lord Cavendish of Hardwick, 1597–1607*, 3 vols (Chesterfield, 2016).

but compound rastra evidently remained in use for many years, featuring in works by Handel and other composers.[8]

The stave ruling of manuscript paper produced with compound rastra presents a challenging imbalance in evidence. Physical evidence of outcome is abundant, occasional errors of length or alignment, confirmed by consistent measurements of rastral spans and the width and spacing of staves, making it readily apparent that ruling was applied by rastra drawing between two and six staves at a time, but there is no direct or documentary evidence of what these tools might have looked like or how they were used.[9] For most of the seventeenth century, single-stave rastra seem to have been very rare, and musicians who needed to add staves to a page normally ruled the lines one at a time with a straight-edge or simply drew them freehand.[10] In this respect, England appears to differ from continental Europe:[11] the existence of single-stave rastra for plainchant was noted in a German calligraphy manual of 1553,[12] and in later centuries the term used in French works of reference for a rastrum is 'pate' or 'patte' (an animal's paw), implying no more points than would draw a single stave.[13] Manuscript paper with staves printed from engraved plates had enjoyed some success in England during the later sixteenth century, patents for

---

[8] See Donald Burrows and M.J. Ronish, *A Catalogue of Handel's Musical Autographs* (Oxford, 1994), pp. xxxvi–xxxvii and 325–8; and, for example, John Eccles, *Inspire us, genius of the day* (1703; GB-Lbl Add. MS 31456); James Hesletine, *Unto thee I will cry* (1707; GB-Lbl Add. MS 30860); John Weldon, *O be joyful in God* (1715–22; GB-Lbl Add. MS 41847), J.E. Galliard, *Julius Caesar* (1723; GB-Lbl Add. MS 25484) and William Croft, *Give the King thy judgements* (1727; GB-Lbl Add. MS 17861, fols 10–18). Illustrative pages from these manuscripts are available online, at https://commons.wikimedia.org/wiki/Category:British_Library_Additional_Manuscripts,_music.

[9] Wolf and Wolf, 'Rastrology', 244–57 and 288–91 list 25 rastra made between the late-seventeenth and nineteenth centuries, none English and all but one single-stave; the exception is a two-stave rastrum made at Nuremberg before 1719 (ibid., 256). For a comprehensive survey of the indirect evidence available, see ibid., 237–67.

[10] Examples online include GB-Lbl Egerton MS 2956, fols 3r, 11v, 15v, 20r and 20v (Purcell, *Yorkshire Feast Song*; additional freehand staves at feet of pages) and GB-Lbl Add. MS 17801, fols 16r–17r (Locke, *Consort for Several Friends*; staves added to flyleaves with a straight-edge).

[11] J.G. Walther, *Musicalisches Lexicon* (Leipzig, 1732) and J.J. Rousseau, *Dictionnaire de musique* (Paris, 1768) respectively define a 'rastrum' or 'patte' in terms which can only mean a single-stave device; see Wolf and Wolf, 'Rastrology', 242, nn. 10–11. The majority of Bach autographs feature single-stave rastra: see E. Winternitz, *Musical Autographs from Monteverdi to Hindemith*, 2 vols (2nd edn, New York, 1965), ii, plates 30–36, and the extensive discussion in R.L. Marshall, *The Compositional Process of J. S. Bach*, 2 vols (Princeton, NJ, 1972), i, 43–61.

[12] Heinrich Holtzmüller, *Liber Perutilis, nunc primum editus, continens Formulas Latinorum & Germanicarum scripturarum* (Basel, 1553); available online at www.e-rara.ch/doi/10.3931/e-rara-16028. Unpaginated, the single relevant page is reproduced in Wolf and Wolf, 'Rastrology', 241, and discussed on pp. 239–40.

[13] Wolf and Wolf, 'Rastrology', 238 and 242.

its sale being granted in 1575 to Thomas Tallis and William Byrd and in 1598 to Thomas Morley,[14] but Morley's patent application itself noted that 'there is many devices by hand to prejudice the press in the printing of ruled paper',[15] implying that the hand-drawing of staves was commercially competitive with printing, surely an economic impossibility unless several staves could be drawn in a single stroke.[16] When in 1612 Morley's widow (by then Susan Hardanville and possibly widowed for a second time) assigned her patent to Edward Allde, it was extended to include hand-ruled paper, although Allde does not seem to have been vigorous in enforcing his privilege.[17]

In spite of the dearth of either surviving artefacts or contemporary documentary evidence, information from a much later source, together with the observable characteristics of seventeenth-century stave-ruling, allows reasonably well-supported conjecture about the nature of the 'devices' mentioned by Morley and, in turn, some plausible speculation as to the factors which enabled the production of manuscript paper with hand-drawn rastra to develop as a minor but significant industry. In his *Art de la réglure des registres et des papiers de musique* (Paris, 1828), A.B. Méguin set out a method for ruling staves for music using, as his title suggests, tools which could also produce rulings of other kinds.[18] The key elements of Méguin's process were a table, an adjustable rectangular frame to hold the paper in position and, for the ruling itself, a slotted wooden bar into which separate pens and spacers were inserted: one version of this bar ('outil fixe'), was permanently set up for a single ruling pattern, with pens and spacers secured by glue; the other ('outil mobile') was more adaptable, with removable pens and spacers locked into place by a screw at one end. The individual pens could have from one to five points, the last kind normally being used only for music, and a guide fixed at the end of the bar ran against one side of the frame, enabling the operator to achieve straight lines.

Méguin describes a contemporary English method of stave ruling apparently more sophisticated than his system, involving self-filling pens beneath which

---

[14] See Iain Fenlon and John Milsom, '"Ruled Paper Imprinted": Music Paper and Patents in Sixteenth-Century England', *Journal of the American Musicological Society*, 37 (1984), 139–63; Teresa Ann Murray, 'Thomas Morley and the Business of Music in Elizabethan England' (PhD dissertation, University of Birmingham, 2010), 149, 150, 153, 163–4, 168–9, 198–9, 209, 212, 249 and 313–17.

[15] Spelling and punctuation modernised: cited thus in Fenlon and Milsom, '"Ruled Paper Imprinted"', 143, and in a diplomatic transcription in Murray, 'Thomas Morley', 163.

[16] Fenlon and Milsom, '"Ruled Paper Imprinted"', 150, observe that although printed manuscript paper remained available in the first decade of the seventeenth century, an extensive survey of contemporary and later sources 'suggests that hand-ruling regained its popularity during the early years of James I's reign and retained it until at least the end of the century'.

[17] Murray, 'Thomas Morley', 248–52.

[18] Wolf and Wolf, 'Rastrology', 259–64. Méguin's illustrations are given on pp. 262–3, which are missing from a digital copy of his work available on the Internet Archive.

the paper was drawn over a roller.[19] Source evidence, however, suggests that in the seventeenth century stave ruling in England followed a process more similar to Méguin's, though differing from it in that Méguin's device accommodated enough individual five-line pens to rule a complete folio-format page in one stroke whereas the seventeenth-century English examples held no more than six, and therefore had to be drawn across the sheet two or three times to achieve the same result. Méguin claims that his process had successfully been put into practice, typically being carried out by women, who could each complete two reams a day despite having to wipe the pens at each ink refill, and asserts that his 'outil mobile' enabled makers of music paper to meet all requirements with a single tool and a stock of 24 five-pointed pens instead of a much larger collection of 'outils fixes'.[20] There is, of course, no proof of how closely the stave-ruling devices used in seventeenth-century England resembled Méguin's design, but the basic principles of the 'outile mobile' in particular correspond with the nature and variety of stave-ruling patterns observable in manuscripts of that time and similar practical considerations must have applied. The ability to rule multiple staves in one stroke of the pen not only accelerated the task but also made it easier to produce a tidy, well-spaced page, and English manufacturers achieved remarkably high standards in this respect. On the other hand, the independence of each five-pointed metal pen could have been critical: the pens were the most complex, and presumably expensive, components, and there would have been good reasons both for ensuring that they could be individually removed and replaced when necessary and for making the device as adaptable as possible to accommodate different requirements for stave widths and spacing.

Méguin instructs that paper intended for different formats should be folded and trimmed before ruling.[21] In contrast, seventeenth-century English sources offer clear evidence that their ruling was applied to complete sheets exactly as they had come from the paper mill, a few manuscripts from the Oxford Music School retaining the deckle edges left by the papermaking process when the mould cover was removed;[22] hand-made papers varied in size but always, apart from cropping of edges, correspond to a complete opening in folio format, so that the stave-drawer ruled up the equivalent of a pair of facing folio pages at a time. As well as the outer margins, then, margins were needed for the gutter; the vertical marginal rulings characteristic of English manuscript paper were evidently applied before the staves and served a practical as well as an aesthetic purpose. Composers and copyists sometimes joined the staves on facing pages with freehand lines, in order to use the full width of the flat unbound

---

[19] Wolf and Wolf, 'Rastrology', 259; Méguin, *Art de la réglure*, 45–6. The tidy and regular appearance of many late eighteenth-century English sources suggests that they were ruled up in this way.

[20] Wolf and Wolf, 'Rastrology', 264; Méguin, *Art de la réglure*, 25–6 and 76.

[21] Wolf and Wolf, 'Rastrology', 261, n. 45; Méguin, *Art de la réglure*, 47–50.

[22] Examples are GB-Ob MSS Mus.Sch.C.98 and E.447–9; see *VdGSIM*, i, pp. 128–30 and ii, 207–11.

sheet – examples in Henry Purcell's hand include GB-Och Mus. 554, fol. 3 (an organ part for Blow's *God is our hope and strength*) and GB-Ob MS Mus.c.26, fols 4–9 (the autograph score of *Let mine eyes run down with tears*) – but instances of such 'stratigraphic' ruling applied with a rastrum across the full width of a sheet are extremely rare.[23]

The vertical alignment of the rulings in either half of a facing pair of rastrum-ruled pages normally coincides with an accuracy unachievable without the use of some form of frame, like the one described by Méguin, and thus provides a useful method of establishing which folios in a bound volume may or may not be conjunct. On paper intended for use in folio format, stave-drawers typically made two to four strokes of a four- or five-stave compound rastrum and aimed to make the distance between stave blocks consistent with the stave spacing fixed within the rastrum itself. For oblong formats, in which the paper would in due course be folded and cut horizontally, they left much wider spaces between the stave blocks to allow for upper or lower margins; composers and copyists sometimes found it convenient to use paper ruled in this way in folio-format scores, as the layout separated systems more clearly than was possible with evenly-spaced staves. Those placing special orders could ask, and presumably pay, for whatever layout they needed, but such arrangements are notable for their rarity: an example exists in the 'Great Set' scorebook, GB-Och Mus. 2, which was ruled throughout using two compound rastra, of two and three staves respectively, to produce discrete blocks of two to six narrow staves,[24] and another is the anthem scorebook GB-Cfm Mu. MS 88, in which the distance between the separate five-stave blocks is too small to allow for folding into an oblong format.[25]

Staves in keyboard manuscripts are sometimes paired, and a more specialised requirement accommodated was that of the lute or lyra viol song, using systems made up of a five-line and a six-line stave separated by a wide space for rhythm stems and text. Two examples from early in the century are GB-Ckc Rowe MS 2 and GB-Lbl Add. MS 15117, both of which seem to have been ruled with two-stave rastra; some uneven stave-ends in the former create an initial impression the lines may have been drawn singly, but measurements and spacing throughout the book are remarkably consistent and the ragged ends are more probably due to the stave-drawer's initial failure to charge the nibs evenly with ink. The production of lute-song rulings appears to have continued

---

[23] Ruling of this kind applied to GB-Och Mus. 1137, fol. 6, probably in the early eighteenth century, may reflect a process of taking stave ruling 'in house' evidenced in some other Oxford manuscripts; see below, p. 42.

[24] *VdGSIM*, i, 172–3. Paper identical in every respect, including stave-ruling, pre-ruled barlines and, for the most part, quiring appears in Matthew Locke's autograph score GB-Lbl Add. MS 17801.

[25] A page of Blow's *Sing we merrily*, partly autograph and partly copied by Purcell, is illustrated in *PM*, 45; the illustration also shows three extra staves added with varying degrees of care.

throughout the century, as in 1690 Henry Playford advertised a blank manuscript book 'of five and six lines'.[26]

To judge from surviving material, no single rastrum configuration lasted for very long, so that the relatively rare instances where different sources share the same rastrum span, stave widths and spacing are likely to reflect some level of relationship between them. The variety of spacing between staves, in particular, suggests that compound rastra were often set up for a particular task and dismantled when it was finished, the five- or six-line pens perhaps being stored in the same way as pieces of type until they were required again; the tool as a whole may, as Méguin explains, have been reconfigured either with different stave widths and spacing or, using another set of pens, for a non-musical purpose. The relationship between the basic structure of Méguin's 'utile mobile' and its various pens parallels that between a printer's forme and his fount of type, and it could be relevant that a rare reference to payment due specifically for ruling staves occurs in a legal case between the printer William Pearson and Henry Playford, alongside charges for printing work Pearson had carried out;[27] the space required for ruling flat sheets of paper, and for laying the just-ruled sheets aside for the ink to dry, may well have been more readily available in a printer's workshop than at a stationer's retail premises.

How much stave ruling added to the cost of paper is difficult to estimate. Records seldom give more information than the quantity of paper purchased and its nominal size, such as 'Royal'; quality is inferred from the price, but a wider range of variable factors come into play, such as the extra costs incurred for transport or through buying paper in quantities much smaller than those for which we have reliable information.[28] The one piece of apparently solid evidence available appears in Pearson's lawsuit, in which he claimed payment of no more than one shilling 'For Ruleing 4 Quire of Imperiall Paper', but the task of ruling both sides of 96 sheets of this large paper is unlikely to have

---

[26] GB-Lbl Harleian 5936, nos. 419–20; see Thompson, 'Manuscript Music in Purcell's London', 614. The year is inferred from an advertisement in *The London Gazette*, 5 June 1690: see Michael Tilmouth, 'A Catalogue of References to Music in Newspapers Published in London and the Provinces (1660–1719)', *Royal Musical Association Research Chronicle*, 1 (1961), pp. i–vii and 1–107, at 9.

[27] Cyrus Lawrence Day and Eleanore Boswell Murrie, 'Playford *versus* Pearson', *The Library*, 17 (1937), 427–47, at 431. The original record of the case is GB-Lna C 10/445/32.

[28] A detailed list of paper types drawn up for the Oxford University Press in the early 1670s, GB-Ob MS Rawlinson D.398, fols 156–7, includes several characteristic of contemporary music manuscripts: the foolscap-sized papers found in many manuscripts cost between 7s. 9d. and 6s. 8d. per ream, while at the other extreme two different types of royal paper were priced at £1 14s. A ream consists of 20 quires, so *pro rata* a quire would cost between about 7d. and 1s. 9d.; these are, however, wholesale prices for substantial quantities. See Martyn A. Ould, *Printing at the University Press, Oxford, 1660–1780*, 3 vols (Seaton, 2015–19), i, 100–2; this account supersedes and corrects previous descriptions, including that in Thompson, 'Manuscript Music in Purcell's London', 608–11, and complements the full transcription of the document in R. W. Chapman, 'An Inventory of Paper, 1674', *The Library*, 7 (1927), 402–8.

amounted to less than a full day's work and the low price suggests that Pearson might have included some cheap stave-ruling in a much more lucrative printing contract. In contrast, a few examples from the years 1620–1640 indicate that a quire of paper described as 'Royal' cost a little under a shilling, whereas one of 'Royal ruled' might be two or three times more expensive, though it is entirely possible that the ruled paper was of a higher quality.[29] At the end of the century, a quire of ruled paper for Westminster Abbey cost two shillings,[30] which again seems to be a significant increase on the cost of any likely unruled equivalent. The overwhelming prevalence of pre-ruled paper in English sources nevertheless indicates that the extra costs of commercial stave ruling were not a deterrent to most prospective purchasers and were almost always outweighed by its advantages.

Although most seventeenth-century English manuscript paper was ruled by compound rastra, some exceptions exist in manuscripts copied or purchased by English musicians abroad or where from choice or necessity composers and copyists in England used paper prepared in a different way. One section (fols 29r–43v) of GB-Lbl Add. MS 31437, a guardbook mainly containing different scores in Matthew Locke's autograph, is entitled 'A Collection of Songs when I was in the Low=Countreys 1648', where the composer had presumably followed prominent Royalists into exile. Each stave line has been drawn individually with a straight-edge to create unusually narrow staves across complete openings, in places leaving a considerable amount of space at the foot of the page to which Locke returned later to add a different work. There is sometimes a marked contrast between the ink colour of the initial and subsequent stages of copying: within either stage, however, the colour of staves and notation tends to correspond, suggesting that the staves were ruled by Locke himself shortly before he copied the music. In this case, a single-stave rastrum suitably narrow for Locke's requirements may not have been available. Single-stave rastra were used in two sets of partbooks belonging to the much-travelled Philip Falle, GB-DRc MSS Mus. D4 and D5, which contain other clues that they were acquired on the continent:[31] English composers represented include William Young, Anthony Poole and Henry Butler, all of whom worked abroad, and spellings in Mus. D4 such as 'Joung' and 'Jenckings' suggest that its copyist was not English. Falle probably bought both of these sets on a visit to Holland between 1694 and 1702, when he was chaplain to King William III.

Exceptions to the rule that cannot be explained by foreign origin fall into two distinct categories: sources which resemble conventional music books in every respect except for their use of paper not ruled by a compound rastrum, and those of a more improvised character, made out of books or loose paper

---

[29] In 1627 'Royal' paper was purchased at 11d. a quire in London; in 1636 New College Oxford paid 3s. 2d. a quire for 14 quires of 'Royal ruled'; Thorold Rogers, *A History of Agriculture and Prices*, vi, 567.

[30] In Westminster Abbey Muniments 47681: 'ffor twelve quire of ruled paper 1-4-0' (i.e., 24s., 2s. per quire). See *PM*, 199.

[31] See *VdGSIM*, ii, 60–63.

clearly intended for another purpose. Several sources in the former category are associated with Oxford, where it is particularly unlikely that conventional music paper was unobtainable, and include manuscripts such as GB-Lbl Add. MSS 17835 and 17840 as well as GB-Och Mus. 11 and 12,[32] in the hands of copyists who worked in the circle of Henry Aldrich; one of them was probably Charles Husbands, who seems to have died in early 1692, and another was definitely Francis Smith (*d*.1698),[33] whose interest in the material aspects of musical culture is evident in his publication with Peter de Walpergen of *Musica Oxoniensis* (1698), set in the 'second Walpergen' typeface which Smith had designed and notable for its early use of the natural sign.[34] It would not be surprising if he or one of his colleagues ventured into stave ruling: the four manuscripts listed above all feature the same 11.5 mm. rastrum and were probably commissioned by Aldrich as part of an extended but self-contained project rather than purchased ready-ruled through the normal commercial channels.

Two rather earlier Oxford volumes contain paper ruled without a rastrum of any kind. One, GB-Lbl Add. MS 30382, is a guardbook housing the personal manuscript scores of Henry Bowman, whose *Songs, for one, two, & three voyces* was published in Oxford in four impressions between 1677 and 1683;[35] even with some of its original material evidently missing, this guardbook contains 91 music folios, all but seven of which have been ruled with a straight-edge. No engraver is credited for the music of Bowman's *Songs*, and marked similarities with his manuscript handwriting suggest that he engraved them himself; an engraver's concern for layout may therefore have influenced his manuscript stave ruling, as on several pages the layout of staves matches the scoring of the music with a precision rarely achieved in sources ruled with compound rastra.

A further surprising instance of single-line stave ruling is GB-Ob MS Mus. Sch.C.71, which belonged to William Noble, a chaplain of Christ Church, Oxford;[36] the volume's contemporary binding contains Simpson's *The Division Viol* (1667) and a substantial manuscript section, mostly ruled with eleven staves drawn one line at a time with a straight-edge.[37] The initial flyleaf of the

---

[32] *PM*, 150 and 152–3. A page of GB-Och Mus. 11 is illustrated in the online *Christ Church Library Music Catalogue*.

[33] *PM*, 309–10 and 313–14.

[34] The colophon includes the words 'Publish'd by Francis Smith, and Peter de Walpergen Letter-Founder, by whom 'twas Cut on Steel, and Cast, by the Directions of the former'. For Walpergen, see D. W. Krummel, *English Music Printing 1553–1700* (London, 1975), 134–8 and 142.

[35] See Cyrus Lawrence Day and Eleanore Boswell Murrie, *English Song-Books 1651–1702* (London, 1940), 59.

[36] Described as 'very well skilled in the practic part of music': Anthony Wood, *Athenae Oxonienses. An Exact History of all the Writers and Bishops who have had their Education in the University of Oxford*, edited by P. Bliss, 4 vols (London, 1813–20), iv, *Fasti*, col. 367; see also J. Foster, *Alumni Oxonienses: the Members of the University of Oxford 1500–1714*, 4 vols (Oxford, 1891–2), iii, 1073.

[37] See *VdGSIM*, ii, 155–8. The Simpson publication bound with the manuscript is *The Division Viol*, not *A Compendium of Practical Music*. The first folio of the manuscript

whole book, bearing the inscription 'Will Noble 1671', is drawn from the manuscript paper stock, suggesting, alongside the unusual but generally consistent ruling, that the manuscript pages were specifically prepared for binding with *The Division Viol*, the dimensions of which are a little too small for conventional twelve-stave ruling but too large for ten-stave. In this source, as well as in Bowman's scorebook, considerations of layout may therefore have tipped the balance against pre-ruled paper. Different factors perhaps applied in GB-Lbl K.1.c.5 and Hirsch III.472, copies of Purcell's posthumous *A Choice Collection of Lessons* (1696) with additional manuscript pages, where the binder would have needed paper ruled for an oblong format; paper with six-line staves in discrete blocks of four was probably available, but it might have saved both delay and expense to draw the staves one line at a time rather than order a small quantity of specialised paper ruled with a compound rastrum.

No constraints of predetermined format or the requirements of music in score can have affected the partbooks GB-Ob MSS Mus.Sch. D.245–7, which initially belonged to their principal copyist, the Gloucester singing-man John Merro (*d*.1639).[38] These three upright quarto books are in handsome seventeenth-century bindings, and each includes a large number of unruled pages towards the end, inviting the conclusion that they were bound as blank volumes and ruled up progressively as new music was added.[39] In reality, their history was probably more complex. Although the single-line stave rulings clearly were applied in broad anticipation of requirements, with between seven and ten staves on most pages, copying did not always work out as expected: some ruled-up pages remained unused; there are frequently spare staves at the feet of pages; and on seven-stave pages, where a wide space was left beneath the ruling, extra staves sometimes had to be added. Moreover, the partbooks are substantial volumes, with almost 150 folios in D.245 and D.246 and over a hundred in D.247; stave ruling and music copying would have been awkward if the books had already been bound, yet both are conspicuously neat. For some reason, then, it appears that Merro began an extensive copying project with a large stock of unruled paper, some or all of which may initially have been intended for notes on theology; at the end of D.245, as well as the inscription 'John Merro his booke' on p. 287, appears a summary on pp. 282–3 of the arguments against the doctrine of predestination set out in a work by Samuel Hoard.[40]

---

section and a few pages at its end were left unruled, an inserted folio (pp. 137–8) is conventionally ruled with a compound rastrum, and pp. 170–2 have fifteen or sixteen staves, narrower than those elsewhere but again drawn with a straight-edge.

[38] A later copyist, who possibly acquired the set after Merro's death in 1639, may have been John Withy of Worcester; see *VdGSIM*, i, 139 and 390–91. For biographical details of Merro, see ibid., 9–10; for the Withy family see Robert Thompson, '"Francis Withie of Oxon" and his Commonplace Book, Christ Church, Oxford, MS 337', *Chelys*, 20 (1991), 3–27 and *VdGSIM*, ii, 7–13. Note that the locations of Worcester records changed between 1991 and 2008.

[39] *VdGSIM*, i, 139–66.

[40] S. Hoard, *Gods love to mankind. Manifested, by dis-prooving his absolute decree for their damnation* ([London], 1633).

Merro's other identified manuscripts, GB-Lbl Add. MSS 17792-6 and US-NYp Drexel MSS 4180-5, are conventionally ruled with a compound rastrum, so it is surprising that similar material was not obtained for D.245-7; a possible reason could be a major outbreak of plague in Gloucester in 1638, which would inevitably have interrupted trade with other cities and perhaps made an extended copying project a welcome occupation.[41] A later Gloucester source ruled without a rastrum is GB-Lbl Add. MS 30932, fols 70r-71v, a copy of two anthems by William King sent c.1673 from the cathedral precentor Edward Jackson to Daniel Henstridge in Rochester; interest in this document naturally focuses on some personal and practical details it reveals (see below), but its musical content is written on twelve staves ruled one line at a time across the whole of one side. Of course, Jackson may simply have chosen not to use available conventional paper, but a possible implication is that even major provincial cathedrals did not routinely hold stocks of rastrum-ruled paper, instead purchasing it in bulk when it was needed for specific projects. Similarly, the composer George Jeffreys did not always have prepared music paper to hand; as steward to the Hatton family, Jeffreys spent most of the Interregnum at Kirby, their Northamptonshire estate,[42] without easy access to London or a major regional centre. His scorebook GB-Lbl Add. MS 10338 mostly contains compound-rastrum rulings,[43] but after the volume was bound he added eight folios from his supply of writing paper,[44] on some of which he drew staves one line at a time to conclude the motet *O Domine Deus* and then to add his anthem *Turn thou us, good Lord*, dated [16]55.

The sources mentioned so far resemble compound-rastrum manuscripts in that they are made of similar types of paper and their staves, if not ruled with a single-stave rastrum, are neatly drawn one line at a time, perhaps with the help of some kind of guide measuring from an initial reference line. Other sources deviate more markedly from the conventional pattern, consisting of paper intended for a different purpose or having freehand stave-lines drawn only as far as is necessary. Both features are apparent in GB-Lbl MS Mus. Dep. 2016/52, which comprises two unrelated documents containing Purcell songs: the second of these is a half-sheet of ordinary writing paper with the songs *She who my poor heart possesses* on one side and *How happy are they* on the other, notated on freehand staves. In this case, any number of social or professional coincidences might have led to the improvisation of manuscript paper at short notice; in contrast, the bass partbook GB-Mch MS Mun. A.2.6

---

[41] N.M. Herbert (ed.), *A History of the County of Gloucester: Volume 4, the City of Gloucester* (London, 1988), 81-4.

[42] See Wainwright, *Musical Patronage*, 115-59, especially at 119.

[43] See ibid., 217-32, and Robert Thompson, 'George Jeffreys and the "Stile Nuovo" in English Sacred Music: a New Date for his Autograph Score, British Library, Add. MS 10338', *Music & Letters*, 70 (1989), 317-41.

[44] Jeffreys used the same stock of paper for letters he wrote to Lady Hatton in February 1649 (GB-Lbl Add. MS 29550, fols 91r-93v): see Thompson, 'George Jeffreys', 324 and Wainwright, *Musical Patronage*, 141.

must have involved a degree of planning, because a companion treble volume, now lost, was involved.[45] Seventy-two of the surviving book's 274 folios have been ruled one line at a time, mostly on one side only; consisting of lightweight paper unsuitable for musical notation, it was perhaps intended for use as a commonplace book, and apart from music now contains an extensive collection of proverbs. Such examples of home-made manuscript paper, however, are notable for their rarity.

The development of technology to aid stave-drawing, whether in England or elsewhere, must have depended upon a coincidence of demand and opportunity: as Méguin's title implies, stave-ruling equipment was related to tools for ruling registers or account books, and it was possibly for this reason that the use of compound rastra flourished in the mercantile hub of London before the end of the sixteenth century. Well-developed formal and informal channels for distribution from London already existed and by no means all the people regularly visiting London from the regions were notably wealthy: as well as merchants, they included clergy and musicians serving in the Chapel Royal and lawyers representing their clients in the London courts, all potentially interested in music and with relatives, friends and colleagues for whom they might either obtain items unavailable at home or arrange introductions into London musical circles.

Perhaps for this reason, in January 1699 John Gostling received 17s from Canterbury Cathedral for 'ruld pap[er] for y^e. Organ book'.[46] John Withy of Worcester, despite his relatively humble status and apparent lack of long-term aristocratic patronage, was a cousin of Richard Withy, a lawyer who must have travelled regularly to London;[47] Thomas Fydell of Norwich, to whom a probable relative of the music publisher John Playford was apprenticed, spent an average of 60 days a year in London between 1600 and 1610 carrying out legal work on behalf of Norwich corporation.[48] Around the start of the century, the accounts of the Cavendish family of Hardwick Hall record a great deal of spending upon musical items at their London house but also reflect their dependence upon London when in Derbyshire: in December 1598 three sets

---

[45] See Robert Thompson, 'The Sources of Locke's Consort "for seaverall friends"', *Chelys*, 19 (1990), 16–43, at 19.

[46] The bill for binding two quarto organ books (GB-CA Music MSS 9–10) and one folio book (probably CA Music MS 11) is dated 4 April 1700, and in the year leading up to 19 November 1700 Daniel Henstridge was paid for extensive copying in all three. Records of the various payments are in GB-CA DCC TB/34, fol. 25, TV/38/15, TV/38/21 and TV/38/32.

[47] For Richard Withy's appointment as 'Attorney in the Common Pleas' for the City of Worcester from 1640 onwards, see Shelagh Bond (ed.), *The Chamber Order Book of Worcester, 1602–1650* (Worcester, 1974), 340; the Common Pleas heard cases only at a 'fixed place', as ordained by Magna Carta, in Westminster Hall.

[48] GB-NWr COL 13/61. See Robert Thompson, 'The Elusive Identity of John Playford', in John Cunningham and Bryan White (eds), *Musical Exchange between Britain and Europe, 1500–1800* (Woodbridge, 2020), 344–56, at 349.

of songs by Thomas Morley were collected from Mansfield,[49] where they had been left by the carrier from London, and in March 1607 one of their servants sent to London for 'ruled books'.[50]

Edward Jackson's transmission copy for Daniel Henstridge (see above) gives a great deal of information about the ways documents could be sent around the country.[51] The sheet had been folded and sent by post as a small packet, annotations beneath the address showing that the cost was 3d to London and 2d onward to Rochester: Jackson suggests that it would be cheaper to exchange material by carrier, asks 'where your Rochester carrier lyes' – where, that is, he stays overnight in London – and requests that large items going to Gloucester be directed to the Bull and Mouth, a coaching inn in Aldersgate, for the Gloucester carrier to collect them. Sources from both the first and the second half of the seventeenth century reveal an established network of wagon and packhorse routes extending throughout the country:[52] John Taylor's *The Carriers Cosmographie* of 1637 lists the places served from London, as does Thomas Delaune's 1681 *The Present State of London*.[53] With the exception of distant coastal towns such as Plymouth and Newcastle, most places of any size appear to have been directly served by one or more waggoners or carriers, in many cases every week.[54] Against this background, Roger North's statement that John Jenkins's more lively ayres were distributed around the country in 'horsloads' is a telling figure of speech;[55] the image of pack-saddles laden with music may be hyperbolic, but it draws upon accepted practice for moving large quantities of goods around the country.

Perhaps because of their regular visits to London and distance from a major regional centre, the Cavendishes appear to have ordered material directly from suppliers in that city; in 1661, Canterbury Cathedral did likewise when it purchased a double set of Barnard's *First Book of Selected Church-Musick*, bound with ruled paper for manuscript additions in each volume, from John

---

[49] Riden, *The Household Accounts*, ii, 61; index entries and cross-references are to sections of the text rather than page numbers, this payment being in section 65.

[50] Ibid., iii, 393 (section 773). The 'ruled books' are not specified as music books, but the servant Nicholas Ham who was to be reimbursed for them had previously bought 'a book to prick viol lessons in'; ibid., 308–9 (section 693).

[51] The relevant part of Jackson's message is transcribed in Thompson, 'Sources and Transmission', 43.

[52] Examined in depth in D. Gerhold, *Carriers and Coachmasters: Trade and Travel before the Turnpikes* (Chichester, 2005). See also J.A. Chartres, 'Road Carrying in England in the Seventeenth Century: Myth and Reality', *The Economic History Review*, 30 (1977), 73–94 and D. Gerhold, 'Packhorses and Wheeled Vehicles in England, 1550–1800', *The Journal of Transport History*, 14 (1993), 1–26.

[53] Thomas Delaune, *The Present State of London: or, Memorials Comprehending a Full and Succinct Account of the Ancient and Modern State Thereof* (London, 1681), 385–435; repr. 1690 as *Angliae Metropolis or, the Present State of London*, 401–41.

[54] To achieve a weekly service, some carriers worked in informal partnerships and others operated multiple teams: see Gerhold, *Carriers and Coachmasters*, 5–9.

[55] Cited in John Wilson (ed.), *Roger North on Music* (London, 1959), 345.

Playford.[56] A flourishing regional book trade nevertheless existed, and at least sometimes handled music manuscript paper: in 1657, the Newcastle bookseller William London's *A Catalogue of the most Vendible Books in England* included an advertisement for 'Paper of all sorts'.[57] In the same and subsequent years, Anthony Wood bought ruled paper in Oxford, on one occasion alongside the printed partbooks of Matthew Locke's *Little Consort*:[58] the vendor is not identified, but a purchase immediately preceding this one was from the bookseller Richard Davis, from whom at other times Wood bought pictures, ink and unspecified paper.[59] Later in the century, Durham Cathedral paid bills for ruled books or paper to the booksellers William Werdon, Hugh Hutchinson and William Freeman,[60] and as some of these purchases were made by two known copyists, William Greggs and Matthew Owen,[61] they are unlikely to have been for anything other than music paper. At Gloucester Cathedral in 1627–8, the bookseller Toby Langford was paid 4s. for 'six quire of ruled pap[er] and Toby Jordan 3s. 4d. for 'five quire';[62] these entries immediately precede a payment for 'pricking', the contemporary term for music copying. The same cathedral's post-Restoration accounts for 1661–2 are more explicit, recording payments of 13s. to 'Mr Langford' for 'rule books for singing' as well as 11s. 3d. to another stationer for 'x quire of rule paper for pricking anthems'.[63] As the regional businesses involved imported most of their printed stock from the capital, and orders for multiple quires of music paper would come in only rarely, it is likely

[56] Carter, 'Music Publishing and Compositional Activity', 49.
[57] See Stephanie Carter and Kirsten Gibson, 'Printed Music in the Provinces: Musical Circulation in Seventeenth-Century England and the Case of Newcastle upon Tyne Bookseller William London', *The Library*, 18 (2017), 428–73, especially at 452–71.
[58] Andrew Clark (ed.), *The Life and Times of Anthony Wood*, vol. 1 (Oxford, 1891), 211, 213, 215, 230 and 237.
[59] Ibid., 286, 433 and 441. Davis was also the printer of one impression of Henry Bowman's *Songs* (see above).
[60] David Pearson, *Book Trade Bills and Vouchers from Durham Cathedral Library, 1634–1740* (unpaginated typescript, [Newcastle upon Tyne], 1986). The relevant payments were made between February 1688 and October 1700; the original documents are in GB-DRc D&C loose papers, boxes 25 and 26.
[61] Brian Crosby, *A Catalogue of Durham Cathedral Music Manuscripts* (Oxford, 1989), 244–5. Hutchinson's bill of 13 February 1688, 'Delivered to Mr Gregs 1 paper book ruled of imperial paper o 18 o' probably refers to one of the large oblong quarto organ books in Greggs's hand, either GB-DRc MS Mus. A25 or MS Mus. A33. On 23 December 1693 Werdon presented a bill for '1 quire of large ruled paper' supplied to Owen.
[62] GB-GL D936/A1/1 (Treasurer's accounts 1609–34), p. 133.
[63] GB-GL D936/A1/2 (Treasurer's accounts 1634–64), p. 256. This and the previous reference were cited in Thompson, 'Manuscript Music in Purcell's London', 606–7; the books have subsequently been relocated from Gloucestershire Archives to the Cathedral Library, rebound and repaginated. I am grateful to Rebecca Phillips, the Cathedral librarian and archivist, for locating the relevant pages and kindly supplying photographs.

that in most if not all cases they acted only as intermediaries between London suppliers of ruled manuscript paper and regional customers.

Around the end of the century, however, in addition to the Aldrich-circle sources already mentioned, the work of the Northumbrian copyist Nicholas Harrison provides evidence of regional production of ruled paper. His keyboard manuscripts GB-Lbl Add. MSS 31465 and 34695 are distinctive not only for their striking calligraphy but also for their shared use of the same single-stave six-line rastrum,[64] though the two books differ in dimensions, paper type and stave layout, with four staves in Add. MS 31465 and six in the much larger Add. MS 34965. Stave ruling is clear and even, but the line ends are less exact than might be expected in a book otherwise copied in an ostentatiously fine calligraphic style, and the occurrence of the same rastrum in both indicates that the device belonged, if not to Harrison himself, to someone close to him. If, as is probable, Harrison derived part of his income from teaching and providing material for his pupils, there would have been a reason for him to create or find a local source of ruled paper, rather than to rely on an expensive, slow and possibly intermittent supply from the south; as outlined above, single-stave rastra were widely used in continental Europe, and it is perhaps more likely than not that the Harrison rastrum was obtained through the overseas North Sea trade rather than from London.

The very fact that such independent production of music manuscript paper is noteworthy in England emphasises the dominance throughout and beyond the seventeenth century of paper ruled with compound rastra, supplied to amateurs and professionals alike through the centralised trade in musical goods developed by John Playford. This dominance led in turn to a general absence of single-stave rastra, the scarcity of home-made rulings of any kind apart from staves added to pre-ruled pages, and the inability of professional musicians to access a single-stave rastrum when one would have been extremely helpful. The lack of any contemporary description of a compound rastrum underlines how far the existence and use of this tool became part of the everyday background of musical culture, taken entirely for granted until musicologists began measuring rastral details in the twentieth century.

---

[64] The copyist of these manuscripts can presumably be identified with Nicholas Harrison of Gateshead, who was paid by Durham Cathedral in 1709 for copying: Crosby, *Catalogue*, 244.

4

The Music Trade in York, 1650–1800: Proprietors and Purchasers

David Griffiths

In 1885 Henry Banks of York, the proprietor of the music shop later known as 'Banks & Son', asserted that he had the 'Largest stock [of music] in England'.[1] A pedigree traces the origin of Banks' music shop in York back to 1756, when Thomas Haxby established a business there that aimed to sell everything that musicians, both amateur and professional, might require.[2] Haxby and Banks were both inheritors of a long tradition of traders supplying music-related goods in York, which can be traced to Anthony Foster, who provided paper for York Minster's partbooks in the 1580s, and John Foster, a seller of music books who died in 1616.[3] The probate inventory of Foster's bookshop lists *c*.750 titles and 3373 identifiable items, including 25 music books.[4] The majority of these volumes are of English secular songs or psalms, but Foster's collection also indicates the early trade in both continental publications and second-hand music books in this city. Following Foster, evidence for the sale of music goods in York is scant until the late seventeenth century and it is the purpose of this chapter to outline the trade in musical goods and services within York between the time of John Foster and the turn of the nineteenth century.

---

[1] *Yorkshire Gazette,* 10 January 1885. Bank's shop, latterly known as 'Banks Musicroom', with premises on Lendal, York, ceased trading on 17 March 2023.
[2] *York Courant,* 29 June 1756. The advertisement refers to 'Gentlemen, Ladies, and others'.
[3] Stephanie Carter and Kirsten Gibson, 'Printed Music in the Provinces: Musical Circulation in Seventeenth-Century England and the Case of Newcastle upon Tyne Bookseller William London', *The Library*, 18/4 (2017), 428–73, at 443 and 445. See also David Griffiths, *A Musical Place of the First Quality: A History of Institutional Music-Making in York c.1550–1990* (York, [1994]), 217–18.
[4] Carter and Gibson, 'Printed Music in the Provinces', 445; John Barnard and Maureen Bell, *The Early Seventeenth-Century York Book Trade and John Foster's Inventory of 1616* (Leeds, 1994).

❧ *Francis and John Hildyard*

The first individual we encounter in this study of York music sellers is Francis Hildyard (d.1731) who, from 1682, kept a shop at the 'Sign of the Bible' on Stonegate.[5] Hildyard traded in a variety of musical goods and services, including the sale of newly published music books such as William Croft's *Musica Sacra* (1724) and Peter Fraser's *The Delightfull Musical Companion* (1726).[6] Hildyard's clients included York Minster: on 24 June 1706 he was paid £1 10s. 'for two Anthem Bookes',[7] and he supplied paper to the Minster in January 1716.[8]

York Minster's use of Hildyard contributes to a growing body of evidence around cathedrals and their use of local stationers for music and music-related stationery services that dates to at least the late sixteenth century.[9] York undoubtedly had a ready market for music amongst the Minster's singing-men and clergy, but also among members of the gentry and professions across the county. The earlier inventory of John Foster includes a list of debtors from not only York but also Leeds and the surrounding towns and villages;[10] this trade with the outlying communities undoubtedly continued through the seventeenth century and into the eighteenth. Less formally, Henry Mace, the 'Sub-Chantor' at the Minster (i.e., the subchanter of the vicars choral), served as a point of contact for subscription to his brother's publication in the 1670s: Thomas Mace's *Musick's Monument* (1676). Subscribers to this work based in Yorkshire included both gentlemen and ladies, as well as clergy and church musicians.[11]

In the eighteenth century, Sir D'Arcy Dawes (c.1694–1732), son of the archbishop of York – Sir William Dawes (1671–1724) – recorded a payment of 15s. for 'music-books of Mr Hildyard' in 1723. D'Arcy Dawes's surviving accounts of 1723–32 list six other payments to Hildyard.[12] Dawes, an amateur musician, was connected to the close-knit community of amateur musicians among the clergy of the Minster that included Edward Finch, William Knight and

---

[5] The sign hangs over the doorway and is inscribed with the date 1682. William K. and E. Margaret Sessions, *Printing in York from the 1490s to the Present Day* (York, 1976), 27.

[6] William Croft, *Musica Sacra* (London, 1724); Peter Fraser, *The Delightfull Musical Companion* (London, 1726). For more on subscribers to musical works, see Simon Fleming and Martin Perkins, *Dataset of Subscribers to Eighteenth-Century Music Publications in Britain and Ireland*, www.musicsubscribers.co.uk.

[7] The payment to Hildyard is recorded in GB-Y E2/5.

[8] GB-Y E2/22.

[9] Carter and Gibson, 'Printed Music in the Provinces', 443.

[10] Barnard and Bell, 'Early Seventeenth-Century York Book Trade', 16–21.

[11] Stephanie Carter, 'Thomas Mace's *Musick's Monument* (1676) and his Subscribers in Late Seventeenth-Century England', in Simon D.I. Fleming and Martin Perkins (eds), *Music by Subscription: Composers and their Networks in the British Music-Publishing Trade, 1676–1820* (London, 2022), 21–38.

[12] GB-Y MS Add. 65/1–4. Dawes also subscribed to Fraser's *The Delightfull Musical Companion* (1726).

Valentine Nalson.[13] Dividing his time between London and York, Dawes records in detail for both cities his purchases of music and musical instruments, his visits to music clubs, and (in London) his trips to the opera. His connection with York Minster is evident in payments to John Cooper and Thomas Benson, both songmen there; one of the payments to Cooper is for copying music, something which the latter undertook on a regular basis for the Minster; the two payments to Benson are likely to have been for the same service.[14]

Francis Hildyard's business was maintained after his death by his son, John (d. 1757).[15] The advertisements the latter placed in local newspapers provide evidence that Hildyard jnr continued trading in music, and in particular the sale of songbooks and psalms intended for domestic use. Books sold by John Hildyard included *The Lark, Containing a Collection of above four Hundred and Seventy Celebrated English and Scotch Songs* (1740) and the fifth edition of *A Sett of New Psalms and Anthems* (1753) edited by the Dorset-based composer, William Knapp.[16] Music was, however, only one part of John's business, as he also published and sold non-musical works, including Charles Cowper's sermon *Self-Love* (c.1751). A 1753 advertisement gives greater detail of the multifarious musical goods Hildyard traded, amongst which we find 'all Sorts of Musical Instruments, Books of Instruction for any Instrument; and the best Roman Strings, fresh imported'.[17]

In 1751, Hildyard jnr published a catalogue that reveals his involvement in the trade in second-hand books.[18] This catalogue lists around 30,000 volumes

---

[13] David Griffiths, 'Music in the Minster Close: Edward Finch, Valentine Nalson, and William Knight in Early Eighteenth-Century York', in Rachel Cowgill and Peter Holman (eds), *Music in the British Provinces, 1690–1914* (Aldershot, 2007), 45–59. Dawes was an amateur keyboard player and, in 1723, paid Mr Davis £11 6d. 'for teaching my wife & me upon the Spinnet'; there are also other payments in Dawes' accounts for tuning spinets. In 1724 he bought a harpsichord from Mr [Jean-Baptiste] Loeillet and a year after that an organ from Mr Harris. He additionally purchased on two occasions a violin and on four occasions a flute. See GB-Y MS Add. 65/1–4.

[14] GB-Y MS Add. 65/1–4.

[15] Robert Davies, *A Memoir of the York Press, with Notices of Authors, Printers, and Stationers, in the Sixteenth, Seventeenth, and Eighteenth Centuries* (Westminster, 1868), 105–6. Hildyard died on 29 January 1757, in which year an elegy to his memory was published.

[16] *York Courant*, 25 September 1739, 7 November 1752 and 12 March 1754. *The Lark* was printed in London for John Osborn.

[17] *York Courant*, 30 October 1753.

[18] John Hildyard, *A Catalogue of Several Libraries and Parcels of Books, Lately Purchased, Consisting of About Thirty Thousand Volumes, In all Branches of Literature, Arts, and Sciences, and in most Languages* (York, 1751). The music is listed on pp. 25–30 of the main sequence (comprising sale item nos. 654–760) and on p. 9 of the Appendix (comprising sale items nos. 205–10). There are copies of the catalogue in the British Library and York Minster Library; it is also available via *Eighteenth Century Collections Online*. ESTC T9143.

alongside 48 items comprising 'a Collection of Natural and Artificial Curiosities', and which included 'A Very curious Skeleton of a Human Foetus', 'The Skin of a Mermaid, stuffed' and 'An artificial Shower of Hail', all of which came with the caveat that 'several of the above Curiosities are little known' and as such 'wrong names may possibly be applied to some of them'.[19] There are 113 lots of vocal and instrumental music, all of which have been listed in Table 4.1; one item, no. 683, is formed from seven different publications 'all neatly bound together ... collected by a Gentleman curious in selecting pieces for that instrument [violin]' (each work has been given a separate entry in the table). The vast majority of the items are printed, although manuscript volumes are represented – such as 'An old book of ninety-nine musical lessons, MSS. 2s 6d',[20] and 'The musick of the favourite songs of several operas, also aires and other pieces of musick curiously wrote by a gentleman (now deceas'd) for his own entertainment, 7s 6d'.[21]

Glancing through the list of items for sale, it is apparent that the majority are secular in nature and composed by musicians not born in Britain.[22] There are approximately equal amounts of vocal and instrumental music, although it is collections of songs that make up the largest number of items, with some volumes consisting of favourite vocal movements from operas and oratorios. Of the instrumental genres, concertos make up the majority, and there are large numbers of trios and solo sonatas; this is perhaps not surprising since such works were popular with musical societies.[23] Most of the published items were issued in London, with a small number issued in Amsterdam and one, the *Manuale Cantus Secundùm Usum* (1682), in Ghent. The only identified work from the British regions is Avison's op 2 concertos, published by Joseph Barber of Newcastle.[24] Hildyard frequently includes the price of a new copy alongside the price by which his copy could be purchased, offering in some cases over 50 per cent off the original selling price. Some works, presumably of a more saleable nature, were offered with a lesser discount; those for an ensemble or orchestra, which were missing one or more parts, had a greater markdown.

---

[19] Hildyard, *A Catalogue*, 23–4.
[20] Ibid., 30.
[21] Ibid., Appendix, p. 9.
[22] This pattern is also evident in other contemporary sale catalogues of new works. See, for example, the four-page catalogue produced by the London-based music publisher Welcker and attached to John Garth's *Six Voluntarys for the Organ Piano Forte or Harpsichord* op 3 (1771). For a discussion of this catalogue, see Simon D.I. Fleming 'Foreign composers, the subscription market, and the popularity of continental music in eighteenth-century Britain', in Fleming and Perkins (eds), *Music by Subscription*, 221–41, at 226–7.
[23] Simon D.I. Fleming and Martin Perkins, 'A Big Data Study: Musical Societies in Subscription Lists', in Fleming and Perkins (eds), *Music by Subscription*, 152–76, at 164–7.
[24] For more on Avison's op 2, see Simon Fleming's contribution on Joseph Barber and William Flackton in this volume.

TABLE 4.1. Music Books in John Hildyard's 1751 catalogue.

Catalogue No	Catalogue Description	Price – New Copy	Price – Hildyard	Possible Publisher and Year of Publication
654	Corelli's Sonatas of three parts, opera 1, 2, 3, 4, for two violins and a bass, with a thorough bass for the organ, &c. the whole 4 operas, bound	£1 1s.	14s.	John Walsh, c.1703
655	—— twelve Sonatas for a violin and bass, opera 5ta, bound	7s.	4s.	John Walsh, c.1740
656	—— six Solos for a flute and a bass, being the second part of his 5th opera	4s.	2s.	John Walsh & John Hare, c.1730
657	—— Grand Concertos, 7 parts, being his sixth and last opera	15s.	10s.	John Walsh, 1712
658	Six Concertos for two flutes and a bass, with a thorough bass for the Harpsicord, transposed from the Great Concertos of Corelli	4s.	2s.	John Walsh, 1720
659	Avison's (organist of Newcastle) Concertos, 7 parts		10s. 6d.	Joseph Barber, 1740
660	Valentini Bizarre per Camera, for two violins and a violoncello	4s.	2s.	John Walsh & John Hare, 1721
661	Albinoni's Concertos, 7 parts, opera 2da	9s.	5s.	John Walsh, c.1732
662	—— Ballettis for two violins and a thorough bass	6s.	3s. 6d.	John Walsh & John Hare, c.1730
663	Six celebrated songs made on purpose for French horns, performed in Handell's operas, 7 parts	5s.	3s.	John Walsh, 1731
664	Harmonia mundi, being six favourite Sonatas, collected from Torelli, Purcell, Bassani, Pepusch, Pez, &c.	5s.	3s.	John Walsh & John Hare, c.1727
665	Harmonia mundi, the second collection, being six Concertos in six parts, collected out of the choicest works of Vivaldi, Tessarini, Albinoni & Alberti	7s.	4s.	John Walsh & John Hare, 1728

TABLE 4.1 continued.

Catalogue No	Catalogue Description	Price – New Copy	Price – Hildyard	Possible Publisher and Year of Publication
666	Vivaldi's, two celebrated Concertos, Cuckow and Extravaganza, 7 parts	4s.	2s.	John Walsh, c.1730
667	Festing's twelve Concertos, in 7 parts, dedicated to the Philarmonick	£1 11s. 6d.	12s.	William Smith, 1734
668	Select harmony, being twelve Concertos, in 6 parts, collections from the works of Antonio Vivaldi, his 6, 7, 8 and 9th opera's, parts, Violino primo principale, alta viola, and a duplicate of organo e violoncello, the rest wanting	Price for the set, 15s.	3s. 6d.	John Walsh, 1730
669	Select harmony, third collection, by Geminiani and others, being six Concertos, in 7 parts, Violino primo Concertino, violin secondo, violoncello el Concertino, alta viola Ripienno, the rest wanting	Price for the set, 9s.	2s.	John Walsh, 1734
670	Babell's Concertos, in 7 parts, the first four for violins and one small flute, the two last for violins and two flutes, the basses wanting	Price for the set, 8s.	3s.	John Walsh, c.1726
671	Alberti's Concertos opera prima, the alta viola part only		1s.	John Walsh, c.1730
672	Geminiani's Concertos, opera terza, the alta viola part only		1s.	John Walsh, c.1730
673	Geminiani's six Concertos, composed from the 5th opera of Corelli's Sonatas, in 7 parts, wanting alta viola	Price for the set, 10s. 6d.	4s.	William Smith, 1726 or John Walsh, 1726
674	Geminiani's Concertos opera terza, the alta viola part only		1s.	John Walsh, c.1730
675	Loeillet's (John) twelve Sonatas, in 3 parts, 6 of which are for two violins and a bass, 3 for two German flutes, 3 for a hautboy and common flute, opera secunda	8s.	4s. 6d.	John Walsh, c.1725

676	Bonporti's Sonatas, or chamber aires for two violins and a thorough bass, opera secunda		4s.	John Walsh, c.1730
677	Bononcini's twelve Sonatas for the chamber, for two violins and a bass, dedicated to the Duchess of Marlborough, the second violin wanting		Price for the set, £1 1s.	John Walsh, 1732
678	Vivaldi's Concertos, opera terza, only the parts for violine e cymbalo violoncello		2s.	John Walsh, 1715
679	Martini's twelve Sonatas for two flutes and a thorough bass		5s.	John Walsh, 1727
680	Courtiville's Sonatas for two flutes		1s. 6d.	John Walsh, c.1701
681	Humphreys's Sonatas for two violins and a bass, opera prima, the bass wanting		Price for the set, 10s. 6d.	John Walsh, c.1736
682	Barsanti's Sonatas, the parts for violin prim. & sec		1s. 6d.	John Walsh, 1727
683[a]	Tartini's six Concertos for eight instruments, opera secunda, complete, Amsterdam		7s. 6d.	Michel-Charles Le Cène, c.1734
683[b]	Tartini's six Concertos for five and six instruments, only the parts for violino principale & organo e violoncello, the rest wanting, Amsterdam	All the eight articles above, £1 11s. 6d.		Michel-Charles Le Cène, 1727
683[c]	Tartini's and Gasparo Visconti's six Concertos for five instruments, opera prima, libro secondo, violino principale part only, Amsterdam			Michel-Charles Le Cène, c.1730
683[d]	Tartini's six Concertos for five instruments, opera prima, libro tertio, wanting only the 2d Ripienno, Amsterdam			Michel-Charles Le Cène, c.1728

TABLE 4.1 continued.

Catalogue No	Catalogue Description	Price – New Copy	Price – Hildyard	Possible Publisher and Year of Publication
683[e]	De Santis Neapolitano six Concertos, opera secunda, violino principale part only, Amsterdam Six Concertos, violino principale part only, Amsterdam N. B. The violino principale part of all the six sets of Concertos above-mentioned are all neatly bound together in one volume, and those and the two following, collected by a Gentleman curious in selecting pieces for that instrument.			Gerard Fredrik Witvogel, 1733
683[f]	Geminiani's six Concertos, opera secunda, the violino principale part only			John Walsh, 1732
683[g]	Vivaldi's twelve Concertos, the violino pincipale part only			John Walsh, 1722
684	Handell's twenty-four overtures for violins, &c. as they were performed at the king's theatre in twenty-seven different operas	£1 1s.	14s.	John Walsh, c.1733
685	Sampson, an oratorio, by Mr Handell	10s. 6d.	7s.	John Walsh, 1743
686	Rosalinda, an opera, in score	£1 1s.	10s. 6d.	John Walsh, c.1750
687	Otho, an opera, by Mr Handell	16s.	7s.	John Walsh, 1729
688	Flavius, an opera, by Mr Handel		5s.	John Walsh, 1723
689	Radamisto, an opera, in score, by Mr Handell	£1 1s.	9s.	John Walsh, 1720
690	Arie Agiunte di Radamisto, opera, dal Handell		4s.	John Walsh, 1720
691	Porus, an opera, by Handell	16s.	6s.	John Walsh, c.1731
692	Astartus, an opera, by Bononcini	16s.	6s.	John Walsh & John Hare, 1721
693	Songs in the opera of Hydaspes		4s.	John Walsh, c.1730

THE MUSIC TRADE IN YORK, 1650–1800   57

694	Favourite songs in the opera of Cyrus	2s. 6d.	1s.	John Walsh & John Hare, 1721
695	—— of Venceslaus	2s. 6d.	1s.	John Walsh, 1731
696	—— of Ormisda	2s. 6d.	1s.	John Walsh, 1730
697	—— of Alcina, 2 collections, imperfect		1s.	John Walsh, 1735
698	Additional favourite songs in the opera of Rinaldo		1s. 6d.	John Walsh, 1731
699	The most celebrated favourite songs in the oratorio of Esther, to which is prefix'd the overture, in score, by Mr Handell	4s.	2s. 6d.	John Walsh, 1732
700	Overture, act-tunes and songs in amorous goddess, composed by Mr Howard		1s. 6d.	John Walsh, 1744
701	Arne's songs in, As you like it and twelfth night, with favourite airs in four other plays and entertainments for two voices		2s. 6d.	William Smith, 1741
702	Gamble's airs and dialogues for one, two, and three voices		1s. 6d.	John Gamble, 1656 or Humphrey Moseley, 1657 or Nathaniel Ekin, 1659
703	A collection of the newest and best songs sung at court and the theatres, 1695, by the best masters, with a thorough bass		1s. 6d.	Henry Playford, 1695
704	Harmonia sacra, or divine hymns and dialogues, with a thorough bass; composed by the best masters, 2 vols.		3s. 6d.	Henry Playford, 1688–93
705	Leveridge's songs, The most celebrated airs and symphonies in Rinaldo fitted for the flute: With these are bound Addison's poems of the Campaign, Peace, and several other poems		2s. 6d.	John Walsh, 1711
706	Dr. Blow's Amphion Anglicus, a work of many compositions for one, two, three, and four voices, with several accompagnements of instrumental musick, and a thorough bass to each song, neatly bound		5s.	John Blow, 1700

TABLE 4.1 continued.

Catalogue No	Catalogue Description	Price – New Copy	Price – Hildyard	Possible Publisher and Year of Publication
707	Sheeles's collection of songs		1s.	John Walsh, c.1727
708	Songs in the Mask of Comus		1s.	William Smith, ?1740
709	Boyce's songs, 2 numbers		1s. 6d.	John Walsh, 1747–8
710	Forty-eight original Scotch aires for a German flute, violin, or harpsicord		1s.	
711	Handell's select duets for two German flutes		1s.	John Walsh, c.1747
712	Forest harmony, a collection of aires, minuets, and marches for French horns		1s.	John Walsh, c.1733–44
713	Select preludes or volentarys for the violin, by the best masters		1s.	John Walsh & John Hare, 1705
714	Collection of song-tunes and symphonies out of operas, fitted for the German-flute	2s.	1s.	
715	Third collection of song-tunes and symphonies	2s.	1s.	
716	Select lessons for a flute, third book by Handell, Hasse, &c.		1s.	John Walsh, c.1733
717	Directions for playing on the flute		1s.	?Benjamin Cooke, c.1730
718	Song-tunes and ariets in Camilla, fitted to the harpsicord	3s.	1s. 6d.	John Walsh & John Hare, 1730
719	Select lessons for the harpsicord		1s.	John Walsh & John Hare, 1705
720	Second book of select lessons for the harpsicord		1s.	
721	Harpsicord master, being instructions for learners		1s.	John Walsh, c.1698–1734

THE MUSIC TRADE IN YORK, 1650–1800   59

722	Keller's rules to attain to play a thorough bass		1s.	John Walsh, c.1730
723	Vanburgh's mirth and harmony, consisting of vocal and instrumental musick	5s.	2s. 6d.	John Walsh, 1730
724	Pepusch's twelve cantatas for one voice, some for a flute and some for a trumpet	9s.	5s.	John Walsh, c.1730
725	British melody, or musical magazine, a collection of sixty of the best songs, aires, &c. set to musick, and transposed for the German and common flute; all corrected, and the fourth part of them set to musick by Lampe. Every song is embellished with a plate, neatly engraven, bound		6s.	James Hodges & Benjamin Cole, 1739
726	The musical entertainer, containing an hundred songs set to musick, and also transposed for the flute. Ornamented each with a cut		10s. 6d.	George Bickham, 1737
727	Three numbers of the 2d vol. of Bickham's musical entertainer		1s.	George Bickham, c.1738
728	A large collection of single songs set to musick, to be sold no less than a dozen together		6d. per dozen	
729	Several small pieces of musick, the price on each.			
730	Musical miscellany, being a collection of choice songs set to the violin, and flute, by the most eminent masters, 6 vols. in 8vo. Bound 1729		12s. 6d.	John Watts, 1729–31
731	Playford's introduction to the skill of musick 1667		1s.	John Playford, 1667
732	—— psalms and hymns, three parts 1700		1s.	Company of Stationers, 1700
733	Ravenscroft's whole book of psalm-tunes, in four parts; and Hopkins's psalms bound with them, 8vo. 1728		1s. 6d.	William Pearson, 1728
734	The genteel companion, being exact directions for the flagellet or recorder		1s.	?Richard Hunt & Humphrey Salter, 1683

TABLE 4.1 continued.

Catalogue No	Catalogue Description	Price – New Copy	Price – Hildyard	Possible Publisher and Year of Publication
735	Singing-psalms in Dutch, with the musick, 240.		1s.	
736	Manuale Cantus secundum usum, F. F. Minorum Recol. Flandriae S. Joseph, in 4 partes divisum, 8vo bound		1s. 6d.	Joannes Kerchovius, 1682
737	Sreeve's divine musick scholar's guide 1741		1s. 6d.	Alice Pearson, 1741
738	Keller's rules for playing a thorough bass, 8vo. 1731		1s.	John Walsh, c.1730
739	A collection of songs set to musick, neatly bound, MSS.		1s. 6d.	
740	Forty-two old songs set to musick, MSS.		1s. 6d.	
741	Anthems set to musick, 2 vols. collection by Mr. Fuller, 8vo		4s.	
742	An antidote against melancholy, being a collection of fourscore merry songs after the manner of suits of lessons. The musick of them entirely new, 8vo 1749		2s. 6d.	Daniel Browne, 1749
743	A treatise on harmony, containing the chief rules for composing in two, three and four parts, dedicated to all lovers of musick, the second edition, altered, enlarged and illustrated by examples in notes, 8vo. bound 1731 N.B. This book is now sold by the author only, and at half a guinea.		6s. 6d.	John Watts, 1730 or William Pearson, 1731
744	A dictionary of foreign words used in musick		1s.	
745	Bononcini divertimenti de Camero, pel violino o flauto, dedicat. al duc di Rutland	5s.	3s.	Mrs. Corticelle, 1722
746	The same book, finely bound, gilt and gilt leaves		5s.	Mrs. Corticelle, 1722
747	Valentini's twelve solos for the violin or violoncello, with a thorough bass for the harpsicord, op. 8va.	6s.	3s.	John Walsh, 1730

748	Marcello's twelve solos for a German flute or violin, with a thorough bass, op. Ima.		2s. 6d.	John Walsh, 1742
749	Birkenstock's twelve solos for a violin, with a thorough bass, op. Ima	7s.	4s.	John Walsh, 1727
750	Loeillet de Gant's twelve sonatas, or solos, for a flute, with a thorough bass, op. 3a.	6s.	2s. 6d.	John Walsh, c.1730
751	Geminiani's twelve solos for a violin, with a thorough bass	6s.	3s.	John Walsh, 1740
752	Galliard's sonatas for a flute and a bass, op. Ima.	4s.	2s.	Thomas Cross, 1711 or John Walsh, c.1721
753	Melande's solos for a violin and bass, op. 2da.	4s.	2s.	John Walsh, c.1725
754	Six sonatas, or solos, fitted for a flute and a bass, by Geminiani and Castrucci		3s.	John Walsh & John Hare, c.1730
755	Abaco's six concertos for seven instruments, op. 5ta. Amst. Another set the same, to be sold together		£1 1s.	Michel-Charles Le Cène, c.1721
756	Abaco's twelve concertos, op. 2da. Ibid. Another set the same, to be sold together, ibid.		£1 1s.	Michel-Charles Le Cène, 1712
757	Abaco's twelve concertos, op. 6ta. Ibid.		£1 1s.	Michel-Charles Le Cène, 1735
758	Abaco's twelve sonatas for the chamber, op. 4ta. Ibid.		10s. 6d.	Michel-Charles Le Cène, 1712
759	An old book of ninety-nine musical lessons, MSS.		2s. 6d.	
760	Nares (organist of York minster) his eight sets of lessons for the harpsichord N.B. This is a subscriber's copy of the first impression. The author does not sell it for less than half a guinea.		7s. 6d.	James Nares, 1747

TABLE 4.1 continued.

Catalogue No	Catalogue Description	Price – New Copy	Price – Hildyard	Possible Publisher and Year of Publication
Appendix, 205	Corelli's 12 sonatas opera 1, 2, 3, and 4, for Violiono [sic] I, Violino 2, & Violencello, 3 vol. half bound, (N.B. The organ part wanting)		9s.	John Walsh, 1705
Appendix, 206	Corelli's 12 sonatas [op 5] or solos for a violin and bass, or harpsichord, half bound		4s.	John Walsh, c.1730
Appendix, 207	Loeillet de Gant's, six sonatas of two parts, for two flutes		2s.	John Walsh, 1728–30
Appendix, 208	Weideman's 12 sonatas, or solos for a German flute, with a thorough-bass for the harpsicord, or violencello		3s. 6d.	John Walsh, 1737
Appendix, 209	Songs in the opera of Calypso and Telemachus, composed by Galliard, the words by Mr Hughes		4s.	John Walsh & John Hare, 1712
Appendix, 210	The musick of the favourite songs of several operas, also aires and other pieces of musick curiously wrote by a gentleman (now deceas'd) for his own entertainment		7s. 6d.	

Of the 119 items listed in Table 4.1, approximately 73 (61.3 per cent) appeared in editions produced by London music publishers, predominantly the Walsh family, although it is not always possible to determine whether Hildyard's copies were Walsh prints or not due to the publication of the same works by others.[25] The difficulty is most obvious in the works by Corelli, which were reissued numerous times both in London and on mainland Europe. Nevertheless, these figures reveal just how important Walsh's business was in supplying printed music to the British regions. In addition, while approximately 98 (82.3 per cent) of items were issued in the eighteenth century, six were published in the seventeenth, indicating that there was still a market for older works. Other items were relatively new: *An Antidote Against Melancholy* had only been published two years previously.[26] Perhaps understandably, given his popularity, Handel is the best represented composer with sixteen separate publications.[27]

John Hildyard's catalogue is important since it provides a snapshot of music sales in York in the 1750s and provides evidence of the trade in second-hand of music away from the metropolis. Here there was clearly a significant demand for such material with little or no stigma attached to purchasing second-hand copies, evident in the high prices charged for some items: a guinea for each set of concertos by the Italian violinist and cellist, Evaristo Felice Dall'Abaco. Hildyard's business was, however, only one element of York's commercial music trade in the eighteenth century since the city had, since c.1660, grown into a centre of organ building.

❧ *Some Early Organ Builders*

One of the earliest organ builders, according to the music historian Sir John Hawkins (1719–89), was 'Preston of York', so named by him in 1776:

> excepting Dallans, Loosemore of Exeter, Thamar of Peterborough, and Preston of York, there was at the time of the restoration scarce an organ-maker that could be called a workman in the kingdom.[28]

Three Prestons were known to have been organ builders in the second half of the seventeenth century: Edward, Roger and William; but their likely

---

[25] To ascertain the publication details for works advertised in Hildyard's catalogue, Library Hub Discover (https://discover.libraryhub.jisc.ac.uk) and Worldcat (www.worldcat.org) were consulted. Details relating to Walsh's imprints can be found in William C. Smith, *A Bibliography of the Musical Works Published by the Firm of John Walsh During the Years 1695–1720* (London, 1948); Charles Humphries and William C. Smith, *A Bibliography of the Musical Works Published by the Firm of John Walsh During the Years 1721–1766* (London, 1968); William C. Smith and Charles Humphries, *Handel: A Descriptive Catalogue of the Early Editions* (2nd edn, Oxford, 1970).

[26] *An Antidote against Melancholy* (London, 1749).

[27] *An Elegy to the Memory of Mr. John Hildyard, Bookseller in York, who died January 29, 1757, aged 46* (York, 1757). ESTC T85961.

[28] John Hawkins, *A General History of the Science and Practice of Music*, 5 vols (London, 1776), iv, 348.

relationship (if any) has not been established. The locations of their work – Carlisle, Gateshead, Ripon and York Minster in the north of England; Southwell in the Midlands; and Cambridge, Ely, Oxford and Salisbury in the south – and the timescale (between 1661 and 1694) suggests that, if the men were related, they were at least two generations.[29] However, no direct connection with York has yet been discovered and they are not elsewhere recorded as working at the Minster.

Robert Dallam of London is known to have built an organ for York Minster in 1634. His grandson, Marc-Antoine Dallam (1673–1730),[30] resident in York from 1719 until death, was paid for repairs to the Minster organ between 1719 and 1730;[31] he is also known to have undertaken repairs and began work on adding a chair organ at Southwell Minster in 1730.[32] Dawes additionally made a payment of five guineas in 1727 to 'Mr Dallum' for setting up an organ.[33]

Ambrose Brownless (or Brownlace) (d.1755) is the last of the York organ builders known before the establishment of Thomas Haxby's business.[34] The first record of any activity as an organ builder occurs in 1744 when he made a proposal 'for Cleaning Repairing and Improving the Organ in Belfrey's Church', that is the church of St Michael-le-Belfrey, York. Attached to the proposal is a testimonial by the York Minster organist, James Nares, who described Brownless as a 'Well Qualifyed Person to Put it [the organ] in order and Add the abovementioned Pipes'.[35] In that same year Brownless was paid £15 5s by St Michael-le-Belfrey, presumably for the work described.[36] He was furthermore paid for various work on the Minster organ between 1749 and 1755;[37] a bill that Brownless submitted on 20 November 1749 includes a proposal for the maintenance of the Minster organ.[38] Brownless additionally did work outside the area, repairing and tuning the organ at Lincoln Cathedral between 1746 and 1753 and repairing the organ at Carlisle Cathedral in 1749.[39]

---

[29] For more on the Prestons, see David Griffiths, 'Preston of York: A Restoration Organ-builder and his Family Connections', *The British Institute of Organ Studies Journal*, 46 (2022), 38–44.

[30] Stephen Bicknell, 'Dallam family', *Grove Music Online*.

[31] GB-Y E2/22 and E2/23.

[32] Paul Hale, *The Organs of Southwell Minster* (Southwell, 1996), 10–11.

[33] GB-Y MS Add. 65/1-4.

[34] Robert Beilby Cooke (ed.), *The Parish Registers of Holy Trinity Church, Goodramgate, 1573–1812* (Leeds, 1911), 286.

[35] York, Borthwick Institute for Archives, St Michael-le-Belfrey Churchwardens' Accounts (1730–52), PR Y/MB 35.

[36] Ibid.

[37] GB-Y E2/23 and E2/PV.

[38] This has been transcribed in Nicholas Thistlethwaite, *The Organs of York Minster, 1236–2021* (Oxford, 2021), 50.

[39] Robert Pacey, *The Organs of Lincoln Cathedral* (Lincoln, 1998), 16; Simon D.I. Fleming, 'The Eighteenth-Century Musicians of Carlisle Cathedral', *Transactions of the*

While not an organ builder, a further York-based instrument maker referred to several times in Dawes' accounts is a Mr [Richard] Vesey. Most of Dawes' payments to him were for tuning spinets: for example, on 21 September 1723 and 6 December 1723, with further annual payments from 1727 to 1730; other payments were for music desks in 1727 and 1729. In 1703 a payment of £1 10s. was made to Richard Vesey by York Minster for 'work done at the Harpsecord in the Schoolehouse' suggesting Vesey's presence in the city since the dawn of the century.[40] Donald Boalch furthermore records a wing-shaped spinet made by Vesey, with an inscription on the nameboard: 'Richardus Vesey Ebor. Fecit'.[41] A payment made to Mrs Vesey for harpsichord strings in 1732, instead of Mr Vesey, seems to confirm the fact that he was the same Richard Vesey who was buried in the church of St Martin-cum-Gregory, York, on 2 April 1732.[42]

While all these instrument makers were relatively minor figures, there was a major shift in 1756 with the establishment of a new business venture by Thomas Haxby, the most important of all individuals involved in the York music trade in the eighteenth century.

Thomas Haxby

Haxby was baptised in York on 23 January 1730, the son of Robert Haxby, a joiner.[43] While nothing is known of Thomas' musical education, it was clearly sufficient for him to be appointed a probationer lay clerk in York Minster choir on 25 January 1751. It seems likely that he, like William Flackton of Canterbury, was a singing boy in the Minster, but this supposition remains unproven since the names of the choristers before the nineteenth century are largely unrecorded.[44] At the same time as his appointment as a Minster songman he was made parish clerk of the church of St Michael-le-Belfrey, York, holding both posts until death.[45] In 1788 he was one of three Minster songmen (the other two were Edward Bennington and John Palmer) 'who are the most useful in that Choir, by Singing Solo Anthems, by their diligent Attendance in the Church, and their good Conduct out of it', for

---

Cumberland & Westmorland Antiquarian & Archaeological Society, 12 (2012), 183–97, at 195.
[40] GB-Y E2/22.
[41] Donald H. Boalch, *Makers of the Harpsichord and Clavichord, 1440–1840* (3rd edn, Oxford, 1995), 672.
[42] Edward Bulmer (ed.), *The Parish Registers of St. Martin-cum-Gregory in the City of York* (York, 1897), 133.
[43] Ibid., 132. See David Haxby and John Malden, 'Thomas Haxby of York (1729–1796) – an Extraordinary Musician and Musical Instrument Maker', *York Historian*, 2 (1978), 43–55; and *eidem*, 'Thomas Haxby—a Note', *York Historian*, 3 (1980), 31–55, at 31.
[44] For more on Flackton, see Simon Fleming's contribution on Joseph Barber and William Flackton in this volume.
[45] GB-Y H 9/1.

which he was awarded a further £6 p.a.[46] He also sang at local concerts, performing at a benefit for Mr. Perkins, the oboist, at the York Assembly Rooms in 1754.[47] In 1758 he became a freeman of the city of York by patrimony, on which occasion he was described as a 'musical instrument maker'.[48] He was later appointed to two municipal offices: in 1771 he was elected as a Common Councilman for Bootham Ward, an administrative area in York, and in 1789 one of six City Chamberlains.[49] He died in 1796, and his obituary notice in the *York Courant* bears witness to the esteem in which he was held within his native city:

> On Monday last [31 October] died, after a painful illness, which he bore with christian [*sic*] fortitude and resignation, Mr. Thomas Haxby of this City; whose kind, warm, and affectionate conduct towards his friends and relatives, and modest, honest, and virtuous demeanour in his intercourse with the world, render his death sincerely lamented, as a private and public loss.[50]

Forty years earlier Haxby had announced the opening of his music shop with the following notice:

> This Day is opened (at the ORGAN in Blake-street, York) A MUSIC SHOP; where Gentlemen, Ladies, and others may be furnished with all Sorts of Musical Instruments and Cases; Bows, Bridges, Strings, and Wire; Music, Vocal and Instrumental, Books of Instruction; blank Books, ruled Paper &c. Wholesale and Retale [*sic*], at reasonable Prices … N.B. Instruments repaired, and kept in Order in Town or Country.[51]

After ten years in business he promoted the opening of a 'New Musical Instrument Warehouse, next Door but one to his Music Shop in Blake-street'.[52] The rainheads on this building – 'TH 1766' – are at the back of the present-day street frontage and not visible, but those on the front, and in the street – 'TH 1773' – are still evident today.[53] In 1788 Haxby disposed of 'all his Stock of Printed Music, and every other Article in the Musical Branch' to Samuel Knapton (for whom see further below) in order to concentrate on the making, repairing, and tuning of harpsichords and pianofortes.[54]

The advertisements Haxby placed in the *York Courant* promoted works composed by musicians of both domestic or foreign extraction; they include Thomas Arne, J.C. Bach, Jonathan Battishill, Thomas Chilcot, Albertus Groneman, Henry Holcombe, Ignaz Holzbauer, James Nares, Gaspare Siprutini, Johann Stamitz, Thomas Thackray and Georg Christoph Wagenseil. The genres available included concerti grossi, symphonies, trio sonatas, psalm and

---

[46] GB-Y E2/24.
[47] *York Courant*, 5 February 1754.
[48] Francis Collins (ed.), *Register of the Freemen of the City of York*, vol. 2: *1559–1759* (Durham, 1900), 262–89.
[49] *York Courant*, 8 August 1771 and 20 January 1789.
[50] Ibid., 7 November 1796.
[51] Ibid., 29 June 1756.
[52] Ibid., 19 August 1766.
[53] *An Inventory of the Historical Monuments in the City of York*, vol. 5: *The Central Area* (London, 1981), 109.
[54] *York Courant*, 14 October 1788.

hymn books, ballad operas, cantatas and collections of dances, works which were suitable for both domestic and public use.[55] In 1768 Haxby boasted that he sold 'All the Music published in England, and great Choice from abroad'.[56] Like Hildyard before him, Haxby subscribed to new musical works for resale in his shop. He appears in 54 lists in the *Dataset of Subscribers*, purchasing six copies of William Randall's editions of Handel's works, and five of those edited by Samuel Arnold. Many works have a North-East connection, including Avison's op 9 concertos (1766–7 – 7 copies), Thomas Ebdon's *Six Sonata's* (*c*.1772 – 12 copies), and his first collection of *Sacred Music* (1790 – 2 copies), John Garth's *Six Sonatas*, op 2 (1768 – 7 copies), T. Kilvington's *Fourteen Country Dances* (*c*.1785 – 12 copies), Edward Miller's *Elegies. Songs, and an Ode* (1770 – 2 copies), *Six Sonatas* (*c*.1769 – 7 copies) and *The Psalms of David* (1790 – 2 copies) and Thomas Wright's *Six Songs* (*c*.1785 – 6 copies).[57]

Haxby was a member of the York Musical Society, for which institution he supplied music between 1768 and 1772.[58] He also provided York Minster with a wide range of services, as revealed in a bill settled on 1 February 1771:

> writing [i.e., copying] a Solo Anthem
> 3 Quires & ¾ of Imperial put into the Books
> Binding 6 Vol^s. Calf Backs — Lettered & Putting an Index to each @ 3/9
> Paid Dr Boyce for his 2. second Vols. of Church Music
> Carriage of D^o
> Paid Duncannon for binding them & 1 of the 1st Vol: in rough Calf & letter'd
> Writing 36 & ½ Sheets into the Church books
> Correcting the Organ Books by Dr Boyce
> Writing 3 Copys of Mr Masons Anthem & the Chorus in loose papers & Score[59]

These services included the binding of books, for which he worked in partnership with other local traders or apprentices, as demonstrated by the payment to 'Duncannon'. Haxby furthermore acted as an agent for London-based music publishers, evident through the Minster's payment for two copies of Boyce's *Cathedral Music*, issued by subscription between 1760 and 1773. The list of subscribers attached to this work reveals that York's Dean and Chapter subscribed to two copies, with the bill indicating that Haxby acted as the middleman, forwarding the payment and subscription details to Boyce or his London-based agent. Boyce's publication appears to have been of great use to the Minster

---

[55] Ibid., 26 October 1762 and 31 December 1765.
[56] Ibid., 16 August 1768.
[57] Fleming and Perkins, *Dataset of Subscribers*. For more on Edward Miller, see Christopher Roberts's contribution in this volume.
[58] York, Explore Library and Archive, York Musical Society Minute and Account Book, Acc. 30: 1a. It is likely that Haxby continued to supply the York Musical Society in a similar way until he gave up selling music; however, the society's accounts for the period 1772–88 have not survived.
[59] GB-Y E2/24 and E2/PV.

choir, since a bill for 12 June 1790 records that the Dean and Chapter paid Haxby for '8 sets (3 Vols each) of Dr Boyce Antient Church Music', along with their carriage from London and the cost of binding.[60] The work purchased was the second edition of Boyce's *Cathedral Music*, published in 1788. Unlike the first edition, the Dean and Chapter are not recorded as subscribers; instead, Haxby provided his own details, with the list recording that he purchased eight copies, presumably the same eight sold to the Minster.

In addition to an array of musical goods and services provided to York Minster, Haxby was engaged to maintain their organ from 1755 onwards, receiving annual payments of six guineas for tuning. He was sometimes paid for other work on the instrument; for instance, in 1760 he received £21 for 'Putting a Dulciana Stop into the Choir Organ & repairing the Furniture &c in the great Organ'.[61] More extensive work was done on the organ in July 1791, presumably in preparation for the three concerts given in the Minster that formed part of the musical festival held in York later that year, for which Haxby was paid £26 5s.[62]

Haxby's career as an organ builder is further demonstrated in the other churches for which he is known to have built organs: Scarborough (St Mary, 1762), Newby Hall (1765), Louth (St James, 1769), and York (St Michael-le-Belfrey, 1785). The work on an organ at Nostell Priory (1767), sometimes attributed to Haxby, has not been clearly authenticated. He was also associated with church organs at Beverley, Halifax, Hull and Leeds, either through submitting bids for building instruments, refereeing those made by others, or for making repairs.[63] Haxby additionally built chamber organs for use at home. In 1761 Haxby made for the lawyer, John Courtney of Beverley, a desk organ, for which he received 36 guineas.[64] Two years later Haxby advertised a 'great Choice of Chamber and Box Organs' for sale, adding that 'new Barrels [were] made to Box Organs'.[65] He installed in 1782, on behalf of the poet and canon at York Minster, William Mason (1724–97), a barrel organ in the church of All Saints, Aston (South Yorkshire) which consisted of two barrels and played twenty-four tunes.[66]

In addition to organ building, Haxby made other musical instruments. Seven spinets which he built between 1763 and 1771 have survived along with two

---

[60] GB-Y E2/PV.

[61] GB-Y E2/23 and E2/PV.

[62] GB-Y E2/PV. The festival also comprised two concerts in the Assembly Rooms.

[63] Maximillian Elliott, 'Thou shalt buzz no more': an examination of the organ-building industry in nineteenth-century York; its origins, growth and prominence' (PhD dissertation, University of York, 2019), 7; Joseph Brogden Baker, *The History of Scarbrough, from the Earliest Date* (London, 1882), 158–9.

[64] Susan and David Neaves (eds), *The Diary of a Yorkshire Gentleman, John Courtney of Beverley, 1759–1768* (Otley, 2001), 39–40. A desk organ is an instrument which gives the appearance of a desk when the keyboard lid is closed.

[65] *York Courant*, 1 March 1763.

[66] Bernard Barr and John Ingamells, *A Candidate for Praise: William Mason, 1725–97, Precentor of York* (York, 1973), 54; Haxby and Malden, 'Thomas Haxby of York', 46–7.

harpsichords (both single manuals, dated 1775 and 1777, respectively).[67] A man of some ingenuity, he was granted in 1770 a patent for an improved harpsichord, presumably done to mitigate a fall in sales due to the increasing popularity of the piano:

A.D. 1770, December 28.—N° 977.

HAXBY, THOMAS.—"A new single harpsichord, containing all the stops of a double one, which by the use of one pedal only, produces every increase, diminution, & variation of tone that a double one is capable of performing.

A single harpsichord of two unisons, octave lute and harp, which by the use of one pedal only (which said pedal has a connection with several sliding tumblers, springs, &c.) produces ten variations of stops, also an increase and diminution of tone (either gradually or instantaneously) from the softest stop to the full harpsichord, or from the full harpsichord to the softest stop."[68]

A harpsichord preserved in York Castle Museum (see Plate 4.1) displays the improvements that Haxby patented. This instrument, however, had no future and by 1772 Haxby had begun to produce fortepianos,[69] twenty-seven of which have survived.[70] Haxby dated all his square pianos and gave each a production number, from which it can be established that he built somewhere in the region of 381 instruments.[71] A cittern and a violin are the only string instruments of his which are known to have survived, and there is now no trace of the 'curious Guittars with eight additional Strings' which he advertised in 1764, nor of the 'Guittars upon a new construction' advertised two years later.[72] Another York instrument maker, John Watson, is known as the maker of a wing spinet, also recorded by Boalch, which has the inscription: 'Johannes Watson Eboraci fecit 1762'.[73] Watson appears to have been in Haxby's employ, as suggested by his presence as one of the two witnesses to the articles of agreement between Haxby and the churchwardens of St James, Louth, for the building of an organ there.[74] It remains to mention three musical works which have Haxby's name in their imprints, and which were published in the 1760s: Matthias Hawdon, *An Ode on the King of Prussia* (c.1760); John Camidge, *Six Easy Lessons for the Harpsichord* (1763); and Thomas Thackray, *Six Lessons for the Guittar* (1765).

---

[67] Boalch, *Makers of the Harpsichord*, 380–82.
[68] *Patents for Inventions. Abridgments of Specifications relating to Music and Musical Instruments. A.D. 1694–1866* (London, 1871), 6–7. Haxby subsequently referred to these improvements in two newspaper advertisements: *York Courant*, 5 March 1771 and 17 March 1772.
[69] Haxby's earliest extant fortepiano is dated 1772 and preserved in the Städtisches Museum, Braunschweig, Germany, https://db2.earlypianos.org/dbport2/PianoGrid12.aspx.
[70] Details of Haxby's piano can be found at *Clinkscale Online*, http://db2.earlypianos.org/dbport2/PianoSearch22.aspx.
[71] Haxby and Malden, 'Thomas Haxby of York', 52–3.
[72] Haxby and Malden, 'Thomas Haxby – a Note', 31; *York Courant*, 3 January 1764 and 19 August 1766.
[73] Boalch, *Makers of the Harpsichord*, 676.
[74] Haxby and Malden, 'Thomas Haxby – a Note', 31.

PLATE 4.1 A single manual harpsichord with pedal by Thomas Haxby.

Following Haxby's death, there were no organ builders in the city until the arrival of John Donaldson in 1791, formerly of Newcastle.[75] He advertised the making of church, chamber and barrel organs, to which he added pianoforte making and repairing. It appears, however, that none of his pianofortes have survived. Attached to his organ workshop, he opened a shop, selling 'Piano Fortes by Broadwood, Culliford, and the other best makers in London'.[76]

---

[75] Roz Southey, *Music-Making in North-East England during the Eighteenth Century* (Aldershot, 2006), 109–10. See also Simon D.I. Fleming's contribution on Stephen Moore in this volume.

[76] *York Courant*, 3 April 1797.

❧ Samuel Knapton

As noted above, Haxby announced in 1788 that he had transferred 'all his Stock of Printed Music, and every other Article in the Musical Branch' to Samuel Knapton.[77] Baptised at Christ Church, York, on 1 November 1756,[78] Knapton became a freeman in 1777, at which time his occupation was described as a peruke-maker (the same occupation as his father). Knapton must have had some musical skill for two years later he was appointed one of the York waits.[79] He retained this post for ten years, resigning around nine months after the opening of his music shop. In the first advertisement for his business, which occupied the same premises as those vacated by Haxby, he undertook to sell:

> every new Musical Production (English and Foreign) procured as soon as published. Also great Choice of Violins, Violoncellos, Tenors, German and English Flutes, Fifes, Hautboys, Clarionets, Bassoons, Harpsicords [sic], and Piano Fortes; Roman Strings, Bows, Music Paper, Wire, and every other Article in the Musical Branch.[80]

Knapton here assured the public 'that all Orders from Town or Country shall be executed with Dispatch, Punctuality, and Integrity', thus acknowledging a clientele outside the city of York. In subsequent advertisements Knapton emphasised the sale of pianofortes 'particularly the Grand Piano Fortes both Upright and Horizontal ... by the first Makers'.[81] He also advised that 'regiments [could be] supplied with complete sets of music and the very best military instruments', thus catering for the needs of local militias. Knapton was, like Haxby, a member of the York Musical Society, and this body made five payments to him. For instance, on 28 April 1794 they 'Paid Mr Knapton for Overture 4s 6d'; in that same year 'Mr Knapton' made a gift to the Society of '35 Concertos by [William] Corbett'.[82] The latter refers to Corbett's *Concerto's or Universal Bizzaries for Four Violins, Tenor Violin a Violoncello and Thorough Bass for the Organ and Harpsichord*, issued in three volumes from 1742. Clearly there was still a need for older works for the use of musical-society members, reflecting the wider interest in such music that reached a peak in 1776 with the founding of the London-based 'Concerts of Ancient Music'.[83]

Knapton subscribed to a number of works, including some that Haxby also purchased. A few were locally produced, and they include Matthew Camidge's

---

[77] Ibid., 14 October 1788.
[78] Walter J. Kaye (ed.), *The Parish Register of Holy Trinity, King's Court (Otherwise Christ Church) York* (Wakefield, 1928), 91. A portrait of Knapton can be found in the York Art Gallery, at www.artuk.org.
[79] Robert Davies, *City of York. The Freeman's Roll* (York, 1835), 41; York, Explore Library and Archives, York Corporation House Books, HB 44, p. 465 and HB 45, p. 353.
[80] *York Courant*, 14 October 1788.
[81] Ibid., 23 January 1797.
[82] York, Explore Library and Archives, York Musical Society Minute and Account Book. Acc. 30: 1a.
[83] Tim Eggington, *The Advancement of Music in Enlightenment England: Benjamin Cooke and the Academy of Ancient Music* (Woodbridge, 2014), 71–3.

Three Sonatas (1797 – 6 copies), William Howgill's *An Original Anthem & Two Voluntaries* (1800 – 2 copies), T. Kilvington's *Twelve Country Dances* (1791 – 6 copies) and Edward Miller's *The Psalms of David* (1790 – 7 copies). We also find him subscribing to works issued in London, including: Domenico Corri's *The Singers Preceptor* (1810 – 6 copies), John Gunn's *The Theory and Practice of Fingering the Violoncello* (1789 – 6 copies), Stephen Storace's *The Favorite Operas of Mahmoud & The Iron Chest* (1797 – 4 copies) and George Surr's *Three Sonatas*, op 1 (1796 – 6 copies).

Samuel Knapton's business continued into the nineteenth century and in 1820 he entered into partnership with his son Philip.[84] At the same time he established a separate enterprise for the printing and publishing of music, in conjunction with John White of Leeds.[85] Samuel Knapton died in 1831, followed two years later by the death of his son.[86]

Joseph Shaw

Eight years after Thomas Haxby had opened his music shop a rival business was established by Joseph Shaw, whose premises were 'at the sign of the Violin and Hautboy', near the Black Swan, one of York's most important eighteenth-century inns and coaching houses.[87] Biographical information about Shaw is hard to distil, since there were at least two other contemporary York musicians with the same surname. Our man was appointed a York wait in 1754, having been approved by the 'Gentlemen Directors who play at the Concert' as the best performer of the candidates for the post.[88] He was then admitted as a member of the York Musical Society in 1770, who paid him for supplying the Society with music in the next year.[89] The initial advertisement for Shaw's music shop has the usual information about instruments and music for sale, but also adds that his shop was a place 'where are made organs, harpsichords, spinnets, &c'; one suspects that the quality of his instruments was not high since none of his instruments have survived. In 1775 he died of 'Gout in his Stomach' and was buried at the church of St Sampson on 29 March.[90] His stock was advertised for sale in May, but his business was still operating in August when subscription

---

[84] *York Herald*, 23 July 1803. A trade card from his time there, with the legend 'Knapton's Music & Musical Warehouse, Coney Street', is among the collections of the York Castle Museum, folder entitled Bill Heads 2. A reproduction can be found in Terry Friedman, *Engrav'd Cards ... of Trades-men ... in the County of Yorkshire* (Bradford, 1976), no. 55.

[85] *Yorkshire Gazette*, 19 August 1820.

[86] *York Herald*, 9 July 1831; *Yorkshire Gazette*, 22 June 1833.

[87] *York Courant*, 24 January 1764.

[88] York, Explore Library and Archives, York Corporation House Books, HB 43, pp. 456 and 459.

[89] York, Explore Library and Archives, York Musical Society Minute and Account Book. Acc. 30: 1a.

[90] York, Borthwick Institute for Archives, PR/Y/SAM/3, Parish Registers for the Archdeaconry of Yorkshire.

tickets for the York August race week concerts were advertised for sale at 'Mrs. Shaw's Music-Shop'.[91]

Haxby's Successors

In his will, Haxby bequeathed to his 'Brother in law Edward Tomlinson & his Son Thomas my Nephew equally between them ... all my Harpsichords Piano Fortes Spinnets Stock of Wood Metal Tools ... use'd in my Workshops [etc.]'[92] Edward had married Haxby's sister in 1767 at the church of St Crux, York, at which time he was described as a musical instrument maker, although it is not known if he was then working for his brother-in-law. Apprenticed to his uncle in 1782, Thomas Haxby Tomlinson took up the freedom of the city after the customary period of seven years, now a musical instrument maker.[93] Ten days after Haxby's death, Edward and Thomas Haxby Tomlinson made the following announcement:

> [We] have entered upon the whole Stock in Trade of the said Mr. Haxby ... at his Shop and Warehouses in Blake-Street, where the business will be carried on in all its branches as formerly. Having been employed by Mr. Haxby for many years past, in assisting him and executing his business, and particularly in finishing all his new Instruments ... [we] hope ... to merit a continuance of that favour and patronage ... so liberally bestowed ... on their worthy Relation.[94]

In addition to the sale of their own pianos, the Tomlinsons sold instruments by other makers, and within two years of taking over the business stocked a wide range of 'new music, vocal and instrumental, books of instructions, ruled books, ruled paper [and] ... every article in the musical branch'.[95] Edward Tomlinson continued in the business until his death in February 1813, and his son Thomas Haxby Tomlinson until his death in May 1846.[96]

Conclusion

This survey of York's music trade has shown that until 1756, when Haxby opened the first specialised music shop, the people of York and its environs relied heavily on general booksellers for the supply of printed music and music-related paraphernalia. Haxby then came to dominate the music trade in York during the second half of the eighteenth century, before selling part of his business – that not concerned with instrument building – to Samuel Knapton in 1788. The former had competition in the form of Joseph Shaw, while Knapton's shop was without competitors until the Tomlinsons established their business

---

[91] *York Courant*, 28 March 1775, 23 May 1775 and 1 August 1775.
[92] York, Borthwick Institute for Archives, Prerogative Court of York Wills, 1797.
[93] Haxby and Malden, 'Thomas Haxby of York', 47.
[94] *York Courant*, 7 November 1796.
[95] Ibid., 19 November 1798.
[96] *York Herald*, 27 February 1813 and 9 May 1846.

in 1796. Both Knapton and the Tomlinsons continued to trade into the next century. Other instrument makers chose York as their base, including Richard Vesey and John Watson, and the city was a centre of organ-building from the Restoration until the establishment of John Donaldson's workshop in the 1790s.

York's rise as a centre of the music trade was undoubtedly due to the presence of its Minster, and we find local businesses providing them with music-copying services, along with the sale of music and its binding, and the maintenance of their organs. It is also interesting that we find evidence of Haxby acting as a gobetween, forwarding the Dean and Chapter's subscriptions to new musical works to London. Haxby and others similarly subscribed to new music themselves and, in a few examples, published music. While York might have been a northern city, the importance of its links with the wider music trade are undeniable, with Haxby and others seeking to make a living by catering to the musical needs of the Minster, and other local and regional inhabitants.

5

Joseph Barber of Newcastle upon Tyne and William Flackton of Canterbury: Booksellers, Music Publishing and the Subscription Market in Eighteenth-Century Britain[1]

Simon D.I. Fleming

Publication by subscription had become, by the eighteenth century, a common method by which composers, editors and authors issued their latest musical and literary works while minimising any personal financial risk. Indeed, for many composers, particularly those who were British born, it could be the only way through which publication might be achieved.[2] Once issued, such works would frequently include a printed list of all those who had subscribed. These lists are of importance to anyone investigating British social history as they shed considerable light on the nature of the subscribers, including status, place of employment, residence and/or musical interests, along with their personal links with the composer.

Britain's booksellers, since the seventeenth century, had been of significant importance to the function of the subscription method for music books, as they were frequently tasked with taking subscriptions on behalf of the composer.[3] By the 1720s, booksellers regularly appear in the subscription lists to new musical

---

[1] I would like to dedicate this chapter to my former colleagues at Queen Elizabeth Sixth Form College, Darlington, and in particular Giles Bayliss, Vicki Boyle, Gary Darby, Steven McGarvie, Beverley Palmer, Jane Spellman, James Stubbs, Roswitha Wagenknecht, Gillian Westlake, Ellie White, Liam Winstanley and Fay Wray.

[2] For a discussion of the prejudice that existed towards British-born composers, whose music was viewed as less commercial than that written by composers from mainland Europe, see Simon D.I. Fleming, 'Foreign Composers, the Subscription Market, and the Popularity of Continental Music in Eighteenth-Century Britain', in Simon D.I. Fleming and Martin Perkins (eds), *Music by Subscription: Composers and their Networks in the British Music-Publishing Trade, 1676–1820* (London, 2022), 221–41.

[3] This was certainly the case in the publication of Henry Purcell's *Sonnata's of III Parts* (London, 1683). Subscriptions could be placed at William Hall's house, or at the music shops run by Henry Playford and John Carr. See Richard Luckett, 'The Playfords and the Purcells', in Robin Myers, Michael Harris and Giles Mandelbrote (eds), *Music and the Book Trade from the Sixteenth to the Twentieth Century* (London, 2008), 45–67, at 53. For a list of self-published books issued in the seventeenth century, including those by subscription, see Rebecca Herissone, 'Playford, Purcell, and the Functions of Music

publications, with their presence providing a modicum of free advertising.[4] It was even commonplace for different publishers to subscribe to each other's publications. Indeed, many of Britain's most important music businesses, the majority of which were located in London, were involved in this practice, including that managed by John Walsh the younger (1709–66). An analysis of their subscriptions indicates a willingness to sell other publishers' works, including some from outside of London, presumably in an effort to make their business the music shop of choice in the capital.[5]

While London remained the most important centre for the printing and publishing of music throughout the eighteenth century, this trade was by no means limited to the metropolis. Two booksellers outside London who had a particularly close association with the subscription method for the publication of music were Joseph Barber (1706–82) of Newcastle upon Tyne and William Flackton (1709–98) of Canterbury. Barber, who was involved in the production of Charles Avison's first sets of concertos, issued between 1740 and 1744, is an early example of a music printer who worked in the north of England. Flackton, on the other hand, was active as a composer and had several of his own works published. However, he opted to have his musical works produced in London by John Walsh. Both Barber and Flackton provide early case studies of printed music traders outside of the capital and their trade networks, thanks to the existence of numerous subscription lists. As such, this chapter reveals the important role localised booksellers had as regional hubs for the production and dissemination of new musical works.

❧ *Publication by Subscription*

While the first book to be issued by subscription in Britain was John Minsheu's *Ductor in Linguas, The Guide into Tongues* (1617),[6] it was not until 1676, with Thomas Mace's *Musick's Monument*,[7] that a music book was issued by subscription, for which a list of subscribers survives.[8] Over the course of the

---

Publishing in Restoration England', *Journal of the American Musicological Society*, 63/2 (2010), 243–90, at 257–60.

[4] It is impossible to say if booksellers, as a rule, subscribed to musical works in the seventeenth century due to the lack of extant subscription lists. For the only list in a seventeenth-century music book, see Stephanie Carter, 'Thomas Mace and the Publication by Subscription of *Musick's Monument* (1676)', in Fleming and Perkins (eds), *Music by Subscription*, 21–38.

[5] John Playford appears to have used a similar approach in the 1650s. See Stephanie Carter, 'Music Publishing and Compositional Activity in England, 1650–1700' (PhD dissertation, University of Manchester, 2011), 42.

[6] Printed in London by Ioannem Browne. For more on the subscription method, see Simon D.I. Fleming and Martin Perkins, 'Introduction', in Fleming and Perkins (eds), *Music by Subscription*, 1–18.

[7] Printed in London by T. Ratcliffe, and N. Thompson.

[8] Stephanie Carter, 'Thomas Mace and Music in Seventeenth-Century Cambridge', *Journal of Seventeenth-Century Music*, 28/1 (2022), at https://sscm-jscm.org/jscm-issues/volume-28-no-1/thomas-mace-and-music-in-seventeenth-century-cambridge/

eighteenth century, the subscription method grew into a well-known vehicle for the publication of music, whether they were newly composed works or new editions of old music. The lists of subscribers attached to these works provide a valuable resource for anyone researching British social history since they frequently contain information that does not survive elsewhere. Nevertheless, such lists can be ambiguous, with mistakes or misspellings creating difficulty for researchers seeking to identify a particular subscriber.[9]

The increasing popularity of the subscription method in Britain was due to the way it enabled authors, composers and editors to publish their latest productions, even if they lacked the necessary capital to undertake such an endeavour themselves. At first, an unpublished work would be promoted through published notices or by word of mouth. A potential subscriber would, most commonly, register their interest with composer, publisher or agent. Then, once printing was complete, they would be expected to forward their promised payment before receiving their copy.[10] Subscribers often had an added incentive through the offer of a discount on the full retail price. There were various reasons as to why an individual might choose to subscribe. Naturally, many would have known the author personally and it is no surprise that, in the average list, a significant number of subscribers lived in the immediate vicinity of the author's hometown or city.[11] Unsurprising too, particularly for musical works, that an appreciable number were professional musicians, some of whom subscribed reciprocally; others, particularly unmarried females, were frequently pupils. Further subscribers may have met the composer or editor at the time a subscription was being promoted, while others would have heard about the subscription through a notice, such as a printed handbill or newspaper advertisement. For some, particularly those from the upper classes, the presence of a list enabled them to publicly demonstrate their patronage of the arts and would certainly have subscribed for pretentious reasons. This would, to a degree, also apply to those individuals wishing to promote their rise in affluence and social status, using the opportunity as a means by which their names might appear alongside more prominent members of British society; the work, to them, may have been of secondary importance to the inclusion of their name on the list. A significant number of the clergy also tended to subscribe, many of whom were talented amateur musicians, and from the 1720s there were also institutions, such as music clubs, choirs or cathedral chapters, which purchased music for use by their members or singers.[12]

---

[9] See Fleming and Perkins, 'Introduction'.
[10] In some cases, subscribers were asked to pay the full subscription at the same time as subscribing or paid in two instalments. See ibid., 10.
[11] Simon D.I. Fleming, 'Avison and his Subscribers: Musical Networking in Eighteenth-Century Britain', *Royal Musical Association Research Chronicle*, 49/1 (2018), 21–49, at 23–6.
[12] For more on the music club and subscription publications, see Simon D.I. Fleming and Martin Perkins, 'A Big Data Study: Musical Societies in Subscription Lists', in Fleming and Perkins (eds), *Music by Subscription*, 152–76.

Music Publishers and Booksellers in Subscription Lists

Along with these other types of subscribers, music publishers or more general booksellers frequently appear in subscription lists. There are several reasons as to why the proprietors of such a business might choose to subscribe to any individual work. While some booksellers could gain some publicity through their presence on a subscription list, it also made financial sense as subscribers tended to receive a discount on the sale price and so copies could then be sold at full price in their shops.[13] What is perhaps most interesting is that publishers would subscribe to works by composers and other publishers with which they had no obvious connection. John Walsh the younger, for example, subscribed to a range of publications, both printed by himself and by his competitors, and purchased multiple copies of many for resale. A list of all the musical works to which he, and his father, John Walsh snr (c.1666–1736), subscribed is given in Table 5.1.

The majority of these publications were not printed by either Walsh, but in some cases they acted as an official agent. This was the case for John Pixell's *A Collection of Songs, with their Recitatives and Symphonies*, op 1 (1759). Printed in Birmingham by Michael Broome, who also engraved the music plates, the title page records that it was 'sold by *Mess. WALSH* and *JOHNSON. LONDON.*'[14] In some cases, Walsh the younger subscribed to an exceptionally large number of copies, taking 31 sets of Boyce's *Twelve Sonatas for Two Violins with a Bass* (1747), a work he also printed for the composer. Walsh clearly expected this work to sell well, and no doubt anticipated a good return on his investment. Nevertheless, of all the composers in Table 5.1, Avison appears the most with Walsh the younger subscribing to four separate works.[15]

The number of copies of Avison's concertos that Walsh purchased grew in parallel to the increasing popularity of Avison's concertos with London audiences. While he did not subscribe to the *Six Concertos in Seven Parts*, op 2 (1740), he was aware of its publication as he brought out a set of eight organ concertos, six of which were based on the concertino parts from this set and designed to work with the already available ripieno parts; they were published as *Eight Concertos for the Organ or Harpsichord* (1747).[16] Walsh went on to pur-

---

[13] Nevertheless, as Feather observed, many businesses would have had the opportunity to purchase new books at wholesale price, whether or not they were issued by subscription. See John Feather, *The Provincial Book Trade in Eighteenth-Century England* (Cambridge, 1985), 55.

[14] For more on the publication of Pixell's op 1, see Simon D.I. Fleming 'John Pixell: An Eighteenth-Century Vicar and Composer', *The Musical Times*, 154/1923 (2013), 71–83, at 78–9.

[15] Walsh also subscribed to six copies of *The First Fifty Psalms* by Benedetto Marcello, produced in an English edition by John Garth in association with Avison.

[16] Of the two remaining 'Walsh' organ concertos, one was based on the second concerto from Avison's first collection of *Two Concertos*, and the other on a published concerto, issued in his second collection of *Two Concertos*. Revised versions of all eight concertos were included by Avison in his *Twelve Concertos in Seven Parts*, op 6 (Newcastle, 1758).

SIX CONCERTO'S
IN
SEVEN PARTS.

DEDICATED to the Honourable

Colonel *Blathwayt*,

BY

CHARLES AVISON, Organist,
in *Newcastle upon Tyne*.

OPERA SECUNDA.

NEWCASTLE:

Printed by *JOSEPH BARBER*, Musick and Copper-Plate Printer;
And Sold by BENJAMIN COOKE at the *Golden-Harp*, in *New-Street, Covent-Garden, London.*
Where may also be had,
SIX SONATA's. In Three Parts. Compos'd by the same Author.

M.DCC.XL.

PLATE 5.1 Charles Avison's *Six Concertos in Seven Parts*, op 2 (1740), Title-page. This image is reproduced from the 'Durham Partbooks', cello part, M2135. For more on these volumes, see Simon D.I. Fleming, 'James Nares' Concerto Grosso and the Durham Partbooks', *Early Music Performer*, 43 (2018), 10–16.

chase one copy of the *Six Concertos,* op 3 (1751), seven of the *Eight Concertos,* op 4 (1755), and fourteen of the *Twelve Concertos,* op 9 (1766–7). Walsh even subscribed to six copies of Avison's *Two Concertos* (1742) issued by Barber in Newcastle.[17]

TABLE 5.1 Musical works to which John Walsh snr and John Walsh jnr subscribed.[18]

Composer	Title	Printer[19]	Year	No. of copies
John Alcock	Six Concerto's in Seven Parts	London, for the author	1750	6
John Alcock	A Morning and Evening Service	John Johnson, for the author	1753	11
John Alcock	The Pious Soul's Heavenly Exercise; or Divine Harmony	Richard Bailye, Lichfield, for the author	1756	12
Charles Avison	Two Concertos The First for an Organ or Harpsichord … the Second for Violins	Joseph Barber, Newcastle	1742	6
Charles Avison	Six Concertos in Seven Parts, op 3	John Johnson	1751	1
Charles Avison	Eight Concertos in Seven Parts, op 4	John Johnson	1755	7
Charles Avison	Twelve Concertos (Divided into Two Set), op 9	Ruth Johnson/ Robert Bremner, for the author	1766[–7]	14
John Bennett	Ten Voluntaries, for the Organ or Harpsichord	London, for the author	c.1750	6
George Berg	Six Concertos in Seven Parts, op 1	John Johnson, for the author	1760	6

[17] Subscriptions for the *Two Concertos* were sought through an advertisement that appeared in the London press. *Daily Gazetteer,* 7 January 1742.
[18] The *Dataset of Subscribers* reveals that there was more than one person named John Walsh that subscribed to music. While it was possible to filter out the majority of these, a few of the subscriptions in Table 5.1 might have been placed by someone else with the same name. John Walsh snr did not die until 1736, but the subscriptions between 1730 and 1736 might have been placed by John Walsh the younger, who had taken an increasing share in the business since c.1730. See William C. Smith and Charles Humphries, *A Bibliography of the Musical Works Published by the Firm of John Walsh during the years 1721-66* (London, 1968), p. viii; *Dataset of Subscribers,* at www.musicsubscribers.co.uk.
[19] Unless stated, printers were based in London.

Composer	Title	Printer[19]	Year	No. of copies
Alessandro Besozzi	*Six Solos for the German-flute, Hautboy, or Violin, with a Thorough Bass for the Harpsichord*	Edmund Chapman	1759	6
William Boyce	*Solomon. A Serenata, in Score, taken from the Canticles*	John Walsh, for the author	1743	12
William Boyce	*Twelve Sonatas for Two Violins With a Bass for the Violoncello or Harpsicord*	John Walsh, for the author	1747	31
Henry Carey	*The Musical Century in One Hundred English Ballads*, vol 2	London, for the author	1740	1
Henry Carey	*The Dramatick Works*	S. Gilbert	1743	1
Richard Carter	*Six Solos For the Use of young Practitioners on the Violin or Harpsichord*, op 1	William Smith	1750	6
Thomas Chilcot	*Twelve English Songs with their Symphonies*	John Johnson	1744	1
Thomas Chilcot	*Six Concertos for the Harpsichord*	John Johnson	1756	1
Thomas Chilcot	*Six Concertos for the Harpsichord*, op 2	[Bath?], for the author	1765	1
Thomas Sanders Dupuis	*Six Concertos for the Organ or Harpsichord*, op 1	London, for the author	1760	6
William Felton	*Six Concerto's for the Organ or Harpsichord*, op 1	John Johnson	1744	6
William Felton	*Eight Concerto's for the Organ, or Harpsichord*, op 7	John Johnson	1761	1
Willem de Fesch	*X Sonatas for Two German Flutes or, Two Violins*, op 7	Benjamin Cooke, for the author	1733	6
Willem de Fesch	*VIII Concerto's in Seven Parts*, op 10	[London?]	1741	6

Composer	Title	Printer[19]	Year	No. of copies
Michael Festing	*Eight Concerto's in Seven Parts*, op 5	William Smith	1739	1
Michael Festing	*Six Sonata's for Two Violins and a Bass*, op 6	William Smith	1742	1
Michael Festing	*Six Solos for a Violin and Thorough-Bass*, op 7	William Smith	1747	2
William Flackton	*The Chase. Selected from the Celebrated Poem of William Somervile, Esqr. Set to Musick … To which is added, Rosalinda; With several other Songs in Score*	John Walsh, for the author	1743	6
William Flackton	*Six Sonatas for Two Violins and a Violoncello or a Harpsichord*	John Walsh, for the author	1758	7
Peter Fraser (pub.)	*The Delightfull Musical Companion for Gentlemen and Ladies being a Choice Collection out of All the latest Operas*, vol 1	Peter Fraser	c.1725	1
Lewis Granom	*A Second Collection of Favourite English Songs*	Thomas Bennett	1753	6
Henry Hargrave	*Five Concertos, the principal Part for the Bassoon or Violoncello*	John Walsh, for the author	c.1765	1
William Hayes	*Six Cantatas Set to Musick*	John Simpson, for the author	1748	7
Henry Holcombe	*Six Solos for a Violin and Thorough Bass With some Pieces for the German Flute and Harpsicord*, op 1	William Smith	1745	6
John Jones	*Lessons for the Harpsichord*, vol 2	London, for the author	1761	1
Joseph Kelway	*Six Sonatas for the Harpischord*	[London]	c.1764	12

Composer	Title	Printer[19]	Year	No. of copies
Richard Langdon	Ten Songs and a Cantata Set to Musick	John Johnson, for the author	1759	6
Benedetto Marcello	The First Fifty Psalms ... adapted to the English Version by John Garth	John Johnson/ Ruth Johnson	1757[–]	6
James Nares	Eight Setts of Lessons for the Harpsichord	John Johnson, for the author	1747	7
John Pixell	A Collection of Songs, with their Recitatives and Symphonies, op 1	Birmingham, for the author	1759	6
Alessandro Scarlatti	Thirty Six Arietta's for a Single Voice with a Thorough Bass for the Harpsichord	Thomas Vandernan	1756	6
John Christopher Smith	Suites de Pieces pour le Clavecin, vol 1	Thomas Cobb, for the author	c.1732	12
William Thomson	Orpheus Caledonius: or a Collection of Scots Songs, vol 1	London, for the author	1733	2
John Travers	Eighteen Canzonets for Two, and three Voices; (The Words chiefly by Matthew Prior Esqr.)	John Simpson, for the author	1746	6
William Walond	Six Voluntaries for the Organ or Harpischord	John Johnson	c.1752	7

Even if Avison's op 2 was published by Barber, copies were made available for purchase in London, for which Avison used the music seller and publisher, Benjamin Cooke, as his official distributor.[20] This information was provided in a newspaper advertisement and on the title page to the music itself (see Plate

---

[20] Cooke was active as a music seller and publisher in London from 1726 until his death in 1743, and issued a number of vocal and instrumental works, some pirated from other publishers. He also published the *VI Concertos in Seven Parts* (1740), attributed to Alessandro Scarlatti, but now thought to be arrangements by Avison. See William Smith and Peter Ward Jones, 'Cooke, Benjamin (i)', *Grove Music Online*; Rosalind Halton and Michael Talbot, '"Choice things of value": The Mysterious Genesis and Character of the *VI Concertos in Seven Parts* attributed to Alessandro Scarlatti', *Eighteenth-Century Music*, 12/1 (2015), 9–32.

5.1).[21] During this period, it was essential that any work issued in the British regions was also made available in the capital if a composer or author wished to maximise their reach and, consequently, their profits. London was then one of the biggest marketplaces for music in the world with a population, at the midpoint of the eighteenth century, of around 675,000; the next biggest town in England, Norwich, had around 50,000 inhabitants.[22] It was only natural that the book trade was London centric, with well-developed links that enabled the spread of books out into the provinces, but, as John Feather has observed, it was not geared for transportation in the opposite direction.[23] To facilitate this reverse flow of books, composers who had their music published in the regions would have felt it a necessity to engage a London-based agent to sell their works in the capital. Cooke had been involved with Avison since the mid-1730s, having sold tickets to Avison's benefit concert held at Hickford's Room, London on 15 March 1734.[24] He went on to publish Avison's set of *VI. SONATAS for two VIOLINS and a BASS*, op 1 (1737).[25] In addition to his role as Avison's London agent for op 2, Cooke subscribed to this work. But, as already noted, the printing of this work was undertaken by Joseph Barber of Newcastle.[26]

Joseph Barber

The Newcastle-based printer and bookseller, Joseph Barber, was born in 1706 in Dublin and baptised on 15 November at the Meeting House in Plunkett Street. His father, also named Joseph, is described as a 'stationer', and probably sold books.[27] By the early 1730s Joseph Barber jnr had moved to Durham, where he set himself up as an auctioneer of second-hand books and prints, advertisements for which appeared in the Newcastle press.[28] Before that decade was over, Barber had relocated to Newcastle where he established his own printing

---

[21] The op 2 was advertised for sale in the *Daily Gazetteer*, 31 May 1740.
[22] See E. Anthony Wrigley, 'Urban Growth and Agricultural Change: England and the Continent in the Early Modern Period', in Peter Borsay (ed.), *The Eighteenth-Century Town: A Reader in Urban History 1688–1820* (London, 1990), 39–82, at 42.
[23] Feather, *The Provincial Book Trade*, 115.
[24] *Country Journal*, 9 March 1734.
[25] *London Evening Post*, 16 August 1737.
[26] Barber does not appear as a music publisher in Frank Kidson, *British Music Publishers, Printers and Engravers: London, Provincial, Scottish, and Irish* (New York, 1900, reprinted 1967). He is, however, included in Charles Humphries and Williams C. Smith's *Music Publishing in the British Isles from the Beginning until the End of the Nineteenth-Century: Second Edition, with Supplement* (Oxford, 1970), 63.
[27] GB-DRu UND/CH1/B128. An investigation into the claim of the family of Joseph Barber of Newcastle upon Tyne to the estate of Charles Barber, late of Calcutta who died in 1799.
[28] *Newcastle Courant*, 9 February 1734, 16 February 1734, 27 September 1735 and 3 January 1736.

business and continued to hold book auctions.[29] An advertisement for July 1739 reveals the range of items that he produced:

JOSEPH BARBER,

Rolling-Press Printer, on the Sand-Hill, Newcastle upon Tyne,

Performs all Manner of Copper-Plate Printing, viz. Copper Plate Advertisements, Coal Certificates, Bills of Parcels for Merchants, Title-Plates, File-Plates for Letters, Tables of Equation for Watchmakers, Coats of Arms and Crests for Gentlemens Libraries, Funeral-Tickets, Plates for Tobacconists, Musick-Plates for Concerto's, &c. or any other Plates Etch'd, Metzotinto [sic], or Engrav'd, as neat as at London.[30]

Perhaps the most interesting reference is that for music plates for concertos. One cannot imagine that there was much demand for such work in the North-East, and it could be that Barber aimed this notice at Avison himself. If so, his strategy clearly worked as Barber was given the task of printing Avison's op 2; indeed, after its publication in 1740, Barber felt confident to describe himself as a 'Musick and Copper-Plate Printer'.[31] In 1741 Barber followed Avison's op 2 with a work described as 'A Curious Copper-Plate Song … Inscribed to the Free Burgesses of Newcastle', which included 'the Musick for the Song, Treble and Bass, on an easy Key … with the Musick transpos'd at the Bottom for both Common and German Flutes'.[32] Then, in 1742, Barber printed another work for Avison, namely his first set of *Two Concertos*. Even though Avison was having his works printed in Newcastle, he decided to have the musical plates engraved in London. Presumably there was no one in Newcastle at that time with the necessary skill. The plates for most of Avison's early works appear to have been produced by Richard Denson (d.1751), whose shop was situated at Long Acre in London.[33] Denson had been engaged to engrave the plates for Avison's op 1 sonatas, and his details appear on the title page of the first edition.

It is evident through comparison that Denson also engraved the plates for Avison's first set of concertos, even though his name does not appear anywhere on the print.[34] Avison evidently had a good working relationship with Denson, which continued following Cooke's death in 1743, when Denson took over as Avison's London-based agent.[35] Copies of Avison's second set of *Two Concertos* (1743) were available from Denson's shop and, while there is no extant copy

---

[29] Ibid., 7 July 1739 and 13 October 1739.
[30] Ibid., 7 July 1739.
[31] Ibid., 29 November 1740.
[32] Ibid., 25 April 1741.
[33] *Daily Advertiser*, Saturday, 27 August 1743.
[34] Denson was a subscriber to Avison's *Two Concertos* and to both volumes of Domenico Scarlatti's *XLII Suites de Pieces Pour le Clavecin* (London, 1739), in its edition by Thomas Roseingrave, to which Avison also subscribed.
[35] While it is impossible to be certain, one suspects that Avison was himself breaking up the different components of the publishing trade for his concertos between London and Newcastle.

of this work, it was presumably also printed by Barber.[36] Also, in 1743, Avison self-published a single concerto as *I Concerto in Seven Parts done from the Lessons of Sig[r]. Domenico Scarlatti*.[37] This work would be incorporated into his set of *Twelve Concertos in Seven Parts ... done from the two Books of Lessons for the Harpsicord ... by Sigr Domenico Scarlatti* (1744), again produced by Denson and Barber. This turned out to be the last time Avison would use Barber for the printing of his concertos and, for the op 3, he had switched his allegiance to John Johnson of London.[38] This also appears to have been the last time Barber printed any music, although he did continue to publish literary works.[39] While we do not know how Barber reacted to the loss of Avison's business, one gets the impression that Avison's subsequent relationship with Barber was not particularly amiable. While Barber subscribed to Avison's op 2 and the 'Scarlatti Concertos', he did not subscribe to any of the composer's later publications. Additionally, when Avison needed an agent for the sale of his latest publications or concert tickets, he looked to other Newcastle-based book and music sellers;[40] in some cases Avison dispensed with an agent entirely and took subscriptions himself, presumably as a way of maximising profits.[41] Nonetheless, other local entrepreneurs, such as Joseph Banks, used Barber as an agent for the sale of their tickets.[42] Barber and Avison were, however, both involved was in the

[36] *Daily Advertiser*, 27 August 1743. The advertisement records that this publication was 'Printed for, and sold by, R. Denson'. In that same year, Barber, presumably with Avison's consent, displayed a collection of paintings in the Newcastle Assembly Room 'on the Concert Night' that he planned to auction. As an important social occasion, this would have been an ideal opportunity for Barber to promote that side of his business. *Newcastle Courant*, 26 November 1743.

[37] The style of engraving to Avison's *I Concerto* is different to his other works and was presumably not produced by Denson, although it may still have been printed by Barber in Newcastle. The title page records that copies could be purchased from Cooke's shop 'at the golden Harp in New-Street Covent Garden' although Cooke's name is not given. Copies could also be purchased from 'M[r] Simpson by y[e] Royal Exchange and M[r] Wamsley in Piccadilly'. The proposal attached to this publication records that subscriptions for the complete set of twelve could be placed with Peter Wamsley. Wamsley's name does not appear anywhere on the parts to Avison's *Twelve Concertos in Seven Parts ... done from the two Books of Lessons for the Harpsicord ... by Sigr Domenico Scarlatti*, not even in the list of subscribers, and one suspects that his services were not retained.

[38] While we do not know who produced the plates for most of Avison's later works, those for the op 6 were engraved by Thomas Baker of Newcastle. Baker added his details to page 2 of the first violin concertino part.

[39] For example, Cuthbert Ellison, *The Babler: in Two Sermons* (1745), and Edward Ward, *The Noble Cuckolds; or the Pleasures of a Single Life, and the Miseries of Matrimony* (1772).

[40] *Newcastle Courant*, 30 June 1753; *Newcastle Chronicle*, 21 June 1766.

[41] *Newcastle Courant*, 1 September 1750.

[42] The tickets were for Banks's annual series of balls. *Newcastle Courant*, 10 April 1762, 26 March 1763, 16 March 1765, 21 February 1767 and 4 February 1769. Barber also sold tickets for performances at the New Theatre in the Bigg-Market. Ibid., 2 July 1768.

fundraising for the new Newcastle Infirmary. Barber not only donated books to this enterprise but also sold tickets for the benefit concert with which Avison participated.[43] By the mid-1760s any animosity between Avison and Barber appears to have subsided as tickets for Avison's concerts were, by then, available from Barber's shop.[44]

Barber, like the Walshes, subscribed to a range of publications for resale, many of which were printed or published by others. For instance, he purchased seven copies of Anthony Munton's *Several Sermons Preached in Newcastle upon Tyne* (1756),[45] and six copies each of William Blennerhassett's *A New History of England* (1751),[46] and John Cunningham's *Poems, Chiefly Pastoral* (1766).[47] Many of these were published in Newcastle, but he also subscribed to works published in Bristol and London.[48] While one might have expected some rivalry between the booksellers in any individual town, it appears that many were willing to work together to promote each other's publications. Barber worked with others to promote his forthcoming publications, including a print he produced of the 'Horse, call'd the Marbled Persian'. Subscriptions could be placed at the 'Keyside Coffee-house' in Newcastle, or with an agent in Sunderland, North-Shields, Morpeth and Durham.[49] An advertisement from two years later reveals that he also worked with agents in Stockton and Alnwick.[50] It is interesting to note that Barber's networks, although not unexpected, extended outwards from Newcastle into other smaller regional centres, as he sought to make it easier for potential customers to subscribe to his upcoming productions. Presumably Barber also used agents in this way when subscribers were sought for Avison's concertos. Not all of Barber's agents were booksellers either. At Durham, subscriptions could be placed with Abraham Taylor, a lay clerk at the Cathedral.[51] Barber also took subscriptions on behalf of others, including for works issued in York and Edinburgh.[52]

---

[43] Ibid., 6 April 1751, 17 August 1751 and 24 August 1751.
[44] Ibid., 22 June 1765 and 30 July 1768.
[45] Newcastle, John White.
[46] Newcastle, John Gooding.
[47] Newcastle, T. Slack.
[48] Barber subscribed to Jonathan Brooks' *Antiquity: Or the Wise Instructor*, 2nd edition (Bristol: S. Farley, 1773), Thomas Hudson's *Poems on Several Occasions* (Newcastle upon Tyne, 1752), Christopher Smart's *Poems on Several Occasions* (London, 1752), John Wignell's *A Collection of Original Pieces* (London, 1762), and John Ryland's *The Preceptor, Or Counsellor of Human Life* (London, 1776). Avison subscribed to both Hudson's and Smart's collections of poems. For a list of Avison's subscriptions see Simon D.I. Fleming, *The Musical World of Charles Avison: Melodic Charm and the Powers of Harmony* (Abingdon, 2025), 38–41.
[49] *Newcastle Courant*, 29 November 1740.
[50] Barber advertised that he would print, by subscription, an image of the statue of James II on horseback, which had once stood in Newcastle. Subscriptions were taken at Durham, Morpeth, Stockton and Alnwick. *Newcastle Courant*, 7 August 1742.
[51] Taylor subscribed to Avison's *Two Concertos* and the 'Scarlatti Concertos'.
[52] *Newcastle Courant*, 17 November 1750 and 26 October 1751.

In terms of music, and music-related works, Barber subscribed to John Alcock's *The Life of Miss Fanny Brown* (1760),[53] and Giovanni Giacomo Androux's *Six Trios for Two German Flutes or Two Violins* (1762).[54] He was also an official seller for some London-published musical works, such as the second edition of Robert Hudson's *The Myrtle* (1755).[55] One might have expected Barber to have subscribed to more musical publications, given that, by the mid-1740s, he had expanded his business into the sale of music and musical instruments. The range of items he sold is evident from the following note that Barber attached to a 1756 advertisement for his circulating library:

> By the above JOSEPH BARBER, are sold German Flutes, and other Instruments; likewise all new Musick, as Sonatæs, Solas, [Solos] Duets, Concertos, Minuets, Country-dances, Books of Instruction for each Instrument, Variety of new Songs set to Musick, &c. &c. One Penny in the Shilling is allowed Discourse for all Musick or Instruments purchased, and the Profit divided with such who teach or deal in the above Articles, having sold Musick above ten Years.[56]

Later advertisements make no reference to his printing business, but for the most part publicise the merchandise he sold, which included tea, telescopes and room hangings, along with powders for fevers, tincture for teeth, stomach pills, oil and snuff.[57] As such, Barber's business was typical of the regional bookseller, who 'needed far more than a good stock of books to make a living'.[58]

---

[53] Printed in Birmingham.
[54] Printed in London by George Terry.
[55] *Newcastle Courant*, 5 July 1755. *The Myrtle* was printed in London by J. Fuller. Subscriptions could be placed at two other booksellers in Newcastle, and those situated at Norwich, Cambridge, Bury St Edmunds, Kings Lynn, Great Yarmouth, and Swaffham (Norfolk). For a list of the music publications that Barber advertised for sale in 1772, see Roz Southey, 'John Hawthorn's shop at the Head of the Side, near the Post Office', *A Handbook for Studies in 18th-century English Music*, 24 (2020), 1–43, at 5.
[56] *Newcastle Courant*, 30 October 1756. While there is no evidence that Barber was a musician, one suspects, given the music side of his business, that he may well have been an amateur. His nephew Charles Barber (d. 1799), who was a Calcutta-based merchant, may have been an amateur musician, evidence of which can be seen in his subscription to William Hamilton Bird's *The Oriental Miscellany, being a Collection of the most Favourite Airs of Hindoostan Compiled and Adapted for the Harpsichord* (Calcutta, 1789). For more on Charles, see Simon D.I. Fleming, 'Subscribers to William Bird's *The Oriental Miscellany* (1789): an insight into late eighteenth-century Anglo-Indian Society', *Consort*, 78 (2022), 40–70, at 59.
[57] *Newcastle Courant*, 3 August 1751, 23 October 1756, 30 October 1756 and 11 November 1758; *Newcastle Chronicle*, 20 April 1765. Other regional booksellers sold a range of goods including music. Take, for example, Robert Martin of Launceston, Devon, who, in addition to books, traded in 'Patent Medicines, Music and Musical Instruments, Perfumery, &c.' See Feather, *The Provincial Book Trade*, 83. Barber's will simply records him as a 'Bookseller and Stationer'. His wife, Eleanor, was the main beneficiary and executor. GB-DRu DPRI/1/1782/B3, Will of Joseph Barber.
[58] Feather, *The Provincial Book Trade*, 87.

Even if Barber's printing activities were not promoted in the press, he may not have stopped that side of his business. Indeed, it may have continued until around 1765 when Joseph Barber's cousin, William (born 1723), set up his own copper-plate printing business in Newcastle, most likely with Joseph's support. His shop was situated near the town's Flesh Market.[59] William was also involved in the printing of music, including that for William Totten's *Several Select Portions of the Psalms, from Tate and Brady's Version, Collected for the Use of Churches, By a Clergyman* (1763), to which a local music teacher, William Thompson, provided the revised and corrected tunes.[60]

Joseph Barber is a rare example of a music printer working in the north of England in the early Georgian period. His Newcastle location does not appear to have been much of a disadvantage, even though the musical plates for these works had to be engraved elsewhere. His skill, however, as a copper-plate printer resulted in his engagement by Avison as the printer of many of this composer's early works. In this role, Barber increased his own prominence, with Avison's works available in London through the use of an agent. Barber himself clearly had good links with the book trade and worked with others in smaller centres in the north of England as he sought subscribers for his latest publications. He also had connections with more distant booksellers, including those in York and Edinburgh. While Barber is an interesting case study, another slightly different example can be found in the Canterbury bookseller and musician, William Flackton, to whose productions Walsh also subscribed.

❧ *William Flackton*

Flackton was born in Canterbury and baptised in the parish church of St Alphege on 27 March 1709.[61] His father, John, was a bricklayer and cathedral

---

[59] GB-DRu UND/CH1/B128; *Newcastle Chronicle*, 12 October 1765. In some ways the careers of Barber's children mirror the various aspects of Joseph's business. One son, Robert (c.1750–?), went into music, and had organist posts at Aberdeen and Manchester. Robert's sister, Maria, also appears to have been an amateur musician, and subscribed to Avison's op 9 concertos. Another son, Joseph (c.1758–1811), moved to Birmingham, where he worked as a landscape painter. David Johnson, 'Barber, Robert (ii)', *Grove Music Online*; Roz Southey, *Music-Making in the North-East of England During the Eighteenth Century* (Aldershot, 2006), 202. See also the subscription list to Thomas Ebdon: *Sacred Music, Composed for the Use of the Choir of Durham* (London, 1790); C.E. Dawkins and R.J. Lambert, 'Barber, Joseph (bap.1758, d.1811), landscape painter', *Oxford Dictionary of National Biography*.

[60] Printed in Newcastle by T. Slack, for W. Thompson, and sold by J. Featherston, bookseller in Hexham. The plates were engraved by Richard Jackson. The name 'W. Barber' appears on the music adjacent to pages 17 and 36. I am grateful to the Bodleian Library, Oxford University, who kindly provided a digital copy of this book. See also Southey, *Music-Making*, 118.

[61] For biographies of Flackton, see W. Shaw and R. Ford, 'Flackton, William', *Grove Music Online*; Sarah Gray, 'Flackton, William (bap.1709, d.1798), bookseller and musician', *Oxford Dictionary of National Biography*; Luke Agati, *William Flackton 1709–1798:*

contractor. Flackton became a chorister at Canterbury Cathedral where, as well as singing for services, he would have been paid a modest salary and have received a free education.[62] The Master of the Choristers at the time, William Raylton (1688–1757), would have provided Flackton's musical training;[63] later his younger brother John was also admitted into the choir.[64] Like many choristers, Flackton received an apprenticeship, learning his trade from Edward Burgess, a bookseller, stationer and cathedral lay clerk. After time spent in London, in 1727 Flackton returned to Canterbury where he set himself up in the book trade; three years later, he was made a freeman.[65] Flackton was later joined in business by his brother John, and subsequently also partnered with two former apprentices, John Marrable in 1774 and James Claris in 1784.[66] Indeed, Flackton's business appears to have been one of the most prominent in Canterbury, and he supplied the Cathedral with music, pens, prayer books, and had books bound for them.[67] He also, much like Barber, dealt in second-hand books and sold whole libraries, advertising the contents in the press and producing catalogues that were available from booksellers in London, Oxford and Cambridge.[68] The library of William Gostling, the well-known singer and antiquarian, was one such library that Flackton sold.[69] He also traded in music manuscripts, and had some volumes pass through his hands that contained autograph manuscripts by Purcell, along with the collectings of Daniel Henstridge, organist of Canterbury Cathedral, and William Raylton, to which Flackton added to. Many of the holographs by Purcell and John Blow in these volumes were obtained by Henstridge while at Rochester, while other seventeenth-century copies were added in Canterbury by subsequent owners. Philip Hayes made use of this collection in 1784–5, from which he made his own copies.[70]

In addition to his bookselling activities, Flackton continued to play a role in the musical life of Canterbury and the surrounding area. Between 1735 and 1752 he was organist of St Mary of Charity, Faversham, and was involved with

---

Organist at Faversham Parish Church, 1735-52, The Life and Times of a Canterbury Musician (Faversham, 2002).

[62] Sarah Gray, 'William Flackton, 1709-1798, Canterbury Bookseller and Musician', in Peter Isaac and Barry McKay (eds), *The Mighty Engine: The Printing Press and its Impact* (Winchester, 2000), 121–30, at 121.

[63] Watkins Shaw, *The Succession of Organists of the Chapel Royal and the Cathedrals of England and Wales from c.1538* (Oxford, 1991), 48–9.

[64] Gray, 'William Flackton', 121.

[65] Joseph Meadows Cowper, *The Roll of the Freemen of the City of Canterbury From A.D. 1392 to 1800* (Canterbury, 1903), 32.

[66] Gray, 'William Flackton', 122.

[67] Ibid., 122.

[68] *Kentish Gazette*, 8 March 1775 and 10 April 1779; Gray, 'William Flackton', 122.

[69] *Kentish Gazette*, 7 February 1778; Watkins Shaw and Robert Ford, 'Gostling, William', *Grove Music Online*.

[70] *Maidstone Journal*, 2 April 1896; Shaw and Ford, 'Flackton, William'. These volumes are GB-Lbl Add. MS 30931-4.

Canterbury's subscription concerts.[71] He was also participated with the Canterbury catch club, established in 1779.[72] Tickets for local concerts and local assemblies could be purchased from his shop.[73]

Unlike Barber, who had his own printing business, Flackton does not appear to have printed anything himself. He was more often used as an official agent, and his name appears in this fashion on the title pages to a number of books, many of which were published in Canterbury.[74] One of the few books he published was the *Kentish Merchant's Pocket Companion* (1769). It was printed for him, and available from several other booksellers in Canterbury, along with those in Rochester, Chatham, Maidstone, Tenderden, Tunbridge, Rye, Lewes, Sandwich, Margate, Dover, Faversham and Ashford.[75] It was clearly the case with Flackton, as we saw with Barber, that he would work with agents in local smaller centres to sell his books.[76]

Much like Barber, Flackton also subscribed to a number of works, including some published in London and Bristol,[77] and took subscriptions for forthcoming books; he was, for instance, an official agent for William Wraight's *Divine Harmony*, printed by Simmons and Kirkby at Canterbury, and published in four parts.[78] Furthermore, he also took subscriptions for William Croft's London-printed *Cathedral Music, or Thirty Select Anthems in Score* (1778),[79] a work to which he himself subscribed.[80] Unlike many of the non-musical works,

---

[71] Gray, 'William Flackton', 123–4.

[72] Ibid., 123. For the Canterbury catch club, Flackton wrote a *Hunting Catch* to the words 'A Glorious Chase it is' and set for three voices and horn, copies of which survive in manuscript in the cathedral archives. See GB-CA, Canterbury Catch Club: vols 5–7, all p. 114, and Gray, 'William Flackton', 124.

[73] *Kentish Gazette*, 19 December 1788, 6 February 1789 and 3 February 1795. According to the author of Flackton's obituary, which appeared in the *Gentlemen's Magazine*, he was 'reckoned a fine performer on the organ and violin.' See *The Gentleman's Magazine* 68, pt. 1 (1798), 170–1.

[74] Peter Vallavine, *Observations on the Present Condition of the Current Coin of this Kingdom* (London, 1742); John Burnby, *The Kentish Cricketers: A Poem* (Canterbury, 1773); George Berkeley *A Caution Against Socinianism* (Canterbury, 1787). Vallavine, a minor canon at Canterbury Cathedral, subscribed to Flackton's *The Chace* (see Table 5.2).

[75] *Kentish Gazette*, 23 August 1769.

[76] This has already been observed by David Shaw in his 'Canterbury's External Links: Book-Trade Relations at the Regional and National Level in the Eighteenth Century', in Isaac and McKay (eds), *The Mighty Engine*, 107–119, at 109–10 and 115.

[77] Flackton purchased twelve copies of Henry Hick's *The Poll for Knights of the Shire to Represent the County of Kent* (London, 1734), six of 'E. W's' *The Lover's Manual. Being a Choice Collection of Poems* (London, 1753), two of George Bickham's *Penmanship in its Utmost Beauty and Extent* (London, 1731), and copies of Charles Moore's *A Full Inquiry into the Subject of Suicide* (London, 1790) and Edward Thomas' Jones's *English System of Book-keeping* (Bristol, 1796).

[78] *Kentish Gazette*, 10 August 1768.

[79] Printed in London by J. French.

[80] *Kentish Gazette*, 25 March 1778.

Flackton's subscription to this work does not refer to his business, and one suspects that he bought Croft's music for personal use. The same was probably also true for his subscription to the first volume of Charles Burney's *A General History of Music, from the Earliest Ages to the Present Period* (1776).[81] Flackton's subscription to Boyce's *Twelve Sonatas* records his position as 'Organist of Faversham in Kent', as does his subscription to John Travers's *Eighteen Canzonets* (1746); these works were again probably purchased for personal use rather than for resale.[82] Flackton appears to have a particularly close relationship with the composer Willem de Fesch, and had previously subscribed to de Fesch's *VIII Concerto's in Seven Parts*, op 10 (1741). De Fesch's subscriptions to both of Flackton's works may have been, in part, a reciprocal act. For William Porter's *Two Anthems a Sanctus, Two Single & Two Double Chants* (c.1795),[83] the subscription is recorded as 'Mess. Flackton and Co. Canterbury', which indicates that these copies might have been purchased for sale in his shop, or perhaps the subscription was placed on behalf of a customer. Another subscription to appear under his business name was to John Barwick's *Harmonia Cantica Divina, or the Kentish Divine Harmonist* (c.1783).[84] In this instance, the subscription was for two copies; Flackton additionally acted as an official agent for this work.[85]

❧ *Flackton's Subscription Lists*

While Flackton published several musical works, only two are known to have been issued by subscription and have extant lists of subscribers. These are *The Chace ... To which is added, Rosalinda; With several other Songs in Score* (1743) and *Six Sonatas for Two Violins and a Violoncello or Harpsichord* (1758).[86] Both works were well received: *The Chace* had 207 subscribers for 254 copies, while his *Six Sonatas* had 137 for 175 copies. What is perhaps most interesting is the geographic spread of Flackton's subscribers. One might expect *The Chace*, as Flackton's first published work, to have had fewer subscribers from outside

---

[81] In four volumes. Printed in London by T. Becket.
[82] Boyce subscribed to both of Flackton's works (see Table 5.2). Flackton clearly had good links with the Chapel Royal and several members of the choir subscribed to Flackton's music. In 1746, the publisher John Simpson sent John Travers, organist of the Chapel Royal, some songs of Flackton's composition to get his opinion of their worth. Travers wrote back on 21 August, advising that 'you may venture to publish any of those songs or all of them if you please for in my opinion they are as worthy the attention of the Publick as many things we have daily published.' These 'songs' were published the following year as part of Flackton's *A Cantata and Several Songs* (London, 1747). Flackton, clearly pleased with Travers' comments, retained the letter. GB-CA: Add. MS no. 30: 'The Flackton Papers': 1. I am grateful to Canterbury Cathedral Library for kindly giving permission to quote from the Flackton Papers.
[83] Printed in London by Preston and Son.
[84] Printed in London by T. Skillern.
[85] *Kentish Gazette*, 14 August 1784.
[86] Both works were printed by Walsh.

Canterbury's environs, but an analysis of this subscription list reveals just how far Flackton's reputation had already spread by 1743.

A good number of Flackton's most distant subscribers were associated with the book trade; they include James Leake of Bath, John Oakey of Cardiff and a Mr Steel of Falmouth (see Table 5.2).[87] Indeed, their locations reveal a link between the booksellers of Canterbury and other regional centres that might have been independent of London.[88] Leake subscribed to a number of musical publications, including works by John Alcock, Thomas Chilcot and William Croft, and presumably planned to sell on his copy of Flackton's *Chace*.[89] Oakey and Steel did not, however, subscribe to any other musical publications;[90] their subscription to Flackton's work may have been an act of support for a respected colleague who they came to know through the book trade; alternatively, their subscriptions might have been placed on behalf of a customer. There were additionally a good number of subscribers to *The Chace* in London, some of whom were involved in the publication and selling of this work. The title page records that this work was 'Printed for the Author, & sold by M[r] Walsh, in Catherine Street, M[r] [Peter] Wamsley, in Piccadilly; and M[r] [John] Simpson, near the Royal Exchange &c.' Walsh, as first in this list, printed the work, while Wamsley and Simpson acted as distributors.[91] Walsh and Wamsley took six copies each, Simpson took twelve.

The advertisement that appeared in the *General Evening Post* reveals that Charles Hitch was another distributor; he subscribed to twelve copies.[92] Prior to publication, subscriptions could be placed at all four businesses, along with 'the Booksellers in Oxford and Cambridge', and at the shops of James Abree in Canterbury, Thomas Clarke of Rochester, Robert Lacy at Maidstone, Thomas Hammond at York, Mr Weaver on London-Bridge, and the aforementioned

---

[87] There are no booksellers, at least described as such, in the subscription lists to Avison's early concertos (printed by Barber).

[88] In his discussion of Canterbury's booksellers, David Shaw discusses their links with other booksellers in the South-East, and with those based in London, but appears unaware of any direct links with other regional centres. See Shaw, 'Canterbury's External Links', 109–18.

[89] Thomas Chilcot, *Six Suites of Lessons for the Harpsichord or Spinet* (London, 1734); John Alcock, *Six Suite's of Easy Lessons for the Harpsichord or Spinnet, with a Trumpet Piece* (London, 1742), William Croft, *Musica Sacra: or, Select Anthems in Score, Consisting of 2, 3, 4, 5, 6, 7 and 8 Parts: To which is added, The Burial-Service, as it is now occasionally perform'd in Westminster-Abbey* (London, 1724). Leake also subscribed to 18 copies of Richard Neale's *A Pocket Companion for Gentlemen and Ladies* (London, 1724). Leake was a general bookseller, and operated a circulating library, one of the first in the country. See Trevor Fawcett, *Georgian Imprints: Printing and Publishing at Bath, 1729–1815* (Bath, 2008), 9; *General Evening Post*, 17 May 1743. For more on Leake, see Matthew Spring's contribution to this volume.

[90] See the *Dataset of Subscribers*.

[91] The arrangement of names on eighteenth-century English imprints is discussed in Feather, *The Provincial Book Trade*, 60.

[92] *General Evening Post*, 17 May 1743.

James Leake of Bath; most of them, as shown in Table 5.2, also subscribed.[93] Indeed, Flackton, perhaps anticipating a wider appeal for his musical works, engaged agents from a wider geographical area. This may have been why this work was advertised in the *General Evening Post*, a newspaper with a country-wide circulation.[94] Flackton's links with the more distant booksellers were not, however, limited to musical publications. For instance, both Leake and Flackton were official distributors for Timothy Smith's translation of *A Treatise of Health and Long Life* (1743), published in London by Hitch.

While it does not appear as though anyone residing north of the English Midlands subscribed to *The Chace*, Thomas Wilson of York, who also took subscriptions for Flackton's *Six Sonatas*, subscribed to the later work. Flackton looked even further afield when seeking subscriptions to his *Six Sonatas*: Robert Akenhead in Newcastle, Robert Williamson at Liverpool and Edward Score in Exeter are all named as agents, even if Flackton appears not to have gained any subscribers from these places.[95] He did, however, have a subscriber from Edinburgh: the bookseller Alexander Donaldson who took six sets.

While Flackton clearly had good working relationships with other booksellers in Britain, this was not the only way by which he sourced books, and in some cases, he used his personal contacts to find material for personal use. Flackton had a particularly close association with the Young family, and both Sir William Young (1725–88) and his wife Elizabeth (1729–1801) subscribed to Flackton's music.[96] Such was the friendship between these two men that when Sir William was undertaking the Grand Tour, Flackton sent him a parcel of books and asked Young to find him a copy of 'the Sonatas of [Carlo] Tessarini'. Unfortunately for Flackton, Young had already left Paris by the time he received Flackton's letter, and so was unable to fulfil his request. He did, however, promise to send Flackton some 'Musick that may Be agreeable to you' in repayment for the books.[97]

---

[93] *London Evening Post*, 25 November 1742.

[94] Feather, *The Provincial Book Trade*, 48. Flackton did, in addition, advertise his work in the local newspaper. See the *Kentish Gazette*, 3 February 1770 and 10 April 1779. Also, GB-CA Add. MS no. 30: 'The Flackton Papers': 29–31, three advertisements for works by Flackton, two press clippings and (31) a handwritten draft advertisement from 1779 for a collection of hymns. See also Agati, *William Flackton*, 35–7.

[95] *London Chronicle*, 3 November 1757. See also GB-CA Add. MS no. 30: 'The Flackton Papers': 32: Printed handbill, dated 5 March 1757, promoting subscriptions to Flackton's *Six Sonatas*.

[96] GB-CA Add. MS no. 30: 'The Flackton Papers': 9. Letter dated 26 January 1770 from William Young to Flackton. Elizabeth Young subscribed to *The Chace* under her maiden name of 'Miss Taylor.' Both she and William, her husband, subscribed as individuals to Flackton's *Six Sonatas*.

[97] GB-CA Add. MS no. 30: 'The Flackton Papers': 3. Letter dated 2 August 1751 from William Young to Flackton. Young here also recorded his intention to 'Hear Scarlatti play five Barrs, that I may not seem to Have Travell'd thro' Italy & lost the greatest Curiosity In It.'

❧ Flackton and Avison

Even though Flackton had an extensive trade network, there is another network evident in his subscription lists through his musician subscribers (as seen Table 5.2). Indeed, some of these subscribers had an association with Avison. Firstly, there is Francesco Geminiani's subscription to Flackton's *Six Sonatas*. Geminiani was Avison's teacher and a subscriber to his opp 2 and 3, and the 'Scarlatti concertos'.[98] Even if we do not know the details of Flackton's relationship with Geminiani, it is clear from earlier studies that the circles of individual musicians overlapped to such an extent that they should collectively be viewed as like an extended family.[99] Walsh, as seen in Table 5.1, also subscribed to both composer's works, as did the London music publisher, John Johnson, and William Boyce.[100] While it is impossible to say whether Avison knew Flackton, Flackton certainly knew of Avison. This was largely through Avison's very public dispute with the Oxford academic, William Hayes, brought about through Avison's publication of his *An Essay on Musical Expression* (1752).[101] Hayes's response to Avison's important treatise, published anonymously as the *Remarks on Mr. Avison's Essay on Musical Expression* (1753), not only sought to undermine Avison's opinions as expressed in his *Essay*, but the Oxonian even devoted fourteen pages to a discussion on the worth of Avison's op 3 concertos in an attempt to undermine the composer's 'musical Merit'.[102] Flackton was greatly affected by the dispute, and feared his own compositions might come in for similar treatment. In a draft letter dated 28 February 1760, and written to Elizabeth Young, Flackton expressed his gratitude to her for her patronage of his set of lessons, but also revealed his fears about how critics might respond to his published works.[103] He wrote: 'I'm pleased when I Reflect on the honour you do me, but on the other hand am Confounded when I think on the meanness of my performance, & the Great Risk I am of being paid in kind, with poor <u>Avison</u>.' Flackton added that: 'Mr Avison was unmercifully Used by the Criticks for publishing some Concertos which they took to pieces with indecency.'[104] Flackton's fear is further manifested in that he sent his *Six Solos Three for a Violoncello and Three for a Tenor [Viola]*, op 2 (1770) for inspection by Carl Friedrich Abel before their publication.[105] Even if we do not

---

[98] Burney noted that Avison 'received instructions from Geminiani'. Burney, *A General History of Music*, iv, 670.
[99] Simon D.I. Fleming, 'William Felton and John Pixell: The Musical Circles of the Vicar Composer', in Fleming and Perkins (eds), *Music by Subscription*, 93–110.
[100] Johnson and Boyce both subscribed to Avison's *Two Concertos*.
[101] Printed in London by C. Davis.
[102] William Hayes, *Remarks on Mr. Avison's Essay on Musical Expression* (London, 1753), 7.
[103] There is no known copy of Flackton's lessons.
[104] GB-CA Add. MS no. 30: 'The Flackton Papers': 5.
[105] See the 'Preface' to the *Six Solos*, where Flackton wrote 'The Author takes this Opportunity of acknowledging his particular Obligations to Mr. ABEL, for inspecting this Work in manuscript before it went to the Press'. This work was printed in London by S. Thompson. Avison has a connection with Abel through his subscription to six copies of Abel's *Six Sonatas for the Harpsicord*, op 2 (London, 1760).

know how widespread such reactions were to the dispute between Avison and Hayes, it nevertheless reveals a negative side of this very public argument and how it impacted on the publication of new music.

Conclusion

While the sale of music could be an important part of a regional bookseller's trade, it was only part of what they offered and, as seen in the case of Joseph Barber, these businesses offered a range of services, including copper-plate printing, and sold a wide selection of non-book products. Such establishments were also important hubs for subscription publication, where a town's inhabitants could subscribe to the latest musical publications, some of which were created by local musicians, while others were produced by composers who had no apparent connection with that place. While Barber is not known to have been a musician, he clearly had enough knowledge to enter the music trade and even acted as Avison's printer during the 1740s. Avison, nevertheless, still felt the need to use a London-based agent and worked with both Benjamin Cooke and Richard Denson to further his presence in the capital; they would have sought subscriptions for Avison's forthcoming publications and have sold these works in their shops to nonsubscribers. John Walsh the younger, the London-based music printer and publisher, had a strong sense of what sold well in the capital and, as Avison's notoriety increased, saw fit to subscribe to more copies of this composer's works. What is clear is that Avison's location in the North-East, and his decision to use Barber as his official printer, did not significantly impede his growth into one of Britain's leading native-born composers.[106]

For Barber, it would have been a significant coup to get Avison's business, more impressive as he did not have the means or ability to engrave musical plates himself. Nevertheless, Barber had a series of trade networks in the North-East of England and further afield, through which he was able to source subscriptions for himself and others, and acted as an agent himself, selling books printed in other parts of Britain. These networks are also evident in the case of William Flackton. He was heavily involved in musical activities, for which he composed a considerable amount of music. The book trade provided him with connections through which he could seek subscriptions for his musical publications, and his bookseller subscribers came from a geographically wide area. Indeed, this study reveals the existence of an intricate web of networks linking booksellers across the nation who subscribed to musical works and acted as agents. Even booksellers located in the same town or city appear to have had good relations with each other, and they often worked together to promote new publications.

While this study into the book trade, music publishing and subscription lists cannot give us a complete picture of the links that such businesses had in

---

[106] For more on Avison's importance as a native-born British composer, see Fleming, *The Musical World of Charles Avison*.

the eighteenth century, it does reveal that geographical distance and location outside London did little to damage the sale of new musical works. Indeed, it is clear from this study that British booksellers were part of a larger web of connections that spread across the whole country and, while these businesses were not independent of London, the trade was in some cases less London centric than one might have expected.

TABLE 5.2 Subscribers of the published works of William Flackton known to have been involved with music or the book trade.

Subscriber as it appears in the source	Source
Rev. Mr. Bailey, Priest of his Majesty's Chapel Royal, and Chaunter of Westminster	Six Sonatas
Mr. [Thomas] Bakewell, in Fleetstreet, London [Seller of prints, maps and paintings]	Chace
Mr. John Beard	Six Sonatas
Mr. William Boyce, Composer to his Majesty's Chapel Royal, and Organist of St. Michael's in Cornhill	Chace
William Boyce, M. D. Organist and Composer to his Majesty's Chapel Royal	Six Sonatas
Rev. Mr. [William] Broderip, Minor Canon of the Cathedral at Canterbury	Chace
Mr. Ben[jamin]. Browne, Organist of St. Mary's, Dover	Chace
John Buswell, M. B. Gentleman of his Majesty's Chapel Royal	Six Sonatas
Mr. Thomas Clarke, of Rochester [Agent]	Chace
Mr. [Robert] Denham, Gentleman of his Majesty's Chapel Royal	Six Sonatas
Mr. Alex[ander]. Donaldson, at Edinburgh, 6 Sets [Bookseller]	Six Sonatas
Mr. [Willem] De Fesch	Chace
Mr. [Willem] Defesch	Six Sonatas
Mr. [Francesco] Geminiani	Six Sonatas
Mr. [Moses] Hawker, [Organist] of Portsmouth	Chace
Mr. Charles Hitch. 12 Books [Agent/Distributor]	Chace
Mr. [John] Hitchcock, Harpsicord and Spinnet-maker, London	Chace
Mr. [John] Johnson, in Cheapside, 12 Sets	Six Sonatas
Mr. [Jacob] Kirkman, Harpsichord-maker	Six Sonatas
Mr. Robert Lacy, of Maidstone [Agent]	Chace
Mr. [Nicholas] Ladd, Gentleman of his Majesty's Chapel Royal	Six Sonatas
Mr. Nicholas Lade, of the King's Royal Chapel, at Windsor	Chace
Mr. [James] Leake, of Bath. [Bookseller and agent]	Chace
Mr. Joseph Mahoon, Harpsicord-maker to his Majesty	Chace

Subscriber as it appears in the source	Source
Mr. [Joseph] Mahoon, Harpsichord-maker to his Majesty	*Six Sonatas*
Mr. William Mount, of Tower-Hill, London [Stationer]	*Chace*
The Musical Society, at Canterbury. 2 Books	*Chace*
The Musical Society, at Canterbury	*Six Sonatas*
The Musical Society, at the Flower-de-Luce, Canterbury	*Chace*
The Musical Society, at the Flower-de-Luce, Canterbury	*Six Sonatas*
The Musical Society, at Faversham	*Chace*
The Musical Society, at Maidstone	*Chace*
The Musical Society, at Rochester	*Chace*
The Musical Society at Sittingbourn	*Chace*
Mr. John Oakey, Bookseller, of Cardiff	*Chace*
Mr. Thomas Page, of Tower-Hill, London [Stationer]	*Chace*
Mr. Charles Peach, Organist of the Cathedral at Rochester	*Chace*
Mr. [William] Savage, Gentleman of his Majesty's Chapel Royal	*Six Sonatas*
Mr. Thomas Sayer, Organist of Dover	*Six Sonatas*
Mr. John Simpson. 12 Books [Instrument Maker]	*Chace*
John Stanley, Batchelor of Musick, Organist of the Temple, and St. Andrew's, Holbourn	*Chace*
Mr. Steel, Bookseller, of Falmouth	*Chace*
Mrs. Thompson and Son, in St. Paul's Churchyard, 12 Sets [Instrument Maker]	*Six Sonatas*
Rev. Mr. [Peter] Val[l]avine, Minor Canon of the Cathedral at Canterbury	*Chace*
Mr. [Thomas] Vandernan, Gentleman of his Majesty's Chapel Royal	*Six Sonatas*
Mr. John Walsh. 6 Books	*Chace*
Mr. [John] Walsh, 7 Sets	*Six Sonatas*
Mr. Peter Wamsley. 6 Books [Instrument Maker]	*Chace*
Mr. Richard Ware, of Warwick-Lane, London [Bookseller]	*Chace*
Mr. [Robert] Wass, Gentleman of his Majesty's Chapels Royal	*Six Sonatas*
Mr. [Edward] Webb, Organist of Windsor College	*Six Sonatas*
Mr. [Charles] Weideman	*Six Sonatas*
Mr. Thomas Wilson [York, Agent]	*Six Sonatas*
Mr. [Henry] Wood, [Vicar Choral] of Litchfield	*Chace*
Mr. Thomas Wood, Organ and Harpsichord maker, at Dover	*Six Sonatas*

6

Distributing Irish Reprints in England: The Activities of Liverpool's John Bridge Pye

Nancy A. Mace

After the passage of the Act of Anne (1710), London booksellers expressed concern about the threat to their profits posed by unauthorised reprints of works produced inexpensively in Ireland and imported into England. Until the Copyright Act of 1801, which extended protections granted by the 1710 statute to the Irish, English copyright holders had no legal way to prevent members of the Irish trade from printing and selling reprints of works purchased by them. They repeatedly argued that these could make their way into the English market, reducing their sales.[1] Like booksellers, members of the London music trade regarded Irish reprints of their music as a threat to their business. Unfortunately, scholars working on the music trade have limited information about the networks by which unauthorised reprints made their way into England and the strategies available to London music sellers to fight the challenge they perceived to their profits for two reasons. First, because Irish music printers were not governed by English copyright law, London music sellers could not sue them directly in British courts for copyright infringement when unauthorised editions appeared in England. Second, research in this area has been hampered by the scarcity of records in Ireland since most court documents before 1922, stored at the Public Record Office in Dublin, were destroyed during the Irish Civil War.

However, a recently discovered Chancery suit filed in 1796 provides a glimpse into one network used to transport unauthorised reprints into England

---

[1] For information about Irish reprints and their relationship to the British market and print trades, see Mary Pollard, *Dublin's Trade in Books, 1550–1800* (Oxford, 1989), 66–92 and 110–35. See also R. Deazley, 'Commentary on *Copyright Act* 1801', (2008) in L. Bently and M. Kretschmer (eds), *Primary Sources on Copyright (1450-1900)*, at www.copyrighthistory.org, which discusses the effect of the copyright act on the Irish print trade. While Pollard and Deazley are primarily writing about the publication of books, their analysis also applies to the trade in printed music. See the discussion of the evidence provided in the booksellers' petition of 1735, discussed in John Feather, *Publishing, Piracy and Politics. An Historical Study of Copyright in Britain* (London, 1994), 71–2.

and the efforts of London music sellers to stop these imports.[2] The suit involved the London firm of Anne Bland and Edward Weller, who accused the Liverpool music seller John Bridge Pye of importing into England and selling unauthorised Irish reprints of popular tunes in violation of the Act of Anne. Their bill of complaint and affidavit offer new details about the activities of these music sellers and reveal one strategy used by members of the London music trade to stifle the traffic in illegal imports from their Irish competitors.

The Case

On 10 November 1796, Bland and Weller filed suit in the court of Chancery against Pye, accusing him of importing from Dublin and selling in England compositions owned by them, thereby damaging their sales. The schedule attached to their complaint and in Edward Weller's affidavit sworn eighteen days after the bill listed some 123 individual titles.[3] To demonstrate possession of these compositions, they asserted that they had duly purchased the copyrights to these musical works from the composers and that afterwards they had entered them with the Stationers' Company, the guild established in 1557 by the Crown to regulate printing.[4] Bland and Weller also pointed out that the works were recent enough that the first fourteen years of copyright protection had not yet expired and that the composers themselves were still alive. Such statements anticipated two common arguments made by the defence in eighteenth-century copyright cases: (1) that the works in question were so old that they were no longer protected by law and (2) that the plaintiffs had no automatic right to the second fourteen years of protection granted under the Act of Anne, since presumably the ownership of a work reverted to the composer or author at the expiration of the first term, which, in theory, the composer could assign to another.[5]

---

[2] The bill of complaint is London, The National Archives (TNA) C12/221/9. Edward Weller swore an affidavit, filed 28 November 1796, located at TNA C31/282, no. 172.

[3] See Tables 6.2 and 6.3 for a complete list of titles. In their schedule, Bland and Weller have two items for op 77, identifying them as parts one and two.

[4] See Tables 6.2 and 6.3 for specific dates on which they entered some of the works listed in the schedule. The entries appeared in *The Stationers' Company Register of Entries* (TSC/1/E/06/12, covering 1 June 1792 to 31 August 1795). The registers for the Stationers' Company are held at Stationers' Hall in London. For a full description of the Company and its activities, see Geoffrey Ashall Glaister, *Encyclopedia of the Book*, 2nd edn (London, 1996), 458.

[5] The Act of Anne (1710) granted authors fourteen years of copyright protection, which they could renew for a second period of equal length if at the end of the first term they were still alive. However, in practice, many music sellers assumed that, when they purchased a musical work, they obtained rights to all twenty-eight years granted by the statute. For a discussion of one conflict over reversionary rights in music, see Nancy A. Mace, 'Charles Rennett and the London Music Sellers in the 1780s: Testing the Ownership of Reversionary Copyrights', *Journal of the Royal Musical Association*, 129 (2004), 1–23. The authors named in this litigation were Charles Dibdin and the organist John Garth of Durham, both of whom had tried to assign their reversionary rights to Charles Rennett.

Their complaint continued by detailing their specific accusations against Pye. They charged that he had arranged to have 'large quantities' of the musical works named in the bill printed in Dublin and had purchased others from Irish music sellers, after which he had imported them into England and exposed them for sale.[6] They maintained that, as printing costs were so much lower in Ireland, he was able to acquire the copies at lower prices than they could print them in England, and, therefore, he could sell them much more cheaply than those that they produced. Thus, Bland and Weller argued, from the sales of these unauthorised editions, Pye had made 'considerable gains', which damaged the sales of their own authorised copies of these works.[7] Although they had themselves and by their agents approached him, asking him to stop selling these illegal copies and demanding that he account for the numbers already sold and the profits he had earned, Pye refused to stop marketing the Irish reprints. They claimed in their bill of complaint that Pye sometimes denied they had any rights to these compositions, even suggesting these works were so old that they were no longer protected by law. As a result, Bland and Weller petitioned the court for relief. They asked that Pye be ordered to identify the Dublin-based printer, requested an injunction to prevent him from selling any more of the disputed works and demanded he be required to provide evidence of the number of copies already sold and his profits. After this accounting, Bland and Weller asked that he be forced to pay them any money he had gained from his illegal activities.

Bland and Weller chose to target an English distributor of Irish reprints because, unlike his sources in Dublin, Pye could be prosecuted for violating the 1710 copyright statute when he sold unauthorised Irish copies in England. Until the 1801 act extended copyright law to include all the United Kingdom, members of the Irish music trade could issue unauthorised reprints of English works without penalty. Throughout the latter half of the eighteenth century, Irish music sellers took advantage of this technicality by printing and selling single sheets of the most popular songs, whose copyright belonged to their English competitors.[8] For instance, on the title page of *The Heaving of the Lead*, taken from the musical entertainment *Hartford Bridge* by William Shield (Covent Garden 3 November 1792), the Dublin music seller Maurice Hime included the following statement:

> At Hime's may be had just published the favorite Rondo, Songs, and Airs in the new Pantomime of Oscar and Malvina [by William Reeve], Price 2^s:2^d, all the favorite Songs in the new Opera of the Pirates [by Stephen Storace], with all [Charles] Dibdins, and [James] Hooks, newest Songs, &c. &c.[9]

---

[6] Quoted in the bill of complaint, TNA C12/221/9.
[7] Ibid.
[8] The practice was so common that compiling a full accounting of unauthorised Irish reprints of popular songs and entertainments is beyond the scope of this essay.
[9] *The Heaving of the Lead A favourite Ballad ... in the new Opera of Hartford Bridge* (Dublin, [n.d.]). James Longman and Francis Fane Broderip entered their copy of *Hartford Bridge*, which contained this song, at Stationers' Hall on 19 November 1792. See *The Stationers' Company Register of Entries* TSC/1/E/06/12. Hime probably

With this statement, Hime revealed his usual practice of bringing out his own editions of the most popular songs printed in London as soon as they appeared. Thus, Bland and Weller as well as other members of the London trade had good reason to regard the Dublin reprints as harmful to their business.

That Bland and Weller focused their attention on a Liverpool music seller was not surprising. During the eighteenth century, Liverpool was an important port of call for ships from Dublin; Karen Cheer estimates that by 1785 about forty percent of all consignments to England from the Irish city went through Liverpool's port.[10] In addition to the town's importance to trade with Ireland and abroad, it also played a central role as a regional shopping centre, distributing consumer goods both in the city and the surrounding areas. As Sheryllynne Haggerty notes, the city had a wide variety of traders, with the percentage of the population engaged in such activities increasing in the last half of the eighteenth century. Members of the print trade, including those who sold music, formed a large group.[11] From 1784 to 1797, when Pye was active, many shopkeepers were connected with the book trade. No fewer than thirty-two booksellers appeared in various sources, and twenty-three others were identified as engravers, many of whom additionally worked in other areas including bookbinding and printing. The music trade was represented by eight businesses: Pye, John Casson, Robert Ferguson, John Gore, Humphrey Hime, Birch Miles, John Sibbald and Joseph Wrenshall. Half dealt exclusively in music and musical instruments; of the others, three sold books as well as music.[12]

---

issued his unauthorised edition of the piece shortly thereafter. *Oscar and Malvina* premiered at Covent Garden 20 October 1791; the libretto was issued by Thomas Cadell in the same year; see *The Air, Duets, Chorusses, and Argument, of the New Ballet Pantomime … called Oscar and Malvina* (London, 1791). Longman and Broderip produced their edition of the overture, songs and chorusses around that time as *The Overture Favorite Songs, Duetts & Chorusses in the Grand Pantomime Ballet of Oscar & Malvina* (London, [n.d.]). Hime's edition would have come out sometime later. Joseph Dale entered William Shield's *The Pirates* at Stationers' Hall on 24 December 1792, suggesting that this Hime edition dated from that period as well. See *The Pirates an Opera* (London, [n.d.]). For the entry, see *The Stationers' Company Register of Entries* TSC/1/E/06/12.

[10] See Karen A. Cheer, 'Irish Maritime Trade in the Eighteenth Century: A Study in Patterns of Trade, Market Structures, and Merchant Communities' (Master's dissertation, Victoria University of Wellington, New Zealand, 2008), 70. For Liverpool's importance for the trade between Ireland and Britain, see L.M. Cullen, *Anglo-Irish Trade 1660-1800* (Manchester, 1968).

[11] Sheryllynne Haggerty, 'The structure of the trading community in Liverpool, 1760–1810', *Transactions of the Historic Society of Lancashire and Cheshire*, 151 (2002), 97–125, at 116 and 151.

[12] M.R. Perkin (ed.), *The Book Trade in Liverpool to 1805: A Directory*, Liverpool Bibliographical Society Occasional Publications, 1 (Liverpool, 1981; repr. 1987). Only Gore, Hime and Pye appear in Charles Humphries and William C. Smith, *Music Publishing in the British Isles*, rev. edn. (Oxford, 1970), 157, 181 and 266.

❧ The Defendant: John Bridge Pye (c.1761–1814)

John Bridge Pye became the defendant in Bland and Weller's suit because he traded not in Ireland but in Liverpool.[13] We only have scattered information about his life and career in the music trade. Born c.1761 in Liverpool, he married Margaret Alice Gibson c.1781.[14] A violinist and music teacher, he worked as a music seller from 1784.[15] His imprint on the title page of Edward Harwood's *The Orient Sun* (c.1785) identified him as a music seller and teacher based at 60 Cable Street, Liverpool.[16] In 1788 he took on Charles Allcock as an apprentice.[17] By 1793 he had a shop located at 15 Lord Street opposite the post office and was described as both a violinist and music seller.[18] He appears to have retired in 1797 when he sold his stock in trade.[19]

Pye published a number of musical works from 1785 onwards (see Table 6.1), of which nineteen were entered with the Stationers' Company between 1787 and 1791.[20] In addition, three more musical pieces printed and sold by him have survived, dating from 1785 to 1791. They represent compositions by seven different composers, all with ties to Liverpool. The best known of these were Charles Henry Wilton (1761-1811), Edward Harwood (1707–1787), and Richard Wainwright (1757–1825). Wilton was a violinist and viola player, who studied under Felice Giardini and performed in London, Gloucester, and finally Liverpool. In addition to the nine works by him printed by Pye, Wilton also brought out four other musical pieces with various London music sellers.[21] Harwood was a professional musician in Liverpool and the composer of hymns, anthems

---

[13] General information about Pye, including his years of activity and the sale of his stock in trade, appears in Perkin, *The Book Trade in Liverpool to 1805*, 23, and Humphries and Smith, *Music Publishing in the British Isles*, 266.

[14] For Pye's birth, see Liverpool Record Office, *Liverpool Church of England Parish Registers* 283 MRY/4/3. For his marriage, see *Lancashire, England, Church of England Marriages and Banns, 1754–1936*.

[15] Although Humphries and Smith (*Music Publishing in the British Isles*, 266) date his music selling business from 1785, Perkin (*The Book Trade in Liverpool to 1805*, 23) gives 1784 as the beginning of Pye's work as a music seller.

[16] Edward Harwood, *The Orient Sun, A Favorite Hunting Cantata* (Liverpool, [n.d.]).

[17] For Allcock's apprenticeship see *The Board of Stamps: Apprenticeship Books*, TNA IR 1/64.

[18] See John Doane, *A Musical Directory for the Year 1794* (London, 1794), 53. By 1796 Pye had moved home to 17 Temple Street, but his music shop remained in Lord Street. See *Gore's Liverpool Directory, or, Alphabetical List of the Merchants, Tradesmen, and Principal Inhabitants, of the Town of Liverpool* (Liverpool, 1796), 138.

[19] The sale of Pye's stock in trade is noted in Perkin, *The Book Trade in Liverpool to 1805*, 23. *Land Tax Redemption Office: Quotas and Assessments* TNA IR23 only has a listing for Pye at his Temple Street address in 1798. Pye and his wife were described as deceased in the will of Edmund Newman Kershaw of Heskin Hall in 1814. Lancashire Archives DDL709.

[20] For the entries, see *The Stationers' Company Register of Entries*.

[21] For Wilton, see Brian Frith and Simon McVeigh, 'Wilton, Charles Henry', *Grove Music Online*.

Plate 6.1 Edward Harwood, *Kind God of Sleep ... Printed by J.B. Pye* (Liverpool, [c.1787]).

and songs, eight of which were issued by Pye.[22] Wainwright spent much of his career as organist at St. Peter's Liverpool; though Pye printed and sold only a single composition by him, he also wrote songs and hymns, which were printed by music sellers in Liverpool and London.[23]

A review of Pye's known publications offers significant insight into the Liverpool music seller's publishing activities. Table 6.1 lists twenty-two works published by Pye, of which twenty were vocal with the majority comprising single songs that only required two to three pewter plates.[24] Pye issued two instrumental works, both by Wilton: *Six Solos for the Violin* and *A Set of Eighteen Lessons for the Piano Forte or Harpsichord*. The title page of *Six Solos for the Violin* provides some clues about the prices Pye charged for different works. The six songs listed went for 6d each. He advertised Wilton's op 3 for 7s. 6d. and op 5 for 6s.[25] He entered nineteen works with the Stationers' Company, which is significant for two reasons. First, the entries demonstrated that he would have been well aware of the risks he ran when he violated Bland and Weller's copyrights by selling unauthorised reprints. That he entered no further works after 1791 suggests that around that time he may have ceased producing his own editions and was only marketing those printed by others.

---

[22] In addition to the Pye editions, Harwood issued works with other music sellers as well.

[23] For Wainwright, see Ronald R. Kidd, 'Wainwright family', *Grove Music Online*. Both Humphrey Hime in Liverpool and Longman and Broderip in London published Wainwright's works. Griffith James Cheese (1751–1804) was organist at Leominster in the 1770s and then Manchester between c.1782 and 1804. For Cheese, see Simon D.I. Fleming and Martin Perkins, *Dataset of Subscribers to Eighteenth-Century Music Publications in Britain and Ireland*, at www.musicsubscribers.co.uk; J.H. Nodal (ed.), *City News Notes and* Queries, vol. 5 (Manchester, 1883), 44. Nothing is known of the other composers whose works were printed by Pye: Miss Carver (three publications), J.F. (one publication) and J.L.B. (two publications).

[24] Ten compositions required two plates; another five, three; two, four; two others, five and six plates each.

[25] He entered *Six Solos* with the Stationers' Company on 21 April 1789. *The Stationers' Company Register of Entries*. The price of *Eighteen Lessons*, op 5, appears on the title page of the British Library copy.

TABLE 6.1 Works published by John Bridge Pye.

Composer	Title	Year printed	Stationers' Entry	Notes
Miss Carver	FREE FROM BUSTLE, NOISE & STRIFE, a favorite CANTATA, set to Music by Miss Carver, of Liverpool, Entd. at Stationers Hall. Price 6d. LIVERPOOL, Printed & Sold by J. B. Pye, at his Music Warehouse, opposite the Post Office, Lord Street, where Music & Musical Instruments are Sold Retail Wholesale & for Exportation, on the same Terms as in LONDON. GB-Lbl G.377.(11.)	1789	22 January 1789	Sold for 6d. 2 music plates, with separate arrangement for the German flute or guitar on bottom of second plate.
———	PATTY THE MILK MAID A FAVOURITE BALLAD Composed by Miss CARVER of Liverpool. Price 6d. Printed & Sold by J. B. Pye at his Music Warehouse opposite the Post Office Lord Street Liverpool. The Violin, Ger. Flute, Guittar, &c. taught to Ladies & Gentlemen. GB-Lbl H.1653.(26.)	1787	11 July 1787	Sold for 6d. 2 music plates, with a separate arrangement for the guitar at the bottom of the second plate.
———	THE QUEEN OF FLOWERS, a favorite SONG set to Music by Miss Carver of Liverpool, Entd. at Stationers Hall. Price 6d. LIVERPOOL, Printed and Sold by J. B. Pye, at his Music Warehouse, opposite the Post Office, Lord Street, where Music & Musical Instruments are Sold Retail, Wholesale & for Exportation, on the same Terms as in LONDON. GB-Lbl G.377.(12.)	1789	22 January 1789	Sold for 6d. 2 plates, with a separate arrangement for the German flute or guitar at the bottom of the second plate.
Griffith James Cheese (1751–1804)	THE VET'RAN SOLDIER Words by Miss Knipe,--Music by Mr. Cheese. Sung by Mr Meredith, at the Festivals, Liverpool, &c. Price 1s/-- Liverpool, Printed & sold by J.B. Pye, Music Warehouse Lord Street, Where every Article in the Music Line may be had. Enter'd at Stationers Hall. GB-Lbl G.377.(13.)	1790	22 September 1790	Sold for 1s. 2 plates.

DISTRIBUTING IRISH REPRINTS IN ENGLAND 107

Edward Harwood (1707–1787)	*ABSENCE A PASTORAL Composed by E. HARWOOD, and Sung at Mr. CASSON'S Concert Liverpool with great Applause. Price 6d. Liverpool: Printed & Sold by J. B. Pye at his Music Warehouse opposite the Post Office Lord Street. The Violin, Ger. Flute, Guittar &c. Taught to Ladies & Gentn.* GB-Lbl H.1653.(29.)	1787	11 July 1787	Sold for 6d. 3 plates, with a separate arrangement for the guitar at the bottom of third plate.
—	*THE BUSY BEES A Celebrated Song Composed by E. Harwood and sung at the Music Hall Liverpool with universal Applause. Price 1s. Liverpool Printed and sold by I. B. Pye at his Music Warehouse opposite the Post Office Lord Street. The Violin Ger: Flute Guittar &c. taught to Ladies and Gentn.* GB-Lbl H.1653.(31.)	1787	11 July 1787	Sold for 1s. 2 plates, with separate arrangements for the guitar and German flute at the bottom of the second plate.
—	*THE CHAIN OF LOVE A favourite Song Compos'd by E. HARWOOD Price 6d. Liverpool. Printed and Sold by J. B. Pye at his Music Warehouse opposite the Post Office Lord Street. NB. The Violin German Flute Guittar &c. taught to Ladies & Gentlemen.* GB-Lbl H.1653.(33.)	1787	11 July 1787	Sold for 6d. 2 plates, with a separate arrangement for the guitar or German flute at the bottom of the second plate.
—	*HAPLESS COLLIN A FAVORITE SONG Composed and Sung by E. Harwood Liverpool Printed and sold by I. B. Pye at his Music Warehouse opposite the Post Office Lord Street. Price 6d. The Violin Ger. Flute and Guittar taught to Ladies and Gentn.* GB-Lbl H.1653.(30.)	1787	11 July 1787	Sold for 6d. 3 plates, with a separate arrangement for the German flute at the bottom of the second plate.
—	*KIND GOD OF SLEEP A Glee now Singing with the utmost applause at all the Principal Concerts COMPOSED by the late E. HARWOOD. Entd at Stationers Hall Price 1s. LIVERPOOL. Printed by J. B. Pye at his Wholesale & Retail Music Warehouse, Lord Street, Where may be had all the above Author's Works.* GB-Ob (W) Harding Mus. G 187 (1)[26]	after 1787	Not entered with the Stationers despite the notation on the title page.	Sold for 1s. 2 plates.

[26] My thanks to Martin Holmes of the Bodleian Library, Oxford, for furnishing a photograph of this work.

TABLE 6.1 continued

Composer	Title	Year printed	Stationers' Entry	Notes
—	LOVE'S FORCE ON THE HEART A favourite SONG by the Author of the Busy Bees. Price 6d. Liverpool. Printed & Sold by J. B. Pye at his Music Warehouse opposite the Post Office Lord Street. GB-Lbl H.1653.(32.).	1787	11 July 1787	Sold for 6d. 2 plates, with separate arrangements for guitar and German flute at the bottom of the second plate.
—	The ORIENT SUN A Favorite HUNTING CANTATA, Composed and Sung By MR. HARWOOD. Printed & sold by J. B. PYE, Music Seller & Teacher No. 60, Cable Street Liverpool, Where may be had a great Variety of new Music & every other Article in the Musical Line, on the most reasonable Terms. GB-Lbl G.808.c.(16.)	1785?	Not entered with the Stationers	No price given.
J. F.	WERTER'S GHOST, Words and Music by J. F. Liverpool. Entered at Stationers Hall. Price 6d. LIVERPOOL, Printed and Sold by J. B. Pye, at his Music Warehouse, opposite the Post Office, Lord Street, where Music and Musical Instrument are Sold Wholesale, Retail, & for Exportation, on the same Terms as in London. GB-Lbl G.377.(24.)	1789	21 April 1789	Sold for 6d. 2 plates, with a separate arrangement for the guitar at the bottom of the second plate.
J. L. B.	THE Joys of Liberty, set to Music by J.L.B. Entd. at Stationers Hall. LIVERPOOL, Price 6d. Printed & Sold by J. B. Pye, at his Music Warehouse, opposite the Post Office, Lord Street, where Music & Musical Instruments are Sold, Retail, Wholesale & for Exportation, on the same terms as in LONDON. GB-Lbl G.377.(6.)	1789	22 January 1789	Sold for 6d. 3 plates, with a separate arrangement for the German flute taking up the whole of the third plate.
—	Universal Love, set to Music by J. L. B., Entd. at Stationers Hall Price 6d. LIVERPOOL, Printed & Sold by J. B. Pye, at his Music Warehouse, opposite the Post Office. Lord Street, where Music & Musical Instruments are Sold, Retail, Wholesale & for Exportation, on the same Terms as in LONDON. GB-Lbl G.377.(7.)	1789	22 January 1789	Sold for 6d. 3 plates, with a separate arrangement for the guitar taking up the whole of the third plate.

Richard Wainwright (1757–1825)	OUR TOPSAILS ATRIP A favorite Sea Song Sung by Mr. DIGNUM at the ANACREONTIC SOCIETY and the Music Hall Liverpool. Composed by R. Wainwright. Printed & Sold by J. B. Pye at his Music Warehouse opposite the Post Office Lord Street Liverpool. Price 6d. GB-Lbl H.1653.(48.)	1787	11 July 1787	Sold for 6d. 2 plates, with a separate arrangement for German flute at the bottom of the second plate.
Charles Henry Wilton (1761–1811)	ANSWER TO Oh NANNY wilt thou gang with me; as sung by Miss Harwood, at the MUSIC HALL LIVERPOOL: Composed by C: H: Wilton. Entered at Stationers Hll. Price 1s. LIVERPOOL, Printed & Sold by J. B. Pye at his Music Warehouse opposite the Post Office, Lord Street, where Music & Musical Instruments are Sold Wholesale Retail & for Exportation, on the same Terms as in London. GB-Lbl G.377.(61.)	1789	21 April 1789	Sold for 1s. 6 plates, with a separate arrangement for German flute or guitar taking up the whole of the final music plate.
———	COOLUN. A Celebrated IRISH AIR with Variations for the PIANO-FORTE OR HARPSICHORD. By C. H. Wilton Price [written in ink] 1/– LIVERPOOL. Printed by J. B. Pye, at his Wholesale & Retail Music Warehouse, Lord Street. Where may be had every new Musical Work as soon as Published. GB-Lbl h.721.w.(10.)	1789?	Not entered with the Stationers	Sold for 1s. 4 plates.
———	DEAR IS MY LITTLE NATIVE VALE, (from an Ode to Superstition) as Sung by Miss Harwood, at the Music Hall, LIVERPOOL: Composed by C. H. WILTON. Entd. at Stationers Hall. Price 6d. Liverpool, Printed & Sold by J. B. Pye, at his Music Warehouse, opposite the Post Office, Lord Street, where Music & Musical Instruments are Sold Retail Wholesale & for Exportation, on the same Terms as in LONDON. GB-Lbl G.377.(63.)	1789	22 January 1789	Sold for 6d. 4 plates, with a separate arrangement for the German flute or guitar at the bottom of the last plate.

TABLE 6.1 continued

Composer	Title	Year printed	Stationers' Entry	Notes
——	*The DEATH of Edwin & Emma, a favorite Song, Sung by Miss Harwood, at the Music Hall, LIVERPOOL; Composed by C. H. Wilton. Entd. at Stationers Hall. Price 6d. LIVERPOOL, Printed & Sold by J. B. Pye, at his Music Warehouse, opposite the Post Office, Lord Street, where Music & Musical Instruments are Sold Retail, Wholesale & for Exportation, on the same Terms as in LONDON.* GB-Lbl G.377.(64.)	1789	22 January 1789	Sold for 6d. 3 plates.
——	*THE MUSICAL CHACE, a favorite Hunting Song as Sung by Mr. Meredith, at the Music Hall LIVERPOOL; Composed by C. H. Wilton. Entd at Stationers Hall Price 6d. LIVERPOOL. Printed & Sold by J. B. Pye, at his Music Warehouse, opposite the Post Office, Lord Street, where Music & Musical Instruments are Sold Retail, Wholesale & for Exportation, on the same Terms as in LONDON.* GB-Lbl G.377.(62.)	1789	22 January 1789	Sold on title page for 6d., advertised later for 1s. 5 plates, with a separate arrangement for the German flute or guitar at the bottom of the last plate.
——	*A SET of Eighteen Lessons for the PIANO FORTE or HARPSICHORD (written in a progressive order and calculated to improve young Practitioners) by C. H. Wilton. Opa V. Entered at Stationers Hall Price 6s. Liverpool. Printed for & Sold by J. B. Pye, at his Wholesale & Retail Music Warehouse, Lord Street—at the Authors No. 3, Houghton Strt. and at all the Music Shops in Town & Country* GB-Lbl g.149.(6.)	1791	1 September 1791	Sold for 6s. Title page and 28 plates.
——	*Six Solos for the VIOLIN, with a THOROUGH BASS for the Harpsichord, Composed by C. H. Wilton. Opera III LIVERPOOL. Price 7s:6d. Printed & Sold by J. B. Pye, at his Music Warehouse opposite the Post Office Lord Street where Music & Musical Instruments are Sold Retail Wholesale & for Exportation on the same terms as in London* GB-Lbl g.221.(3.)	1789	21 April 1789	Sold for 7s. 6d. Title page and 32 plates. Lists several works by Wilton, among which is Wilton's op 2, printed by Thomas Skillern of London.

Although Bland and Weller did not name any specific Irish music trader from whom Pye had purchased copies, one likely possibility was the Dublin printer Maurice (or Morris) Hime. Originally from Liverpool, Hime was in partnership with his brother Humphrey by 1789 with a shop at 15 Castle Street, not too far from Pye's establishment.[27] Given that both Hime and Pye were in the music trade and operated in close proximity, they very likely knew each other. Certainly, their business coincided: the song 'The Earth is Toper' (c.1796), sold under Humphrey Hime's imprint, included that the composition was available at 'J.B. Pye's music shop Nº. 17 Lord Street.'[28] Between 1791 and 1792, the Hime brothers' partnership ended, and Maurice moved his operation to Dublin, where he occupied premises at 34 College Green from that time until 1814. By 1795 he was married to the daughter of prominent Dublin music seller Elizabeth Rhames, who is known to have issued unauthorised editions of music originally published in London.[29] While Hime may not have been the only Dublin music seller with whom Pye dealt, he could certainly have been one of Pye's connections into the trade of inexpensive unauthorised reprints from Ireland.

A large part of Hime's business in Dublin involved printing popular English songs for export to England, an activity that provided him with a substantial profit for over two decades.[30] Even after 1801, Hime continued to defy the copyright statute by issuing his own editions of popular English works. For example, in 1815 the English composer and music seller John Whitaker sued

[27] For Hime's partnership with his brother and activities in Liverpool, see Perkin, *The Book Trade in Liverpool to 1805*, 13; Humphries and Smith, *Music Publishing in the British Isles*, 181.

[28] The full title was *The Earth is a Toper: Translated from the Greek of Anacreon. By Dr. Cogan. Set to Music by Harmonicus. And Sung by Mr. Meredith, at the Music Hall Liverpool. Entd. at Stationers Hall. Price 1s.* Hime entered the composition with the Stationers's Company on 16 December 1796. The entry with the Stationers Company is TSC 1/E/06/13, covering 4 September 1796–29 April 1799. The mention of Pye is part of the imprint itself.

[29] For Hime's activities in Ireland and relationship to Elizabeth Rhames, see Mary Pollard, *A Dictionary of Members of the Dublin Book Trade 1550–800* (London, 2000), 289–90; Humphries and Smith, *Music Publishing*, 181. For information about the Rhames family and their activities, see *Dictionary of Members of the Dublin Book Trade*, 487–90; Humphries and Smith, *Music Publishing*, 272. Though Elizabeth Rhames died in 1795, music under her imprint or that of her family continued to appear until 1806.

[30] For Hime's activities around printing and selling unauthorised reprints of English works, see Michael Talbot, *The Business of Music* (Liverpool, 2002), 68–9; D.W. Krummel and Stanley Sadie, *Music Printing and Publishing* (London, 1990), 288. See also 'Hime, Maurice,' in *The Dublin Music Trade*, at http://dublinmusictrade.ie/node/203. One composer whose works Hime and others frequently reprinted was James Hook. Edith B. Schapper (ed.), *The British Union-Catalogue of Early Music Printed Before the Year 1801*, vol. 1 (London, 1957), 490–505 lists seventy-eight Irish reprints of Hook's compositions; of those twenty-six (one third) carried Hime's name.

Hime for copyright infringement in Dublin's Court of Exchequer.[31] Asking for damages of £5000, Whitaker accused Hime of producing and selling pirated copies of three songs he had written: 'Silent Kisses', 'Love and the Aeolian Harp' and 'Mary, Mary, list, awake', all composed around 1808 and 1809 to words by the poet Leigh Hunt (1784–1859).[32] After a lengthy trial, the jury dismissed the arguments of Hime's attorneys, awarding a victory to Whitaker and setting an important legal precedent in the history of copyright law.[33]

The Accusers: Anne Bland and Edward Weller

In filing their Chancery suit against Pye, Anne Bland and Edward Weller did not name the composers of the listed 123 compositions (see Tables 6.2 and 6.3). However, all the titles can be identified as works by James Hook (1746–1827). Hook's music was a likely target for Irish printers since, as well as being a well-known organist, he was a popular and prolific composer. In addition to instrumental pieces and music for the theatres, from 1767 until c.1807 Hook composed more than 2,000 songs for the pleasure gardens at Marylebone and Vauxhall.[34] From 1767 he sold to music sellers for publication each year two or three collections of seven to nine songs. In addition, several London music sellers – including Peter Welcker, the Thompsons and John Preston – issued various editions of the songs from the pleasure gardens and single pieces written by Hook.[35] Irish music sellers reproduced his most popular tunes as single sheets, printed on fewer plates and with paper inferior to that used on the authorised London editions.

Bland and Weller dealt extensively in Hook's compositions. Bland traded between 1784 and 1792, operating from her London shop at 23 Oxford Street. In 1792 she entered into partnership with Weller, who may have been a pianoforte

---

[31] The full proceedings appeared in print: *Musical Copyright. Proceedings on a Trial Before the Hon. Baron George, in the Court of Exchequer, Dublin, May 18th, 1815* (London, 1816). The case merited a full summary because, in addition to the copyright issues raised by the case, it also attracted attention as John Whitaker, himself a popular composer, had set to music lyrics written by the well-known author Leigh Hunt.

[32] The full titles were the following: John Whitaker, *No. 1. Silent Kisses Written by Leigh Hunt Esqr.* (London, [n.d.]); Whitaker, *No 2. Love and the Æolian Harp* (London, [n.d.]); and Whitaker, *No 3 Mary, Mary, list! Awake!* (London, [n.d.]).

[33] One indication of the trial's importance is that a volume reproducing a complete transcript of the proceeding was printed. In addition, other accounts of the case appeared in London newspapers: for instance, a full transcript of the proceedings in *Saunders's News-Letter*, 25 May 1815 (pp. 2–3) and 26 May 1815 (p. 2); and 'Observations on the trial – Whitaker *v*. Hime,' in *The Examiner*, Sunday, 11 June 1815 (pp. 14–15).

[34] Pamela McGairl, 'Hook, James', *Grove Music Online*.

[35] Welcker printed collections of Hook's songs between 1769 and 1775; the Thompsons, between 1767 and 1789; Preston, between 1783 and 1796. See entries in Schapper (ed.), *The British Union-Catalogue*, i, 492–93.

maker, and their joint enterprise continued until c.1818.[36] Between 1791 and 1801 Bland and Weller issued each year one of Hook's annual collection of Vauxhall songs; in addition, the firm sold single pieces not included in the collected editions.[37] They appear to have been particularly concerned about the possibility that others might illegally reprint Hook's compositions since they were the most conscientious about entering these publications with the Stationers' Company. Of the seventy-seven examples that appeared in the entry books from 1790 until 1796 when the suit was filed, sixty (almost seventy-eight percent) named Bland and Weller as proprietors.[38] As Tables 6.2 and 6.3 indicate, among them were the collections for the years 1793 to 1796 as well as fifty-four individual songs (one in 1792; eleven in 1793; eighteen in 1794; fifteen in 1795; nine in 1796) and the musical entertainment *Jack of Newbury*.[39] By entering their copies with the Stationers' Company, they demonstrated that they considered Hook's works valuable enough to merit the costs involved in registering his work and providing the requisite deposit copies.[40] If they had to sue for copyright infringement, then, Bland and Weller had anticipated another common defence in such cases: that they had not established their ownership according to the statute.[41] Therefore, they were prepared to take action against anyone in England they found selling these unauthorised editions.

[36] For information on Edward Weller, see Humphries and Smith, *Music Publishing*, 327, where he is listed as manufacturing pianofortes after his partnership with Anne Bland. For information about Bland and Weller, see ibid., 76; Krummel and Sadie, *Music Printing and Publishing*, 178.

[37] Schapper (ed.), *The British Union-Catalogue*, i, 492–93.

[38] See *The Stationers' Company Register of Entries* TSC 1/E/06/11-13. In this count I include *Jack of Newbury*, which Hook entered himself 20 May 1795. Bland and Weller almost certainly purchased the copyright from him since they later brought out copies of individual songs under their own imprint.

[39] They also entered two instrumental compositions: *Three Sonatas for the Pianoforte or Harpsichord dedicated to Miss Isabella Sutton*, op 72, in 1793; and *Six Sonatas for the Pianoforte or Harpsichord dedicated to the Right Honourable Lady Lydia Turnour*, op 77, in 1795. A review of Stationers' Company entries up to 1800 reveals that after the suit, they continued to enter their copies of Hook's compositions with the Stationers. In 1797 they entered seventeen Hook works, and in 1800 another two. Only Longman and Broderip, with four entries in 1799, and Hodsoll, with another in 1800, registered Hook compositions at Stationers' Hall between 1797 and 1800.

[40] Because of the expense involved, book and music sellers did not ordinarily enter all their works with the Stationers' Company. See Nancy A. Mace, 'The Market for Music in the Late Eighteenth Century and the Entry Books of the Stationers' Company', *The Library*, 10/2 (2009), 157–87, at 160–1.

[41] For the requirement that proprietors had to enter their copies with the Stationers' Company in order to claim protection under the law, see R. Deazley, 'Commentary on the *Statute of Anne* 1710', (2008) in Bently and Kretschmer (eds), *Primary Sources on Copyright (1450–1900)*. Later the court in *Beckford v. Hood* (1798) ruled that entry with the Stationers' Company was not necessary in order to establish ownership legally. See R. Deazley, 'Commentary on *Beckford v. Hood* (1798)', (2008) in Bently and Kretschmer (eds), *Primary Sources on Copyright (1450–1900)*.

However, Bland and Weller weakened their position since not all the compositions listed in the suit appeared in the Stationers' Company entry books. Although they asserted in their bill of complaint that they had entered all these works, the records of the Company indicate that they had in fact registered just three of the five song collections and forty-four of the eighty-two single songs. Even though all the title pages of the song collections included the phrase 'Entered at Stationers' Hall', only those printed in 1793, 1794 and 1795 appeared in the Company's records. Hook himself had entered *Jack of Newbury* on 20 May 1795; since Bland and Weller issued under their own imprint individual songs from the entertainment, including 'Donna Della' and 'When the Mind is in Tune', they most likely purchased the copyright from Hook sometime after the first edition of the collected songs appeared.[42] Of the individual titles named in the suit, Bland and Weller asserted on forty-seven first pages that they had entered the compositions with the Stationers' Company when three – 'I Sigh for the Girl I Adore', 'Some Wives are Good' and 'The Sweet River Dee' – did not appear in the entry books.[43] Their practice was not unusual. Frequently, music sellers claimed on title pages that a work had been 'entered at Stationers Hall' even when it had not, presumably to deter their competitors from producing unauthorised reprints.

Though Bland and Weller had not entered all the works mentioned in the lawsuit, they would have had sufficient grounds to sue Pye as long as they could identify any compositions registered by them that he had reprinted or sold as unauthorised copies. They probably did not know which specific pieces he had imported; therefore, as did plaintiffs in many such cases, they listed a large number of titles in order to improve their chances of finding at least one that he had illegally marketed.[44] To avoid any ambiguity, they identified each individual song that appeared in the collections from 1791 to 1795 and included selected pieces from *Jack of Newbury* and *Look Ere You Leap* even though they had entered the works under the collection's title. Such entries would offer

---

[42] For the Bland and Weller copies, both printed in 1795, see James Hook, *Donna Della, The much Admired Song* (London, [n.d.]); and *When the Mind is in Tune A Favorite Song* (London, [n.d.]).

[43] James Hook, *I sigh For the Girl I adore, A Favorite Song* (London, [n.d.]); *Some Wives are Good! A Favorite Comic Glee For Three Ladies & Three Gentlemen* (London, [n.d.]); and *The Sweet River Dee, A Favorite Song* (London, [n.d.]).

[44] For this common practice, see, for example, TNA E112/1684, no. 3268 (Longman and Broderip [L&B] v. John Fielding), E112/1690, no. 3450 (L&B v. William Sibbald), E112/1691, nos. 3456 (L&B v. Thomas Williams), 3457 (L&B v. John Bland), 3460 (L&B v. Samuel Babb), 3461 (L&B v. Robert Massey) and 3466 (L&B v. Francis Roome). In these Exchequer suits and others filed by Longman and Broderip in the 1780s against several music sellers both in London and elsewhere, the plaintiffs attached to the bills of complaint a full transcript of their sales catalogue. In some of these suits, the defendants argued that Longman and Broderip had no right to claim protection because they had not entered the works with the Stationers' Company as required by statute. See, in particular, the answers of William Sibbald (March 1784) in E112/1690, no. 3450; and John Bland (February 1784) in E112/1691, no. 3457.

copyright protection to each individual piece in these collected works although it was not specifically named in the registration.

Had Pye decided to mount a defense against their bill, he could have argued, as did many defendants, that he had every right to import and sell some of these compositions because Bland and Weller had not established their right to those not registered with the Stationers' Company as required by law.[45] The items in Tables 6.2 and 6.3 demonstrate that at least fourteen reprints issued by Dublin printers fell into this category. Thus, if Pye had imported these compositions, he could have argued that he was legally entitled to do so. However, because at least thirty-three of the forty-six copies with Dublin imprints appeared in the Stationers' Company records, the London music sellers would have had sufficient grounds for their suit if Pye had imported any of the other compositions.[46]

A central part of Bland and Weller's complaint was their assertion that Dublin printers produced copies more cheaply, enabling them and those importing such copies to price them lower than their English competitors. A comparison of the reprints listed in Tables 6.2 and 6.3 with the authorised editions produced by Bland and Weller provides support for this assertion. The London music sellers printed songs in folios comprising one large sheet folded in half, yielding four sides. Of the copies listed that Bland and Weller marketed as single songs, twenty-three came from two plates printed in such a way that the music appears on facing pages with two blank pages on the other two sides, a convenient arrangement for a musician since it avoided page turns. Six of these songs included a separate arrangement on the second plate for either German flute or guitar. With the exception of 'Why is Love' (1794), marketed at 1s., all sold for 6d. a copy.[47] Thirty other pieces were produced using three plates, with one blank on the recto of the first page. On the final page of twenty-one of these copies appeared a separate arrangement with words for such instruments as the guitar, flute or German flute. Bland and Weller sold all of these editions for 1s. a piece. Another seven required four plates, using up both recto and verso of a folio's four sides; five of these included lines for multiple instruments in score, thus necessitating the larger number of plates. Even though the printing costs of these editions were undoubtedly higher, Bland and Weller also advertised these copies for 1s.

---

[45] For example, see the defendants' answers in TNA E112/1690, no. 3450 (Longman and Broderip v. William Sibbald) and E112/1691, no. 3457 (Longman and Broderip v. John Bland).

[46] We have no way of knowing exactly how many unauthorised reprints of Hook's works were issued. I have not been able to locate any catalogues for the Dublin music sellers who frequently reprinted popular English tunes: for example, Maurice Hime, Elizabeth Rhames and her family, or Edmund Lee. What I have found suggests that Hime produced unauthorised copies most often; of the reprints in Tables 6.2 and 6.3, twenty-five carried his imprint; another eight, that of Rhames, Hime's in-laws. Other Dublin printers represented in the tables include the following: Edmund Lee, who issued four; Benjamin Cooke, six; McDonnell, one. Two other songs appeared in *Walker's Hibernian Magazine*.

[47] James Hook, *Why is Love so past Defining. A Favorite Glee* (London, [n.d.]).

A physical comparison of the Irish reprints in Tables 6.2 and 6.3 with the authorised copies printed by Bland and Weller reveals that one way the Irish music sellers reduced their costs was by cutting the number of plates required for each piece and using inferior paper. The tables include forty-four reprints of thirty works listed by Bland and Weller in their schedule.[48] Every one of the Irish editions was on a single sheet with the verso blank. If they were using the same size sheets as the London music sellers, then, they would have cut them in half, allowing them to produce twice the number of copies per sheet. In addition, each employed a single plate instead of the two or three typical of the Bland and Weller publications. If the Irish reprint included a separate arrangement for instruments such as the guitar or German flute, it appeared at the bottom of the single page. In order to fit everything on one plate, the engraver had to make the musical lines and notes much smaller than those in the English editions of the same works. Except for the use of fewer plates, the Irish editions, though compressed, were virtually identical to English versions. The only variation in some cases was in the printer's choice to omit separate instrumental accompaniments. The difference in price between a ream of better-quality paper used by Bland and Weller and that employed by Irish printers like Hime would have been substantial, reducing further Irish printers' expenses.[49] Finally, Irish printers did not have to lay out money to the composer for the copyright. Irish music sellers could therefore produce their versions of these English songs more cheaply than their London competitors.

While Irish music sellers like Hime could clearly produce reprints for much less than Bland and Weller, they would only undercut the English music sellers if they priced their copies low enough to attract buyers away from the higher-quality London prints. Unfortunately, prices do not usually appear on the Irish single sheets, nor have any sales catalogues from Irish music traders survived. None of the Irish reprints in Tables 6.2 and 6.3 identify the price of a copy. However, an examination of various Hime editions in the British Library provides some information about the typical prices charged by him for single sheet songs. For example, Hime's printing of *Roy's Wife of Alldivalock, a much admir'd Duett* (c.1800) listed prices for eleven compositions, for each of which Hime charged 6d Hibernian (or about 5½ d in English currency).[50] Therefore, Hime and the other

---

[48] I have omitted the two reprints of songs that appeared in *Walker's Hibernian Magazine* because they appeared in quarto rather than folio as part of a letterpress printing.

[49] In discussing the cost of printing letterpress books in Dublin as compared to English editions, Mary Pollard notes that paper was cheaper in Ireland, and the wages of those engaged in the print trade were lower than those earned by their English counterparts. Although she is discussing book printing, we can reasonably assume that her analysis can also apply to music printing. See Pollard, *Dublin's Trade in Books, 1550–1800*, 110–35.

[50] *Roy's Wife of Alldivaloch a much admir'd Duett. Price 6 ½ Dublin Publish'd by Hime at his Musical Circulating Library No 34 College Green*. Hime also charged 6d. Hibernian in five other instances. In his printing of *The Ram of Derby A favorite Glee by Callcott*, which he sold for 1s. 1d., he listed several other works with prices, among them *The Red Cross Knight*, sold by Robert Birchall for 1s. 6d., and advertised for 6d. Hibernian;

Dublin music sellers probably charged 6d. Hibernian for music that Bland and Weller advertised for 6d. and 1s. in English money, suggesting that these London music sellers had sufficient grounds to claim that Pye and the Irish music sellers were damaging their profits by selling reprints at cheaper prices.

We do not know what Pye's response to Bland and Weller's charges was, for the suit did not progress further than the bill of complaint and Edward Weller's affidavit. As in many such copyright cases, the bill itself was probably enough to achieve its intended goal since it curtailed the actions of a defendant who knew that he had a weak argument against the charges levelled against him.[51] It cannot be coincidence that Pye sold his stock in trade the following year, and it may well have been Bland and Weller's suit that played a central part in Pye's decision to leave the music trade, especially if a large part of his business involved unauthorised Irish reprints.

Conclusion

Even though Bland and Weller's suit went no further than the original filings, it offers new information about the activities of a Liverpool music seller in the last decade of the eighteenth century and reveals one route by which unauthorised Irish reprints made their way into England. It also shows a strategy for fighting music piracies available to members of the London music trade, who had no direct legal way to combat the perceived threat posed by cheap Irish reproductions of popular songs. If they could identify an English music seller importing the unauthorised editions, as Bland and Weller did in this instance, they had a strong argument for an injunction and accounting when they brought their complaint to Chancery. In this case, Bland and Weller's detailed list of Hook's compositions and their haphazard registrations with the Stationers' Company emphasize the highly competitive trade of printed works by popular composers in the English music market in the latter half of the eighteenth century.

The Friar of Orders Gray, sold by Birchall for 1s. 6d., and advertised for 6d. Hibernian; *the Erl King*, sold by Birchall for 2s. 6d., and advertised for 1s. 1d. Hibernian. Callcott advertised these works in a catalogue, *Catalogue of Music Composed by I.W. Callcott*, a copy of which survives at the end of the British Library's edition of John Wall Callcott (1766–1821), *The Complaint. Written by Mr. Rannie* (G.806.a.(3.)). Robert Birchall purchased the rights to all these works from Callcott on 17 January 1807. See *Musical & dramatic curiosities exhibited by C. Lonsdale* (Newberry Library, MS folio V 209.52, fo. 12r, item 58). He subsequently printed and sold them at the same prices Callcott originally charged. Hime also sold copies of *Oscar and Malvina*, advertised by Longman and Broderip for 6s., for 2s. 2d. See fn. 9 for the relevant imprints. For the value of Irish currency, see John J. McCusker, *Money and Exchange in Europe and America 1600–1775* (Chapel Hill, 1992), 34–9. The table on p. 39 indicates that in 1775, the latest date given by McCusker, £100 of Irish money was worth approximately £108.06 in English sterling. Thus, 6d. of Irish money was worth about 5s. 5d. in English currency.

[51] See, for example, TNA E112/1691, nos. 3456, 3461 and 3466; E112/1708, no. 3895 (Longman and Broderip v. John Wilks).

TABLE 6.2 Song Collections and Musical Entertainments mentioned in the lawsuit against John Bridge Pye by Anne Bland and Edward Weller.[52]

Collection title	Collection's works named in suit	Dublin reprints	Comments
A Collection of favorite SONGS Sung by Mr. Darley, Mr. Duffy, Miss Leary, Miss Milne & Mrs. Addison, at VAUXHALL GARDENS Composed by Mr. Hook. Book 1st. 1791. Entered at Stationers Hall Price 3s [GB-Lbl G.379.b.(8.)]	'The Cottager's Daughter' 'I'm in Haste' 'While High the Foaming Surges Rise' 'The Rose with Sweet Fragrance Delights' 'Die an Old Maid' 'I Loo Him Dearly' 'My Shepherd Gone Away'	'The Cottager's Daughter': printed by Edmund Lee [GB-Lbl H.1601.g.(.98)], E. Rhames [GB-Lbl H.1654.n.(.5)], M. Hime with watermark dated 1796 [GB-En JM 990] 'I'm in Haste': printed by E. Rhames, c.1795 [GB-En Add Mus 1114l], Hime, c.1800 [GB-En Add Mus 10464] 'While High the Foaming Surges Roll': printed by Hime [GB-En Add. Mus 7503] 'The Rose with Sweet Fragrance': printed by E. Rhames [GB-En JM 1000]	Not entered in *Entry Books of the Stationer's Company* (SC). Each song printed by Bland has a separate titlepage, with the price for each 6*d*. so that the songs could be sold individually. All the songs in the collection are named individually in court documents.
A Collection of favorite SONGS Sung by Mr. Darley, Mr. Clifford, Miss Leary, Miss Milne & Mrs. Addison, at VAUXHALL GARDENS Composed by Mr. Hook. Book 1st. 1792. Entered at Stationers Hall Price 3s. London. [GB-Lbl G.379.b.(10.)]	'I Never Will Be Married' 'Molly of the Mead' 'Jockey of the Green' 'She Never Thinks of Me' 'I'll Die for No Shepherd Not I' 'The Veil A Favorite Song' 'William of the Ferry' 'Fye for Shame'		Not entered in SC. Each song has a separate titlepage, with the price for each 6*d*. so that the songs could be sold individually. All the songs in the collection are named individually in court documents.

[52] The Bland and Weller Catalogue of 1800 was the source for some works I was unable to locate elsewhere. *A Catalogue of New Songs, Duetts, Catches, and Glees, Printed and Published by Messrs. Bland & Weller* (London, [c.1800]), GB-Lbl 7896.h.40.(1.)). Except for the song collections, musical works did not usually have a publication date in the imprint; without external information, then, such as registration with the Stationers, the dates given in the table for the Irish reprints are in most cases estimates. Therefore, I have included Irish reprints carrying publication dates of 1800, presuming that they may very well have been issued before Bland and Weller filed their suit.

A Collection of Favorite SONGS Sung by Mr. Darley, Mr. Clifford, Mrs. Franklin, Miss Milne, Mrs. Addison & Mrs. Mountain, AT VAUXHALL GARDENS. Composed by Mr. Hook. Entered at Stationers Hall Book 1st. 1793. Price 3s. [GB-Lbl G.379.(1.)]	'The Silver Moon' 'Then Say my Sweet Girl Can You Love Me' 'Two Bunches a Penny Primroses' 'Yarrow Vale' 'The Contented Shepherd' 'Never Say No, When You Wish to Say Yes' 'Let Others Wreaths of Roses Twine' 'My Dear Willy' 'Sweet Patty'	'The Silver Moon': printed in *Walker's Hibernian Magazine*, January 1794 [GB-En JM 1016], by Edmund Lee [GB-En JM 1015], by Hime [GB-Lbl H.1601.f.(56.)] 'Then Say My Sweet Girl': printed by E. Rhames [GB-En JM 5929] 'The Contented Shepherd': printed by Hime [GB-En JM 987] 'Never Say No': printed by Hime [GB-En JM 955]	Entered in *SC*, 7 June 1793. All the songs in the collection are named individually in court documents.
A Collection of Favorite SONGS Sung by Mr. Dignum, Mr. Taylor, Mrs. Franklin, Miss Milne, Master Phelps & Mrs. Mountain, AT VAUXHALL GARDENS. Composed by Mr. Hook. Entered at Stationers Hall. Book 1st. 1794. Price 3s. [GB-Lbl G.379.(3.)]	'The Sweetest Flower of Yarrow' 'Sweet Girl by the Light of the Moon' 'A Smile from the Lovely Brown Maid' 'The Caledonian Laddy' 'Few are so Happy as Ellen and I' 'I Hope to Marry Charley' 'A Bumper, A Friend, and the Girl of Your Heart' 'He Loves his winsome Kate'	'Sweet Girl': printed by Hime [GB-En Add Mus 7638], by B. Cooke, c.1795 [GB-En Add Mus 9819] 'The Caledonian Laddy': printed by Rhames [GB-En Add Mus 1139], by Edmund Lee [GB-En JM 983], by Hime with a watermark dated 1795 [GB-En JM 981]	Entered in *SC*, 27 May 1794. All the songs in the collection are named individually in court documents.
A Collection of Favorite SONGS Sung by Mr. Dignum, Mr. Taylor, Mrs. Franklin, Miss Milne, Master Welsh, & Mrs. Mountain, AT VAUXHALL GARDENS, Composed by Mr. Hook. Entered at Stationers Hall. Book 1st. 1795. Price 3s. [GB-Lbl G.379.(5.)]	'Rosy the Wine is the Key' 'Ah Welladay Poor Anna' 'A Dance Round the Maypole' 'How Gaily Roll'd the Moments on' 'Love thou Strange Capricious Boy' 'Donald of Dundee' 'So Dearly I Love Johnny O' 'Lubin of the Hill'	'Ah welladay poor Anna': printed by Hime, c.1800 [GB-En Add Mus 7410] 'Donald of Dundee': printed by Hime, c.1800 [GB-En Add Mus 9629] 'Lubin of the Hill': printed by Hime, c.1800 [GB-En Add Mus 7557]	Entered in *SC*, 8 June 1795. All the songs in the collection are named individually in court documents.

TABLE 6.2 continued

Collection title	Collection's works named in suit	Dublin reprints	Comments
Jack of Newbury, an Opera, in Three Acts with a Masque, in honor of the Royal Nuptials performed with Universal Applause at the Theatre Royal, Drury Lane, Compos'd and humbly dedicated to His Royal Highness the Prince of Wales, By James Hook, Op. 80. London: Printed for the Composer [1795] [GB-Lbl D.287.(1.)]	'Donna Della' 'The blush that o'er the Virgin Cheek' 'Fair Ellen was a Gentle Maid' 'Gentle Hymen at thy feet' 'The lordly Oak the forrests pride' 'More sweet than thrush or woodlarks note' 'O happy day when folks shall say' 'My love is Young' 'There was Cormac O'Con' 'Twangdillo' 'What is a passion I avow' 'When a Man is determined' 'where Liffy rolls in Silver Stream' 'The wings of Love by fortune decked' 'When the Mind is in Tune'	'When the Mind is in Tune': printed by B. Cooke, c.1795 [GB-Lbl H.1601.t.(8.)], by Hime [GB-En JM 3556]	Entered by James Hook in SC, 20 May 1795. Songs listed individually in suit and many sold separately for 1s. each under the imprint of Bland and Weller, indicating that they had purchased the copyright from the composer.
Look ere you Leap A Favorite Serenata Sung with Universal Applause By Mr. Darley, Mr. Loder, Mr. Evans, Master Shepherd & Mr. Clifford, Miss Leary, Miss Milne & Mrs Addison, AT VAUXHALL GARDENS, Written by Mr. Vint, Set to Music by Mr. Hook. Op. 69 Price 2s: 6d [GB-Lbl G.239.a.(2.)]	'Swains a truce with your deceiving' 'What the deuce is here to do' 'Hark hark to the Voice of the Musical Swain' 'Swain I mean your truth to try' 'Tempests having ceased to jar'		Not entered in SC. First performed on 2 June 1792.

TABLE 6.3 Individual Songs mentioned in the lawsuit against John Bridge Pye by Anne Bland and Edward Weller.

Song Title	Dublin Reprints	Comments
ADIEU TO DELIGHT. A Favorite Song Sung by Master Phelps, at Vauxhall, COMPOSED BY MR. HOOK. Entered at Stationers Hall. Price 1s. Written by Mrs. Plowden [GB-Lbl H.1651.c.(28.)]		Entered in *Entry Books of the Stationer's Company* (SC), 22 August 1794.
Away to the Woodlands away A Favorite Glee for 3 Voices Sung with Universal Applause AT VAUXHALL GARDENS Composed by Mr. Hook. Pr. 1s/- London [GB-Lbl H.1651.c.(56.)]		Not entered in SC.
THE BONNY COLLIER'S DAUGHTER A Favorite New Song Sung with Universal Applause by Mr Dignum at Vauxhall Gardens. Composed by Mr. Hook. Enter'd at Stationers Hall. Price 1s. [GB-Lbl H.1651.a.(31.)]		Entered in SC, 14 July 1795.
The British Fair with Three Times Three A Favorite Song, Sung by Mr. Taylor, with Universal Applause at Vauxhall Gardens, Composed by Mr. Hook. Entered at Stationers Hall. Price 1s. [GB-Lbl H.1651.a.(21.)]	Printed by Hime, c.1795 [GB-En JM 980]	Entered in SC, 26 June 1794.
British Loyalty, OR KING, LORDS, & COMMONS A Favorite Song Sung at Vauxhall Gardens. Composed by Mr Hook. Entered at Stationers Hall. Price 1s. The Words by Mr. Vint. [GB-Lbl H.1651.a.(25.)]		Entered in SC, 2 June 1794.
The British Tar, A Favorite Medley SONATA, for the Piano-Forte or Harpsichord. Composed, Selected & Arranged By Mr. Hook. Price 2s/6d. [GB-Lbl g.352.f(5.)]		Not entered in SC.
BRITONS STRUCK HOME, LED THE WAY BY LORD HOWE, A Favorite Song, Sung with Universal Applause, at Vauxhall Gardens, COMPOSED BY MR. HOOK. Entered at Stationers Hall. Price 1s. The Words by Mr. Upton. [GB-Lbl H.1651.a.(28.)]		Entered in SC, 26 June 1794.

TABLE 6.3 continued

Song Title	Dublin Reprints	Comments
THE CAPTIVE QUEEN A Favorite New Song as now Singing at the Principal Concerts, with the greatest applause, Composed by Mr. Hook. Pr. 1s. [GB-Lbl H.1651.c.(19.)]		Not entered in SC.
Come Buy my Water Cresses. A Favorite Song, Sung by Master Phelps at Vauxhall, Composed by Mr. Hook. Entered at Stationers Hall. Price 1s. Written by Mr. Upton. [GB-Lbl H.1651.c.(29.)]		Entered in SC, 26 July 1794.
The Cottage in the Grove, A Favorite Song, Sung by Mr. Dignum, at Vauxhall Gardens, Composed by Mr. Hook. Entered at Stationers Hall. Price 1s. The Words by a Lady. [GB-Lbl H.1651.c.(17.)]	Printed by Hime, c.1800 [GB-Lbl G.426.kk.(43)]	Entered in SC, 13 August 1794.
Dear little Cottage Maiden A Favorite SONG Sung by Master Phelps at Vauxhall Gardens Composed by Mr. Hook. Entered at Stationers Hall. Written by Mr. Upton. Price 1s [GB-Lbl H.1651.a.(20.)]		Entered in SC, 26 August 1793.
THE DYING NEGRO A Favorite Song Sung by Mr. Clifford, AT VAUXHALL GARDENS, Composed by Mr. Hook. Price 6.d. [GB-Lbl H.1651.b.(42.)]	Printed by Hime [GB-Lbl H.1601.f.(40.)], by J. Hill [GB-En JM 998]	Not entered in SC.
The Eccho Song. Sung with Universal Applause By Miss Milne, Eccho Master Shepherd AT VAUXHALL GARDENS. Composed by Mr. Hook. Price 6d. [GB-Lbl G.239.b.(14.)]		Not entered in SC.
FOR WE SHALL BOTH GROW OLDER A Favorite Song Sung by Master Welch, AT Vauxhall Gardens, COMPOSED by MR. HOOK. Entered at Stationers Hall. Price 1s [GB-Lbl H.1651.a.(39.)]		Entered in SC, 12 June 1795.
'For you ye Fair' (not found)		Listed in the 1800 catalogue under duetts, sold for 6d.

The Happy Milk Maid A Favorite SONG Sung by Miss Milne at Vauxhall Gardens Composed by Mr. Hook. Entered at Stationers Hall. Written by Mr. Vint. Price 1s. [GB-Lbl H.1651.(16.)]	Printed by Hime, ?1800 [GB-Lbl H.1601.g.(79.)]	Entered in SC, 26 August 1793.
Hark the Martial Fife and Drum, A Favorite New Song, Sung by Mrs. Mountain, at Vauxhall Gardens COMPOSED BY MR. HOOK. Entered at Stationers Hall. Price 1s. The Words by Mr. Vint. [GB-Lbl H.1651.b.(33.)]		Entered in SC, 21 June 1794.
HITHER MARY HITHER COME A Favorite Song Sung by Mastr. Phelps with Universal Applause AT VAUXHALL GARDENS Composed by Mr. Hook. Entered at Stationers Hall. Price 1s. [GB-Lbl H.1651.c.(30.)]	Printed by Hime [GB-En JM 909], by Edmund Lee, c.1795 [GB-En Add. Mus 12374], by *Walker's Hibernian Magazine*, July 1794 [GB-En JM 2797]	Entered in SC, 31 May 1793.
'I know a thing or two' (not found)		
I Never Lov'd any Dear Mary but You A Favorite Song, Sung with Universal Applause, by Mr. Dignum, AT Vauxhall Gardens. COMPOSED BY MR. HOOK Entered at Stationers Hall Price 1s. The Words by a Lady. [GB-Lbl H.1651.a.(29.)]	Printed by F. Rhames, c.1800 [GB-En Add Mus 6500], by B. Cooke, c.1795 [GB-En JM 2845], by Hime, c.1800 [GB-En JM 920]	Entered in SC, 29 May 1794.
I sigh For the Girl I adore, A Favorite Song Sung by Master Phelps with Universal Applause, At Vauxhall Gardens, Composed by Mr. Hook. Entered at Stationers Hall. Price 1s. The Words by Mr. Anderson. [GB-Lbl H.1651.c.(26.)]	Printed by B. Cooke [GB-En JM 926]	Not entered in SC.
In Dublin City lives a Youth A Celebrated Irish Song Sung by Mrs. Mountain at Vauxhall Gardens Composed by Mr. Hook. Entered at Stationers Hall. Written by Mr. Upton. Price 1s. [GB-Lbl H.1651.(19.)]		Entered in SC, 10 August 1793.
KATE OF DOVER, A Favorite Sea Song, Sung with Universal Applause by Mr. Dignum, AT VAUXHALL GARDENS. Composed by Mr. Hook. Entered at Stationers Hall. Price 1s. The Words by Mr. Anderson. [GB-Lbl H.1651.a.(36.)]		Entered in SC, 9 June 1795.

TABLE 6.3 continued

Song Title	Dublin Reprints	Comments
Keep your Distance A Favorite Song Sung by Mrs. Franklin At Vauxhall Gardens Composed by Mr. Hook. Enterd at Stationers Hall. Price 6d. Written by Mr. Pitt. [GB-Lbl H.1651.a.(37.)]		Entered in SC, 21 August 1795.
THE KING and CONSTITUTION A NEW Song, Adapted for the Piano Forte or Harpsichord, COMPOSED BY MR. HOOK. Enterd at Stationers Hall. Price 1s. [GB-Lbl H.1651.b.(20.)]		Entered in SC, 22 December 1792.
Let's Tie the Knot my Sally. A Favorite Song Sung by Master Shepherd at VAUXHALL GARDENS Composed by MR. HOOK. The Words by Mr. Upton Price 6d. [GB-Lbl H.1651.b.(46.)]	Printed by Hime [GB-Lbl H.1601.f.(23.)], by F. Rhames, c.1800 [GB-En JM 330]	Not entered in SC.
Listen Listen to the Voice of Love. A Favorite New Song. Sung with the Greatest Applause by Master Welsh, at Vauxhall Gardens. Composed by Mr. Hook. Enterd at Stationers Hall. Price 1s. [GB-Lbl H.1651.c.(18.)]	Printed by McDonnell [GB-Lbl G.353.(13.)], by Rhames, c.1800 [GB-En JM 943], by Hime, c.1795 [GB-En Add. Mus 11313]	Entered in SC, 14 July 1795.
LITTLE BIRD WITH BOSOM RED. Sung with the Greatest Applause at THE READINGS & MUSIC FREEMASONS HALL By Messrs. INCLEDON, STREET, &c. And at Vauxhall Gardens, Composed by Mr. Hook. Enterd at Stationers Hall. Price 1s. [GB-Lbl H.1651.c.(48.)]		Entered in SC, 25 June 1795.
The Little Waist DEFENDED. A Favorite New Song Sung by Mrs. Mountain, At Vauxhall Gardens, Composed by Mr. Hook. Enterd at Stationers Hall Pr. 1s. Written by Mr. Upton. [GB-Lbl H.1651.a.(40.)]		Entered in SC, 15 August 1795.
Love shall be my Guide, A Favorite Song Sung by Miss Milne At Vauxhall Gardens Composed by Mr. Hook. Enter'd at Stationers Hall. Price 6d. Written by Mr. Fox. [GB-Lbl H.1651.a.(38.)]		Entered in SC, 21 August 1795.

Title	Imprint	SC Entry
The Lovers Quarrel A Favorite Dialogue, Sung with Unbounded Applause By Mr. Darley & Miss Leary, At Vauxhall Gardens. Composed by Mr. Hook. The Words by Mr. Upton. Price 6d. [GB-Lbl H.1651.b.(19.)]		Not entered in SC.
LUCY GRAY OF ALLENDALE A Favorite Song Sung by MASTER PHELPS.at Vauxhall Gardens. Composed by Mr. Hook. Entered at Stationers Hall. Price 1s. The Words by Mr. Anderson. [GB-Lbl H.1651.c.(27.)]	Printed by B. Cooke, c.1795 [GB-En Add. Mus 9631]	Entered in SC, 2 June 1794.
THE MODEL, A Favorite Song Sung with Universal Applause by Mr. Dignum, at Vauxhall Gardens. Written by MILES PETER ANDREWS ESQR. Composed by Mr. Hook. Entered at Stationers Hall. Price 1s. [GB-Lbl H.1651.a.(30.)]		Entered in SC, 29 May 1794.
MUIRLAND WILLY, A Favorite Song Sung by Mrs. Franklin. at Vauxhall Gardens, Composed by Mr. Hook. Entered at Stationers Hall. Price 6d. The Words by Mr. Anderson. [GB-Lbl H.1651.b.(44.)]	Printed by B. Cooke, c.1794] [GB-En Add. Mus 9634]	Entered in SC, 17 June 1794.
My heart is devoted dear Mary to thee, A Favorite Song Sung by MR. DARLEY, at Vauxhall Gardens, Composed by Mr. Hook, Pr. 1s. [GB-Lbl G.379.c.(41.)]	Printed by Hime, c.1795 [GB-En Add. Mus 13004]	Not entered in SC.
No Waist at all. A New Song. SUNG BY MR. TAYLOR. At Vauxhall Gardens. Composed by Mr Hook. Enter'd at Stationers Hall. Price 6d. The Words by Mr. Taylor [GB-Lbl H.1651.a.(35.)]		Entered in SC, 21 August 1795.
The Pleasures of Hunting & Drinking, A Favorite Song Sung by Mr. Taylor with Universal Applause. AT Vauxhall Gardens, Composed by Mr. Hook. Entered at Stationers Hall. Price 1s. [GB-Lbl H.1651.a.(33.)]		Entered in SC, 16 June 1795.
POOR ANNETTE THE SAVOYARD A Favorite Song Sung by Miss Milne, at Vauxhall Gardens, COMPOSED BY MR. HOOK. Entered at Stationers Hall. Price 6d. [GB-Lbl H.1651.a.(24.)]	Printed by Hime [GB-En JM 872]	Entered in SC, 21 August 1794.

TABLE 6.3 continued

Song Title	Dublin Reprints	Comments
The Press Gang forc'd my Love to go. A Favorite Scotch Song, SUNG BY MRS. MOUNTAIN, AT Vauxhall Gardens. Composed by Mr. Hook. Entered at Stationers Hall. Price 1s. The Words by Mr. Anderson. [GB-Lbl H.1651.a.(32.)]		Entered in SC, 18 June 1795.
The ROYAL SOLDIER'S Farewell A Favorite New Song Sung with Universal Applause by Mr. Sedgwick at Vauxhall Gardens, Composed by Mr. Hook. Entered at Stationers Hall. Price 6d. [GB-Lbl H.1651.a.(6.)]		Entered in SC, 14 December 1793.
Since Life's a Jest, A Favorite GLEE for Three Voices Sung with the greatest Applause At Vauxhall Gardens, Composed by Mr. Hook. Entered at Stationers Hall. Price 1s. [GB-Lbl H.1651.c.(55.)]		Entered in SC, 25 June 1795.
Six SONATAS FOR THE Piano-Forte or Harpsichord. With an Accompaniment FOR THE GERMAN FLUTE or VIOLIN. Humbly Dedicated to the Right Honorable Lady Lydia Turnour, COMPOSED BY MR. HOOK. Op. 77. Enter'd at Stationers Hall. Book I. Price 10s. 6 [GB-Lbl g.142.6]		Entered in SC, 30 January 1795. Book 2, listed separately in the court documents, also entered on the same date.
The Soldier's Adieu A Favorite GLEE For Three Voices Sung with UNIVERSAL APPLAUSE at Vauxhall Gardens. Composed by Mr. Hook. Entered at Stationers Hall. Price 1s. [GB-Lbl H.1651.c.(47.)]		Entered in SC, 26 August 1793.
Some Wives are Good! A Favorite Comic Glee For Three Ladies & Three Gentlemen. Sung with Universal Applause at Vauxhall, Composed by Mr Hook. Enter'd at Stationers Hall. Price 6d [GB-Lbl H.1651.c.(52.)]		Not entered in SC.
Sweet Girl Adieu 'tis Glory Calls afar, A Favorite Dialogue Sung by Mr. Dignum & Mrs. Franklin at Vauxhall Gardens, Composed by Mr. Hook. Entered at Stationers Hall. Pr. 6d [GB-Lbl H.1651.a.(23.)]		Entered in SC, 1 September 1794.

Sweet lovely Rose of Burford Dale. A Favorite Song SUNG BY MR. CLIFFORD, AT Vauxhall Gardens Composed by Mr. Hook. Price 6d. The words by Mr. Upton. [GB-Lbl H.1651.b.(16.)]	Printed by Hime [GB-Lbl H.1601.f.(11.)]	Not entered in SC.
'Sweet notes inspired by love divine' (not found)		Listed in the 1800 catalogue under duetts; sold for 1s.
The Sweet River Dee, A Favorite Song, Sung with Universal Applause By Miss Youens at Vauxhall Gardens, Composed by Mr. Hook. Entered at Stationers Hall. Price 6d. [GB-Lbl H.1651.a.(26.)]		Not entered in SC.
Tell the Maid I Love her, A Favorite Song, SUNG BY MR. TAYLOR, at Vauxhall Gardens, Composed by Mr. Hook. Entered at Stationers Hall. Price 6d. [GB-Lbl H.1651.a.(27.)]	Printed by Hime, c.1795 [GB-En Add. Mus 11310]	Entered in SC, 22 August 1794.
THEN CEASE YE FINE FELLOWS. A favorite Song. Sung by Miss Leary. At Vauxhall Gardens, COMPOSED by MR. HOOK. Price 6d. [GB-Lbl G.808.e.(21.)]		Not entered in SC.
Three SONATAS for the Piano Forte or Harpsichord. With an Accompaniment for the VIOLIN or FLUTE, Composed & Dedicated by Permission to Miss Isabella Sutton, BY JAMES HOOK. Op. 72. Entered at Stationers Hall. Price 7s/6d [GB-Lbl g.147.7]		Entered in SC, 16 February 1793.
''Tis not so sweet as her I love' (not found)		
Tom Careless, A Favorite Song, Sung by Mr. Dignum, at Vauxhall Gardens, Written by Edward Topham Esqr. Composed by Mr. Hook. Entered at Stationers Hall. Price 1s. London [GB-Lbl H.1651.a.(22.)]	Printed by Hime, c.1795 [GB-En JM 1029]	Entered in SC, 13 August 1794.
The True Honest Heart, A New Song Sung by Mr. Taylor with the greatest applause At Vauxhall Gardens, Composed by Mr. Hook. Enter'd at Stationers Hall Price 1s. [GB-Lbl H.1651.a.(34.)]		Entered in SC, 3 July 1795.

TABLE 6.3 continued

Song Title	Dublin Reprints	Comments
The Way to Keep him, A Favorite Song Sung by Mrs. Mountain, with Universal Applause At Vauxhall Gardens, Composed by Mr. Hook. Entered at Stationers Hall. Price 1s. [GB-Lbl H.1651.b.(47.)]		Entered in SC, 18 June 1793.
'We'll laugh and dance thro' life together' (not found)		Listed in the 1800 catalogue under duetts; sold for 1s.
'what tho' the one have God in Store' (not found)		
WHEN LUCY WAS KIND A Favorite Song Sung by Master Phelps, At Vauxhall Gardens, Composed by Mr. Hook. Entered at Stationers Hall. Pr. 1s. [GB-Lbl H.1651.c.(31.)]		Entered in SC, 13 June 1793.
Why is Love so past Defining. A Favorite Glee, For Four Voices, Sung with Universal Applause, at Vauxhall Gardens, Composed by Mr. Hook. Entered at Stationers Hall. Price 1s. [GB-Lbl H.1651.c.(57.)]		Entered in SC, 2 June 1794.
With Horns & Hounds in Chorus. A much admired Hunting Glee, Sung with the greatest applause at Vauxhall Gardens, Composed by Mr. Hook. Entered at Stationers Hall. Price 1s. [GB-Lbl H.1651.c.(58.)]		Entered in SC, 2 July 1794.
Ye true British Sportsmen, A Favorite Hunting Song Sung by Mr. Clifford, At Vauxhall Gardens Composed by Mr. Hook. Entered at Stationers Hall. Price 1s. The Words by Mr. Stafford. [GB-Lbl H.1651.a.(19.)]		Entered in SC, 18 June 1793.
You'll Conquer your Man A Favorite SONG Sung by Mr. Sedgwick at Vauxhall Gardens, Composed by Mr. Hook. Entered at Stationers Hall. Written by Mr. Upton. Price 1s. [GB-Lbl H.1651.(24.)]		Entered in SC, 26 August 1793.

7

Edward Miller of Doncaster: The Composer and the Music Trade

Christopher Roberts

In the eighteenth century, the publishing of music was the chief method by which a composer could disseminate their work, enabled by the support of other individuals, of which printers, publishers and music-sellers were the most important. One musician who had a particularly close involvement with the trade in printed music was the Doncaster-based organist, Edward Miller (1735–1807). At least fifteen of his music and pedagogical publications were issued between 1756 and 1800 by London music publishers, including three by Longman and Broderip, one of the foremost and largest English music-sellers of the late eighteenth century, and two by the firm's successor Broderip and Wilkinson (see Table 7.1).[1] Miller's music was distributed widely across England, as admirably demonstrated by the impressive subscription list to his monumental work, *The Psalms of David, for the Use of Parish Churches* (1790). This work advocated the use of simple tunes and the training of church choirs to improve congregational singing, and features a list of over 2600 subscribers, making it the most successful musical publication by subscriber numbers to be published in eighteenth-century Britain.[2] While Miller's career and profes-

---

[1] At least five of Miller's musical works were published by subscription for which the lists of subscribers survive: *A Collection of New English Songs and a Cantata* (1756); *Six Sonatas for the Harpsichord; with an accompaniment to three of them, for a Violin, or German Flute* (c.1768); *Elegies, Songs, and an Ode of Mr. Pope's, with Instrumental Parts*, op 3 (c.1770); *The Psalms of David, for the Use of Parish Churches* (1790); and *Dr Watts's Psalms and Hymns* (1800). For a full list of Miller's publications, see Christopher Roberts, '"I esteem my lot fortunate, in residing in this happy country": Edward Miller, Social Networking and Music Making in Eighteenth-Century Doncaster', in Stephanie Carter, Kirsten Gibson and Roz Southey (eds), *Music in North-East England, 1500–1800* (Woodbridge, 2020), 89–108.

[2] On 4 February 1791 the *Stamford Mercury* reported: 'The list of subscribers to Dr Miller's Psalms, is supposed to contain more names than has ever before appeared to any book published in this kingdom'. See also similar reports in *Newcastle Courant*, 12 February 1791 and *Cumberland Pacquet*, 15 February 1791. Publication by subscription was customary for large collections or new editions of church music which were expensive to produce: for instance, the collections of *Cathedral Music* by William Boyce (1760), Maurice Green (c.1770), William Croft (c.1775), Samuel Arnold (1790),

sional music network has received attention elsewhere,[3] this chapter focuses on the 108 music traders who subscribed to the book: booksellers, music-sellers, stationers, engravers and printers. In doing so, this chapter explores the community of music traders across the country and the importance of their role in the dissemination and circulation of printed music in late eighteenth-century England.

TABLE 7.1 The published music of Edward Miller.

Title	Date	Place and Publisher
A Collection of New English Songs and a Cantata	1756	London: John Johnson
Six Solos for a German Flute, with a Thorough Bass for the Harpsichord or Violoncello	1761	London: John Johnson
Six Sonatas for the Harpsichord; with an accompaniment to three of them, for a Violin, or German Flute	c.1768	London: [Peter] Welcker
Six Solos for a German Flute with Instructions for double Tonguing and a Thorough Bass for the Harpsichord or Violoncello [second edition]	1769	London: J[ames] Longman and Co.
Elegies, Songs, and an Ode of Mr Pope's, with Instrumental Parts	c.1770	London: Printed for the author[4]
Institutes of Music or easy Instructions for the Harpsichord	1783	London: [James] Longman and [Francis] Broderip
Elements of Thorough Bass and Composition	1787	London: [James] Longman and [Francis] Broderip
Anthem for Voices and Instruments also a Hymn Composed for the Use of Sunday Schools	1789	[London]: Printed for the author[5]

Matthew Camidge (1790), William Hayes (1795), Thomas Sanders Dupuis (1797) and Thomas Ebdon's *Sacred Music* (1790). See Simon D.I. Fleming, 'The patterns of music subscription in English, Welsh and Irish cathedrals during the Georgian era', *Early Music*, 48/2 (2020), 205–23; Simon D.I. Fleming and Martin Perkins, *Dataset of Subscribers to Eighteenth-Century Music Publications in Britain and Ireland*, at www.musicsubscribers.co.uk.

[3] Roberts, '"I esteem my lot fortunate, in residing in this happy country"', 89–108.
[4] Probably by Robert Bremner. I am grateful to Simon D.I. Fleming for this suggestion.
[5] The title page advises that the publication was 'to be had at all the Music Shops' but offers no indication of a publisher. 'Vincent Fecit' is included beneath the opus number. However, this is believed to be the engraver of the plate. I am grateful to Charles Doran at Princeton University Library Special Collections for this information.

Corelli's Six Sonatas Opera IIIzo [I] Adapted for the Organ / Six Sonatas Opera Ivto [II] Adapted for the Piano Forte or Harpsichord	1789	London: [James] Longman and [Francis] Broderip
The Psalms of David, for the Use of Parish Churches	1790	London: William [Richard Beckford] Miller
Twelve Progressive Lessons for the Pianoforte or Harpsichord with an Accompaniment for the Flute or Violin	1791	London: William [Richard Beckford] Miller
Sixteen Easy Voluntaries for the Organ	1797	London: [John] Preston
Twelve Canzonets for the Voice and Piano Forte	c.1799	London: [George] Goulding, Phipps and [Thomas] D'Almaine
The New Flute Instructor	1800	London: Printed for the author by [Francis] Broderip and [Charles] Wilkinson
Dr. Watts's Psalms and Hymns	1800	London: Printed for the author and sold by [Francis] Broderip and [Charles] Wilkinson

❧ *Edward Miller and Publication by Subscription*

Composers often utilised subscription publication to minimise the financial risk involved in printing their music and to make sure there was enough demand to at least cover their costs.[6] In addition to encouraging their personal contacts and networks to subscribe, advertisements would often be placed in both local and national newspapers. While payment had to be made before individuals received their copies, subscribers tended to be offered a cheaper rate

---

[6] For the subscriber and reviews of subscription lists to musical works, see Stanley Sadie, 'Music in the Home II', in H. Diack Johnstone and Roger Fiske (eds), *The Blackwell History of Music in Britain: The Eighteenth Century*, vol. 4 (Oxford, 1990), 313–54; David Hunter, 'The Publishing of Opera and Song Books in England, 1703–1726', *Notes*, 47 (1991), 647–85; Jennifer Burchell, 'Musical Societies in Subscription Lists: An Overlooked Resource', in *A Handbook for Studies in 18th-Century English Music* (Oxford, 1998), 1–75; David Hunter and Rose M. Mason, 'Supporting Handel through Subscription to Publications', *Notes*, 56/1 (1999), 27–93; Margaret Seares, 'The Composer and the Subscriber: A case study from the 18th century', *Early Music*, 39/1 (2011), 65–78; Simon D.I. Fleming, 'Avison and his Subscribers: Musical Networking in Eighteenth-Century Britain', *Royal Musical Association Research Chronicle*, 49 (2018), 21–49; Simon D.I. Fleming, 'The Gender of Subscribers to Eighteenth-Century Music Publications', *Royal Musical Association Research Chronicle*, 50/1 (2019), 94–152; Amélie Addison, 'William Shield's *A Collection of Favourite Songs* (c.1775)', in Carter, Gibson and Southey (eds), *Music in North-East England, 1500–1800*, 241–60; Simon D.I. Fleming and Martin Perkins (eds), *Music by Subscription: Composers and their Networks in the British Music-Publishing Trade, 1676–1820* (Abingdon, 2022).

compared to nonsubscribers (for instance, a copy of Miller's *Psalms of David* was 7*s*. 6*d*. to subscribers and 10*s*. 6*d*. to nonsubscribers).[7] However, securing enough subscribers was not guaranteed. In 1760, Miller attempted to entice subscribers for a new collection of guitar lessons through an advertisement placed in the *York Courant*:

> PROPOSALS for printing by Subscription, A Set of LESSONS for the GUITTAR, composed in an easy familiar Stile, natural to that Instrument. *By* EDWARD MILLER, *Organist of Doncaster*. Most of these Lessons have an Accompanyment for another Guittar. Some Rules are also added for playing these and other Lessons in Taste. The Subscription is Five Shillings, to be paid on Delivery of the Book, which will be published as speedily as possible. Subscriptions are taken in at Johnson's Music Shop in Cheapside, London; at Haxby's Music Shop in York; and by Mr. Miller, at Doncaster. *Also shortly will be published*, Six Sonatas for two Violins or German Flutes, and a Bass. Composed by Mr. Miller.[8]

As the promoted publication appears not to survive in print, it was probably never published due to a lacklustre response. Another advertisement from 1761 is for Miller's collection of 'Six Solos for a German Flute, Hautboy or Violin, with a Thorough Bass for the Harpsichord or Violoncello' (presumably his *Six Solos for a German Flute, with a Thorough Bass for the Harpsichord or Violoncello*).[9] Subscribers were asked to send their names to Thomas Miller at his shop in Bungay (Suffolk) and delivery of the publication would be made by the end of the year at a cost of 5*s*. In instances where not enough subscribers were secured to cover the production costs, the composer, publisher or a wealthy patron could have covered the expenses themselves.[10] This appears to have been the case with Miller's *Six Solos for a German Flute*: the title page indicates that the work was 'Printed for John Johnson', suggesting that Johnson (*d*.1761) took responsibility for publishing the collection; perhaps Miller was too busy to source subscriptions himself and therefore moved away from the subscription method on this occasion.[11] Using dedications and commendations from benefactors and other professional musicians was a common marketing strategy used to attract subscribers, as demonstrated in an advertisement from 1769, in which Miller incorporates an excerpt from a letter by Charles Avison:

---

[7] *Bury and Norwich Post*, 19 May 1790.
[8] *York Courant*, 8 April 1760.
[9] *Norwich Mercury*, 20 June 1761.
[10] For example, see Stephen Rose, 'The composer as self-publisher in 17th-century Germany', in Erik Kjellberg (ed.), *The Dissemination of Music in Seventeenth-Century Europe: Celebrating the Düben Collection* (Bern, 2010), 239–60; Stephen Rose, 'The Price of Italophilia: Wriothesley Russell and Nicola Cosimi's Sonate da camera (London, 1702)', unpublished paper, 19th Biennial International Conference on Baroque Music, Royal Birmingham Conservatoire, 15 July 2021; Stephanie Carter, 'Thomas Mace and the publication by subscription of *Musick's Monument* (1676)', in Fleming and Perkins (eds), *Music by Subscription*, 21–38.
[11] I am grateful to Simon D.I. Fleming for this suggestion. It is important to note that not all advertised works published by subscription were accompanied by a list of subscribers.

PROPOSALS For PRINTING by SUBSCRIPTION, (Dedicated to the Rev. Mr. MASON,) A COLLECTION of ELEGIES, Odes, *and* Songs. The MUSIC composed by EDWARD MILLER, of DONCASTER. The Subscription, Half a Guinea, to be paid on Delivery of the Book, which will *certainly* be in March 1770. Subscribers are requested to send their Names to Mr. Miller, Mr. Haxby at York, or to Mr. Bremner in the Strand, London. *Copy of a Letter from Mr.* Avison, *Organist at Newcastle-upon-Tyne, to Mr.* Miller. 'Sir; I have perused all your Vocal Music, and do, with Truth, assure you, that in forty Years Acquaintance with Music, I have seen but few Productions more promising than yours'.[12]

With *Psalms of David*, Miller clearly believed he was doing something new and inventive, describing the work in the preface as 'the *first* publication of congregational psalmody that has appeared since the Reformation'. He also here expressed a hope that it would produce a 'reformation in the performance of psalmody'. Nicholas Temperley later acknowledged the importance of Miller's publication, describing it as 'a landmark in the reform of town psalmody'.[13] However, the importance of this collection and the high level of anticipation it generated is most obviously demonstrated through its list of subscribers.

Of Miller's 2600 subscribers, it is not surprising that members of the music trade subscribed to the largest number of copies of *Psalms of David*, undoubtedly for resale in their shops. Two of these individuals were also family members: Thomas Miller (1731–1804), Edward's older brother and bookseller in Bungay, and William Richard Beckford Miller (1769–1844), Thomas's son and the publisher of this collection; they each subscribed to 25 copies. Other subscribers include John Rackham (c.1760–1824), a bookseller, printer and proprietor of a circulating library in Bury St Edmunds (34 copies) and Myles Swinney (d.1812), a Birmingham bookseller, printer and journalist (25 copies). The places provided in the subscription list cover a large swathe of the country,[14] and this is similarly evident from the geographical spread of those members of the commercial music trade. As demonstrated in Table 7.2, Bristol, Bury St Edmunds, Chelmsford, Doncaster, London, Newcastle upon Tyne, Norwich, Oxford and York all had provision for at least three proprietors selling printed music. However, the list also demonstrates a well-established trading of printed music in the smaller market towns and ports in the 1790s, including Beccles, Berwick upon Tweed, Eye, Halifax, Whitby and Whitehaven.

---

[12] *Leeds Mercury*, 5 September 1769.
[13] Nicholas Temperley, *The Music of the English Parish Church: Volume 1* (Cambridge, 1979, reissued 1983), 215.
[14] 397 subscribers to Miller's *Psalms of David* came from Yorkshire; see Fleming and Perkins, *Dataset of Subscribers*. This is the largest identified group by county followed by Lincolnshire (165), Suffolk (117), Essex (114), Norfolk (111), Nottinghamshire (101), Cambridgeshire (71), Northamptonshire (67), Derbyshire (67), Gloucestershire (66), Lancashire (61), Northumberland (56), Warwickshire (53), Middlesex (48), Shropshire (42), Staffordshire (33), City of London (33) and Somerset (32). See Table 7.2.

Edward Miller's Music Publishers

Miller's network in the commercial music trade ranged from local contacts in Yorkshire to connections in London, which was not atypical for regional musicians during this period.[15] Although there is no surviving evidence of Miller's interactions with his publishers, it is probable that he sought to capitalise on the expertise, marketing power and networks of specialist London contacts to publish his music and pedagogical works (see Table 7.1) rather than their regional counterparts. Indeed, London-based music publishers were better placed then their regional counterparts to disseminate Miller's works across Britain and even abroad.

During his teenage years, Miller appears to have regularly travelled to London: he was a flautist in Handel's London oratorio orchestra in 1753 and even attended rehearsals at Handel's house in Brook Street.[16] The title page of his earliest surviving publication, *A Collection of New English Songs and a Cantata* (1756), records that this work was sold in London by John Johnson (Miller's publisher) and 'by the author, at Mr. Wass[']s in old Fish Street'. Robert Wass (d.1764), a singer at the Chapel Royal, was a regular bass soloist in Handel's oratorio performances between 1752 and 1756;[17] perhaps Miller was lodged with the singer at the time of publication. Johnson referred to himself as a musical instrument maker, and combined music publishing with other aspects of the music trade including the sale of instruments, manuscript paper and accessories. On his trade card Johnson recorded the sale of:

> all Sorts of Musical Instruments, Viz: Bass-Violins, Viols, Violins, Hautboys, German & English Flutes, Harpsichords, Spinnets, French horns, Trumpets &c Also Variety of the newest Concertos, Sonatas, & Solos for all Instruments now in Use. Books of Instructions, rul'd Books & Paper, Songs, Reeds, Wire for harpsichords, & [th]e best Roman Strings. Wholesale & Retail.[18]

It is likely that Miller was introduced to the London publisher through his musical connections or even visited Johnson's shop for supplies when in the capital. It is worth noting that some of Miller's regional counterparts also used Johnson as their main publisher; he published Avison's *Six Concertos in Seven Parts*, op 3 (1751) for instance.

From an early stage, Miller composed relatively simple music that not only catered for amateur musicians but fitted well into the catalogues of publishers and stationers. His *Six Solos for a German Flute, with a Thorough Bass for the Harpsichord or Violoncello* (1761) and *Six Sonatas for the Harpsichord; with an*

---

[15] See, for example, Simon D.I. Fleming's contribution on William Flackton in this volume.

[16] Edward Miller, *The History and Antiquities of Doncaster and its Vicinity, with Anecdotes of Eminent Men* (Doncaster, 1804), 309. See also Roberts, "'I esteem my lot fortunate, in residing in this happy country'", 89–108.

[17] Donald Burrows, *Handel and the English Chapel Royal* (Oxford, 2005), 592.

[18] Reproduced in Jenny Nex, 'Longman & Broderip', in Michael Kassler (ed.), *The Music Trade in Georgian England* (Farnham, 2011), 9–93, at 13.

accompaniment to three of them, for a Violin, or German Flute (c.1768) was well pitched to be added to the list of publications by the instrumental music specialist Peter Welcker (d.1775): the four-page catalogue Welcker attached to John Garth's *Six Voluntarys for the Organ Piano Forte or Harpsichord*, op 3 (1771) includes an array of harpsichord music by foreign and British composers, including Luigi Boccherini (1743–1805), J.C. Bach (1735–1782), John Garth (1721–1810) and James Nares (1715–1783).[19] The second edition of Miller's *Six Solos for a German Flute* (1769) was published by Johnson's former apprentice, James Longman (1745–1803).[20] Longman had only commenced his own business a year earlier, at 26 Cheapside, and may have embarked on this early venture having seen the success of the first edition, issued during his apprenticeship. Longman was to join forces with Francis Fane Broderip (d.1807) in 1773, establishing one of the most successful music publishing houses in London. The firm of Longman and Broderip issued a range of music from solo and chamber music, songs with easy accompaniments, pieces arranged from popular operas and theatre works of the day, and instruction books.[21] They also ran a music circulating library at their Cheapside shop, offering subscribers 'every publication, ancient and modern, that England, France, Holland and Germany have produced, or may in future';[22] a second shop at Haymarket offered the same service.[23] They continued as Miller's publishers for the composer's pedagogical works – *Institutes of Music or easy Instructions for the Harpsichord* (1783) and *Elements of Thorough Bass and Composition* (1787) – both of which suited the firm's published catalogues.[24]

Despite Longman and Broderip's prominence as music publishers, Miller's *Psalms of David* was published by the composer's nephew, William Miller. What is perhaps more surprising is that William was entrusted with such a substantial publication, given he had only started his business earlier that year.[25] William

---

[19] The first page of Welcker's catalogue is reproduced as Figure 12.1 in Simon D.I. Fleming, 'Foreign composers, the subscription market, and the popularity of continental music in eighteenth-century Britain', in Fleming and Perkins (eds), *Music by Subscription*, 221–41.

[20] For a detailed biographical account of Longman's business, see Nex, 'Longman & Broderip', 9–93.

[21] Between 1770 and 1790 Longman and Broderip issued instruction books for the harpsichord, piano, flute, oboe, bassoon, clarinet, bagpipe, violin, guitar, mandolin, harp, cittern and viola. See Adrienne Simpson, 'A short-title list of printed English instrumental tutors up to 1800, held in British libraries', *Royal Musical Association Research Chronicle*, 6 (1966), 24–50.

[22] *The London Courant*, 21 March 1782.

[23] *Parker's General Advertiser*, 27 January 1783.

[24] Longman and Broderip's 1782 catalogue is attached to Michael Arne's (c.1740–86) *The Overture, Songs, Duetts, Catch, Choruses, & Comic-tunes, with the Marches, and Dances, in the Procession of the New Pantomime Called The Choice of Harlequin Or The Indian Chief* (London, 1782); see Fleming, 'Foreign composers, the subscription market, and the popularity of continental music in eighteenth-century Britain', 221–41.

[25] See J.M. Alter, 'Miller, William Richard Beckford', *Grove Music Online*.

subscribed to multiple copies of his uncle's works (25 copies of *Psalms of David* and 6 copies of *Dr Watts's Psalms and Hymns*), presumably to support his relation and to sell in his own shop at 5 Old Bond Street, London. He continued publishing music, issuing Miller's *Twelve Progressive Lessons for the Pianoforte or Harpsichord* (1791) and Karl Weiss's *Three Quartetts for a Flute, Violin, Tenor, and Violoncello*, op 5 and op 6 (*c*.1800).[26] It may have been the success of *Psalms of David* that led to William Miller's appointment as official bookseller to the Duke of Clarence in 1790.

While London guitar and violin maker John Preston (*d*.1798) subscribed to six copies of *Psalms of David*, Edward Miller later engaged Preston to publish his *Sixteen Easy Voluntaries for the Organ* (1797). Preston must have already been well acquainted with Miller's music, as a catalogue from *c*.1783 includes the Doncaster composer's *Elegies, Songs, and an Ode of Mr Pope's, with Instrumental Parts* (*c*.1770).[27] In 1789 Preston's son Thomas entered the business and continued alone after his father's death. After purchasing the plates and stock of several other publishing firms, including Robert Bremner (1789), Thomas Skillern the elder (*c*.1803), H. Wright (*c*.1803) and Wilkinson and Co. (*c*.1810), Preston reprinted many publications, most notably those Handel oratorios he acquired from H. Wright (formerly Wright and Wilkinson), the successor of Walsh and Randall.[28] Interestingly, Preston also reissued Miller's *Psalms of David* in *c*.1818, having presumably acquired the original plates himself – an indication that there was still demand for Miller's work almost thirty years after its first publication. As for Miller, in 1800 he returned to working with Francis Broderip, as part of Broderip and Wilkinson; they published in 1800 Miller's *New Flute Instructor* and *Dr Watts's Psalms and Hymns*.

Even though Miller, through his publishing activities, had successfully cultivated business relationships with several prominent London-based music publishers, some of which involved family members, this does not tell the full story of the dissemination of Miller's monumental work throughout Britain. However, evidence of regional networks – important in the wider circulation of *Psalms of David* – are revealed though a more detailed analysis of the subscription list.

❧ *The Sellers of Edward Miller's Psalms of David*

While Miller's music was readily available in the published sale catalogues of London music sellers, regional traders – including booksellers, music-sellers,

---

[26] Fleming and Perkins, *Dataset of Subscribers*; Charles Humphries and William C. Smith, *Music Publishing in the British Isles from the beginning until the middle of the nineteenth century* (Oxford, 1970), 234.

[27] Reproduced in Yu Lee An, 'Music Publishing in London from 1780 to 1837 as reflected in Music Publishers' Catalogues of Music for Sale: A Bibliography and Commentary' (PhD dissertation, University of Canterbury, 2008), 193.

[28] D.W. Krummel and Stanley Sadie, *The New Grove Handbooks in Music: Music Printing and Publishing* (London, 1990), 381–2.

general stationers and engravers – were crucial in the dissemination of his publications at a local level across England. By selling concert tickets, sheet music, musical instruments and associated goods, this trading community was an important component in the commercial dissemination and availability of musical goods and services across the regions in the eighteenth century. Moreover, these regional sellers frequently acted as agents, promoting popular music performed in local theatres, concerts and pleasure gardens as well as advertising the latest musical publications in local newspapers.[29] Many of the advertisements for Miller's *Psalms of David* that appeared before publication recommended those wishing to subscribe to give their names to the editor or a local agent. For instance, in Northampton, interested parties were advised to visit the shop of William Burnham.[30] Some local agents publicised that the 'Lists of the Subscribers … may be seen' during a visit to their shop;[31] others identified notable subscribers as a means of enticement:

> The List at present contains the Names of His Majesty, their Royal Highnesses the Prince of Wales, the Duke of York, and many of the Nobility, Gentry, and others: Among the Clergy, are a respectable Number of Right Reverend Bishops, Deans, Archdeacons, &c. already amounting upwards of 1000 Names.[32]

One advertisement from September 1790 records that subscriptions could be placed with twelve sellers identified in the subscription list, spread geographically between London and Yorkshire, with several in towns situated along the Great North Road, the main route between London and Edinburgh. They were: John Preston, London; Richard Newcomb, Stamford; William Brooke, Lincoln; James Taylor, Retford; Caleb Preston, Boston; James Wier, Horncastle; Thomas Marsh, Louth; John Albin, Spalding; Mr Bright, Melton Mowbray; William Allin and John Ridge, Newark; Thomas Hookham, London;[33] and Richard Firth, Oxford.[34] It is clear from this notice that as well as disseminating music in their localities by selling copies of musical works in their shops, these businesses were also important in that they could encourage their customers to purchase and subscribe to new music (for which they would have received a proportion of the proceeds). The sellers, however, appear to have had mixed success in procuring subscribers to Miller's collection: for instance, seventeen subscribers were identified as residents of Stamford (Lincolnshire), six from Newark (Nottinghamshire), five from Louth (Lincolnshire) and two from Spalding (Lincolnshire).[35] Not all official agents subscribed to the work themselves. John Corri and James Sutherland, who ran a music shop in Edinburgh, did not subscribe, nor did Thomas Blagden of Winchester (and

---

[29] For example, see the extensive newspaper advertisements placed by Leeds music-seller John Binns (*c*.1744–1796) below.
[30] *Northampton Mercury*, 3 April 1790.
[31] *Stamford Mercury*, 30 July 1790.
[32] *Northampton Mercury*, 11 September 1790.
[33] *Stamford Mercury*, 10 September 1790.
[34] *Northampton Mercury*, 11 September 1790.
[35] See Fleming and Perkins, *Dataset of Subscribers*.

printer of the *Hampshire Chronicle*), or bookseller Thomas Skelton of Southampton.[36] Subscriptions could additionally be placed at 'Messrs. Bull, Meyler's and Marshall's Libraries' in Bath, no doubt an attempt to secure subscribers from amongst 'the company'.[37]

Between the 108 sellers identified in the subscription list attached to Miller's *Psalms of David* (listed in Table 7.2), 428 copies were purchased. The largest groups of sellers were based in Yorkshire (26), London (10), Lincolnshire (8), Suffolk (8), Norfolk (7) and Bristol (5). Miller had served as organist of St George's Church, Doncaster for over 30 years (having been appointed in 1756), and the high number of Yorkshire sellers reflects not only his notoriety among the local populace but supports the concept that most subscribers in any list came from the composer's immediate environs.[38] Miller also had close familial associations with Norfolk and Suffolk. Just over half of the sellers (56) purchased two or more copies of the work. The vast majority identified, perhaps as a means of promoting their business, recorded in the list their occupation as a bookseller (63), music-seller (18) or printer (10), as demonstrated in Table 7.2.

TABLE 7.2 Sellers identified in the subscription list of Edward Miller's *Psalms of David* (1790).[39]

Names	Occupation	Place	Copies
Suffolk (73 copies)			
Mr. [John] Rackham	Bookseller	Bury	34
Mr. T[homas] Miller	[Bookseller]	Bungay	25
Mr. [Peter] Gedge	Bookseller	Bury	6
Mr. [John] Shave	Bookseller	Ipswich	3
Mrs. Horth	Bookseller	Beccles	2
Mr. P[hilip] Deck	Bookseller	Bury	1
Mr. [T.] Leatherdale	Bookseller	Eye	1
Mr. [Robert] Loder	Printer	Woodbridge	1
Yorkshire (71 copies)			
Mr. [William] Tess[e]yman	Bookseller	York	12
Mr. S[amuel] Knapton	Musicseller	York	7

[36] *Norfolk Chronicle*, 16 January 1790; *Derby Mercury*, 22 July 1790 and 26 August 1790; *Bath Chronicle and Weekly Gazette*, 14 January 1790. For more on Banks, see Charles Beare, 'Banks, Benjamin', *Grove Music Online*.

[37] *Bath Chronicle*, 15 July 1790. For more information on 'the company', see Matthew Spring's contribution to this volume.

[38] Fleming, 'Avison and his Subscribers', 43–6; Fleming, 'The Patterns of Music Subscription', 219–21.

[39] I am grateful to Simon D.I. Fleming for his assistance in identifying the sellers in the subscription list and for reviewing newspaper advertisements to enable those sellers identified with an asterisk (*) to be included.

Names	Occupation	Place	Copies
Mr. W. Bewley	Music-seller	York	6
Mess. Soulby and [John] Hurst	Musicsellers	Wakefield	6
Mr. J[ohn] Todd	Bookseller	York	6
Mr. George Clarke	Bookseller	Whitby	4
Mr. [?Jonas] Browne	Bookseller	Hull	3
Mr. [John] Lyndley	Bookseller	Pontefract	3
Mr. [Edward] Petch	Stationer	Selby	3
Mr. [Joseph] Gales	Printer	Sheffield	2
Mr. [Thomas] Haxby	[Printer and Music-seller]	York	2
Mr. [Thomas] Sanderson	Printer	Doncaster	2
Mr. [Lawrence] Whitaker	Bookseller	Beverley	2
Mr. [John] Binns	Bookseller	Leeds	1
Mess. [Dickinson] Boys and [William] Sheardown	Books[ellers]	Doncaster	1
Mr. [W.] Brameld	Bookseller	Swinton	1
Mr. T[homas] Cockshaw	Bookseller	Barnsley	1
Mess. [William] Edwards and Sons	Booksellers	Hallifax [sic]	1
Mr. Gale	Bookseller	Whitby	1
Mr. [William] Mather*	Organist [and music seller]	Sheffield	1
Mr. [John] Meggitt	Bookseller	Wakefield	1
Mr. John Milnes	Bookseller	Halifax	1
Mr. S. [?John] Nicholson	Bookseller	Bradforth [sic]	1
Mr. G[eorge] Peacock	Printer of the York Courant	[York]	1
Mr. E[dward] Porter	Music-seller	Leeds	1
Mr. [Thomas] Smith	Bookseller	Doncaster	1
London (49 copies)			
Mr. W[illiam] Miller	Bookseller	Old Bond-street	25
Mr. [James] Cooper	Music Seller	Gerrard-street	6
Mr. T[homas] Hookham	Bookseller	New Bond-street	6
Mess. [John] Preston and Sons	Music-sellers	Stran[d]	6
Mr. [John] Caulfield	Engraver	London	1
Mr. [William] Charron	Engraver	London	1

Names	Occupation	Place	Copies
Mr. Draper	Stationer	Fetter-lane	1
Miss Seagoe	Printseller	High-street, St. Giles's	1
Mr. [William] Skelton	Printseller	Hay-market	1
Mr. G[eorge] Smart	Music-seller	No. 331, Oxford-street	1
Lincolnshire (36 copies)			
Mr. J. Newcombe	Music-seller	Stamford	14
Mr. [William] Allen	Printer and Bookseller	Grantham	12
Mr. [William] Brooke	Bookseller	Lincoln	3
Mr. C[aleb] Preston	Bookseller	Boston	3
Mr. John Albin	Bookseller	Spalding	1
Mr. J[ohn] Drury*	[Bookseller]	Lincoln	1
Mr. [Thomas] Marsh	Bookseller	Louth	1
Mr. [James] Weir	Bookseller	Horncastle	1
West Midlands (34 copies)			
Mr. [Myles] Swinney	Bookseller	Birmingham	25
Mr. [Thomas] Pearson	Bookseller	Birmingham	6
Mr. [Noah] Rollason	Printer and Bookseller	Coventry	3
Bristol (28 copies)			
Mr. W[illiam] Bulgin	Bookseller	Bristol	6
Mr. J[ames] Norton	Bookseller	Bristol	6
Mr. [John] Percival	Music-seller	Bristol	6
Mr. [John] Rudhall	Printer	Bristol	6
Mr. [Thomas] Howell	Musicseller	Bristol	4
Essex (28 copies)			
Mr. [William] Clachar	Bookseller	Chelmsford	15
Mr. W[illiam] Stanes	Bookseller	Chelmsford	12
Mr. R[ichard] Creak Stanes	Bookseller	[Chelmsford]	1
Oxfordshire (16 copies)			
Mr. [Richard] Firth	Music Seller	Oxford	14
Mr. [William] Jackson	Printer	Oxford	1
Mr. [Philip] Jung	Music-seller	Oxford	1
Tyne and Wear (12 copies)			
Mr. [Edward] Humble	Bookseller	Newcastle	6
Mr. J[oseph] Whitfield	Bookseller	Newcastle	4
Mr. [William] Ch[a]rnley	Bookseller	Newcastle	1
Mr. [Solomon] Hodgson	Bookseller	Newcastle	1

Names	Occupation	Place	Copies
Norfolk (10 copies)			
Mess. [William] Yarrington and [Richard] Bacon	Booksellers	Norwich	3
Mr. W[illiam] T. Roberts	Bookseller	Norwich	2
Mr. Christ[opher] Berry	Bookseller	Norwich	1
Mr. [John] Crouse	Printer and Bookseller	Norwich	1
Mess. [John Dawson] Downes and [John] March	Booksellers	[Great] Yarmouth	1
Mr. [Thomas] Fortin	Bookseller	Swaffham	1
Mr. W[illiam] Stevenson	Printer and Bookseller	Norwich	1
Northamptonshire (10 copies)			
Mess. [John and Charles] Lacy's [*sic*]	Booksellers	Northampton	8
Mr. J. [Thomas] Burnham	Bookseller	Northampton	2
Merseyside (9 copies)			
Mess. [Morris and Humphrey] Himes	Music-sellers	Liverpool	7
Mr. [John] Gore*	[Bookseller and stationer]	Liverpool	2
Derbyshire (9 copies)			
Mr. F[rancis] Roome	Bookseller	Derby	6
Mr. [John] Drewry	Bookseller	Derby	3
County Durham (8 copies)			
Mr. [Lewis] Pennington	Bookseller	Durham	6
Mr. [William] Appleton	Bookseller	Darlington	1
Mrs. [*sic*] R[obert] Christopher	Bookseller	Stockton	1
Nottinghamshire (6 copies)			
Mr. J[ohn] R[ichard] Medley	Bookseller	Retford	2
Mr. [James] Taylor	Bookseller	Retford	2
Messrs. [William] All[i]n and [John] Ridge	Music-sellers	Newark	1
Mr. G[eorge] Burbage	Printer	Nottingham	1
Leicestershire (4 copies)			
Mr. Bright	Bookseller	Melton Mo[w]bray	3
Mr. H[enry] Valentine	Music-seller	Leicester	1
Northumberland (4 copies)			
Mr. [William] Phorson	Bookseller	Berwick upon Tweed	4

Names	Occupation	Place	Copies
Cambridgeshire (3 copies)			
Mrs. [sic] [John] Jenkinson	Bookseller	Huntingdon	1
J[ohn] and J[oseph] Merrill	Booksellers	Cambridge	1
Mr. [John] Wynne	Music-seller	Cambridge	1
Kent (3 copies)			
Messrs. [James] Simmons and [George] Kirkby	Booksellers	Canterbury	3
Cumbria (3 copies)			
Mess. [John] Ware and son	Printers	Whitehaven	3
Somerset (2 copies)			
Mr. Rich[ard] Cruttwell	Printer	Bath	1
Mr. J[ames] Lint[e]rn	Music-seller	Bath	1
Wiltshire (2 copies)			
Mr. B[enjamin]. Banks*	Musical Instrument Maker	Salisbury	2
Greater Manchester (2 copies)			
Messrs. [William] Sudlow and [William] Wainwright	Music-sellers	Manchester	2
Staffordshire (1 copy)			
Mr. [H.] Mycock	Bookseller	Uttoxeter	1
Buckinghamshire (1 copy)			
Mr. J[ohn] Pearson	Bookseller	Newport Pagnel[l]	1
Cheshire (1 copy)			
Mr. [Thomas] Poole	Bookseller	Chester	1
Lancashire (1 copy)			
Mr. [Henry] Spencer	Bookseller	Burnley	1
Devon (1 copy)			
Messrs. [Robert] Trewman, and Son	Printers and Booksellers	Exeter	1
Shropshire (1 copy)			
Mr. T[homas] Wood	Printer	Shrewsbury	1

Yorkshire instrument maker and music shop proprietor Thomas Haxby (1729-1796) had long been a supporter of Miller and regularly accepted subscriptions for the composer's publications;[40] Haxby subscribed to seven copies of Miller's *Six Sonatas for the Harpsichord; with an accompaniment to three of them, for a Violin, or German Flute* (*c.*1768), two of *Elegies, Songs, and an Ode* (*c.*1770), and two of *Psalms of David* (1790);[41] it is likely that Haxby added these copies to the stock in his York-based music shop. Haxby was a supporter of local and regional musicians, publishing pedagogical music books such as *Six Easy Lessons for the Harpsichord* (1764) by John Camidge (organist at York Minster) and local musician Thomas Thackray's *Six Lessons for the Guittar* (*c.*1765).[42]

In addition to Haxby, Miller's other York-based subscribers include booksellers William Tesseyman (12 copies) and John Todd (6 copies), music-sellers Samuel Knapton (7 copies) and W. Bewley (6 copies), and George Peacock, the printer of the *York Courant* (1 copy). While Peacock may well have purchased his copy for personal use, the others undoubtedly intended them for resale. However, it is evident that, even though these local booksellers were, in many ways, in direct competition with each other, they anticipated sufficient demand for copies among the residents of York and its environs.

Another Yorkshire-based subscriber was the Leeds printer, bookseller and music-seller John Binns (*c.*1744–1796). He placed multiple newspaper advertisements that highlighted the quality and diversity of his music stock.[43] An amateur violin and cello player, he published a *Dictionarium Musica* (London, 1770, 2/1790 and 3/1791) under the pseudonym John Hoyle.[44] Binns was considered

---

[40] For example, see *York Courant*, 25 May 1762.

[41] For further information on Haxby, see D. Haxby and J. Malden, 'Thomas Haxby of York (1729–1796): an Extraordinary Musician and Musical Instrument Maker', *York Historian*, 2 (1978), 43–55; Margaret Cranmer, 'Haxby, Thomas', *Grove Music Online*; and David Griffiths' chapter in this volume.

[42] Humphries and Smith, *Music Publishing in the British Isles*, 176.

[43] *Leeds Intelligencer*, 10 February 1767, 24 October 1769, 8 January 1771 and 4 June 1771.

[44] The *Leeds Intelligencer* announced on 3 July 1770: '*This Day is published,* BY JOHN BINNS, *Bookseller, In* BRIDGGATE, LEEDS, Price TWO SHILLINGS and SIXPENCE, DICTIONARIUM MUSICA: Being a Compleat Dictionary or Treasury of MUSIC. Containing a full Explanation of all the Words and Terms made Use of in Music, both Speculative, Practical, and Historical. All the Terms and Words made Use of by the *Italians,* are also inserted. The Whole compiled from the best Antient and Modern Authors, who have wrote on the Subject. BY JOHN HOYLE, MUSICIAN. *At* J. BINNS's *Shop may be had,* Music and Musical Instruments of all Kinds whatever; and every other Article in the Musical Branch. He assures his Friends, and the Public in general, That he has it in his Power, and is determined to serve them in the best Manner with them, and on a low Terms as any where in London'. This work was derived chiefly from the dictionary published by James Grassineau in 1740; see Jamie C. Kassler, 'Binns [Hoyle], John', *Grove Music Online*; Humphries and Smith, *Music Publishing in the British Isles*, 359.

'most indefatigable in business, and his bibliographical knowledge was excelled by few'.[45] He sold schoolbooks, concert tickets, oratorio texts and sermons,[46] along with musical instruments:

> To be Sold, a Double HARPSICHORD, with two Setts of beautiful Keys made of Snake Wood, with four Stops, and in exceeding fine Condition; the Maker, Christian Frederick Pintz. – It may be seen at J. BINNS'S MUSIC-SHOP in Leeds: Where are several HARPSICHORDS and SPINNETS for Sale, of various Prices; and most other Kinds of Musical Instruments, as cheap as in London.[47]

In addition to subscribing to a copy of Miller's *Psalms of David*, Binns purchased six copies of Thomas Jackson's *Twelve Psalm Tunes* (London, 1788) and single copies of *A Plain and Easy Introduction to Practical Music* (London, 1771) by Thomas Morley and Stephen Storace's *Collection of Original Harpsichord Music* (London, 1778). He furthermore subscribed to the numerous printed collections of Handel's music issued by William Randall.[48] Towards the end of the eighteenth century, Binns was beginning to have competition from Edward Porter who also owned a music shop in the city – although Porter mostly sold concert tickets,[49] he also purchased a copy of Miller's *Psalms*.

In his native county of Norfolk, Miller had loyal followers.[50] The Norwich printer and bookseller Christopher Berry (1725–1770), who subscribed to one copy, also subscribed to Miller's first work *A Collection of New English Songs and a Cantata* in 1756 and his son Christopher Berry jnr (1749–1828) subscribed to Miller's *Psalms of David*.[51] Just as in York, we find several other Norwich-based booksellers subscribing to Miller's *Psalms of David*: William T. Roberts (2 copies) and William Yarrington and Richard Bacon (1745–1812), who were partners in the *Norwich Mercury* (3 copies).[52]

---

[45] Charles Henry Timperley, *A Dictionary of Printers and Printing, with the Progress of Literature, Ancient and Modern: Bibliographic Illustrations, Etc.* (London, 1839), 791, quoted in Henry R. Plomer, with George Herbert Bushnell, Ernest Reginald McClintock Dix and Alfred W. Pollard, *A Dictionary of the Printers and Booksellers who were at work in England, Scotland and Ireland from 1726 to 1775* (Oxford, 1932), 26.

[46] *Leeds Intelligencer*, 24 September 1765, 24 September 1771, 18 February 1772 and 11 October 1774; *Leeds Mercury*, 10 October 1769; *Leeds Intelligencer*, 8 February 1774 and 1 July 1777. In a catalogue of books for 1796 Binns described himself as 'Bookseller, Printer, Stationer, Print-Seller, and Music-Seller' (*Leeds Intelligencer*, 19 October 1795).

[47] *Leeds Intelligencer*, 10 September 1776.

[48] See Fleming and Perkins, *Dataset of Subscribers*.

[49] For example, see *Leeds Intelligencer*, 28 December 1795.

[50] See Roberts, '"I esteem my lot fortunate, in residing in this happy country"', 89–108.

[51] Plomer, et al., *A Dictionary of the Printers and Booksellers who were at work in England, Scotland and Ireland from 1726 to 1775*, 23. See also David Stoker, 'The Berry family of Norwich: The rise and fall of a book trade dynasty', *Publishing History*, 74 (2014), 67–95; David Stoker, '"To all booksellers, country chapmen and others": How the rural population of East Anglia obtained its printed materials (1570–1800)', in Giles Mandelbrote, Robin Myers and Michael Harris (eds), *Fairs, Markets and the Itinerant Book Trade* (London, 2007), 107–36.

[52] David Stoker, 'The Norwich Book Trades Before 1800', *Transactions of the Cambridge Bibliographical Society*, 8/1 (1981), 79–125, at 81 and 123.

Familial connections into the commercial trade could also be important for the dissemination of a composer's printed works across England. For instance, the relations of Thomas Mace (d.1706) acted as subscription agents in York and Norwich for the publication of his *Musick's Monument* (1676) over 100 years earlier.[53] In a similar vein, Miller's older brother, Thomas, ordered six copies of *A Collection of New English Songs and a Cantata*, seven copies of *Six Sonatas for the Harpsichord*, twenty-five copies of *Psalms of David* and six copies of *Dr Watts's Psalms and Hymns* for his bookshop in the Market Place in Bungay.[54] It is highly likely that Thomas and other family members were actively encouraging subscriptions and shared news of Edward's upcoming publications with their customers and contacts to maximise sales.

However, the largest number of subscription copies of Miller's *Psalms of David* was not taken up by a family member but by John Rackham, bookseller, printer, stationer and proprietor of a public circulating library on Angel Hill, opposite the old Abbey Gate, in Bury St Edmunds with 34 copies.[55] Rackham had begun his library by 1781 when he advertised that books from his stock of 1600 were available to borrow for 1d a night, 4s a quarter, 7s for six months or 12s a year.[56] This was clearly a successful enterprise as, by 1803, his inventory had increased to 6,200 books and Rackham claimed to have the largest circulating library across the region of Suffolk, Norfolk, Cambridgeshire and Essex.[57] Rackham's library stock may have included copies of works to which he subscribed, including Joseph William Holder's *A Favourite Collection of Songs Adapted for the Voice, Piano-Forte* (London, 1789), Charles Dibdin's *The Musical Tour* (Sheffield, 1788) and the collections of Handel's vocal music arranged by John Clarke (London, 1809, 1810 and 1819).[58] Presumably Rackham purchased 34 copies of Miller's *Psalms of David* not only for resale purposes but for supplementing his library stock. It is also important to note that local booksellers could be important instigators in producing and commissioning local history books for their towns and regions: Edmund Gillingwater's book *An Historical and Descriptive Account of St Edmund's Bury* was printed 'by and for' Rackham in

---

[53] Carter, 'Thomas Mace and the publication by subscription of *Musick's Monument*', 21–38.
[54] Thomas Miller, bookseller and grocer, was a successful businessman and attracted significant custom to his shop; see J.M. Blatchly, 'Miller, Thomas (1731–1804)', *Oxford Dictionary of National Biography*.
[55] Rackham's will is available at The National Archives, PROB 11/1643/234.
[56] *Ipswich Journal*, 24 March 1781.
[57] *Bury and Norwich Post*, 12 October 1803. See also David Addy, 'St Edmundsbury: The Eighteenth Century and Napoleonic Wars from 1700 to 1812', *St Edmundsbury Chronicle*, at www.stedmundsburychronicle.co.uk/Chronicle/1700-1812. A token for Rackham's library survives in London, British Museum (SSB,187.21.2). It displays an open book and the text 'Payable at Rackham's Circulating Library, Angel Hill, Bury'. The reverse shows a view of the Abbey Gate directly opposite to Rackham's premises. See also Richard Dalton and Samuel H. Hamer, *The Provincial Token-Coinage of the 18th Century* (London, 1910; reprinted 1967).
[58] Fleming and Perkins, *Dataset of Subscribers*.

1804.[59] In that same year, Miller's own *The History and Antiquities of Doncaster and its Vicinity* (1804) was published by Doncaster printer William Sheardown.

While it is clear that there was a wealth of general booksellers across several regions subscribing and selling Miller's publication and other music books, and responding to consumer demand within their localities, this trend continued outside the areas with which Miller had an obvious close association. This includes the West Midlands, with the Birmingham-based printer, typefounder, bookseller and journalist Myles Swinney, who purchased twenty-five copies of Miller's *Psalms of David*. He appears to have had an interest in locally-composed vocal music since he also purchased two copies of Robert Broderip's *A Miscellaneous Collection of Vocal Music*, op 9 (London, 1791) and one of Jeremiah Clark's *Ten Songs*, op 4 (London, 1791).[60] Swinney, like other sellers, had a diverse business and utilised the added marketing power of self-published newspapers to communicate with customers and generate sales, although these subscriptions suggest Swinney was reacting to local demand for particular repertoire instead of advertising extensively in newspapers.[61]

Conclusion

It is evident from the impressive subscription list attached to *Psalms of David* that Edward Miller's music was distributed widely across England, with regional booksellers, music-sellers, stationers, engravers and printers having a significant role in the book's dissemination into local music markets. The majority of these traders would have stocked these copies in their shops; others may have added to their circulating library catalogues. This chapter demonstrates the diversity of services and goods in the commercial music trade across the country in the late eighteenth century: successful and enterprising sellers employed a variety of marketing strategies to appeal to customer taste by advertising in newspapers, publishing and selling music and educational tutor books for the domestic music market and acting as subscription agents.

As is evident from this study of Miller, a regional musician could develop and maintain strong relationships with a network of London publishers, many of whom were important supporters that assisted and promoted works and accepted subscriptions. However, more important for a national circulation and dissemination of Miller's *Psalms of David* appear to be the widespread community of commercial traders in music, servicing their localities across regional Britain. Family connections continued to be important as they were in the seventeenth century for extending and promoting a music book's dissemination

---

[59] Edmund Gillingwater, *An Historical and Descriptive Account of St. Edmund's Bury, in the County of Suffolk* (St Edmund's Bury, 1804).
[60] Fleming and Perkins, *Dataset of Subscribers*.
[61] Swinney printed the *Birmingham Chronicle and Warwickshire Journal* from 1771 (a continuation of the *Warwickshire Weekly Journal*); see Plomer, et al., *A Dictionary of the Printers and Booksellers who were at work in England, Scotland and Ireland from 1726 to 1775*, 241.

but in the case of *Psalms of David*, Miller also relied upon family members to facilitate publication. By focussing on composing music and pedagogical books for amateur musicians, Miller enhanced his own reputation and secured the support and endorsement of London-based publishers. This no doubt helped raise the composer's profile and enabled him to publish *Psalms of* David, a work that turned out to be the most successful musical publication, by number of subscribers, issued in eighteenth-century Britain.

8

Thomas Underwood and his Successors: The Music Shops of Eighteenth-Century Bath

Matthew Spring

Bath, in the latter part of the seventeenth century, had all the appearances of a quiet market town.[1] With a population of c.2000,[2] it was heavily reliant on its natural springs for producing bottled water and for supplying its famous baths. Though its origins as a spa date from Roman times, the city's fortunes began to improve in the sixteenth century with the visit of Mary of Moderna, Queen to James II; she attributed her success in producing the Old Pretender, James Francis Edward Stuart (1688–1766), to Bath's thermal waters. Queen Anne then visited in 1692, 1702 and 1703 to relieve her persistent gout.[3] What made Bath special for the Romans, Queens Mary and Anne, and the eighteenth-century 'company' (i.e., the well-healed visitors who stayed in Bath for health and leisure) were the 'chalybeate' waters, believed beneficial for health.[4] The quotidian drinking of the waters and bathing in the hot baths was known as 'the cure', and had long incorporated a good degree of entertainment and social interaction among the well-healed visitors that constituted 'the company',[5] in which music played a prominent role.

The decades that followed the 1705 appointment of Richard 'Beau' Nash (1674–1762) as Master of Ceremonies saw Bath's advancement as a centre of leisure and gambling.[6] Bath's spa 'season' gradually evolved into an autumn

---

[1] City status was granted in 1590.

[2] For estimations of Bath's size in the later seventeenth century, see Graham Davis and Penny Bonsall, *A History of Bath: Image and Reality* (Bath, 2006), 66.

[3] Ronald S. Neale, *Bath: A Social History 1680–1850* (London, 1981), 16. For a contemporary account from May 1716, see Daniel Defoe, *A Tour Through the Whole Island of Great Britain* (Harmondsworth, Penguin modern edition 1971, orig. 1724-6), 359–61.

[4] Doctors William Oliver and Robert Peirce were among the most successful of Bath's physicians in propagating the idea that Bath's waters would cure a host of ailments. See Neale, *Bath*, 13–16.

[5] Davis and Bonsall, *A History of Bath*, 112.

[6] Nash was Bath's first officially recorded 'Master of Ceremonies', though the role was developed by his predecessor Captain Webster, for whom Nash acted as deputy until Webster's untimely death in a duel. See Davis and Bonsall, *A History of Bath*, 117–22; Trevor Fawcett, *Bath Entertain'd, Amusements, Recreations and Gambling at the 18th Century Spa* (Bath, 1998), 4–10.

and spring period that extended from the end of September until mid-May.[7] The months out of season were initially described as 'desolate as a Wilderness' but, as the eighteenth century progressed, the summer developed its own programme of entertainments.[8] The city, which was centred around the abbey, expanded outwards from its medieval walls,[9] while its population increased to upwards of 30,000 people in full season by 1800; most new building work was, unsurprisingly, based on speculative investment in dwellings for short stay occupancy.[10] Bath's commercial heart grew to such a degree that Trevor Fawcett thought 'perhaps only the shops of London's West End, so dazzling to foreign tourists, outshone the later eighteenth-century emporia of Bath'.[11] As part of the commercialisation of leisure, a music trade developed in Bath that grew steadily from before the mid-eighteenth century to peak in the early to mid-nineteenth century.[12] Along with specialised music shops, individual musicians sold and hired music from their homes; Bath's celebrated toyshops, warehouses (diversified shops that sold a varied range of goods) and repositories (early forms of department stores) also sold musical instruments as a part of their business interests.[13]

---

[7] Davis and Bonsall, *A History of Bath*, 113 and 120–1.

[8] Edward Ward, *A Step to the Bath with a Character of the Place* (London, 1700), 16. In summer months the Bath pleasure gardens (of which there were several) developed public breakfasts, teas, gala events and evening concert seasons, particularly after 1766. See Matthew Spring, 'Vauxhall Gardens: the provision of music in Bath's pleasure gardens and walks, and the development of Grand Gala Concerts, a combination of pleasures "after the manner of Vauxhall"', *Bath History Journal*, 15 (2019), 74–92, at 79–80.

[9] Davis and Bonsall, *A History of Bath*, 83.

[10] Ibid., 83–112. The population rose to 34,163 in 1801 a ten-fold increase in a hundred years. See Rowland Mainwaring, *Annals of Bath, from the Year 1800 to the Passing of the New Municipal Council* (Bath, 1838), 11.

[11] Trevor Fawcett, 'Eighteenth-Century Shops and the Luxury Trade', *Bath History Journal*, 3 (2003), 49–75, at 50.

[12] Trevor Fawcett, *Bath Commercialis'd, Shops, Trades and Market at the 18th-Century Spa* (Bath, 2002), 74–6; Kenneth Edward James, 'Concert Life in Eighteenth-Century Bath', 2 vols (PhD dissertation, Royal Holloway, London, 1987), i, 65–9.

[13] A good example of a diversified store that included musical instruments was the repository of William Glover and J.L. Newman that occupied the discontinued Assembly Rooms in the Terrace Walk *c.*1782–1783. See Fawcett, 'Eighteenth-Century Shops and the Luxury Trade', 72.

Table 8.1 Timeline of Bath music shops, 1740–1800.

	Underwood	Milgrove (& Brooks)	Tylee	Whitehead	Lintern	Mathews	Ashley
1740	Began c.1740.						
1750							
1760	Quit in 1762. Restarted c.1769.	Began 1762.	Began c.1765.				
1770	Died 1777.	Brooks left 1774. Milgrove's became a toyshop.	Ceased trading in 1771.	Began 1773.			
1780				Moved trade to home from 1786.	Began c.1780. James Lintern joined by Walter Lintern in c.1786.	Began c.1789.	
1790							Began c.1798.
1800		Ceased trading in 1808.				Ceased trading in 1805.	Ceased trading in 1812.

Before c.1740, musical goods were available from general bookshops in Bath, not unlike the situation in other regional towns and cities.[14] While extant records are scarce, there was a trade in printed music in Bath from at least the early eighteenth century. Bookseller Henry Hammond, who was in business no earlier than 1690, sold music books in c.1711–1713 to Claver Morris (1659–1726/7), a wealthy Wells physician. During the latter's visits to Bath, he purchased from Hammond: '4 Sets of Play-House Airs', 'Corelli's 12 Solos [op 5], with his Graces to them', 'the 2ᵈ & 4ᵗʰ Operas of Massiti's Solos' and 'Gasparini Visconti's 1ˢᵗ Opera of Solos'.[15] Additionally, in September 1712 Morris purchased William Corbett's '5ᵗʰ Opera being 6 Sonatas of 3 Parts for Violins & for Flutes for 8s' direct from the composer.[16] Hammond's successor, James Leake, likewise included music in his stock, advertising the sale of works by the prolific song-composer Henry Carey (1687–1743);[17] during the 1720s Leake developed a circulating library, one of the first in the country.[18]

Table 8.1 reveals that, by the 1760s, there were two or three music traders in the city at any one time. The numbers rose in the first decades of the nineteenth

---

[14] Stephanie Carter and Kirsten Gibson, 'Printed Music in the Provinces: Musical Circulation in Seventeenth-Century England and the Case of Newcastle upon Tyne Bookseller William London', *The Library*, 18/4 (2017), 428–73.

[15] Harry D. Johnstone, 'Claver Morris, an Early Eighteenth-Century English Physician and Amateur Musician Extraordinaire' *Journal of the Royal Musical Association*, 133/1 (2008), 93–127, at 124. These publications are Arcangelo Corelli, *Sonate a Violino e Violone o Cimbalo … Troisième Edition ou l'on à joint les Agréemens des Adagio de cet Ouvrage*, op 5 (Amsterdam, [c.1710]) or John Walsh's *XII Sonata's or Solos for a Violin, a Bass Violin or harpsicord … haveing ye graces to all ye adagio's and other places*, op 5 (London, [c.1711]); Michele Mascitti, *Sonate da Camera a Violino Solo col Violone o Cembalo*, op 2 (Paris, 1706), *Sonate a violino Solo e Basso, e Sonate a due Violini, e Basso*, op 4 (Paris, 1711), or Walsh's reissues of the two works by Mascitti from c.1712; Gaspero Visconti, *Sonate à Violino, é Violone, ò Cembalo*, op 1 (Amsterdam, 1703) or *Gasperini's Solos for a Violin with a through Bass for the Harpsicord or Bass Violin*, op 1 (London, 1703). See William C. Smith, *A Bibliography of the Musical Works Published by John Walsh during the Years 1695–1720* (London, 1948), 38, 120 and 128–9. For more on Claver Morris, see Edmund Hobhouse, *The Diary of a West Country Physician A.D. 1684–1726* (London, 1934); Harry D. Johnstone, 'Instruments, Strings, Wire and other Musical Miscellanea in the Account Books of Claver Morris (1659–1727)', *Galpin Society Journal*, 60 (2007), 29–35. For more on Henry Hammond, see Trevor Fawcett, *Georgian Imprints, Printing and Publishing in Bath 1729–1815* (Bath, 2008), 9.

[16] William Corbett, *Six Sonata's a 3 ☐ for two Flutes or two German Flutes and a Bass*, op 5 (London, 1712). See Johnstone, 'Claver Morris', 125.

[17] Charles Humphries and William C. Smith, *Music Publishing in the British Isles: from the beginning until the middle of the nineteenth century* (Oxford, 1970), 225. See also Stephen Banfield, *Music in the West Country: Social and Cultural History across an English Region* (Woodbridge, 2018), 171–2. For more on Carey, see Gillespie, Norman. 'Carey, Henry', *Grove Music Online*.

[18] Fawcett, *Georgian Imprints, Printing and Publishing in Bath 1729–1815*, 9; Fawcett, *Bath Commercialis'd*, 8. For more on Leake, see Simon Fleming's contribution on Joseph Barber and William Flackton in this volume.

century and reached its peak with six to eight businesses listed in Bath's directories.[19] While London and Edinburgh were undeniably the largest and most important centres of the commercial music trade, Bath had a sizeable market with seven dedicated music shops over the course of the eighteenth century, and all situated within a narrow geographical area. In comparison, evidence for music shops in neighbouring Bristol does not emerge until 1745 when the music seller Richard Haynes Plomer was first known to be active; the trade in that city grew to five dealers by 1775, although they all combined their music businesses with other occupations (music teacher, stationer, toy seller, cutler or publican) – perhaps a consequence of a limited market.[20] Indeed, Stephen Banfield describes Bristol at this time as 'not particularly forward in the provision of music sellers' and unlike Bath which he characterised as the 'west country's … Mecca for conspicuous consumption'.[21]

The services that Bath's music businesses provided made them increasingly integral to the musical life of the city. Some were led by members of the resident musician families, and collectively they provided commercial spaces for the trial, hire and sale of instruments and their accessories (strings, bridges, reeds, rosins, etc.). All sold music; some ran circulating music libraries, published music or were venues for public demonstrations and performances. They were places where teachers could be secured, musical events advertised and tickets purchased. Some shops promoted themselves as musical instrument makers, though there is little evidence of instrument making in Bath before the early nineteenth century.[22] Their services provided customers, keen to improve their musical skills, with the facility to hire teachers and instruments alike during their time in Bath and to furnish themselves with new music. Our journey through the history of Bath's specialist music shops begins with Thomas Underwood who established his business in c.1740.[23]

---

[19] Matthew Spring, 'Music Shops and the Music Trade in Eighteenth-Century Bath', 50/1 *Brio* (2013), 3–16, at 3; Matthew Spring, 'The Musical Life of Bath, 1800–1850' in Nicholas Temperley (ed.), *Musicians of Bath and Beyond, Edward Loder (1809–1865) and his Family* (Woodbridge, 2016), 2–41, at 38–9. Music sellers and music shop owners listed in the Bath Directories between 1805 and 1819 were: James Lintern, John Ashley, Matthew Patton, Charles White, Andrew Loder, John David Loder, Martin Pittman and John Phillpott; though not all in the same years.

[20] Banfield, *Music in the West Country*, 172–3.

[21] Ibid.

[22] Underwood, Milgrove and Lintern all styled themselves as 'instrument makers' but their advertisements do not list the instruments they made, and no examples of their work survive. There were a few instrument makers in eighteenth-century Bath among them: John Holland, organ builder; John Morris, violin maker; Edward Boehman, pianoforte maker; and John Simcock, who devised and made the Bell Harp, an instrument both plucked and swung while played to give a pulsating sound. See James, 'Concert Life in Eighteenth-Century Bath', i, 384.

[23] *Bath Chronicle*, 19 April 1770. The advertisement (dated 21 February) states that Underwood had been thirty years in the music trade, suggesting he began trading around 1740.

ॐ *Thomas Underwood (fl.1740–1777)*

Underwood's first known advertisement from 1746 reveals that, in addition to the selling or letting of 'all Sorts of MUSICAL INSTRUMENTS', he sold strings, paper and music 'all as Good, and as Cheap as at any Place in *England*'.[24] Items could be purchased at wholesale or retail prices and he listed a variety of instruments, some of which were archaic or novel in the mid-eighteenth century: 'Lutes, Bamborines, [Tambourines] Kits [pocket violins] and Shells [Castanets?] and Mute Violins'. He furthermore advised that 'People in the Country may have any Thing they want, by speaking to the Newsmen'.[25] Bath's newspaper proprietors had a retinue of 'newsmen' and 'hawkers' who distributed print to a circuit of neighbouring cities, towns and villages and, as with later Bath music shops, Underwood aimed his trade at outlying shops as well as individuals outside Bath.[26] By 1770 Bath's newsmen had circuits that took in such cities and towns as Bristol, Frome, Devizes, Chippenham, Wells and Glastonbury but also went as far afield as Salisbury, Sherborne, Taunton, Cirencester and Marlborough, as well as villages around Bath.[27]

Underwood, like other Bath businessmen, took on apprentices; indenture documents survive for two: Thomas Atwood, who began his apprenticeship in March 1749,[28] and Benjamin Milgrove (also spelt Millgrove, 1731–1810).[29] These records make no mention of music selling or the retail trade, but only instruction in the 'Art or Mistery of a Musical Instrument maker'.[30] Underwood always styled himself as a 'Musical Instrument-Maker' and presumably had undergone a maker's apprenticeship himself, although there is no clear evidence he was active in that field. Business may have been patchy and difficult as on at least two occasions he announced abandoning the trade. In 1752 he advertised a week-long stock sale of instruments, music and strings, 'with many other Articles to [sic] tedious to mention' as he was 'going to leave off Business'; he does it again in 1762 announcing that he has 'quitted business', this time passing his trade to Milgrove in partnership with John Brooks.[31] Underwood continued to advertise regularly in the *Bath Advertiser* and *Journal* during the 1750s and, from March 1757, 'Let or Sold Guitars'.[32] He additionally publicised 'an Engine

---

[24] *Bath Journal*, 3 February 1746.
[25] Ibid.
[26] Kevin Grieves, 'Spreading the News: The Distribution of Bath Newspapers in the Eighteenth Century', *Bath History Journal*, 15 (2017), 58–73, at 60–1.
[27] Ibid.
[28] James, 'Concert Life in Eighteenth-Century Bath', i, 340. Other named apprentices were John Jones, 1744; James Sheppard, 1753; Anthony Cottle, 1761; Christopher Kempson, 1762; and William Besley, 1768. London, The National Archives (TNA), IR 1, Board of Stamps: Apprenticeship Books. Atwood's indenture document is found at Bath City Archives, Sydenham scrapbooks, p. 845.
[29] Bath City Archives, BC/21, 'Bath Freeman's Apprentice Register', p. 75.
[30] James, 'Concert Life in Eighteenth-Century Bath', i, 341.
[31] *Bath Chronicle*, 14 October 1762.
[32] For example, *Bath Advertiser*, 5 March 1757.

[used] to wire Gold or Silver Strings to any Size', that he sold 'the best Dutch Wire for Harpsichords, Hautboy and Bassoon Reeds, Pitch Pipes, Taber and Pipes', and that he could supply 'all the new Country-Dances or Minuets fitted for any Instrument before they are printed'.[33] From 1757 he offered the new metal strung 'guittar' (a form of cittern) alongside a range of guitar music.[34] Underwood's advertisements for the 'guittar' suggest that he hoped to profit from the sudden popularity of this instrument, as did other Bath traders: guittars by the London harpsichord- and piano-maker Johannes Zumpe (1726–90) were on sale at Charles Gill's pastry shop in 1759.[35]

During his long career as a music shop owner, Underwood periodically advertised that the new music available from his shop had 'just been printed', some of which was by Bath composers, and he accepted subscriptions for forthcoming publications.[36] James George's set of *Six Concertos in Seven Parts* (1756) were, according to the title page, 'Engrav'd and Printed by the Author at BATH' and listed by Underwood as 'just published' in his advertisements for 1755 and 1756.[37] They had also been publicised a decade earlier, in 1746, suggesting that the 1755 edition might have been a reissue.[38] George was a musician in the Pump Room Band and dedicated this set to Nash.[39] The title page, which emphatically states that Bath was the place of its engraving and printing, suggests the city in the mid-eighteenth century had printers and engravers able to produce music editions, even if there is little corroborative evidence.[40]

[33] Ibid., 5 March 1757.
[34] Ibid., 23 August 1758.
[35] *Bath Journal*, 29 October 1759. The guitar appears to have been particularly popular in Bath, where Ann Ford was painted, holding the instrument, by Gainsborough in 1760. Ford, later Mrs Thicknesse, produced a tutor for the instrument around this time. Ann Ford, *Lessons and Instructions for Playing on the Guitar* (London, c.1760). See Christopher Page, *The Guitar in Georgian England* (London, 2020), 38–62; Peter Holman, *Life After Death: The Viola Da Gamba in Britain from Purcell to Dolmetsch* (Woodbridge, 2010), 135–48; Panagiotis Poulopoulos, 'The guittar in the British Isles, 1750–1810', (PhD dissertation, University of Edinburgh, 2011).
[36] For example, *Bath Chronicle*, 28 March 1771, includes an advertisement for a newly printed treatise for the German Flute and that subscriptions for a set of duets by Luke Heron of Dublin were accepted by Underwood.
[37] *Bath Advertiser*, 3 October 1755 and 25 December 1756.
[38] James George, *Six Concerto's in Seven Parts, Four for Violins, one for a German Flute, one for a Violincello and Tenor and Thorough Bass for the Organ, or Harpsichord, composed by James George* (Bath, 1756). George's set was first advertised by Underwood in the *Bath Journal* for 27 October 1746 (at half a guinea per set).
[39] George is listed by Francis Fleming as one of the musicians of the Pump Room Band to be allowed a deputy. See *The Life and Extraordinary Adventures, the Perils and Critical Escapes of Timothy Ginnadrake, that chequer'd Fortune*, 3 vols (Bath, 1771), iii, 103.
[40] George Steart was a copper plate and music printer based in Bath, who operated at the end of the eighteenth century. He printed Venanzio Rauzzini's *A Periodical Collection of Vocal Music ... Vol. I* (Bath, 1797). See Humphries and Smith, *Music Publishing in the British Isles*, 300.

A diversification that Underwood pioneered in Bath was the promotion of performances by visiting artists within his music shop or adjoining premises. In 1760 he had sufficient space in his 'great Music Shop' to accommodate an impromptu band performance in celebration of a British naval victory.[41] The first specified performer promoted was a Mr Cartwright in December 1761:

> In a Parlour at Mr Underwood's, adjoining to his Music-Shop, in Stall-Street, Mr Cartwright, Jun. Will perform every Day (Sundays excepted) on the MUSICAL GLASSES, between the hours of Twelve and Three, and from Six to Eight in the Evening. Admittance 2s 6d.[42]

In these entertainments Underwood clearly hoped to emulate the London success of novelty acts, such as Frederic Theodor Schumann's performance on the musical glasses at Cox's Rooms, London, held between August and October 1761.[43] Similarly, Underwood's advertisement of December 1761 includes a notice that 'Two of the Original LEARNED DOGS from the Hay-market, London [will perform]; one of which Reads, Writes, and Casts Accounts, &c. The other performs a Hornpipe, in the Character of Nancy Dawson at Drury Lane'.[44]

Though Underwood announced that he was giving up his shop to Benjamin Milgrove and John Brooks in 1762, he had re-entered the business by 1765 with the establishment of a 'Concert Room, in Major Bolton's Court'.[45] At this venue he promoted all sorts of exhibitions, including the performance of an 'Invisible Agent, A New Phaenomenon': a 'wonderful Apparatus' that could communicate invisibly so that 'two friends at a great Distance communicate through thoughts'. There was also a 'SIBYL', a 'Learned Mermaid', and the 'Enchanted Needle';[46] in December 1765 it was advertised that, at 'Mr Underwood's Concert-Room', one might see the 'Nostradamus, or the Necromancer in the Bottle'.[47] By the end of the decade Underwood had returned to advertising a shop that sold and leased a variety of instruments, including Scotch and Irish

---

[41] Fawcett, *Bath Commercialis'd*, 75. This performance presumably commemorated the Battle of Restigouche of 28 June–8 July 1760.

[42] *Bath Chronicle*, 31 December 1761, 21 and 28 January 1762.

[43] The advertisements in the *Bath Chronicle* for 21 and 28 January 1762 are explicitly titled 'MUSIC on the GLASSES, In the Manner of Mr SCHUMAN'. See Peter Holman, 'Ann Ford Revisited', *Eighteenth-Century Music*, 1/2 (2004), 157–84, at 174.

[44] *Bath Chronicle*, 21 January 1762. Nancy Dawson was the stage name for Ann Newton (c.1728–1767) who rose to fame dancing the hornpipe between the acts of *The Beggars Opera* in the Covent Garden production of 1759 and then at Drury Lane in 1760. See Philip H. Highfill (ed), *A Biographical Dictionary of Actors, Actresses, Musicians, Dancers, Managers and Other Stage Personnel in London, 1660–1800* (Carbondale, IL, 1975) 239.

[45] *Bath Chronicle* for 1765–6, for example 19 December 1765.

[46] *Bath Chronicle*, 17 October 1765. Drawing from classical mythology, a sybil was a prophetess at a holy site capable of seeing into the future.

[47] *Bath Chronicle*, 19 December 1765, 26 December 1765 and 13 February 1766. It was claimed to be a distillation of the astrologer, 'chopped to Pieces, and boil'd down in a

bagpipes, dulcimores and aeolian harps.[48] In February 1770 he announced his 'Experience of thirty Years in this City for his own proficiency in the Business of Instrument Maker, &c' with the opening of a 'SHOP in the PUMP-ROOM PASSAGE'.[49] Underwood continued in business until his death in 1777, by which time there were a number of other similar businesses operating in the city (see Table 8.1) including the one managed by Underwood's apprentice, Milgrove.[50]

❦ Underwood's Successors: Milgrove, Tylee and Whitehead

Benjamin Milgrove must have completed the usual seven-year apprenticeship with Underwood in June 1762, around the same time that an agreement was made to take over his master's shop in partnership with local cellist John Brooks (*d*.1787).[51] An advertisement that appeared in September and October 1762 announced that 'Mr Underwood, Musical Instrument-Maker and Music-Seller, in Stall-Street [has…] QUITTED BUSINESS in Favour of Benj. Millgrove and Jn. Brooks'.[52] This seems to have been an amicable signing off as the same advertisement states that 'All Persons indebted to Mr UNDERWOOD, are desired to pay their respective Debts to him, at his former Dwelling-House; or to the sa'd Millgrove and Brooks, who are authorized to receive the same'.[53]

While there is no evidence that Underwood was a musician (unless he personally taught guittar), Milgrove had a full and varied career as a performer and composer.[54] He was active for most of his long adult life as a musician in the city's numerous ensembles and played several instruments, including violin, horn and guittar at a professional level.[55] He composed and published his own music, including a tutor for guittar, and was attached to Lady Huntingdon's

---

Liquid' and then brought back to life with his head 'to rise and descend at Pleasure out of the Mouth of a common Glass-Bottle'.

[48] *Bath Chronicle*, 5 October 1769: 'Ladies and Gentlemen taught to play on the Guittar'.

[49] *Bath Chronicle*, 22 February 1770, 12 April 1770 and 19 April 1770.

[50] Underwood sold Davidson Russel's collection of vocal music, titled *The Butterfly*, from his shop (*Bath Chronicle*, 18 March 1773). Russel was a violinist, cellist and composer, and the last advertisement to mention Underwood was for 'Subscriptions for *Six New Anthems*', 'as sung as St James's Church' by Russel (*Bath Chronicle*, 10 April 1777). For a record of Underwood's death, see Taunton, Somerset Record Office, D\P\ba.ab/2/9/1 (microfiche).

[51] His apprenticeship document is dated 2 June 1755 so he would have completed seven years in June 1762. Bath City Archives, BC/21, 'Bath Freeman's Apprentice Register', p. 75.

[52] *Bath Chronicle*, 30 September 1762 and 14 October 1762.

[53] Ibid.

[54] Matthew Spring, 'Benjamin Milgrove, the Musical 'Toy man', and the 'guittar' in Bath, 1757–1790', *Early Music*, 4/2 (2013), 317–29. *Bath Chronicle*, 5 October 1769: '*Ladies and Gentlemen taught to play on the* Guittar'.

[55] *Bath Herald*, 20 August 1797. Here, Milgrove records 'the practice and study of [the horn for] more than forty years'.

Chapel in Bath (probably its first organist).[56] He was furthermore a successful director of music at Bath's musically ambitious Villa Gardens, then in competition with the well-established Spring Gardens concerts of the Hanoverian-born musician and composer William Herschel (1738–1822).[57] The rivalry must have been friendly, since Milgrove received Herschel's support when the musical director and composer, Thomas Linley snr, cut Milgrove out of work at Bath's New Assembly Rooms.[58] Herschel subsequently employed Milgrove as a musician in a rival subscription concert series at the old Assembly Rooms.[59] With his considerable energy and a diversified portfolio of professional musical activities, Milgrove became the epitome of the successful home-grown Bath musician of the late eighteenth century. In 1774 Milgrove, looking to expand his business interests, acquired the neighbouring premises in Wade's Passage and, from 1778, styled it as a 'toyshop'.[60] Bath's toyshops often sold musical instruments and here Milgrove continued to purvey music, instruments and all necessary accessories, and to hire out and teach guittar.[61] Given the diversification of music shops, the transition to a toyshop may have been more one of emphasis than stock.

Another of Bath's leading musicians to open a music shop was Joseph Tylee (1736–1794), assistant organist at the Abbey from c.1765 and full organist from February 1767.[62] Tylee sold 'all Sorts of Music and Musical Instruments [… and] Guittars', along with 'All Sorts of Instruments Tun'd, and Lett by the Week' from his shop in Queen's Square.[63] However, it seems that the music shop was

---

[56] Spring, 'Benjamin Milgrove, the Musical 'Toy man', and the 'guittar' in Bath', 326. His *Forty Lessons for One and Two Guittars* (London, 1762) was 'Sold by the Author and comp. at the Music-Shop in Stall-Street, Bath' (*Bath Chronicle*, 16 December 1762). Milgrove also had published three books of hymns: *Sixteen Hymns As they are sung at the Right Honourable Countess of Huntingdon's Chappel in Bath* (?London, 1768); *Twelve Hymns A they are sung at the Countess of Huntingdon's Chappel in Bath* (?Bath, 1771); *Twelve hymns and a favourite lyric poem written by Dr Watts* (?Bath, 1781). His hymn tunes live on, both in *The English Hymnal* and especially within evangelical communities in America. Percy Dearmer and Ralph Vaughan Williams (eds), *The English Hymnal with Tunes* (Oxford, 1933), nos. 177 and 196. Milgrove's tunes are named 'Harts' and 'Mount Ephraim'.

[57] Herschel was active in Bath between 1766 and 1782 before accepting an appointment as personal astronomer to George III. Michael Hoskin, *Discoverers of the Universe, William and Caroline Herschel* (Princetown, 2011), 20 and 57–68.

[58] The New Assembly Rooms opened in 1771. See James, 'Concert Life in Eighteenth-Century Bath', i, 175–90.

[59] Ian Woodfield, *The Celebrated Quarrel between Thomas Linley (senior) and William Herschel: An Episode in the Musical Life of 18th Century Bath* (Bath, 1977), 13.

[60] Spring, 'Benjamin Milgrove, the Musical "Toy man", and the "guittar" in Bath', 321.

[61] For Bath's toyshops, see Fawcett, 'Eighteenth-Century Shops and the Luxury Trade', 65–71; Vanessa Brett, *Bertrand's Toyshop in Bath: Luxury Retailing, 1685–1765* (Wetherby, 2014), 85–6.

[62] David Falconer and Peter King, *The Organs and Organists of Bath Abbey* (Bath, 2001), 70.

[63] *Bath Chronicle*, 30 May 1765.

of less interest to Tylee than the renting out of a house at Belvidere, Lansdowne Road, since the advertising for his music business is tacked onto notices for his property.[64] His broad approach to commercial interests continues with a notice in November 1765 for fine textiles and lace acquired from 'E. Grey from Chancery-Lane. London, [and] Now at Mr Tylee's Music-Shop in Queen's Square'.[65] A month later, his house was again advertised, adding that from his music shop 'Ladies may now be supplied with HARPSICHORDS on Hire or Sale, having receiv'd more new ones from Mr. *Kirckman* last Week'.[66] Tylee is an example of a Bath musician, part of a musical family, who used his stable employment as an organist to support and embark on other forms of economic activity that the expanding city, with its well-healed visiting clientele, could support. The Linley family similarly embarked on building projects (not least the Margaret Chapel), the Bath violinist John Grant kept a lodging house used by many visiting musicians; the Herschel family used their musical employments to support their developing interest in astronomy and telescope making.[67]

Tylee made a significant move in early 1770 when he opened a shop close to the Pump Room with an attendant musical instrument maker *in situ*, 'opposite Ladies Coffee Room', for which he 'hath procured a Stock of the best Instruments, and a curious Assortment of printed music'; music was sent to Tylee 'three times a Week from London'.[68] The advertisements for this new shop are more elaborate and detailed than before, quite possibly a deliberate ploy to mitigate the impact of Underwood's new shop. Tylee's new store seems to have been a substantial venture and a new beginning, although his advertisements suggest he did not operate the shop himself but was its financial backer.[69] As well as listing instruments, both for sale and hire, music for purchase included 'All the New Minuets, Dances, &c that are performed at BATH, and are not yet in Print, and those that are … transposed, on the shortest Notice, and adapted to any Instrument … Likewise the Cotillons, Dances, Minuetts, &c neatly

[64] Ibid.
[65] Ibid., 21 November 1765.
[66] Ibid., 5 December 1765. Harpsichords made by members of the London-based Kirkman family were among the most esteemed instruments of the time. Fanny Burney described Jacob Kirkman as 'the first harpsichord maker of the times'. See Donald Howard Boalch, revised by Peter Williams and Charles Mould, 'Kirkman', *Grove Music Online*.
[67] James, 'Concert Life in Eighteenth-Century Bath', 637, 700 and 753. For the Herschel family's telescope-making business, see James Mullaney, *The Herschel Objects and to Observe Them* (New York, 2007), 10–14.
[68] *Bath Chronicle*, 15 March 1770. Interestingly, the advertisements for 15 and 29 March 1770 have it as 'opposite the Ladies Coffee Room, near the Pump-Room' yet those for April and May have it as 'opposite the Pump-Room, near the Ladies Coffee-Room'. This suggests either a move from one side of Pump Room forecourt to another, or a mistake.
[69] The advertisements for 1770 (for example, *Bath Chronicle*, 29 March 1770) note that 'As the person who attends the Shop hath for many years worked for the Music Shops in Bath, etc. … as well as teaching the flute'.

printed on Cards at 2s 6d each Pack'.[70] The production of manuscript music continued to be an important mode of musical dissemination in the 1770s and, in continuation of the service offered by Underwood, he offered to supply bespoke manuscripts of the most recent dances from the Assembly Rooms. Such copying services were to continue into the nineteenth century. It may be that Tylee's shop did not last more than a year as there is no surviving evidence of the business after 1771 although his son, Henry Dixon Tylee, was running a music library in 1800.[71]

There was a further entrant to the market in 1773 when Thomas Whitehead (d.1793) moved to Bath following the death of Evelyn Pierrepoint, the 2nd Duke of Kingston (1715–1773), for whom Whitehead had served as a 'travelling valet' and viola player in the ducal band.[72] Similar to Tylee, Milgrove and Brooks, Whitehead was active as a professional musician; he played the horn within the city's several professional ensembles, performing in Bath's pleasure gardens,[73] and was a regular player for Bath's Royal Theatre.[74] Whitehead also worked in Bristol where he performed and ran another shop; indeed, he was robbed on a return journey to Bath in 1780.[75] He certainly published music in Bath including Thomas Shaw's *Six Favourite Minuets in Eight parts, as Performed in the Assemblies in Bath* (Bath, 1774), although the place of printing is unknown.[76] He also took on apprentices as two are mentioned as performing for free alongside him in the 1782 charity performance of Handel's *Messiah*.[77]

Whitehead exemplifies the precariousness of the music trade in eighteenth-century Bath as his business seems to have deteriorated by 1786 when he was forced to sell his stock at low prices. He promised to sell 'very Cheap' a 'Lot of Musical Instruments', adding that he 'is remov'd from his Music-Shop [...to] opposite the Theatre' [in Orchard Street] to a house where he continued to hire out instruments and teach guittar.[78] Whitehead continued to perform on the horn and to conduct business from his home where he traded in

---

[70] *Bath Chronicle*, 29 March 1770.
[71] *Robbins' Bath Directory* (Bath, 1800), 95.
[72] James, 'Concert Life in Eighteenth-Century Bath', i, 4; Thomas Whitehead, *Original Anecdotes of the late Duke of Kingston and Miss Chudleigh* (London, 1792), 117 and 126.
[73] *Bath Chronicle*, 20 May 1779.
[74] Bath Archives, BRL, Ms 26988, Theatre Log Book of the Orchard Street theatre for 1774. See James, 'Concert Life in Eighteenth-Century Bath', ii, 1049.
[75] *Bath Chronicle*, 13 July 1780. Also, James, 'Concert Life in Eighteenth-Century Bath', ii, 1030.
[76] Humphries and Smith, *Music Publishing in the British Isles*, 331.
[77] *Bath Chronicle*, 9 May 1782.
[78] *Bath Journal*, 6 October 1786. Unusually he gives prices for the hire of his instruments; prices were graded with the shortest per month hire relative to the most expensive and yearly prices about a third to a quarter of the bought price. Thus, a harpsichord could be hired for a month at 15s., a quarter at £2 2s. and a year at £6 6s.; a piano-forte for a month at 10s. 6d., a quarter at £1 11s. 6d., and a year at £4 4s.; a guittar for a month at 5s., a quarter at 12s. and a year at £2 2s.

instruments made by London-based Longman and Broderip.[79] He gave benefit concerts in 1788 and 1791,[80] advertising that following 'a number of unforeseen misfortunes, [he] is much distress'd and involv'd in several small debts, and the promise of the concert will be appropriate towards the discharge of the same'.[81] He published his *Original Anecdotes of the late Duke of Kingston and Miss Chudleigh* in 1792, and in the 'Advertisement' to this book makes clear he was doing so 'as a means of adding to the little he now gets by his profession'.[82] In c.1792 he relocated to Bristol, where he died shortly after.[83]

In 1780, with Milgrove's business growing and Whitehead at the peak of his trade, Bath's commercial community saw the entrance of the most successful of all Bath's eighteenth-century music-shop owners and one who would remain in business for nearly forty years. James Lintern's shop was to become the model for Bath's music businesses in the early nineteenth century and it may be that his growing success contributed to Whitehead's business troubles.

❧ James Lintern (c.1755–1816)

James Lintern's business was a more prestigious enterprise than those which went before. In some respects, it followed the model set by Longman and Broderip in London, though on a more modest scale, in that its work encompassed many aspects of the trade, dealing in instruments and music, publishing, selling tickets and accommodating visiting musicians, and ultimately gaining a royal appointment.[84] Lintern's business was not initially propitious, since he went bankrupt in early 1781.[85] He cannot have been in business long at this time, since he was aged only 25.[86] An auction of his stock consisted of 'fine ton'd piano fortes by *Beck*, guittars, violins, tenors, basses, Germain flutes, and a great quantity of new and old music by the most eminent composers'; it also listed the disposal of his

---

[79] *Bath Journal*, 5 October 1787. Here Whitehead gives more prices for hiring his instruments by the week, month and year. He also offers to supply a 'Band of Horns and Clarionets, and Music for Balls'.

[80] *Bath Chronicle*, 15 May 1788.

[81] *Bath Journal*, 31 October 1791.

[82] Thomas Whitehead, *Original Anecdotes of the late Duke of Kingston and Miss Chudleigh* (London, 1792), p. iv. This book records how Whitehead had been promised a legacy of £200 in the duke's will, to be paid ten years after the duke's death. Whitehead had mortgaged the legacy for £150 on the failure of his music business but the duke's family obstructed the payment of the legacy leaving Whitehead financially stricken. Ibid., 176–9.

[83] *Bath Chronicle*, 17 October 1793.

[84] Jenny Nex, 'Longman and Broderip' in Michael Kassler (ed.), *The Music Trade in Georgian England* (Farnham, 2011), 9–93, at 10.

[85] *Ipswich Journal*, 13 January 1781. The Lintern family came from Twerton just outside of Bath and James's father Walter was a blacksmith in Twerton. James was one of at least five children born to Walter and his wife Hannah between 1755 and 1764. See Bath Record Office, Twerton parish registers.

[86] Bath Record Office, Twerton parish registers. James Lintern was baptised on 2 March 1755.

'Household Furniture, consisting of four-post and other beds, mahogany dining and tea tables, chairs, pitchers, pier looking glasses. Kitchen and other furniture'.[87] Despite bankruptcy,[88] Lintern had returned as a shop owner by October 1782 when his business was listed in an advertisement for Bath musician James Cantelo's (d.1804) *Twenty-five new Cotillons* (1782), having relocated from Stall Street to the Abbey Churchyard – a more advantageous location situated in the heart of Bath.[89]

Of all the advertised services available at Lintern's shop, the most extensively promoted was as a distributor of tickets to Bath concerts – especially performer-promoted benefit concerts, breakfast concerts or musical events at the pleasure gardens. Events that were not part of the regular series of subscription balls and concerts needed bespoke promotion and ticketing, which was administered through the music shops (including for some concerts outside Bath) and for which Lintern undoubtedly received commission.[90] By October 1784 Lintern had rebranded his shop as a 'Musick Warehouse',[91] indicating an enlargement or, at the very least, a statement of ambition. The nomenclatures 'music warehouse' and 'music repository' were increasingly adopted in London, Bath and elsewhere after 1785 to suggest a larger shop space with a wider variety of stock to peruse and purchase;[92] for example, John Johnson's shop in London, where James Longman served his apprenticeship, was styled a 'musick-warehouse'.[93] Lintern advertised a variety of keyboard, string and wind instruments (including reed and brass), under all sorts of terms – hire, outright purchase, part-exchange, and the sale and purchase of second-hand instruments. All instruments were warranted, could be trialled or exchanged, 'or the full money returned. Deducting the hire'.[94] The range of instruments and the flexibility of arrangements of hire or purchase remained a feature of Lintern's business, evident from a 1796 advertisement (Plate 8.1).

Having labelled his premises a 'warehouse', Lintern preceded this with the additional title 'Musick Library' from 1787.[95] Bath had a tradition of circulating libraries among its several booksellers, including that managed by James Leake in the 1720s; their lending stock typically included songbooks.[96] Lintern developed this idea in Bath specifically for music; it was the demand for song sheets that he aimed to satisfy on the principle that payment of a subscription

---

[87] *Bath Chronicle*, 8 February 1781.
[88] Ibid., 1 March 1781. Here a 'Certificate' of conformity was noted – presumably this allowed him to restart trading.
[89] *Bath Chronicle*, 31 October 1782. Cantelo's collection was printed in London 'for the author'.
[90] For example, Lintern offered tickets for the annual concert at Oakley Wood-house, near Cirencester. *Bath Chronicle*, 3 August 1786.
[91] *Bath Chronicle*, 14 October 1784.
[92] Banfield, *Music in the West Country*, 173–5.
[93] Nex, 'Longman and Broderip', 85.
[94] *Bath Chronicle*, 1 August 1793. Here Lintern is selling the instruments of 'a Gentleman' and, unusually, the advertisement gives each instrument's worth and the sale price.
[95] *Bath Chronicle*, 8 November 1787.
[96] Fawcett, *Bath Commercialis'd*, 8–9; Fawcett, *Bath Entertain'd*, 24–5; Alec Hyatt King, 'Music Circulating Libraries in Britain', *The Musical Times*, 119/1620 (1978), 134–8, at 135.

Plate 8.1 Lintern's Royal Appointment, *Bath Chronicle*, 24 November 1796.

would allow the customer to hold a limited number of items over an agreed time, but that they could be freely exchanged for other items without further cost. Lintern's claims were bold as to the extent of his stock: 'Every Musical Publication may be had at the above warehouse'.[97] That Lintern had a huge stock of music is suggested by the sale of 'a collection of some Thousands of New and Old songs' at half price,[98] and the admission that 'near a Thousand of the most favourite SONGS' were stolen from the shop counter in January 1790, for the return of which Lintern would pay two guineas reward.[99]

Lintern also promoted a number of teachers and performers from and through his shop, and, like Underwood, hosted exhibitions. In 1783 enquiries for a Mr Peck as a teacher of the organ, harpsichord and piano-forte could be left at the shop.[100] In 1788 a 'Mr Boynton, organist, [who] teaches pianoforte &

[97] *Bath Chronicle*, 8 November 1787.
[98] Ibid., 13 October 1785.
[99] Ibid., 14 January 1790.
[100] Ibid., 20 November 1783. There were several members of the Peck family of musicians working in Bath during this period, but this was probably Robert Peck (d.1795). See James, 'Concert Life in Eighteenth-Century Bath', ii, 865.

harpsichord, [could…] be heard at Lintern's music shop, Abbey Church Yard'.[101] The services of Philip Seybold, 'harp master', were advertised in the 1790s alongside the sale of a 'New harp'.[102] Ensembles of performers could also be hired through the shop: 'a party of the Principal Catch and Glee Singers will be ready to attend Publick or Private Parties on the shortest notice, by applying as above'.[103]

In addition, Lintern published small collections of popular dance tunes in easy versions for keyboard: for instance, *Ten Country Dances, and four Cotillions … for 1797*.[104] The arranger is not mentioned, and these modest publications were seasonal and linked to the current dances and tunes performed at the New Assembly Rooms. This kind of publication became particularly popular in the early nineteenth century and was an important staple for new music businesses after 1805.[105] Lintern certainly promoted local composers; an advertisement for 16 October 1788 lists only works by composers local to Bath.[106]

Despite the broad range of specialist music services that comprised James Lintern's business, he was not averse to selling non-musical goods. Lintern's shop acted as a hub of Bath's wider commercial life in its own right. For instance, Daniel Fellow sold gold and silver pens and portable inkstands there;[107] Miss Payne, a milliner from 'Dover St[reet] London, returned from Paris' was advertised as selling from Lintern's shop;[108] Signor Rovere offered drawing and painting lessons;[109] and paintings and miniatures by Mr Ogier were sold there.[110] It seems that Lintern was open to ad hoc business opportunities as and when they arose, including the renting out of apartments upstairs; in January 1790 they were rented to the Polish 'dwarf' Count Joseph Boruwlaski (1739–1837), the most celebrated performer of the day on the guittar.[111] Lintern's trade included the role of agent and distributor for the London firm of Thomas and William Maurice Cahusac and he jointly published dance music with them; for example, a collection of *Thirteen Favorite New Dances* (1800).[112] Lintern

---

[101] *Bath Chronicle*, 30 October 1788.
[102] Ibid., 25 November 1790, 29 December 1790 and 20 January 1791.
[103] Ibid., 31 December 1789.
[104] *Ten Country Dances, and four Cotillions … for 1797*, printed for and sold at J. and W. Lintern's Music Warehouse, Bath, listed in Frank Kidson, *British Music Publishers, Printers and Engravers* (London, 1900), 161.
[105] For example, Charles White and John David Loder. See Spring, 'The Musical Life of Bath', 38–9.
[106] *Bath Chronicle*, 16 October 1788. Composers mentioned are Henry Harington, James Brooks, Venanzio Rauzzini and John Ashley.
[107] *Bath Chronicle*, 14 December 1786.
[108] Ibid., 13 November 1788 and 4 December 1788.
[109] Ibid., 1 March 1792.
[110] *Bath Journal*, 12 January 1795.
[111] *Bath Chronicle*, 7 January 1790; *Memoirs of Count Joszef Boruwlaski* (Durham, 1820), 56.
[112] *Thirteen Favorite New Waltzes and Country Dances* (London, 1800), published by T. & W.M. Cahusac and J. & W. Lintern. For Thomas Cahusac, see Frank Kidson, 'Cahusac, Thomas (i)', *Grove Music Online*.

was also listed first in a long list of regional agents selling works for the music selling, publishing and instrument making firm of Longman, Clementi and Company in 1800.[113]

After entering into a partnership with his younger brother Walter (1760–1806) in 1789, James Lintern's business continued to prosper and was not significantly affected by the Bath banking collapse of March 1793; the brothers were among a list of leading Bath businessmen that pledged to continue to receive the cash notes drawn on the Bath banks that were failing.[114] The Linterns' success led to their royal appointment to the Duke of York, celebrated in print with the national anthem quoted on a treble stave (see Plate 8.1). The success of the Lintern family continued into the nineteenth century with James's nephew, George Packer, taking over the business in 1816.[115] However, the Linterns were not without competition, and two other musicians to try their luck with a music shop in Bath in the late eighteenth century were James Mathews and John Ashley.

James Mathews (1744–1821) and John Ashley (1760–1830)

James Mathews (also spelt Matthews) was a comic singer and a larger-than-life character with a number of commercial interests, including an inherited butchery business; however, his main interest was performing across Bath's venues.[116] In 1789 he promoted his own concerts, held at his 'New Music Warehouse in Market Street', from where he sold instruments, music,[117] and a 'full range' of accessories.[118] He additionally ran a music library where 'the company' could hire music.[119]

Mathews was additionally a concert promoter. One entertainment put on for Mathew's benefit, and which he organised, was based on selections from the hugely popular poem by Edward Young (poet, author, and later Dean of Salisbury, 1683–1765), 'Night Thoughts on Life, Death and Immortality'. It took place in February 1789 at the New Assembly Rooms under the direction of local

---

[113] David Rowland, 'Clementi's Music Business' in Kassler (ed.), *The Music Trade in Georgian England*, 125–57, at 131.
[114] *Bath Chronicle*, 14 March 1793.
[115] TNA, PROB, 11/1591/135, will of James Lintern of Bath, proved 11 April 1817.
[116] James, 'Concert Life in Eighteenth-Century Bath', ii, 805.
[117] Mathew's published music in collaboration with London music shops, for instance, the song, 'Tis Memory's Aid, A New Song by a Young Lady, the Words from Hayley, published for I Mathews, Music Seller, Milson Street, Bath', is printed on the reverse of a catalogue belonging to the London-based music dealer, William Gawler. Copy from the collection assembled by Simon D.I. Fleming, held at GB-DRu, Fleming 416.
[118] James, 'Concert Life in Eighteenth-Century Bath', ii, 808; *Bath Journal*, 7 December 1789.
[119] *Bath Chronicle*, 4 July 1799.

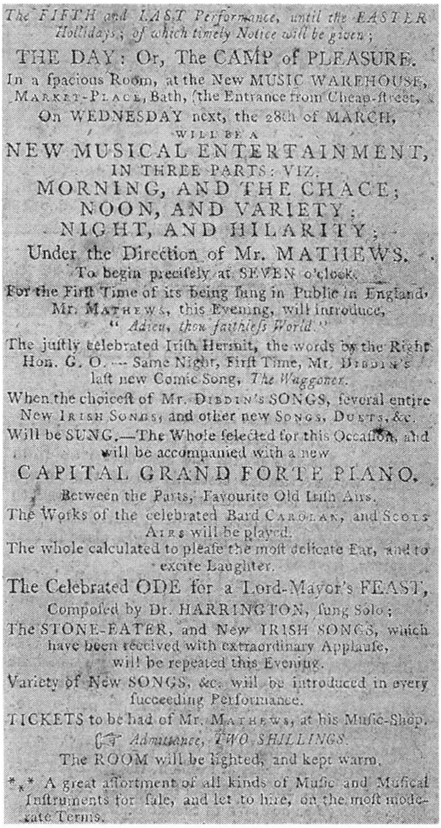
The FIFTH and LAST Performance, until the EASTER Hollidays; of which timely Notice will be given;

THE DAY: Or, The CAMP of PLEASURE.

In a ſpacious Room, at the New MUSIC WAREHOUSE, MARKET-PLACE, Bath, (the Entrance from Cheap-ſtreet,

On WEDNESDAY next, the 28th of MARCH,

WILL BE A

NEW MUSICAL ENTERTAINMENT,

IN THREE PARTS: VIZ.

MORNING, AND THE CHACE;

NOON, AND VARIETY;

NIGHT, AND HILARITY;

Under the Direction of Mr. MATHEWS.

To begin preciſely at SEVEN o'clock.

For the Firſt Time of its being ſung in Public in England, Mr. MATHEWS, this Evening, will introduce,

" *Adieu, thou faithleſs World.*"

The juſtly celebrated Iriſh Hermit, the words by the Right Hon. G. O. --- Same Night, Firſt Time, Mr. DIBDIN's laſt new Comic Song, *The Waggoner.*

When the choiceſt of Mr. DIBDIN's SONGS, ſeveral entire New IRISH SONGS, and other new SONGS, DUETS, &c. Will be SUNG.—The Whole ſelected for this Occaſion, and will be accompanied with a new

CAPITAL GRAND FORTE PIANO.

Between the Parts, Favourite Old Iriſh Airs, The Works of the celebrated Bard CAROLAN, and SCOTS AIRS will be played.

The whole calculated to pleaſe the moſt delicate Ear, and to excite Laughter.

The Celebrated ODE for a Lord-Mayor's FEAST,

Compoſed by Dr. HARRINGTON, ſung Solo;

The STONE-EATER, and New IRISH SONGS, which have been received with extraordinary Applauſe, will be repeated this Evening.

Variety of New SONGS, &c. will be introduced in every ſucceeding Performance.

TICKETS to be had of Mr. MATHEWS, at his Muſic-Shop.

☞ *Admittance, TWO SHILLINGS.*

The ROOM will be lighted, and kept warm.

*** A great aſſortment of all kinds of Muſic and Muſical Inſtruments for ſale, and let to hire, on the moſt moderate Terms.

PLATE 8.2 Advertisement for James Mathews' concert, 'The Day: Or, the Camp of Pleasure', *Bath Herald*, 24 March 1792.

pianist and singing teacher Thomas Billington.[120] In early 1792 Mathews went on to use his own premises as the venue for a series of themed entertainments, with a varied selection of solo and ensemble vocal music accompanied by the piano.[121] Titled "THE DAY, Or, The CAMP of PLEASURE', it was performed in 'a spacious Room' within his 'New MUSIC WAREHOUSE, Market-Place'. Mathews directed the shows and sold the tickets from his shop.[122] At two shillings, the tickets were inexpensive relative to most concerts (5s.) but most significantly they took place on the commercial premises: 'The ROOM will be lighted, and kept warm' (see Plate 8.2).[123] These entertainments and Mathews'

[120] Ibid., 5 February 1789; another was 'Duncan's Victory' of 1797 performed in the 'Great Room' of the Spring Gardens 'with Military Band in attendance', (*Bath Journal*, 13 November 1797). Billington was brother-in-law of the more famous Mrs Elizabeth Billington (née Weichsell), a favourite with Bath audiences in the 1780s and 90s. Edward Young's poem, *The Complaint: or Night-Thoughts* was written *c.*1742–45 and had a high reputation in the later eighteenth century. An illustrated version was produced by William Blake, and published in 1797. See James, 'Concert Life in Eighteenth-Century Bath', ii, 485–6.

[121] *Bath Herald*, 24 March 1792.

[122] Ibid.

[123] Ibid.

own comic songs were influenced by those developed by the hugely popular performer, mimic, and composer Charles Dibdin (1745–1814) who developed his celebrated comic one-man 'table entertainments' and toured them extensively.[124] Mathews had attempted unsuccessfully to develop a career in London in 1785-90, working with Dibdin with whom he sang at The Royal Circus and The Haymarket.[125]

The Ashleys were another well-established Bath musical family that diversified into a music business for a period in the late 1790s and maintained a shop until 1812. The business was established by John Ashley (c.1760–1830), a singer, oboist, bassoonist, piano teacher and composer of light and topical songs, some of which achieved a degree of popularity.[126] He dealt in instruments and music which he sold from his shop.[127] While his brother Joseph (another bassoonist) left Bath for London, James remained active as a musician in the town for some fifty years. His business was declared bankrupt in October 1814, but this did not prevent his continuation as a leading musician in Bath until well into the 1820s.[128]

Ashley and Mathews were primarily professional performers (and composers of light and comic songs) who operated commercial music businesses as a side line, in the tradition of Tylee. This is in contrast to the larger and more successful businesses of Underwood and Lintern, who were traders who diversified. In the middle we find Milgrove, who was able to maintain a dual focus on performance and trade – although, even for him, trade seems to have won out in his declining years.

Conclusion

Bath was unquestionably an important regional centre of the music trade in eighteenth century Britain. There was clearly a burgeoning trade in books at the start of the century, with the shops managed by Hammond and Leake dominating the trade. As in other regional centres, Bath's booksellers offered music books from at least the early eighteenth century. These general booksellers, drawing on demand, supplied music to visitors from communities around

---

[124] For recent scholarship on Dibdin, see John Franceschina, *The Musical Theatre of Charles Dibdin*, (Cambridge, 2024).

[125] James, 'Concert Life in Eighteenth-Century Bath', ii, 807; Charles Dibdin, *The Musical tour of Mr Dibdin; in which ... previous to his embarkation for India ... he finished his career as a public character* (Sheffield, 1788), 22.

[126] The online catalogue of popular songs that were published by John Ashley has over forty items. For instance, 'The poor orphan maid, a favorite ballad', written and composed by J. Ashley (London, 1805) and 'The celebrated Quakers song "My names's Obadiah" sung by Mr Edwin at the Theatres Royal, Bath and Bristol, pub/printed for the author, Bath c.1810'. See William Waterhouse, 'Ashley [of Bath], John', *Grove Music Online*.

[127] *Bath Journal*, 31 October 1796. See *Bath Directories* for 1800, 1805 and 1812.

[128] Ashley's bankruptcy was listed in *The Star*, 31 October 1814.

Bath and to short-stay members of 'the company'. More specialist music shops began to open in Bath from the 1740s onwards in line with the city's expansion and related increase in luxury consumption and desire for culture. Thomas Underwood established the first dedicated music shop in *c*.1740, with the sale, maintenance and hire of instruments his main concern during its early years. Seeing of an opportunity for profit, he upscaled his provision with the sale of sheet music and diversified into food stuffs and organising exhibition performances, for which there was clearly considerable demand. In all these activities he set a precedent that later music businesses followed.

In the 1760s and 70s there were, at times, three music shops in Bath, and owners like Tylee and Milgrove sought to combine their business ventures with a professional life as a Bath musician, a trend that continued into the next century. By the final decades of the eighteenth century, music and musical goods were available from specialised music shops and warehouses (centred around the Abbey and Market Place), but also from toyshops, as well as the homes of some individuals. Bath's increasing importance as a spa town facilitated the growth of the music business, with visitors looking to purchase tickets, hire instruments and sheet music, or engage the services of a teacher. The emphasis on the hire of music and instruments reflects the transient nature of Bath's elite clientele, with visitors typically remaining there for short periods of time. Indeed, the seasonality of Bath's musical activity encouraged businesses to diversify into unrelated areas of trade, such as the sale of consumables such as food and drink, along with pens and paintings. They also developed a trade with the surrounding towns and villages; in this regard, Bath was undoubtedly more of a regional hub than has previously been acknowledged.

Music was imported from London several times a week and most of the sheet music available in Bath was printed and published in the capital, though a certain amount was privately published for Bath's composers and music traders. Evidence also suggests that some music printing took place in the city, although this part of the trade remained small. In the absence of larger businesses printing music, shops instead supplied the latest dance music, as performed at the Assembly Room, in manuscript form.

This discussion of the commercial music trade in eighteenth-century Bath reveals that, if firms wished to be successful, they had to diversify and adapt in response to Bath's changing clientele, the desire for luxury consumption and the general shifting of the commercial landscape. The concept of the specialist music shop outside London and Edinburgh was still a relatively new phenomenon, but gradually the rather itinerant, seasonal nature of the music businesses of Underwood and Milgrove gave way to the larger and lavish 'music warehouses' of Mathews and Lintern. Bath reached its zenith as a spa resort for the wealthy in the second half of the eighteenth century and the music trade – as part of the fabric of this economy – kept pace with its development, and the ever-changing pursuit of leisure.

9

Thomas Bewick's Dealings with North-Eastern Musicians, 1770–1800

Roz Southey

Thomas Bewick (1753–1828) of Newcastle upon Tyne is familiar for his engravings of north-eastern wildlife and fauna. His best-known book, *A History of British Birds*, was first published in Newcastle upon Tyne in 1797.[1] What is perhaps less known is that Bewick was head of a business that provided more every-day items for local residents. In 1767, he was apprenticed to the engraver, Ralph Beilby (1744–1817), and became Beilby's partner in 1777, a partnership which lasted until 1797, after which Bewick set up on his own. The books connected with the partnership and Bewick's own business survive in the Tyne and Wear Archives (TWAM) in Newcastle;[2] these include ledgers, cash and purchase books, day and weekly workbooks, subscription and debt books, as well as letters to Bewick and members of his family in the early nineteenth century, and various miscellaneous papers relating both to the family and to the business. The records cover a period from 1752 – when Beilby ran the business and before Bewick became an apprentice – until well into the nineteenth century; customers included local gentry, shopkeepers and professional clients, for whom Bewick (or rather his apprentices, in most cases)[3] produced items such as visiting cards, seals, tickets for events, letter heads for tradesmen's bills, and other miscellaneous domestic items.

This study deals with the period from 1777 until the turn of the century, and with transactions with members of the musical community, both in the North-East and further afield. There are limitations to what can be deduced from the

---

[1] For an account of Bewick's life and work, see Jenny Uglow, *Nature's Engraver, A life of Thomas Bewick* (London, 2007). Bewick's *A History of British Birds* was published in two volumes – Land Birds in 1797 (printed by Sol. Hodgson) and Water Birds in 1804 (printed by Edward Walker), with a supplement in 1821. Thomas Ebdon, organist of Durham Cathedral, subscribed to the first volume.

[2] Under the catalogue number TWAM 1269/1–257.

[3] Bewick and Beilby are known to have had around thirty apprentices between them over a considerable number of years. Bewick was always eager to develop his apprentices' talents and to encourage them, and entrusted them with many commissions. Bewick said of Beilby: 'I think he was the best master in the world for teaching boys, for he obliged them to put their hands to every variety of work', Thomas Bewick, *A Memoir, written by himself* (Newcastle, 1862), 59.

records – they are, for instance, not always consistent in the information they record or in their terminology, and are sometimes vague or cryptic; nevertheless, they can complement information from other sources and throw new light on musical activities in North-East England. Even more importantly, they allow a behind-the-scenes glimpse of practical aspects of professional musicians' lives, showing how a non-musical trade could provide an essential service to musicians in a crucial and often overlooked aspect of their work – the critical task of marketing themselves and their music.

❧ *Thomas Bewick and Music*

Bewick's own tastes in music ran to the vernacular. He remembered with fondness the days when Newcastle's streets rang with the songs of ballad singers, regretting the change in political circumstances which had seen the singers' suppression;[4] he talked of the 'exhilarating, wild notes of the Northumbrian pipes',[5] although he admitted that he preferred vocal music to instrumental.[6] His opinion of art music was scathing: 'I have ever been much disgusted to hear and see these spoiled performers, quavering and spinning out with unnatural falsetto voices until almost spent. … I could never sit to hear any of them; as it appeared to me to be anything but music, or music run mad'.[7] He called people who liked this kind of music 'coxcombical connoisseurs and a vitiated, aping public';[8] even the more popularly-based music of the theatre did not appeal to him.[9]

He endeavoured to pass on his love of vernacular music to his son, Robert, and encouraged him to learn the Northumbrian pipes, hiring as his teacher the former wait, John Peacock; Peacock was the preeminent player of the pipes at the time, modifying the instrument by adding extra notes and writing down many local tunes in a book published in 1801.[10] In his *Memoir*, Bewick described Peacock as 'our inimitable performer', admiring 'his old tunes, his lilts, his pauses, and his variations' and talked of encouraging him to teach as many pupils as possible, to ensure the music did not die. Peacock taught Robert for at least two years, 1798–1799. Bewick also hired another former wait, John Aldridge, to teach Robert, although it is not clear precisely the subject of the lessons.[11]

---

[4] Ibid., 60: 'During times of war, ballad singers and their often iconoclastic songs tended to be seen as subversive and dangerous'.
[5] Ibid., 81.
[6] Ibid., 131.
[7] Ibid.
[8] Ibid.
[9] Ibid.
[10] John Peacock, *A favourite Collection of tunes with variations adapted for the Northumbrian pipes, violin or flute* (Newcastle, 1801). Peacock was a rare example in the area in playing both traditional music and art music, being part of the local concert band – although it is not clear which instrument he played in the band.
[11] TWAM 1269/5, Cash books.

But business was business and Bewick's customers included representatives of almost every section of the musical community in the area, whether he liked their productions or not: waits and organists; sellers of music (both in bookshops and in music-shops); dancing masters; actors and theatrical musicians; members of the musical personnel – both singers and organists – from Durham Cathedral; and even a circus manager. The list of musicians who found Bewick's services useful or even indispensable is long and extensive (see Table 9.1). Most came from Newcastle or were based in the town (26 customers out of 38), or towns in the surrounding area such as Gateshead, Durham and Sunderland (a further 9 customers), but two came from further afield: from Hull (Mr Southern, a dancing master),[12] and Beverley (George Lambert, organist of the minster) in Yorkshire. It is not clear why these non-local musicians chose to employ Bewick; Lambert certainly had Newcastle links, subscribing to *Six Songs* by Newcastle composer, Thomas Wright, in the mid to late 1780s, and may well have known Matthias Hawdon, his predecessor at Beverley Minster, who was a customer of Bewick. A third musician who initially appears to have been from outside the region, Robert Barber from Manchester, was a native of Newcastle and had originally used Bewick's services while resident there.

Four local musical organisations are also known to have employed Bewick: the Musical Societies of Newcastle and Sunderland; the gentlemen who organised subscription concerts in the town of Morpeth, north of Newcastle; and the Newcastle Volunteer Band. Two local gentlemen's societies who held or sponsored concerts from time to time – the Freemasons, and the Gentlemen of the Forest Hunt – also used Bewick's services. The Newcastle Volunteer Band had been started, and was run, by composer Thomas Wright, who held the post of organist of St Andrew's church in Newcastle and was the foremost promoter of concerts in Newcastle in the 1790s. Wright organised concerts for his own benefit, for the benefit of the Volunteer Band, and for the benefit of another band which he ran, the Armed Association Band; he may have been involved in other musical organisations as well. There may have also been other transactions that involved musical bodies if individuals organising their affairs conducted business with Bewick under their own names, rather than that of the organisation they represented.

TABLE 9.1 Musicians listed in Bewick's records.

Name	Profession	Residence	Dates in Bewick's records
Individual musicians			
John Aldridge	Wait	Newcastle	1798, 1799
Joseph Austin	Comedian [actor]	Newcastle	1773, 1778, 1787
Charles Avison jnr	Organist, concert promoter	Newcastle	1782, 1783, 1785, 1787, 1788, 1789, 1792, 1793

[12] Little is known of Southern – he may in fact be the Mr Southeran, a dancing master in Wakefield, whose marriage was noted in newspapers in July 1789. *Cumberland Pacquet*, 8 July 1789; *Sheffield Register*, 4 July 1789.

THOMAS BEWICK'S DEALINGS WITH NORTH-EASTERN MUSICIANS 171

Name	Profession	Residence	Dates in Bewick's records
Edward Ayrton	Organist	Gateshead	1789
John Banks	Dancing master	Newcastle	1794, 1802, 1804
Joseph Barber	Book and music seller	Newcastle	1771, 1774
Robert Barber[13]	Organist, composer, concert promoter	Newcastle/ Manchester	1773, 1783, 1788, 1789, 1790, 1792
James Cawdell	Theatre manager	Durham	1785
John Donaldson	Organ-builder and clockmaker	Newcastle	1781
Thomas Ebdon	Organist, composer, concert promoter	Durham	1773, 1775, 1797
Ivy Greg	Dancing master	Newcastle	1777, 1778
William Gregg	Dancing master	Newcastle	1784, 1788
Matthias Hawdon	Organist, composer, concert promoter	Newcastle	1777, 1779, 1780, 1781, 1783, 1784, 1785, 1787, 1788
Thomas Hawdon[14]	Organist, concert promoter	Newcastle	1780, 1802
John Hawthorn	Watchmaker, music seller, wait	Newcastle	1771, 1777
Humphries	Circus manager	Newcastle	1790, 1794
Adam and Alexander Kinlock	Dancing masters	Newcastle	1780, 1782, 1784, 1785, 1786, 1787, 1788, 1789, 1790, 1791, 1793, 1794, 1795, 1796, 1797, 1798, 1799, 1800, 1804
Mrs Mapples	Comedian	Newcastle	1781
La Mask	Comedian	[passing through Newcastle]	1793
G. Lambert	Organist	Beverley	1778
Edward Meredith	Singer	Durham	1780, 1787, 1788, 1789, 1790, 1791
Charles Munden	Theatre manager	Newcastle	1789
Nevions	Comedian	[passing through Newcastle]	1793
Nuns	Comedian	[passing through Newcastle]	1781

[13] Son of Joseph Barber.
[14] Son of Matthias Hawdon.

Name	Profession	Residence	Dates in Bewick's records
John Peacock	Wait	Newcastle	1798, 1799
Andrew Picken	Dancing master	North Shields	1777
John Simpson	Music teacher, tuner, organist	Newcastle	1777
Christopher Smith	Musician at theatre company	Newcastle	1774, 1778
Southern	Organist	Hull	1778
Sutton	Circus	Newcastle	1794
John Thompson	Breeches maker, wait	Sunderland	1774, 1779, 1780, 1782, 1795
Thomas Thompson[15]	Organist, teacher, concert promoter, composer	Newcastle	1794, 1796, 1799, 1800, 1802
Charles Edward Whitlock	Theatre manager	Newcastle	1785, 1786, 1787, 1788, 1789, 1790
Thomas Wright	Composer, concert promoter	Newcastle	1778, 1793, 1794, 1795, 1796, 1797, 1800
William Wright	Music-shop owner, composer	Newcastle	1800
Bodies and organisations			
Gentlemen of the Forest Hunt		Newcastle	1777
Morpeth concert organisers		Morpeth	1785
Newcastle Musical Society		Newcastle	1780, 1781
Newcastle Volunteer Band		Newcastle	1801
St George's Lodge of Freemasons		Sunderland	1778
Sunderland Musical Society		Sunderland	1777, 1779

Some of these customers, such as Andrew Picken, a dancing master in North Shields, only had dealings with Bewick once; this may be because they did not often need engraving services, because they could not afford Bewick's prices or, in the case of musicians from some distance, that there were other

---

[15] Son of John Thompson.

engravers closer to hand. There is also the possibility that some of these customers engaged Bewick for a one-off special occasion, to add to an event's prestige. Three customers, associated with touring theatre companies or the circus, were in the area for only a short time and naturally had limited dealings with Bewick. Others, however, came back repeatedly. Adam Kinlock was a Scotsman who settled in Newcastle in the 1780s and became the town's best-known and most successful dancing master of the period; he trained up his son, Alexander, who set up on his own before inheriting his father's dancing school after Adam's early death in 1799.[16] It is not always possible to be certain whether Bewick's records are referring to the father or the son – the books usually refer merely to a 'Mr Kinlock' – but between 1780 and 1800, Bewick fulfilled orders for one or the other of them almost every year.[17]

Services provided by Bewick

Despite being known principally for the intricate and delicate engravings of wildlife which illustrated his books, much of Bewick's income came from much smaller everyday tasks. Bewick undoubtedly learnt the importance of these miscellaneous orders from his master, Ralph Beilby, who would take on any engraving task, no matter how small.

> He undertook everything, which he did in the best way he could. ... This readiness brought him in an overflow of work, and the work-place was filled with the coarsest kind of steel stamps, pipe moulds, bottle moulds, brass clock faces, door plates, coffin plates, bookbinders [sic] letters and stamps, steel, silver, and gold seals, mourning rings, &c. He also undertook the engraving of arms, crests and cyphers, on silver, and every kind of job from the silversmiths; also engraving bills of exchange, bank notes, invoices, account heads, and cards.[18]

Visiting cards were the most common requirement for almost all Bewick's customers.[19] For musicians, visiting cards were a form of publicity, invaluable to

---

[16] For a brief biography of the Kinlocks, see Roz Southey, *Music-Making in North-East England during the Eighteenth Century* (Aldershot, 2006), 214.

[17] The elder Kinlock, Adam, died in an accident in 1799 and his son took over the dancing school; orders from that period onwards, therefore, were definitely placed by the son.

[18] Bewick, *A Memoir*, 58.

[19] Bewick also printed playing cards, usually for use in the card assemblies which accompanied music assemblies and other events. The accounts, however, do not always make clear which cards are being referred to. In some cases, however, the cards are referred to as being in packs and the purchase refers to distinct numbers of packs; these would seem to be playing cards. References elsewhere simply to an overall number of cards, for example 200, 500, etc, would seem to be references to visiting cards. In addition, concert promoters in the area did not hold card assemblies at the same time as their concerts, or, as far as can be discerned, have any association with the formal card assemblies. It is unlikely, therefore, that they would purchase such things except for private use.

tradesmen expected to pay personal visits to any gentleman or lady they hoped to interest in tickets for concerts or subscriptions to publications. Cards were sold by the pack – the number of cards in a pack is not recorded – and came in two sizes: the normal variety and large (exact dimensions are not given). Prices for packs varied according to the quality of card used and the complexity of the design; the customer paid for the engraving of a plate (usually between 7s. 6d. and 15s.), and then for the packs which were printed from the plate (usually between 6d. and 1s. a pack). The plates could be kept and reused; many orders refer to the printing of packs from a pre-existing plate. Most cards were printed in black but for a slightly higher price, a customer could obtain coloured cards, red being particularly popular. Printing in colour also applied to tickets for events (see below): the Kinlocks seem to have favoured regularly changing the colour of the tickets for their yearly balls, using, for instance, green in 1784, red in 1786, brown in 1788 and blue in 1790, perhaps in an attempt to avoid attendees trying to use outdated tickets.[20] They also sometimes used different colours for cards as well – green in 1784, for instance.[21]

Another essential publicity item was the door-plate, for which Bewick charged the relatively small sum of 5s. Musicians often taught in their own homes; in an age when the modern system of numbered addresses was not in use, a door plate with name and profession on it therefore enabled someone to be easily found. At least three Newcastle musicians paid Bewick for such a plate. Matthias Hawdon, organist of St Nicholas, principal concert promoter in the town in the 1780s, and one of Bewick's most frequent customers, ordered a doorplate in 1777;[22] Thomas Wright ordered one in 1778.[23] Wright's inclusion in Bewick's records at this point is informative as he was not a native of Newcastle and the precise timing of his arrival in the town is unknown; the first certain recorded reference to him otherwise is in an advertisement for a performance at the theatre in April 1784.[24] He was a musician with Stephen Kemble's theatre company; that company had originally been peripatetic but decided to make Newcastle its permanent base when the new Theatre Royal was opened there in 1778 – exactly the moment at which Wright ordered the door plate, implying that he too had decided to settle permanently in the town.[25] It appears to have

[20] TWAM 1269/13, Day book: 24 March 1784, 15 April 1786, 22 March 1788 and 27 April 1790. The colour continued to change regularly throughout the 1790s. A case of cheating by attempting to reuse old tickets is recorded in 1750 in the books of the Edinburgh Musical Society, when two gentlemen were accusing of altering the date on tickets. Edinburgh, Public Library, qYML 28 MS, Edinburgh Musical Society, Sederunt (Minute) books, ii, 18. Quoted in Jennifer Macleod, 'The Edinburgh Musical Society: Its Membership and Repertoire, 1728–1797' (PhD dissertation, University of Edinburgh, 2001) 71–2.
[21] TWAM 1269/13, Day book, 27 March 1784.
[22] TWAM 1269/12, Day book, 22 October 1777.
[23] TWAM 1269/1, Cash book, 21 October 1778.
[24] *Newcastle Courant*, 21 March 1784; *Newcastle Chronicle*, 27 March 1784.
[25] For most of the eighteenth century, theatre companies in the North-East were peripatetic, touring a considerable portion of the north. By the last decades of the

been common practice for musicians to have a plate produced for their door as soon as they arrived in a new place.[26]

The third customer who bought a plate from Bewick was John Simpson. Little is known of Simpson's early history; he was a native of Newcastle and held a benefit concert in the town in June 1775, probably as an advertisement for a small teaching practice[27] – he also advertised that he had musical instruments for sale, a common practice with music teachers.[28] His principal source of income, however, seems to have been from tuning; he was prepared to travel a considerable distance to tune instruments, which was not the case for other musicians in town, and he therefore obtained a great deal of patronage amongst the ladies and gentlemen with country houses.[29] In September 1777, however, he was appointed organist of St John's church,[30] and immediately ordered his door plate from Bewick – it was in effect an acknowledgement of his taking a step up in the world in becoming a salaried musician.

Bewick's company also engraved another item essential for any business: letterheads and bills. John Hawthorn, who conducted business at the top of the winding steep hill called the Side, was principally a watchmaker but also served as a wait. His shop sold a great deal of music which he advertised in local newspapers twice a year.[31] In 1771, Hawthorn ordered a 'steel block', which was described as being 'with Fiddles';[32] this cost him 1s. 6d. and was almost certainly the engraving for a letterhead. The cost was similar to that paid three years later by the Newcastle book- and music-seller, Joseph Barber of Amen Corner behind St Nicholas's church, when he ordered an engraving to be used as a book plate for volumes in his circulating library, and which included music.[33] One slightly enigmatic entry suggests that Bewick also designed, or at least altered, the masthead on organist Thomas Thompson's bills (see below).[34] On slightly different lines, the Sunderland Musical Society asked for a medal, although it is not clear what the medal was used for; it cost 15s.[35]

---

century, however, the company, under the management of Stephen Kemble, settled in Newcastle. Southey, *Music-Making in North-East England*, 47–8.

[26] Hawdon was a native of Newcastle but had been resident in Yorkshire since 1751; Wright's origins are unknown but he was probably from Yorkshire.

[27] *Newcastle Courant*, 17 June 1775.

[28] Ibid., 25 March 1797.

[29] Ibid., 17 June 1775.

[30] TWAM 1269/12, Day book, 22 October 1777; *Newcastle Courant*, 27 September 1777.

[31] For Hawthorn's business, see Roz Southey, 'John Hawthorn's shop at the Head of the Side, near the Post Office', in Colin Coleman and Katharine Hogg (eds), *A Handbook for Studies in 18th-Century English Music*, 24 (2020), 1–44.

[32] TWAM 1269/11, Day book, 8 November 1771.

[33] Ibid., 1 March 1774.

[34] TWAM 1269/22, Ledger, 26 October 1780.

[35] TWAM 1269/1, Cash book, 18 September 1777. In addition to these strictly musical services, Bewick often engraved domestic items for his musical customers. In 1780, he engraved a name on a dog collar for Matthias Hawdon and at nearly the same period, engraved animals on coat buttons for a Sunderland musician.

There were also several other items which, while not strictly musical in themselves, could be employed in a musician's daily life. Bewick enjoyed a considerable trade in seals, for instance, which were a common everyday necessity for anyone who wanted to write a letter, but could also be a kind of minor advertisement when made distinctive by the use of initials. Bewick made a steel seal for Hawdon with a cypher (probably Hawdon's initials intertwined), which cost him 7s. 6d.; four other musicians also ordered seals, including Thomas Ebdon, organist of Durham Cathedral, With prices between 6s. 6d. and 9s. 6d.[36] Likewise, Bewick's frequent provision of engraved cutlery for musicians may have been related only to domestic matters, perhaps owing to a feeling on the part of the purchaser that he had attained a certain status in society, but in some cases the cutlery may also have been used in professional life. In 1802, for example, Alexander Kinlock had a miscellaneous selection of cutlery and other items engraved with his monogram: four tablespoons, six teaspoons and tongs, five salt shovels, a mustard pot, a cream pot and six tea pots. Kinlock married about this time so the cutlery may have been part of his preparations for married life; the purchase of six tea pots, however, seems rather more than one household would need and suggests that some may have used by pupils or Kinlock's relations.[37] Kinlock also asked Bewick for a plate to label his trunk, paying 1s. 6d. for it in 1793.[38] As dancing masters were still accustomed to travelling extensively from town to town to set up temporary dancing schools, this trunk too, and the purchase from Bewick, may have been needed in a professional context.

❧ Bewick's Tickets and the Case of Matthias Hawson

The most significant expense for many of Bewick's musical customers was the printing of tickets for concerts and similar events. One of these tickets survives in the back pocket of a diary for 1777, which Bewick took with him on a walking trip to the Lakes. The credit-card sized ticket has an elaborate border of cherubs, musical instruments and greenery surrounding the word SUBSCRIPTION, followed by 'No. –' and a space presumably for the addition of a name or ticket number. If it dates from the year of the diary and was for Newcastle, it must have been for Matthias Hawdon, newly returned to his native town from Yorkshire – an order which might refer to this very ticket survives in Bewick's accounts for 13 November 1777.[39] Alternatively, the ticket may have been intended for the Durham organist Thomas Ebdon who was also organiser of the subscription series there. It had almost certainly been engraved on copper and has Ralph Beilby's name flourished in one corner, but was probably never used: the word 'subscription' had been misspelt and the 'c' omitted.[40]

---

[36] TWAM 1269/12, Day book, 12 June 1773.
[37] TWAM 1269/14, Day book, 24 April 1802.
[38] Ibid., 21 October 1793.
[39] TWAM 1269/12, Day book, 13 November 1777.
[40] Newcastle, City Library, Bewick Collection, 446, *Ladies Journal* (1777).

PLATE 9.1 A concert ticket in the Bewick Collection, Newcastle.

The printing of tickets as recorded in Bewick's accounts not only illustrates support services for musicians but also helps throw new light on musical life and institutions in the town, supplementing often scanty evidence from local newspapers. For instance, the books record that the Newcastle Musical Society ordered tickets on five separate occasions between 1779 and 1781.[41] The Society is a shadowy organisation – there is little indication as to its activities, and the evidence which does exist is contradictory.[42] It has long been known that members played privately for their own pleasure but Bewick's records constitute the only direct evidence that they also held public concerts. Their orders for tickets were in midsummer (usually late July), and in autumn (October/November); the Society's summer concerts may have been held in Race or Assize Week when the town would be crowded with visitors. These concerts may have been a benefit for a professional musician employed by the Society; a decent turn-out was expected as the Society ordered 100 tickets on each occasion.

The information provided by Bewick's accounts and their recording of ticket orders is probably most significant in the case of Matthias Hawdon, the organist of St Nicholas's church. Hawdon ran concerts in Newcastle during the latter half of the 1770s and the first half of the 1780s, and was one of Bewick's longest-lasting customers, buying tickets over a ten-year period from 1777 to 1787. Most of what we know about Hawdon's concerts comes from advertisements in

---

[41] TWAM 1269/12, Day book, 2 October, 1779, 19 July and 29 November 1780, 25 July and 10 November 1781.

[42] See Southey, *Music-Making in North-East England*, 79–81 for details of musical societies in the North-East.

local newspapers and very occasional reviews, providing a sparse account of his activities; comparing Bewick's accounts with the newspaper reports, however, fleshes out this information considerably and reveals the truth behind some of Hawdon's bland statements aimed for public consumption.

Hawdon had been a pupil of Newcastle's best-known musician of the period, Charles Avison; his first post was as organist of Holy Trinity, Hull, in 1751, from where he moved to Beverley Minster in 1767.[43] After the death of Avison in 1770, the post of organist at St Nicholas's church (and, by virtue of that position, principal concert promoter in Newcastle) was taken over by Avison's elder son, Edward, but the latter died early in 1776. Hawdon applied for, and obtained, the job. He may not fully have realised the situation in his hometown. He had considerable experience in organising concerts in Yorkshire but he came back to a town in which public concert-giving was at a low ebb. Public music-making had collapsed almost entirely in Newcastle in the wake of Charles Avison's death in 1770 when it became apparent that it had been only his personal influence keeping the subscription series going. Attempts to continue it by his son were hampered by illness and lack of public interest. It is not known to what extent Hawdon was aware of the problems when he returned to Newcastle but his purchases from Bewick indicate the ups and downs of his attempts to keep public music-making and, in particular, the subscription concert series afloat (see Table 9.2).

In November 1777, Hawdon mounted his first subscription series in the town, offering six concerts with the assistance of the choir from Durham Cathedral and 'a numerous band of performers'. The *Newcastle Courant* commented on the first of the series that there had been 'a polite company' of nearly 500 music-lovers;[44] it was for this series that the surviving subscription ticket was probably intended. Unfortunately, Bewick records only the engraving of a plate for the ticket and does not indicate how many tickets were ordered;[45] in 1779, however, the accounts do record that Hawdon ordered 200 subscription tickets for the series of that year. If he had ordered a similar number the previous year, the newspaper review was probably an exaggeration; each ticket did admit one gentleman or two ladies, but that would only allow for a maximum of 400 people – in addition, to get anywhere near 500 people, the audience must have been overwhelmingly female. However, anyone who wished only to attend an individual concert – a visitor to the town, for instance – could have turned up at the door and obtained a 'nightly' ticket, which would possibly have increased the audience size at individual concerts. This might not have required a printed ticket – anyone paying the cost at the door may simply have received a receipt in exchange; however, on at least one occasion (see below) Hawdon did indeed have tickets printed for this eventuality.

In any case, to order 200 tickets seems rather optimistic – Charles Avison had once commented that the series had never attracted more than 140

---

[43] Ibid., 210.
[44] *Newcastle Courant*, 22 November 1777.
[45] TWAM 1269/12, Day book, 13 November 1777.

subscribers even in its heyday.[46] If the newspaper reports were anywhere near correct, the large number attending the 1777 and 1778 concerts may have been owing to the novelty of a revived series and a new promoter.[47] This does not seem to have lasted and numbers of attendees appear to have dwindled dramatically as the novelty wore off: in 1780, Hawdon ordered only 50 for the mid-year Assize Week Concert which would normally have been expected to attract a much larger audience than the subscription series – which contrarily seems unduly pessimistic.[48] However, such mid-year concerts may have attracted a far higher proportion of people simply turning up on the night, rather than buying a ticket in advance; no newspaper reports survive to indicate either way.

It seems that Hawdon may have been feeling his way by trial and error. Certainly in 1780, he appears to have been trying to promote the subscription series more effectively by hiring an added attraction in the form of a known and admired vocal soloist, Miss Harwood from Lancashire.[49] To showcase her charms and abilities and to allow music-lovers to judge whether she was worth the cost of a subscription ticket, he took the precaution of holding a pre-series concert;[50] her reception must have been encouraging as he once more ordered 200 tickets from Bewick, splashing out a little by ordering 150 of the tickets in the more expensive red.[51] However, when it came to Miss Harwood's benefit at the end of the series in January 1781, Hawdon asked for only 100 tickets, suggesting that the series, and Miss Harwood, had not been as popular as he had hoped.[52] It seems that Hawdon may have once more been over-optimistic.

Whatever disappointment this series caused must, however, have been dissipated by a series of oratorios Hawdon promoted at Easter 1781.[53] Newcastle did not have a history of liking oratorios – before Hawdon's return there had been only one other recorded complete performance of an oratorio in the town, and the fact that it was never repeated suggests it had not been popular.[54] But in Yorkshire, where Hawdon had lived and worked so long, oratorios were immensely popular,[55] and he had no hesitation in promoting a small festival in Newcastle in 1778, only two years after his return.[56] This was obviously successful enough to tempt him to do another. In 1781, he offered a three-day festival with *Messiah* and *Judas Maccabaeus* the prime attractions, for which

---

[46] *Newcastle Journal*, 4–11 November 1758.
[47] Ibid.
[48] TWAM 1269/12, Day book, 14 August 1780. 'This week the Assemblies and Concert have been very crowded, and the town has been honoured with a numerous and genteel company', *Newcastle Courant*, 19 August 1780.
[49] *Newcastle Courant*, 14 October 1780.
[50] Ibid., 21 October 1780.
[51] TWAM 1269/12, Day book, 29 November 1780.
[52] Ibid., 24 January 1781.
[53] *Newcastle Courant*, 17 March 1781.
[54] Ibid., 1 September 1763.
[55] See Southey, *Music-Making in North-East England*, 131–33 for Hawdon's experiences with oratorios in Yorkshire.
[56] *Newcastle Chronicle*, 15 August 1778.

he hired a number of high-quality performers, including Miss Harwood and two of the most popular singing-men from Durham Cathedral, tenor William Evance and bass Edward Meredith, in addition to the celebrated chorus singers from Hay and Shaw Chapel in Lancashire, and Robert Jobson, a well-known violinist from Leeds. No expense was spared: the performances were accompanied with trumpets, French horns and kettle drums, none of which were instruments commonly heard in Newcastle or played by local musicians.[57] For this festival, Hawdon ordered 500 tickets from Bewick, although he did opt for the cheapest variety printed in black.[58] Only one week later, he went back and ordered another 250 tickets and only ten days after that, in the last week before the performances, he ordered another 200.[59]

Yet that seems to have been the high point of Hawdon's time in Newcastle. For the next subscription concert in January 1782, he had to apologize in local papers for confining the subscribers to the small Assembly room – he had done so, he said, because of the cold weather and 'the smallness of the number of Subscribers'.[60] No evidence survives in Bewick's accounts to show how many tickets Hawdon had ordered for this series, but for the series the following year (1783) he ordered only 50, suggesting that the number of subscribers was indeed small, although he had also had printed 50 tickets for people who did not subscribe but expected to be able to buy a ticket at the door – it is impossible to say how many people turned up for these 'nightly tickets' and the number would in any case have been dependent on the weather. This was a great come down from his optimism of only a few years earlier when he had anticipated 200 subscribers. He also cut his expenses in 1783 by having an old ticket plate altered rather than buying a new one.[61]

Bewick does not record any purchases of tickets by Hawdon between 1783 and 1784, even though Hawdon collaborated with Thomas Ebdon of Durham on a Newcastle subscription series in early 1784 and an oratorio performance in January 1785.[62] Hawdon then ordered 100 tickets for his concert in Assize Week in July 1785 – typically, he spent more than he strictly needed to, ordering the tickets to be printed in red.[63] The *Newcastle Chronicle* commented that 'the assemblies and concert this week have been uncommonly numerous and splendid'.[64] But in December that year Hawdon advertised that he would not hold a winter subscription series, citing ill health and the lack of support he had received: 'the support', he wrote, 'has not of late been any way adequate to

---

[57] *Newcastle Courant*, 17 March 1781. On the rare occasions this kind of instrument was heard in Newcastle, performers were usually recruited from military bands belonging to regiments quartered in Tynemouth.

[58] TWAM 1269/12, Day book, 24 March 1781.

[59] Ibid., 31 March and 9 April 1781.

[60] *Newcastle Courant*, 12 January 1782.

[61] TWAM 1269/12, Day book, 9 January 1783.

[62] *Newcastle Courant*, 17 January 1784 and 22 January 1785. Nor does any record survive for an order in Ebdon's name for these concerts.

[63] TWAM 1269/13, Day book, 18 July 1785.

[64] *Newcastle Chronicle*, 30 July 1785.

the expence'.[65] Local newspapers record that he held only three more concerts, all for his own benefit: in February 1787, August 1787, and in Assize Week 1788.[66] The August concert in 1787 earned a very short review in the *Newcastle Courant*, which said that it had been 'honoured with a numerous and brilliant company',[67] but Bewick's accounts show that he had only ordered 50 tickets (in red), so the review may be exaggerated or the audience swollen by purchases of tickets on the door.[68] The following year, Hawdon was more optimistic about his chances of attracting a large audience and had 200 tickets printed, ordering a cheap plate at 5s., but making up for the economy by printing the tickets in red.[69] He may have known in advance of the visit to the town of the Duke and Duchess of Northumberland; they certainly attended his concert and no doubt brought with them many of their friends and social hangers-on.[70] Although it is impossible to be certain how many people bought tickets at the door for either of these two latter concerts, it is clear that in 1787 Hawdon was anticipating that most people attending the concert would make the decision on the night, weighing up the concert's attractions against other competing events, but that in 1788, because of the attendance of the Duke and Duchess, he judged that more people would wish to secure a ticket in advance.

In fact, Bewick's accounts show that throughout this period Hawdon had been in severe financial straits; only four months after that triumph with the Easter oratorios, the books record Hawdon's bankruptcy.[71] Almost certainly, the income from the oratorios – good though it obviously was – had been exceeded by expenditure. Hawdon's debts to Bewick amounted to £4 7s. 6d., which was to be paid in five annual payments of 17s. 6d. but there were other creditors as well, and Bewick records that Hawdon had been forced to agree that £60 of his annual income be set aside every year to pay off his debts, suggesting that the total was around £300 – a serious sum.[72] Hawdon was still buying tickets and visiting cards from Bewick between 1781 and 1785, and it is not clear whether these costs were added to his existing debts or whether Bewick demanded

---

[65] *Newcastle Courant*, 3 December 1785.
[66] Ibid., 3 February 1787 and 12 July 1788.
[67] Ibid., 11 August 1787.
[68] TWAM 1269/13, Day book, 11 August 1787: As noted previously, each ticket usually admitted one gentleman or two ladies to the concert but even if only ladies had attended there could not have been more than 100 in the audience, and it is highly unlikely that there were no gentlemen at all. There is no record of nightly tickets being printed for the event.
[69] TWAM 1269/13, Day book, 19 July 1788.
[70] *Newcastle Courant*, 26 July 1788.
[71] TWAM 1269/22, Ledger, 28 July 1781.
[72] The £60 to be set aside amounted to Hawdon's entire salary as organist of St Nicholas's Church, plus income from such activities as teaching. Given Hawdon's failing health, his teaching practice must have been a struggle at this time too and in 1788, his son, Thomas, who had been working as organist in Hull, returned home to help support his father. *Newcastle Courant*, 29 November 1788. Matthias Hawdon died in March 1789. Ibid., 21 March 1789.

payment on receipt of the goods. Bewick did not receive the last of the money Hawdon owed him until 1787.[73]

There were certainly concerts for which organisers ordered substantial numbers of tickets: the gentlemen who ran the Morpeth subscription series, for instance, ordered 200 tickets for the 1786 series.[74] But most of Bewick's customers who wanted tickets for concerts in Newcastle and the North-East, like Hawdon, ordered small numbers – it was clearly a minority interest. In November 1780, the Newcastle Musical Society expected to sell no more than 100 tickets for their concert;[75] even Edward Meredith, a singing man from Durham Cathedral whose popularity in the region in the 1780s was such that Matthias Hawdon once felt obliged to apologise for his absence,[76] ordered only 100 tickets for his benefit in early 1787 at the height of his popularity.[77] (Meredith was the regular soloist in the Morpeth concert, which may account for the gentlemen's optimism as to the number of tickets they could sell.)[78] Charles Avison jnr, the younger son of the composer, also had only 100 tickets printed in March 1787, although in July of the same year, he ordered 200 for an event of which a record does not survive; Avison was one of the musicians in the local theatre company and may have been having a benefit there, consisting of plays, which would attract a larger audience.[79] Thomas Wright ordered only 60 tickets for his subscription series in January 1794.[80]

Special occasions, and special efforts, could, however, attract a larger audience. Thomas Thompson, son of the breeches-maker and music-seller, John Thompson, was organist of All Saints from 1794 and St Nicholas from 1795; in 1794 (aged only 17), he was promoting his yearly benefit when he ordered 325 tickets from Bewick.[81] Benefits usually attracted a much larger audience than subscription series, and were often held at busy times of the year like Assize and Race Weeks; promoters of such concerts therefore tended to be more extravagant with their offerings in order to attract those who did not usually attend musical events. For this concert, Thompson offered as soloists one of the singing-men from Durham and a popular and attractive actress from the local theatre company, and stressed that the music was 'intirely new', always an attraction in Newcastle which much preferred new music to older repertoire.[82] He also pandered to patriotic sentiment – the war with France was well under way – by performing a sumptuous version of 'God Save the King' with full

---

[73] TWAM 1269/22, Ledger.
[74] TWAM 1269/13, Day book, 30 January 1786.
[75] TWAM 1269/12, Day book, 29 November 1780.
[76] *Newcastle Courant*, 23 July 1785; *Newcastle Chronicle*, 23 July 1785.
[77] TWAM 1269/22, Ledger, 24 March 1787.
[78] *Newcastle Courant*, 31 December 1785 and 7 January 1786.
[79] TWAM 1269/13, Day book, 10 March and 30 July 1787.
[80] TWAM 1269/14, Day book, 11 January 1794.
[81] TWAM 1269/14, Day book, 16 September 1794.
[82] Thompson conveniently ignored the fact that the singing man proposed to perform an aria by Handel. *Newcastle Courant*, 9 March 1782.

band and choir, and a number of 'new Military Pieces'.[83] He was lucky too in having attracted the patronage of the Lady Mayoress. His reward for all this was apparently the 'numerous' attendance of 'the most fashionable company in this town and neighbourhood', including the Duke of Norfolk who was visiting the region.[84]

Even this, however, paled into insignificance beside the number of tickets routinely ordered by dancing masters. Adam and Alexander Kinlock regularly asked Bewick for very high numbers of tickets (see Table 9.2). In 1785, the same year that Hawdon stated publicly that there was no support for concerts in Newcastle, the Kinlocks anticipated selling 400 tickets for their annual ball – they had printed 500 for the previous year.[85] Public concert-making collapsed almost completely across the North-East in the 1790s under the pressure of the French Revolutionary Wars, being represented solely by the performances of two military bands, but the Kinlocks found no diminution in their business, except for one inexplicably anomalous year: 1797.[86] Concerts might have been considered a trivial pursuit in such critical times but dancing was not; it was, of course, an activity that could be carried on in the privacy of the home or after private social occasions such as dinners, and was therefore not necessarily a public display of inappropriate frivolity.[87]

Bewick's accounts also potentially cast light on another puzzle. As noted earlier, the two Kinlocks worked together for some time after their arrival in Newcastle before the son, Alexander, set up on his own. There is no clear evidence for when this might have taken place but a surprisingly low order for tickets in March 1787 may suggest that this was Alexander's first attempt at a ball not long after setting up his own school.

---

[83] *Newcastle Courant*, 27 September 1794.
[84] Ibid., 11 October 1794.
[85] TWAM 1269/13, Day book, 16 April 1785.
[86] TWAM 1269/14, Day book, 22 April 1797. There is no suggestion in local papers that this was a particularly difficult year for entertainments.
[87] These figures for attendances at concerts in Newcastle, and the cost of printing tickets, can be compared to figures available elsewhere. For instance, Jennifer Macleod, in her dissertation about the Edinburgh Musical Society, notes that in the early 1730s, the average number of tickets ordered for concerts in 1730 was around 50, rising to around 80 in 1831. Prices for the plates for these tickets are not recorded separately but may be included in the global figures for printing: in 1730, the price for 50 tickets appears to have been between £4 12s. 6d. and £6 7s. 6d. Macleod also refers to expenses for 1783, a period much closer to Hawdon's time, but the entries in the Society's minute books do not appear to contain as much detail as the earlier entries. The printer of the Musical Society's tickets in 1763 was Charles Esplin. Macleod, 'The Edinburgh Musical Society', 74–81.

TABLE 9.2 Tickets purchased by Matthias Hawdon, and Adam and Alexander Kinlock.[88]

Year	Date	Purchaser	No. tickets	Plate cost
1777	13 November	Hawdon		15s.
1779	21 July	Hawdon	100	
	13 October/13 November[89]	Hawdon	200 (100 black, 100 red)	
1780	11 March	Kinlock	500	7s. 6d.
	14 August	Hawdon	50	
	2 November	Kinlock	300	
	27 November	Hawdon	200 (50 black, 150 red)	
1781	24 January	Hawdon	100 (blue)	
	24 March	Hawdon	500	
	31 March	Hawdon	250 (black)	
	9–11 April	Hawdon	200	
1782	7–12 January	Hawdon	50	
	13 April	Kinlock	400	2s. 6d. (altered plate)
1783	9 January	Hawdon	100 (50 subscription tickets, 50 nightly tickets)	2s. 6d. (altered plate)
1784	27 March	Kinlock	600 (green)	
1785	16 April	Kinlock	400	
	18 July	Hawdon	100 (red)	
1786	15 April	Kinlock	500 (red)	
1787	31 March	Kinlock	250	
	11 August	Hawdon	50 (red)	
1788	22 March	Kinlock	450 (brown)	
	19 July	Hawdon	200	5s. (altered plate)
1790	27 April	Kinlock	500 (blue)	
1791	2 April	Kinlock	500 (red)	

[88] Drawing up this table is complicated by the fact that Bewick's records do not always use the same terminology throughout – several orders are recorded twice, using the words 'cards' and 'tickets' interchangeably.

[89] Both dates are listed in Bewick's records.

1794	31 March	Kinlock	500 (black)	
1795	1 April	Kinlock	500	10s. 6d.
1796	1 April	Kinlock	500 (red)	
1797	1 April	Kinlock	500 (blue)	
	22 April	Kinlock	50 (blue)	
1798		Kinlock	500 (red)	
1799	6 July	Kinlock	400	7s. 6d.
1800	5 April	Kinlock	800 (black)	3s. 6d.
1802	25 March	Kinlock	300	

Payments and Debts

The account books also throw new light onto another critical part of musicians' lives – finances. Particularly in periods of war, such as the French Revolutionary Wars, music was often regarded as a trivial pastime, decreasing the number of attendees at public events and increasing costs, leaving musicians in a difficult position. The financial capabilities of musicians could be critical and Bewick's accounts detail the difficulties faced by many of them, although it is worth pointing out that Bewick himself does not seem to have increased his prices over the inflationary period of the French Revolutionary Wars. The cost of engraving a plate for concert or ball tickets, for instance, remained steady at between 7s. 6d. and 15s.

Hawdon's difficulties have already been noted. Other customers were more efficient in business and paid promptly. The Kinlocks, for instance, almost always paid on receipt of the goods; their balls were clearly profitable, and father and son had plenty of money to pay their debts. They rarely paid high prices for their ticket plate, paying 7s. 6d. in 1780,[90] altering a plate in 1782 at a cost of 2s. 6d.,[91] then buying a new one for 10s. 6d. in 1795.[92] The younger Kinlock then purchased a new ticket after his father's death in 1799.[93] It is possible that the plates bought in the 1780s were in fact purchased when father and son ran separate schools and that both of them prudently used the same plate for as many years as possible.

Charles Avison jnr was less skilful in his financial management.[94] In 1777, Avison had left Newcastle for St Petersburg, presumably to teach and perform

---

[90] TWAM 1269/12, Day book, 11 March 1780.
[91] TWAM 1269/22, Ledger, 15 April 1782.
[92] TWAM 1269/13, Day book, 16 April 1785.
[93] TWAM 1269/14, Day book, 6 July 1799.
[94] Charles was not the only member of his family to patronise Bewick. One of the earliest references in the accounts, dating to 1768, the year after Bewick was apprenticed to Beilby, was a slightly enigmatic order from 'Miss Avison' – almost certainly Jane Avison, daughter of the composer, who asked for a 'stone' to be engraved; this may, the

to English residents there.[95] However, he had returned to his native town within five years and set himself up as a teacher and concert promoter. In 1783, shortly after his return, he promoted a concert for which he purchased an engraved plate from Bewick at the high cost of 15s., from which he printed 200 tickets.[96] It is worth noting that in this same year, Hawdon was having an old plate altered at a cost of 2s. 6d. and was printing only 100 tickets from it, and that only two years later Hawdon was complaining about the general lack of support for music in Newcastle. Avison may have found out the hard way that Hawdon was right; neither Bewick's accounts or the local papers record an attempt by Avison to hold another concert until 1787, and on that occasion, as noted earlier, he spent a mere 5s. on the plate and printed only 100 tickets.[97]

The 1787 tickets were for a concert to be held in Freemasons' Hall in Newcastle, a concert sponsored by the masons for Avison's benefit – like many musicians in the area, Avison was himself a member.[98] Although the Freemasons were promoting Avison, it was clearly up to him to cover the expenses, paying for them out of the profits on the night: the only thing the Freemasons' support seems to have guaranteed was an audience. Perhaps this was not numerous enough to cover the expenses, even after cutting costs on engraving the ticket plate; Avison did not pay Bewick's bill, being listed in the outstanding debts book as owing 10s. 4d.[99] Three months later, he ordered tickets for his second concert that year; despite the outstanding debt, Bewick seems to have fulfilled this order. But by 1792, Avison was listed as being in debt to Bewick by £1 1s.,[100] and this increased eventually to £1 10s. 10d.[101] Bewick lost patience and took out a summons at a cost of 6d., adding it to Avison's bill – the only known time he took out a summons against a musician.[102] Avison paid 9s. of the debt straight away but there is no record of the outstanding amount ever being settled. He died in 1795, in such debt that acrimonious arguments arose about his possessions which were to be sold to pay his creditors, leaving his wife and children in severe difficulties.[103] Bewick was clearly only one of many debtors.

---

context suggests, have been a cameo 'set with Garnets'; the job cost her £1 5s. TWAM 1269/11, Day book, 20 October 1768.

[95] For a brief biography of Avison, see Southey, *Music-Making in North-East England*, 200–1. Avison's cousin, William, was engaged in the Baltic trade with Hull and was resident in Narva; it is possible, therefore, that Avison might have travelled north with a view to collaborating with him in some way. At present, however, there is no evidence as to Avison's exact activities in the region.

[96] TWAM 1269/22, Ledger, 10 October 1783.

[97] TWAM 1269/13, Day book, 30 June 1787.

[98] *Newcastle Courant*, 3 March 1787.

[99] TWAM 1269/230, Outstanding debt book, n.d.

[100] TWAM 1269/231, Outstanding debt book, n.d.

[101] TWAM 1269/13, Day book, n.d.

[102] Ibid.

[103] Avison died on 30 March 1795, *Newcastle Chronicle*, 4 April 1795. The advertisement of a meeting of his creditors makes it clear that his main income came from teaching and from selling books and instruments, as well as his organist's salary. Ibid., 4 July 1795.

Like Hawdon, Avison was living in difficult times for musicians and could not cope financially.

Another customer who struggled, though not as disastrously as Avison, was Thomas Thompson. For his benefit concert of 1794, with its aristocratic audience, he splashed out 15s. on the cost of the engraved plate, which suggests the design must have been intricate. There is no indication of the finances of this concert but as Thompson seems to have paid his debt to Bewick without fuss and promptly, the event was probably profitable. But in July 1796, Thompson was one of the promoters of an ambitious oratorio festival that attracted 'audiences, which were genteel, but not very numerous';[104] as a consequence, he and his collaborator lost nearly 120 guineas owing to the 'enormous expence incurred … by the engagement of performers of eminence'.[105] This loss seems to have hit Thompson hard – thereafter he seems to have eschewed concert promotion for many years, devoting himself instead to his large teaching practice and to composition.[106]

Sometimes circumstances intervened to prevent prompt payment. In March 1787, Edward Meredith, the bass singer from Durham Cathedral, ordered a plate for concert tickets from Bewick together with 100 tickets.[107] This was for a bespoke concert for the Gentlemen of the Forest Hunt to mark the end of the hunting season and, unlike Avison's Freemasons' concert, was 'honoured with a very great company'.[108] (It is clear from advertisements for other concerts that Meredith had a wide and lively repertoire of hunting songs.) The tickets, together with two packs of visiting cards, cost Meredith 15s. 10d., and he added a further debt of around 7s. the following year when ordering 100 tickets more for another concert from the gentleman, again greatly patronised.[109] However, no sooner had Meredith incurred the second debt than he left the area permanently for Liverpool – Bewick seems to have taken no action to recover the debt but it is likely that he had mentally written it off.[110] But Meredith came back to Newcastle in early 1791 to sing in

---

Two years later, Avison's creditors met 'to compel their Attorney to make a Dividend, from the Produce of the sale of the deceased Effects' and demanded to know what was to become of 'Things of Value' which had not been sold but were thought to be in the possession of Avison's wife. *Newcastle Courant*, 8 July 1797.

[104] *Newcastle Courant*, 6 August 1796. However, the *Newcastle Chronicle* said that the oratorios were 'well attended'. *Newcastle Chronicle*, 6 August 1796.
[105] *Newcastle Chronicle*, 6 August 1796.
[106] In 1813, Thompson took part, with his father, in a number of concerts put on in Newcastle by a choral group; no further details of these can at present be found. Newcastle, Central Library, L780.79: concert programmes.
[107] TWAM 1269/22, Ledger, 24 March 1787.
[108] *Newcastle Courant*, 31 March 1787.
[109] TWAM 1269/22, Ledger, 7 January 1788; *Newcastle Courant*, 29 March 1788.
[110] See Roz Southey, 'Managing a musical career in the eighteenth century: the interweaving of patronage and commercialisation in the careers of Charles Avison and Edward Meredith', in Roz Southey and Eric Cross (eds), *Charles Avison in Context: National and International Musical Links in Eighteenth-Century North-East England* (Abingdon, 2018), 179–213.

an oratorio festival and made one of his first calls a visit to pay his outstanding debt of £1 2s. 6d.[111]

In some cases, the nonpayment of a debt to Bewick may have been a way of balancing the books on a short-term basis for a musician in temporary difficulties. Thomas Wright seems to have been a tolerably prompt payer until the early 1790s. However, in early 1794 he put on a subscription concert series in Newcastle, ordering a plate he already owned to be altered at a cost of a mere 1s. 6d. and printing only 60 tickets from it.[112] The subscription series in the town had been moribund since Hawdon gave up in 1785; Wright had been petitioned by some music-lovers to revive it,[113] but it was undoubtedly a risky venture in the uncertain times, with the war continuing abroad and inflation rising at home. In addition, this was a difficult period for Wright personally;[114] after a short period as organist of St Andrew's church, he had argued violently with the churchwardens and thrown the organ keys back in their faces in a fit of pique. He was making ends meet with teaching, and had also established two military bands in the town, whose patriotic concerts the public could feel comfortable attending, but he seems to have suspended his usual practice on paying bills promptly – Bewick had to wait at least three years for the 3s. 3d. spent on the subscription concert expenses.[115] However, Wright continued to purchase goods from Bewick for some years – a ticket plate and visiting cards in 1801, for instance – so Bewick may have considered him for the most part tolerably reliable.[116]

☙ Conclusion

Bewick's accounts throw new light on musical life in North-East England from an unusual standpoint – a service which was itself non-musical but which offered support of various kinds to musicians. The records of the famous tradesman are informative for the minutiae and practicalities of musician's lives: the everyday struggles to make ends meet; the acquisition of visiting cards to flatter genteel customers by calling on them; the purchase of door plates so that pupils could find them easily. They show the need for seals to secure letters, a good letterhead for bills, and even cyphers on cutlery which might be used by pupils. They illustrate the cost of these everyday items and the decisions to be made when ordering: how much to spend on a plate from which to print the tickets, how many tickets to order, whether to indulge

---

[111] TWAM 1269/22, Ledger, 20 April 1791.
[112] TWAM 1269/14, Day book, 11 January 1794.
[113] *Newcastle Courant*, 7 December 1793 and 1 February 1794.
[114] For an outline of Wright's career, see Southey, *Music-Making in North-East England*, 228.
[115] TWAM 1269/232, Outstanding debt book, 2 January 1794; TWAM 1269/233, Outstanding debt book, January 1797.
[116] TWAM 1269//14, Day book, 4 April 1801.

a little in the matter of colour, the weighing up of expenses against potential income – and how many times musicians got those calculation wrong. The accounts also flesh out the sparse account of musical life available from local newspapers and demonstrate how much of a minority interest music was, particularly in time of war. Such surviving primarily non-musical sources have generally received little attention, despite the rich detail they can provide on the hidden aspect of musicians' lives, and the goods and services which were vital for musicians to function as professionals.

10

Makers, Repairers, Teachers, Dealers and Printers: The Music Trade Network in Late Eighteenth-Century West Midlands

Martin Perkins

In the multifaceted sphere of music, where a 'consumer' may attend or participate in concerts, purchase sheet music or accessories, receive music tuition, or acquire a musical instrument, there are potentially considerable overlaps between the people who work in the trade. In eighteenth-century Britain, most professional musicians forged freelance careers: as William Weber noted, in order to maintain a living, 'a musician had to "undertake" … a variety of enterprises as performer, composer, arranger, and, most important of all, as teacher'.[1] Although the most common forms of employment for professional musicians were as teachers, performers, concert promoters and composers, the subsidiary trades that facilitated these activities – instrument making and maintenance, music printing and selling, etc., – were undertaken as much by these professionals as others.

By the mid-eighteenth century, a growing number of individuals, often referred to as the 'middling sort', were able to experience culture more readily than before, that the elite – nobility and gentry – already enjoyed.[2] The increased financial security and resulting gain of leisure time enabled them to experience music on similar terms to the elite: as an audience – attendance at public concerts, opera and theatre – but also as practising amateurs making music at home and in musical clubs and societies. The result was increased sales of printed music and musical instruments and, therefore, the subsidiary trades that served both the concert platform and private music room. In the Midlands, where the geographical spread of employment opportunities was far wider than London, there was a greater diversity in the portfolio of trades and services offered by those serving the communities there.

The case studies presented here centre on two important yet contrasting settlements in the West Midlands – Birmingham and Worcester – and fall broadly into two categories: professional musicians who turned to subsidiary

---

[1] William Weber, *The Musician as Entrepreneur, 1700–1914: Managers, Charlatans, and Idealists* (Bloomington, 2004), 11.

[2] Margaret Hunt, *The Middling Sort: Commerce, Gender and the Family in England, 1680–1780* (London, 1996), 2–4.

trades as part of a portfolio career, and printers and craftspeople who adapted to serve the music industry. It is no coincidence that some of the individuals discussed here were employed by the church: such an environment was perfect for providing regular employment for professional musicians whilst allowing them relative freedom to explore other avenues of employment around their daily duties of the choir. Specialist knowledge of music was required for many supporting industries, and so it is not surprising that cathedral musicians found themselves engaged in the commercial music trade.

From the early eighteenth century, Birmingham experienced a steady rise in population and status through innovations in commerce and manufacturing. The resulting rise of the professional class – merchants, traders and professionals – created a demand for, and fostered the development of, a full gamut of cultural activities. In 1715 a new church – St Philip's (now Birmingham Cathedral) – was built to ease the strain on the principal church, St Martin's, due to the town's rapidly-growing population. Soon after, London organ builder Thomas Swarbrick (c.1675–c.1753) was engaged to build an organ for St Philip's, and Barnabas Gunn (c.1680–1753) appointed to play it.[3] Dancing master William Sawyer opened his 'Great Room' in 1740 to host public assemblies, concerts and balls, and the 'New Hotel' with a large ball room was built in 1772 to serve the growing need for public events.[4] Pleasure gardens at Duddeston, modelled on the popular London gardens, were established by 1755 and located a mile to the east of the town; the existing King Street Theatre gained competition from a new theatre erected on New Street in 1765.[5]

In contrast, 30 miles south-west of Birmingham, Worcester's music scene was much older and centred around the long-established cathedral choir. Like Birmingham, Worcester was well served with subscription and benefit concerts, often held at the Guildhall or at public houses.[6] Nevertheless, the musical highlight, established from at least 1715, was the annual meeting of the choirs of Worcester, Hereford and Gloucester.[7] By the end of the eighteenth century, the 'Three Choirs Festival' had become an important social event, attracting audiences from town, county and country to see the most admired vocal and instrumental performers in Britain. Many of Worcester Cathedral's lay clerks

[3] *National Pipe Organ Register* (NPOR – https://npor.org.uk/), organ D02783; Terry Slater, *The Pride of the Place: The Cathedral Church of St Philip, Birmingham, 1715–2015* (Birmingham, 2015), 74.

[4] James Bisset, *A Poetic Survey Round Birmingham* (Birmingham, 1800), 10; 'Sawyer William, Dancing Master', *Sketchley's Birmingham, Wolverhampton & Walsall Directory, 1767* (Birmingham, 1767).

[5] John Money, *Experience and Identity: Birmingham and the West Midlands, 1760–1800* (Manchester, 1977), 87.

[6] The Crown, an old coaching inn in Broad Street, hosted concerts, such as the 'Concert of Vocal and Instrumental Music for the Benefit of Mr. and Miss Marshall held in the Long Room at the Crown'. *Berrow's Worcester Journal*, 6 December 1770.

[7] For a thorough discussion of the establishment and origins of the Three Choirs Festival, see Anthony Boden and Paul Hedley, *The Three Choirs Festival: A History* (Woodbridge, 2017).

sought employment away from the cathedral, performing elsewhere in the city and the wider region, offering musical services such as teaching, tuning harpsichords and organs, or acting as agents to instrument makers and music publishers. As such, they played an important role in keeping the cogs of the regional music trade turning. The mechanisms and organisation needed for such events and activities to take place were, in some cases, highly intricate and dependent on cooperation between many parties. The careers of these professional musicians who served the whole region were influenced by the supply and demand of the industry they served and competition from others who either expanded their existing activities as locals or arrived in the region from elsewhere.

This chapter begins with an investigation of instrument and music dealing in Worcester, with an emphasis on cathedral musicians-turned traders, James Chew and James Radcliffe, and the activities in the city of London-based organ builder, William Gray. The subsequent comparison of trading in Birmingham focusses on William Fletcher and the rivalry between Michael Woodward and Henry Laycock. The business activities of dancing master-turned instrument dealer, James Farlo, in Birmingham and across Worcestershire serves as an example of a music trader, who came into conflict with printer and dealer Thomas Holl. Examples of how music and instruments were procured through private networks conclude this chapter.

Worcester Music and Instrument Dealers

James Chew was a lay clerk at Worcester Cathedral from at least 1748 until his death in 1790; he received additional payments for tuning the cathedral harpsichord and organ.[8] Chew's activities as an organ builder and harpsichord maker are not well documented, and it is possible that he did not build many instruments.[9] It is more likely that most of his freelance work was as a peripatetic tuner, visiting clients in the region to tune and service their keyboard instruments.[10] In 1771 Chew tuned and repaired instruments belonging to the

---

[8] Chew subscribed to William Hayes's *Six Cantatas* (London, 1748), where he is listed as 'Mr. James Chew, Lay-Clerk in the Cathedral at Worcester'. He appears in Worcester Cathedral treasurers accounts up to and including the year 1789-90. See Worcester Cathedral, Treasurer's Book, A57–64 (1752–80), p. 15.

[9] His name does not appear in *NPOR*, and the Worcester Cathedral treasurer's books only ever list him as tuning organs, not repairing. He is however recorded as a 'Harpsichord Maker' in seven lists in Simon D.I. Fleming and Martin Perkins, *Dataset of Subscribers to Eighteenth-Century Music Publications in Britain and Ireland*, at www.musicsubscribers.co.uk. They include: Capel Bond, *Six Anthems* (London, 1769); Joseph Harris, *Eight Songs* (London, c.1767); Philip Hayes, *Six Concertos* (London, 1769); and Benjamin Thomas, *Six Canzonets* (Gloucester, c.1767).

[10] For another example of an eighteenth-century peripatetic tuner, see Gillian Sheldrick (ed.), *The Accounts of Thomas Green: Music Teacher and Tuner of Musical Instruments, 1742–1790* (Hertford, 1992).

Vernon family at Hanbury Hall, eight miles north of Worcester. A bill records that Chew repaired 'Miss Vernon's Harpsichord, and tune'd her Clavichord &c: at Hanbury'.[11] The money owed to Chew was settled the following January with a payment of £3 3s., made via the Vernons' harpsichord teacher and Worcester's cathedral organist, Elias Isaac, who itemised Chew's tuning work on his own bill.[12] Whilst one can only speculate as to the extent of the repairs undertaken, they cannot have involved much more than replacing strings, plectra, or regulation of the action, given that the repairs were done *in situ*.

For more extensive instrument repairs, Chew may have needed to stay away from Worcester or transport instruments to work on at his own premises. Between 1779 and 1781 Chew undertook repairs to a harpsichord belonging to keen amateur musician Sir Samuel Hellier (1736–1784), a minor landowner who lived on the outskirts of Wombourne, Staffordshire (a village situated five miles from Wolverhampton and thirteen from Birmingham). Hellier's interests in music and philanthropy were such that he formed a small orchestra comprising estate workers and villagers, and purchased instruments and music for their use.[13] The considerable distance of twenty-six miles to Worcester (over twice the distance than to Birmingham) is perhaps indicative of the scarcity of repairers in the region, and perhaps of the complete absence of them in Birmingham. In a letter to his estate manager, John Rogers, in late September 1781, Hellier wrote:

> I sent my Harpsichord above Two Year's ago to be alter'd to Mr. Chew at Worcester … I desire you will give Mr. Chew a Line inform him of my anxiety about my Harpsichord t[ha]t I have been a long while absent in London, but t[ha]t if it is ready … you will apply to ye glass house or some Convenient Waggon from Stourbridge to bring it home &c.[14]

Hellier's concern over the transportation of his harpsichord continued the following week, by which time he had decided that Chew himself would need to send the harpsichord back, rather than for Rogers to fetch it: 'I hope Mr. Chew will pack it Exceedingly well … Let me know w[ha]t improvemen[ts] are made to it & how it play's & if it keeps well in Tune[.]'[15]

The problem of transporting a delicate yet large instrument was more complicated than Hellier imagined, and he subsequently resolved that Rogers should journey with the harpsichord to ensure its safety. Rogers was instructed to supervise loading the harpsichord onto a boat at the Worcester quay, travelling with it upriver as far as Stourport-on-Severn, where it would be transferred to a canal boat and sailed up the Staffordshire and Worcestershire navigation to

---

[11] Worcester, Worcestershire Archive and Archaeology Service (WAAS), BA7335/24/170. This instrument is not the clavier organum now housed at Hanbury Hall.
[12] WAAS, BA7335/24/169, Mr. Isaac's Bill 18 January 1772.
[13] Catherine Frew and Arnold Myers, 'Sir Samuel Hellier's "Musicall Instruments"', *The Galpin Society Journal*, 56 (2003), 6–26.
[14] Letter to John Rogers, the Woodhouse, Wombourne, from Sir Samuel Hellier, 27 September 1781. Private collection, used with permission.
[15] Ibid., Letter to John Rogers, 2 December 1781.

a wharf at Wombourne, half a mile west of the village. From there 'it sh[oul]d be Carried by hand and not in any Carriage upon a hand Barrow or otherwise[.] these things Complied with I See no objection to its Coming by water and ye Sooner ye Better'.[16] The repair of Hellier's harpsichord and its return to Wombourne was presumably a success since, the following year, he asked Chew to make repairs to the organ at Wombourne church.[17] Chew further worked on Hellier's own organ, located in the purpose-built music room in the grounds of The Wodehouse.[18] These instances reveal that Chew would travel to clients where it was convenient (to Hanbury Hall, for example) or to where the instrument was located in cases where moving the instrument was impractical (Wombourne, Staffordshire).

Following his death in 1790,[19] Chew's business was taken over by George Partridge, a former apprentice of London harpsichord maker Jacob Kirkman (1710-92). Partridge had married Chew's daughter, Frances, in 1780.[20] An announcement in the *Hereford Journal* for 14 July 1790 stated:

> George Partridge, Musical Instrument Maker, From Mr. Kirkman's, London, and Successor to the late Mr. Chew, – Takes this opportunity of returning his most grateful acknowledgements to the Nobility and Gentry for their favours conferred on him, humbly soliciting a continuance of them, as it will ever be his highest ambition to deserve them … Organs, Harpsichords, and other Music Instruments are carefully and expeditiously repaired on the most reasonable terms.

For instrument sales in the second half of the eighteenth century, customers could turn to other local traders. Stourbridge musician, Thomas Caddick, promoted his musical instrument business in the local newspaper, using performance as part of his sales strategy. In 1762 Caddick advertised a free performance of 'several Select Pieces of Instrumental Music' to be given in Worcester, when, at the same time would be sold 'a neat Chamber Organ, built by the famous Christopher Smith; and also a new Table-Organ, at a reasonable Value, by Thomas Caddick, who will furnish any Person, with Organs or Harpsichords, at reasonable Rates'.[21] Little is known of Caddick's formative years, but in 1760 he had repaired the organ Abraham Adcock (1709–1773), a London-based

---

[16] Ibid., Letter to John Rogers, 22 December 1781.
[17] Ibid., Letter to John Rogers, 21 September 1782.
[18] Ibid., Letter to John Rogers, 16 January 1783.
[19] Chew's son, also named James, is recorded as a chorister at Worcester Cathedral between 1765 and 1767. Although the account books do not list individual chorister names for subsequent years until 1776-7, it is likely that the 'Chew' listed from this time until 1790 is still the father. He was listed in the 1791 *Worcester Royal Directory* (Worcester, 1791) as 'James Chew, organ builder and harpsichord maker, Palace row' despite having died the previous year.
[20] Frances was baptized on 10 February 1758. Birmingham, Library, DRO 53, Archive Roll: M142 Baptisms, Marriages and Burials, 1538–1812.
[21] *Aris's Birmingham Gazette*, 15 November 1762.

musician and organ builder, had hired to St John's, Wolverhampton.[22] Caddick continued to operate as a musical instrument dealer and organ maker. He took the trouble to list all thirty of the tunes played on an eight-stop barrel organ he was selling in an advertisement of 1766; a further advertisement, from 1770, was for a five-stop barrel organ containing thirty-two tunes.[23]

James Radcliffe, another member of Worcester's cathedral choir, was active in the wider music trade in the late eighteenth century. A younger contemporary of James Chew, Radcliffe joined the choir in 1777, with family members Charles and John (probably sons) joining him from 1780–1.[24] As a freelance musician, Radcliffe held concerts throughout the 1780s and 90s including a benefit concert in November 1781 at Worcester Guildhall.[25] He directed music meetings elsewhere in the county, including Kidderminster in 1784, and Evesham in 1791.[26] He started advertising his services as a harpsichord tuner and music copyist in 1787: one newspaper advertisement records that 'Harpsichords, Forte Pianos, Spinnets and other Musical Instruments, tuned and repaired in the neatest manner … by Mr Radcliffe, … who begs leave to Solicit the Patronage of the Nobility, Gentry, &c. in Worcester and its vicinity … Music neatly, and correctly copied'.[27] Whether or not Radcliffe's appeal to the nobility and gentry – seeking new clients – marked the beginning of a new business venture, he was presumably in direct competition with his lay clerk colleague, James Chew. The following year his services had expanded to include 'Music, vocal or instrumental, taught in the most expeditious method, and after the manner of the most approved masters'.[28] Perhaps this advertisement – an attempt to elevate himself from a mere tuner to that of teacher – indicates that he sought the greater financial reward from teaching, which could easily be done alongside tuning activities at his client's homes.

Radcliffe's branching out into teaching may have been a result of increased competition in the tuning or repairing market. In August 1788 Worcester bookseller William Smart announced that William Gray, 'from London, tunes and repairs Harpsichords and Piano Fortes'.[29] Smart, acting as Gray's representative, assured readers of *Berrow's Worcester Journal* that they may 'depend on his giving satisfaction. His intention is to come from London every six months'.[30] William Gray and his brother, Robert, had traded in London for several years

---

[22] Stafford, Staffordshire Record Office, D/SSR/44/287: 'Extracts from Copy of Chapel-Wardens' Accounts Dating from 1760'. For more Adcock, see www.abrahamadcock.com.

[23] *Aris's Birmingham Gazette*, 3 March 1766 and 26 February 1770.

[24] It is possible that John and Charles were sons of James, but they are not recorded as being choristers in the cathedral treasurer books before appearing as lay clerks.

[25] *Berrow's Worcester Journal*, 22 November 1781.

[26] Ibid., 17 June 1784 and 7 April 1791. Evesham's music meeting took place on the 3–4 May.

[27] Ibid., 8 February 1787.

[28] Ibid., 28 February 1788.

[29] Ibid., 28 August 1788.

[30] Ibid.

as organ builders and harpsichord and piano makers.[31] William Gray's visits to Worcester to tune keyboard instruments suggest a local demand for this service that was beyond the capacity of Chew and Radcliffe. Yet, it is likely that these visits were networking expeditions for a greater prize: the Gray brothers were subsequently chosen to build a ten-stop organ for St Swithun's, Worcester, completed in 1793.[32]

Radcliffe's aforementioned advertisement reveals there was also a local demand for music copying. This service may have been offered to amateur or professional customers: to create a second basso continuo part for a sonata so that the cellist and harpsichordist did not need to share a score; or creating ripieno parts for concertos and symphonies. Radcliffe was not an instrument maker, or a music publisher: as a singer first and foremost, his portfolio of music trade activities was distinctly different from the London model. Focusing on his singing career, he left the Midlands in 1795 after his appointment as a lay clerk at Durham Cathedral, where he continued to work as a music copyist.[33]

Worcester was understandably a centre of music production in the Midlands. Members of the cathedral choir facilitated a commercial trade in other musical services and goods, supplementing their cathedral income as instrument makers and repairs or sellers of musical goods. In contrast, the rapid industrial development of Birmingham through the eighteenth century provided a growing market for a wealth of opportunities for commercial music traders and encouraged an influx of traders from outside the town.

Birmingham Music and Instrument Dealers

The building of St Philip's church resulted in a growth in musical activities in the town, and the subsequent founding of the Blue Coat School, situated adjacent to St Philip's in 1724, supplied the church with choristers.[34] Perhaps attracted by the growth in music-related opportunities, music engraver, Michael Broome (c.1700–1775) arrived in the town in 1733.[35] Formerly a singing master in Isle-

---

[31] Draft trade card of Robert & William Gray, c.1793, British Museum, Heal, 88.38; Nicholas Thistlethwaite, *Organ-building in Georgian and Victorian England: The Work of Gray & Davison, 1772–1890* (Woodbridge, 2020), 62.

[32] NPOR organ no. N03625. *NPOR* records the organ as being built in 1795, yet the inaugural concert was held on 10 December 1793 (*Aris's Birmingham Gazette*, 5 December 1793, advertisement; *Berrow's Worcester Journal*, 12 December 1793, review).

[33] Simon D.I. Fleming, 'A Century of Music Production in Durham City 1711–1811: A Documentary Study' (PhD dissertation, University of Durham, 2009), 49. Radcliffe's *Church Music* (London, 1801) includes music he had originally written for use at Worcester; ibid., 265. See also Brian Crosby, *Durham Cathedral Choir: Biographical Details of Masters of the Choristers, and Organists, Lay-Clerks, and Boys, with a Supplement on Minor Canons. Part 2: 1660–1812* (unpublished manuscript in the possession of Simon D.I. Fleming).

[34] Slater, *The Pride of the Place*, 62.

[35] David Hunter, 'English Country Psalmodists and Their Publications, 1700–1760', *Journal of the Royal Musical Association*, 115/2 (1990), 220–39, at 225–6.

worth, Middlesex,[36] he served as a parish clerk and trained Blue Coat boys as choristers for St Philip's.[37] Broome's own publications included collections of sacred and secular vocal music, and he engraved the musical plates for several Midlands composers.[38] Another Birmingham-based centre of parochial music was St Bartholomew's, a chapel of ease to the older St Martin's, which opened in 1749.[39] One of its choristers was James Kempson (1742–1822), who founded the 'Musical and Amicable Society' in 1762; he was assistant conductor of the Oratorio Choral Society for over fifty years and the first clerk of St Paul's church, Hockley, Birmingham, built in 1777.[40] Kempson is also known to have engraved music, specifically John Pixell's *Odes, cantatas, songs &c*, op 2 (1775).[41] Broome and Kempson maintained steady careers in music performance and teaching with occasional work in other areas of the music trade. Yet the Birmingham music scene was also served by musicians who turned away from performance and by merchants and shop owners who acted as agents for London music publishers and instrument makers. Four examples serve well to illustrate the backgrounds and focus of the individuals involved, as well as how the markets in the Birmingham area overlapped.

William Fletcher was a musician and music dealer who owned premises in Bull Street, Birmingham, from the early 1770s. He acted as a ticket agent for events in Birmingham such as concerts at the fashionable Duddeston Gardens.[42] He printed John Pixell's *Odes, cantatas, songs &c*, op 2, and subscribed to six sets, no doubt for resale in his shop.[43] However, it appears that Fletcher gave up his music shop soon after as he is not listed in trade directories after this.[44] It is likely that he is the same Mr Fletcher who subscribed to Jeremiah

[36] Charles Humphries and William C. Smith, *Music Publishing in the British Isles from the beginning until the middle of the nineteenth century* (Oxford, 1970), 87–8.
[37] Joseph Sutcliffe Smith, *The Story of Music in Birmingham* (Birmingham, 1945), 11; Margaret Handford, *Sounds Unlikely: Six Hundred Years of Music in Birmingham* (Birmingham, 1992), 15.
[38] Publications include Coventry organist John Barker's *A Select Number of the Best Psalm Tunes* (Birmingham, c.1750), Wolverhampton organist James Lyndon's *Six Solos* (Birmingham, 1751) and John Alcock's *Divine Harmony* (Birmingham, 1752).
[39] Joseph Sutcliffe Smith, *The Story of Music in Birmingham* (Birmingham, 1945), 12–14. This St Bartholomew's church is not to be confused with St Bartholomew's, Edgbaston (known as Edgbaston Old Church), where John Pixell was vicar.
[40] Monumental inscription, St Paul's, Hockley.
[41] For more on Pixell, see Simon D. I. Fleming, 'John Pixell: an eighteenth-century vicar and composer' *The Musical Times*, 154/1923 (2013), 71–83.
[42] *Aris's Birmingham Gazette*, 19 August 1771. 'For the Benefit of Mr. Blonck. At Vaux-Hall Gardens, on Thursday next … a Concert of Vocal and Instrumental Music … Tickets … to be had at … Mr. Fletcher's Music Shop in Bull-Street'.
[43] On the title page of this work is printed 'Birmingham: Printed and sold for the author by William Fletcher, 1775.'
[44] He is not listed in Pearson and Rollason's *The Birmingham Directory* (Birmingham, 1777) or *The Birmingham, Wolverhampton, Walsall, Dudley, Bilston, and Willenhall Directory* (Birmingham, 1780).

Clark's *Six Sonata's* (1779) and to John Alcock's *Harmonia Festi* (1791), but as these were for just one copy each they were probably for personal use rather than resale.[45] Fletcher held an annual concert from at least 1772 at Mrs Sawyer's Great Room and later in the Great Room in the New Hotel where he performed as singer and violinist.[46] His focus turned to performing and teaching from the 1780s onwards; by 1792 his family was living in Church Street and he and his three daughters featured in many of the local performances.[47] The family was listed in Joseph Doane's *A Musical Directory for the Year 1794*, which notes they had performed at the Handel commemoration performances at Westminster Abbey. By the early 1800s they had moved to Newhall Street, where they had 'convenient Apartments to receive such of their Pupils as may prefer to honour them with their Attendance'.[48] There is some evidence that Fletcher dealt in musical instruments in the early 1800s, but none of the advertisements at the time mention this aspect of the family's trade.[49]

Perhaps the reason Fletcher closed his music shop in the late 1770s was the appearance of a rival trader, William Hall, who in 1778 extensively promoted his Birmingham 'Music Ware Room' at the New Hotel.[50] His advertisements from October and November that year reveal he had for sale the latest publications by the Italian violinist Felice Giardini (1716–1796) and the Irish composer Thomas Carter (1769–1800). Also available were copies of Thomas Willet and Raynor Taylor's *Buxom Joan*, first performed at London's Haymarket theatre earlier that season.[51] The listing of specific composers and works reveals Fletcher's focus on the sheet music that Birmingham audiences demanded, with Hall providing the latest works from the London stage and concert platform. However, he was clearly aiming to establish a one-stop music shop by also offering 'a large and elegant Assortment of Organs, Harpsichords, Piano-Fortes, and Spinnets' for sale, and 'Organs, Harpsichords, Piano Fortes, and Spinets, and all other Instruments repaired and tuned in Town and Country ... and Barrels made

---

[45] Jeremiah Clark, *Six Sonata's for the Harpsichord or Pianoforte with Accompanyments for Two Violins and Violoncello* (London, 1779); John Alcock, *Harmonia Festi, or a Collection of Canons; Cheerful & Serious Glees, & Catches* (Lichfield, 1791).

[46] For example, a 'Grand Concert of Vocal and Instrumental Music', 19 December 1793. *Aris's Birmingham Gazette*, 16 December 1793.

[47] *Birmingham Directory, for the year 1792* (Birmingham). A concert advertisement provides a good example of the Fletchers' activities: 'Mr. Fletcher's Concert and Ball, will be at the Hotel Great Room, on Thursday the 13th of November instant. ... Act II. Overture – Song, Miss J. Fletcher, Harp Accompaniment – Quartet, Messrs Bird, Fletcher and Miss Fletchers, for Violins, Tenor, and Violoncello'. *Aris's Birmingham Gazette*, 10 November 1794.

[48] *Aris's Birmingham Gazette*, 11 April 1808.

[49] William Waterhouse, *The New Langwill Index: Dictionary of Musical Wind-instrument Makers and Inventors* (London, 1993), 119, lists a William Fletcher (fl. 1805–7)' as a brass maker living in Church Street.

[50] *Aris's Birmingham Gazette*, 24 April 1778.

[51] Ibid., 12 October 1778. *Buxom Joan. A burletta, ... First performed, 25th June 1778.* (*John Larpent Plays*, Huntingdon Library (US), LA 449).

to Organs of any Size, on the shortest Notice'.[52] His business must have been significant enough to warrant taking rooms large enough to display the wide selection of keyboard instruments his advertisements boasted. The location of his 'Music Ware Room' at the prestigious hotel (then just seven years old), where concerts and assemblies were held, was surely a deliberate decision, the cost of which may have been a gamble Hall lost. His venture did not last long: no further evidence of Hall's activities can be found after 1779.

Filling the gap left by Hall was Michael Woodward, who had a shop in New Street, Birmingham from at least 1780, and was probably resident from 1777.[53] In his first advertisements, Woodward describes himself as a 'Musical Instrument-Maker, from London', supplying 'Ruled Books, and Paper, Music of all Sorts, Vocal and Instrumental, and every Article in the Musical Way'.[54] Woodward is known to have built an organ for St Nicholas's, Loxley (Warwickshire) in 1780,[55] and was responsible for moving the organ, built by Richard Bridge (d.1758) for Charles Jennens (1700–1773), to Great Packington Hall in 1792.[56] Woodward's activities as a music seller can be deduced through an examination of the music to which he subscribed.[57] These included seven copies of Edward Miller's *The Psalms of David for the use of Parish Churches* (1790 – in which he is described as an 'Organ Builder'), Jeremiah Clark's *Ten Songs* (1791 – 'Mr. Woodward, Music-seller, Birmingham'), and six copies of John Page's, *A Collection of Hymns* (1804 – where the description of his trade reverts to 'Musical Instrument Maker, Birmingham'). Although Woodward continued to advertise his services as a seller of sheet music, his main reputation was as a maker and one he was willing to defend in the press:[58]

> At the lowest London Prices, and free of all Expence of Carriage and Packing Cases.
>
> M. L. Woodward, Organ Builder, Harpsichord and Forte Piano Maker, from London, … Musical Instrument and Music Warehouse, New street, Birmingham, […supplies] Instruments of all Descriptions, from the most trifling to the most

---

[52] *Berrow's Worcester Journal*, 12 October 1778.
[53] He was listed in *The Birmingham, Wolverhampton, Walsall, Dudley, Bilston, and Willenhall Directory* (1780). Laycock in *Aris's Birmingham Gazette*, 21 November 1791, stated that Woodward had been in Birmingham 'for fourteen years'.
[54] *Aris's Birmingham Gazette*, 20 May 1782.
[55] NPOR, organ no. 3102.
[56] NPOR, organ no. 5888. This organ was until recently thought to have been the work of Thomas Parker, and originally built in 1748 for Gopsal Hall, Jennens' Leicestershire residence; the instrument was enlarged by John Snetzler (1710–1785) in 1777. Jennens bequeathed the seven-stop instrument to his second cousin, Heneage Finch (1715–1777), 3rd Earl of Aylesford, who had the instrument first in Packington Hall before moving it to the estate chapel of St James, where it resides today.
[57] Fleming and Perkins, *Dataset of Subscribers*.
[58] In 1807, Woodward let his New Street premises to James Lates, organist of Magdalen College, Oxford, for teaching 'the Ladies and Gentlemen of Birmingham and its Vicinity … Piano Forte, Singing, Thorough Bass, and Composition'. *Aris's Birmingham Gazette*, 12 October 1807.

elegant and superb; also fine Roman Violin, Violoncello, Harp and Guittar Strings, Reeds of all Kinds, German Wire of all sizes, and every other Article in the musical Way.

(Beware Pretenders). As many Persons have, and do, unskilfully undertake to repair and tune Musical Instruments, to the great Injury of the same, M. L. Woodward, who is the only Person in or near Birmingham ... bred to the Business, thinks it his Duty to inform the Public, that he repairs and tunes Church and Chamber Organs, Harpsichords, Forte Pianos, Spinnets, Violins, Violoncellos, and every other Musical Instruments, on the best and most approved Principles, and on reasonable Terms, in Town or Country. Instruments bought and sold on Commission. New Songs, Music, &c. constantly on Sale. Some fine old Violins to be sold cheap.[59]

Woodward's 'Beware of Pretenders' warning may well have been aimed at Henry Laycock, who had previously lived in Derby but proudly promoted his London origins in his own advertisements in the Birmingham newspapers.[60] The first of these came on 31 October 1791, in which Laycock set himself up in direct competition with Woodward: 'Laycock, from London, Organ-Builder, makes and repairs all Kinds of Musical Instruments. Organs made to play by Water and Clock-work. For Sale an excellent Finger-Organ, with eighteen Stops and two Rows of Keys; an excellent Chamber-organ and some Barrel Organs'.[61] If Woodward's earlier caution to his customers was not clear enough, his next advertisement, placed in the *Gazette* the following week, made it very plain to whom he referred:

Whereas a Person who calls himself *Laycock* and pretends to be a Musical Instrument Maker, has not only endeavoured to get Fame by Imposition and Falsehood, but has taken very illiberal Means to traduce my Reputation in my Profession of Organ-Builder &c. After a Residence of fourteen Years in this Place, the Satisfaction I have given my Employers is, I presume, A Testimony of Approbation the itinerant *Laycock* cannot boast of.[62]

The quarrel escalated over the following fortnight, and Laycock made a public threat of legal action countering Woodward's 'Beware of Pretenders' warning with:

Beware of Puffers! – Michael Woodskull, the Birmingham Organ Builder, did well to appeal to the public Discernment, for a Decision on the Difference, in point of Merit, between him and Mr. L. Nevertheless, the Calumnies which he says Mr. L. has circulated, if false, would certainly have proved of no Account, and therefore unworthy of his Notice; and, if true, they are no longer Calumnies. Let the galled Jade wince – However, Mr. Woodskull had better be cautious of his Language in future; it is not impossible but an Action may be commenced

[59] Ibid., 22 August 1791.
[60] *Derby Mercury*, 13 April 1786. 'Henry Laycock, Willow-Row, Derby, Musical Instrument and Cabinet-Maker, from London, makes violins, violoncellos, and bows'.
[61] *Aris's Birmingham Gazette*, 31 October 1791.
[62] Ibid., 7 November 1791.

against him for his Abuse; which would have been done 'ere this, was he not too contemptible for Notice. – Sorry am I that the Town of Birmingham should have been so imposed on for fourteen years.[63]

Whilst it is unclear how this public argument ended, Laycock's name is absent from the newspapers after 1791. Woodward, on the other hand, continued to advertise his sheet music and instrument business well into the nineteenth century.[64]

As well as larger music warehouses, Birmingham saw several smaller music shops and traders in the late eighteenth century. Birmingham dancing master, James Farlo, ventured into the music trade in the late 1780s. By September 1782 he had opened a school in rented rooms in Park Street 'where young Ladies and Gentlemen will be taught … every Part of Dancing in the most polite and graceful Manner'.[65] The following January he had acquired a house in nearby Corbett's Alley where he set up an assembly room and held a school.[66] He was clearly intending to benefit by renting his new premises, advertising that 'The Assembly Room, which is fitted up in an elegant Manner, may be had four Days in the Week for Balls, Concerts, Exhibitions, &c. upon reasonable Terms'.[67] His business expanded and he ran an evening school, practice balls every Tuesday evening, a fortnightly subscription ball and fencing lessons, and held a school in Wolverhampton.[68] He published his own set of dances later that year[69] and, by 1785, he was also teaching at schools in Walsall and Bilston.[70] In 1788 it appears he went into partnership with a London dancing master, 'Mr Wallis', who 'having engaged with Mr. Farlo, as Partner (whose Business was more than he could attend himself) … opened a School'.[71] Whilst Wallis took over the running of the premises in Corbett's Alley, Farlo relocated from Birmingham to Old Swinford, in Worcestershire, where he opened another school.[72]

By the early 1790s, Farlo had ventured into selling sheet music and musical instruments by opening a shop in Bromsgrove, a town situated midway between Birmingham and Worcester. In 1794 he boasted 'violins, violas, violoncellos, bassoons, hoboys, clarinets, German flutes, fifes and all sorts of musical instruments, with every article in the music branch considerably under

---

[63] Ibid., 21 November 1791.
[64] For example, Ibid., 5 May 1823. See also Humphries and Smith, *Music Publishing in the British Isles*, 341.
[65] *Aris's Birmingham Gazette,* 23 September 1782, 13 January 1783 (advertisement for school), 24 February 1783 (advertisement for letting out rooms for lodgings).
[66] Ibid., 13 January 1783.
[67] Ibid., 14 October 1782.
[68] Ibid, 13 January 1783.
[69] Ibid., 10 February 1783. 'Twenty-four New Country Dances and Cotillons, published by J. M. FARLO, may be had at the Academy, Price 6d.'.
[70] Ibid., 21 February 1785.
[71] Ibid., 8 September 1788.
[72] Ibid., 7 July 1788. Advertisement for school assistant for 'Mr. Farlo, Dancing Master, at Old Swinford, near Stourbridge, Worcestershire'.

the customary prices. Musical instruments bought, sold, or exchanged; and instruments let out to hire'.[73] Operating closer to Worcester, Farlo found himself in competition with a newly established printer, paper manufacturer and bookbinder, John Holl; he had arrived from London with his son, Thomas, in 1788.[74] The Holls had a shop on Worcester high street and owned a paper mill at nearby Hurcott. They had started stocking musical instruments at their shop by 1791 but the following year they dissolved their partnership with John taking over the paper mill and Thomas undertaking the bookselling and musical instruments business.[75] This was probably to separate the risks associated with each venture rather than as a result of any disagreement: John Holl was declared bankrupt in November 1793, and it is likely the business had been struggling before the partnership ended.[76] Perhaps in response to this setback and in an attempt to branch out from printing, Thomas Holl heavily promoted his musical instruments business: an advertisement placed in October 1793 announced he sold 'several excellent Instruments, consisting of an Organ, Piano Fortes, Guittars, a very capital Patent Flute, by Potter, a Cremona Violin, and a number of common [violins] and a choice assortments of New Instruments of every description, and the latest Publications, Songs, &c'.[77]

The proximity of Farlo and Holl's shops (twelve miles from Worcester to Bromsgrove), and the timing – after John Holl's business had gone under, and whilst Thomas was building up the music side of his – must have put a strain on these businesses, with the rivalry played out in the newspaper. On 25 November 1793, Farlo was obliged to quell rumours of a 'False Report' that he intended to sell his stock of books, stationary and medicines, and 'leave the country'.[78] In an attempt to save face he informed 'his Friends, and the Public in general that he had never a Thought of leaving Bromsgrove, much more the Country, nor of declining his Business in the Dancing Line', assuring the readers that he 'continues the Wholesale Bookselling and Stationary Business to Schools, and the Music Business Wholesale and Retail as usual, at very reduced Prices'.[79] Yet, in January 1794 Farlo announced to readers of *Aris's Birmingham Gazette* that he was opening a new Academy for Dancing, back in Birmingham, with an intention to hold fortnightly subscription assemblies and obtain more permanent premises.[80] Six months later he had decided to

---

[73] Ibid., 16 January 1794.
[74] *The Worcester Directory* (Worcester, 1788); Cooper, *The Worcester Book Trade in the Eighteenth Century* ([Worcester], 1997), 15. John and Thomas Holl traded under several names, including John Holl (1788), J & T Holl (1791–2), as T Holl & Co (1794–5), and with other partners. *British Book Trade Index*, at www.bbti.bodleian.ox.ac.uk.
[75] *London Gazette*, 21 June 1792.
[76] Ibid., 6 March 1784.
[77] 877 *Berrow's Worcester Journal*, 10 October 1793.
[78] *Aris's Birmingham Gazette*, 25 November 1793.
[79] Ibid.
[80] Ibid., 13 January 1794.

sell up his Bromsgrove business, and placed the following advertisement in the *Worcester Journal*:

> Cheap Music, well worth the Attention of Musical Societies and Musical Persons in general, now on Sale at J. Farlo's Music Warehouse, High Street, Bromsgrove, a large Stock of Violins by the best Makers, and the finest Tones, from Half a Guinea upwards; Violincellos; all Sorts of Fifes, German Flutes, English and Italian Hautboys, Clarinets, Bassoons, &c. by the best Makers. Violin Bows at 1s each; Screw Bows from 18d upwards; the best Roman and silvered Strings for Violins, Violincellos, &c. Reeds of all Sorts, Pegs, Bridges, &c. Instruction Books for every Instrument, with a large Assortment of new Songs, Overtures, Marches, &c. and every Article in the Musical Line, much under the customary Prices. An elegant new fine toned Piano Forte to be sold greatly under its Value, also a very good Second Hand one for Nine Guineas, worth double, made by Beck. Instruments lent out on Hire. N.B. Any Instruments bought at this Shop will be exchanged, if not approved of within one Month.[81]

The following August, Farlo's stock of books, stationary, and musical instruments was auctioned,[82] and he appeared before the bankruptcy court that October.[83] It is not clear if the failure of Farlo's business was down to competition with the Holls, a shortage of customers, or bad business decisions, such as the sale of inferior products. Thomas Holl certainly had a strong network through his printing and book selling activities, and often served the music industry by selling concert tickets and taking subscriptions to music publications. He printed concert programmes for Worcester's Three Choirs meetings, and took subscriptions for Jeremiah Clark's *Ten Songs*, op 4.[84] His association with Worcester Cathedral continued until at least 1801: he was paid for providing 'Music Books, &c', alongside lay clerks who were paid for copying and William Smart (who had represented William Gray's keyboard tuning and repair work in 1788), who was paid for 'Paper, Books, etc.'.[85]

Although there was evidently a significant amount of competition among the larger music traders in the Midlands, there were a significant number of smaller-scale enterprises that were set up by individuals who aspired to a portion of the market, often in conjunction with activities such as teaching and performing. This provided the seller with the benefit of avoiding the costs and risks associated with establishing a dedicated shop. It provided the purchaser with a personalised experience and eliminated the need of visiting a store or contacting a more distant business through correspondence. While some, who had a residence in London, would purchase music during trips to the capital, even they would still use personal connections to secure new music when

---

[81] Ibid., 21 July 1794.
[82] Ibid., 10 August 1795.
[83] Ibid., 13 October 1795.
[84] Thomas and John Holl, *Performance at the College-Hall, Worcester, August the 6th, 1788. Selection of Music, from Handel*. Worcester: Printed by J. Holl, in the High-Street; advertisement for Jeremiah Clark's *Ten Songs* (*Aris's Birmingham Gazette*, 25 August 1791).
[85] Worcester, Cathedral Library, A307 Treasurer's Book 1800–01.

resident in the Midlands. The final section of this chapter looks at two examples of families who used their personal links with individuals to acquire music on their behalf.

Private Networks of Music Trading

While the music shops and warehouses of Birmingham and Worcester undoubtedly served residents and visitors well, other means of acquiring music included the direct method of sharing music, with teachers and other professionals selling directly to their clients. James Chew, who tuned and repaired the Vernon family instruments, also billed them for music he acquired for them. The Vernon family, who resided in rural Worcestershire, had a good reason for acquiring music by this method, since it would not have always been convenient to make the journey to a shop. Whilst we cannot assume they did not purchase some music directly from shops, or used other agents either in London or the Midlands, a music teacher, who was well informed about new works and where to acquire them, could easily serve as a consultant.

The wealthiest families, who enjoyed the convenience of a London residence for the Season, had the option of purchasing music direct from dealers or through the services of their country music tutors. The Coventry family, whose country seat was Croome Court in Worcestershire, employed Charles Rousseau Burney (1747–1819) as their music tutor between at least 1764 and 1774.[86] Bills for instructing Maria and Anne, the daughters of George (1722–1809) 6th Earl of Coventry, also list items of printed music.[87] Burney's bill from May 1766 itemises the music: 'Song's in Tho[ma]s. & Sally' (Thomas Arne's highly popular pastoral opera from 1760 and surely an easy work to acquire), but also 'Isabelle and Gertrude, a French Opera'.[88] Adolphe Benoît Blaise's *Isabelle et Gertrude* was produced the previous year and only published in full by the French publisher Louis-Balthazar de La Chevardière (1730–1812). This may have been obtained by Burney at one of the London music shops, such as those managed by Peter Welcker or Robert Bremner; they presumably acted as agents for continental publishers but there is no evidence of this particular work in contemporary catalogues; its popularity may have been too fleeting to warrant inclusion. This points to the scarcity of the work and shows how valuable a gobetween the family music teacher was in procuring it.

We can compare this method of acquiring music by this important Midlands family with the more direct method of purchasing from a music shop thanks to two receipts from Robert Bremner. The bill to the Earl dated 26 June 1771 included 'The 2d, 3d, and 4 no of Orlando – 0:8:0': Pietro Alessandro Guglielmi's *Le pazzie di Orlando* premiered at The King's Theatre on 23 February

---

[86] Charles Rousseau Burney was a nephew and pupil of the celebrated musicologist Charles Burney. See Kerry S. Grant, 'Burney, Charles', *Grove Music Online*.

[87] WAAS, 705:73 BA14450/149/17 (45): *The Rt. Hon'ble the Earl of Coventry's acc[oun]t from Feb 11, 1764 to Apr 28 inclusive*. This bill itemised '12 Books' for 12s. total.

[88] WAAS, 705:73 BA14450/149/17 (35): *The Rt. Hon'ble the Earl of Coventry's acc[ount] w[i]th Ch. Barney, to May 11th 1765 inclusive*.

1771.[89] One further bill from Bremner, addressed to Lady Coventry and dated 24 February 1781, includes Antonio Sacchini's *Mitridate*, first performed 23 January that year. Both methods of acquiring music – from music publishers direct and via the music teacher – were used by the family.

A similar example comes from Samuel Hellier, who, like much of the nobility, spent the season in London and the summer months at his country estate. In Hellier's case there are no surviving receipts from London music dealers, but the letters he wrote to his estate manager John Rogers reveals how he procured music via music teachers: 'I have sent Books of Instruct[ion]s. one for the Horn & one the Hautboy & a gamut'.[90] In February 1767, he wrote 'I find some Musick Books were sent by Mr. Eller of Birmingham & given to W[illia]m Dalton for me I desire they may be immediately got from Dalton & sent Carefully packed up to me here all of them as they are much wanted I ought to have had them Two Month's ago.'[91] Two years later, his band of music was still a going concern, and Hellier continued to give instructions for Rogers to help with music books:

> I have sent you Walland's Voluntaries pray keep t[he]m very clean as I bo[ugh]t the Book for myself but you are welcome to the use of it I have likewise sent you somethings pretty Marches as in 4 Parts … I have also sent Down Eight small Musick Books one for Each – Performer (Viz: 1st Horn; 2^d Horn; First Hautboy; 2^d Hautboy; First Bassoon; 2^d Bassoon; First Clarinet; 2^d Clarinet pray Let them be Letter'd so & keep them Clean & w[he]n Mr. Eller comes They will be ready for him to Instruct them.'[92]

Just as the landed gentry used the services of music teachers to source music, so too did the merchant and professional classes. A notable example was Matthew Boulton (1728–1809), an important figure in eighteenth-century Birmingham and pioneer of mass-production manufacturing with the use of factories. His Soho Manufactory, built in 1766 a few miles north of the town centre, was among the first factories that fuelled the Industrial Revolution and strengthened Birmingham's status as the city of 1000 trades.[93] Boulton's daughter Anne (*c*. 1767–1829) was educated at home, rather than at a London boarding school owing to delicate health, and her music teacher was Joseph Harris (1743–1814), organist of St Martin's, Birmingham from 1771.[94] Items of music on Harris's bills between 1786 and 1793 included sonatas and duets by Ignace Joseph Pleyel, Johann Christian Bach and Muzio Clementi, and arias by Giovanni Paisiello, Giuseppe Sarti, Stephen Storace and Ferdinando Bertoni.[95] Harris acted as

---

[89] WAAS, 705:73 BA14450/355/1 (15): 26 June 1771.
[90] Letter, Hellier to Rogers, 11 January 1767. Private collection.
[91] Ibid., 28 February 1767.
[92] Ibid., 21 January 1769. The work referred to here is the *Six Voluntaries for the Organ* (London, 1752) by William Walond (1719–1768).
[93] Jennifer Tann, 'Boulton, Matthew (1728–1809), manufacturer and entrepreneur'. *Oxford Dictionary of National Biography*.
[94] Shena Mason, 'Hark, I hear Musick! Music and the Boultons of Soho House' (private manuscript research report, Birmingham, 1999), 6.
[95] Birmingham, Library, Mathew Boulton Papers, Ms.3782/13/142/1.

intermediary between client and music dealer: a music agent in all but name who facilitated the trade in music in the region.

❧ Conclusion

The various aspects of the music business in Worcester and Birmingham reflects, in many ways, the multifaceted careers and circumstances of the people involved. Professional musicians in salaried positions supplemented their income with freelance work as keyboard technicians and instrument builders, performers, teachers and impresarios. While this is perhaps unsurprising, one theme that emerges from this case-study of the eighteenth-century Midlands region is the importance of these related trades to the individuals involved. James Chew and James Radcliffe, for instance, managed their duties as lay clerks with peripatetic teaching, performing and keyboard tuning, and some activity in harpsichord and organ building and maintenance. Conversely, there are examples of instrument builders and stationers, whose primary income did not come from performance, diversifying by selling sheet music, and instruments and accessories. John and Thomas Holl's branching out from paper production and book manufacture to the sale of musical instruments is particularly unusual, but they presumably felt there was a local demand and subsequent opportunity for profit despite the existence of local competition in the form of James Farlo.

The trade in musical instruments during this period was principally carried out by the well-advertised music warehouses and shops of Worcester and Birmingham, which primarily dealt in new instruments from London makers. Again, the variety of business practices owed much to the individual traders, whether they were trained instrument builders such as Michael Woodward, or musicians such as James Farlo and James Radcliffe. There could moreover be considerable rivalry between individual traders: examples include the sheet music and instrument dealers, Farlo and the Holls, and the instrument makers Michael Woodward and Henry Laycock. The nature of these entrepreneurs – as agents for a variety of music-related trade – differed from the smaller-scale activities of instrument repairers or music copyists. Overheads for a shop-front business must have been high and the profits from reselling products from London-based publishers and instrument makers low, so that little could have been gained through cooperation. While the musical scene of the West Midlands was understandably influenced by what was happening in the capital, the area's development as an industrial powerhouse helped draw people in, many of whom had a desire to participate in music-related activities. This, in turn, drew others in who sought to provide for the needs of local inhabitants. Even musicians in an old cathedral city such as Worcester were able to capitalise on the growth of interest in music, primarily due to the rising music-related demands by a growing middle class. It was these demands that dictated the working practices of musicians and music traders alike, with many sensing the opportunity to make a profit through the provision of music-related services, or from the sale of music and its related wares.

11

'Quacks in the Musical ... Science'? The Curious Case of Stephen Moore, Piano Maker, and the Organ of St Paul's Chapel, Aberdeen

Simon D.I. Fleming

The eighteenth century was, in many respects, a golden age of organ building in Britain. Many churches and cathedrals had lost their instruments during the English Civil Wars, and while there had been a move to replace them following the restoration of the monarchy in 1660,[1] most of these same institutions sought to improve or replace these instruments over the course of the eighteenth century. Others had new organs installed with the aim of improving the quality of music that accompanied worship. This increase in demand led to a growth in the number of organ builders.[2]

In many cases, those engaged to construct or rebuild these instruments would reside a considerable distance from the town or city in which the organ was located and were unable to provide regular maintenance. Some organists were able to tune their own instruments, and perhaps even make minor repairs; for instance, Henry Valentine, organist of St Martin's Church, Stamford Baron, Northamptonshire, was in 1725 paid 'for mending the organ'.[3] Even so, organs would still require periodic servicing from a professional builder. For that reason, the offer from of work from a visiting organ builder could be a Godsend, saving on the cost of engaging a more distant professional. In some cases, however, people would be engaged to make repairs without limited proof of their ability.[4]

---

[1] Stephen Bicknell, *The History of the English Organ* (Cambridge, 1996, rpt 2001), 104–21.
[2] For an in-depth discussion of organ building and builders during the eighteenth century, see ibid., 122–93.
[3] Simon D.I. Fleming 'Music and Concert Promotion in Georgian Stamford', *The Consort*, 73 (2017), 61–83, at 62.
[4] 'Quacks' were particularly common in the medical profession. See Roy Porter, 'Before the Fringe: "Quackery" and the Eighteenth-Century Medical Market', in Roger Cooter (ed.), *Studies in The History of Alternative Medicine* (Basingstoke, 1988), 1–27. From a musical standpoint, the most infamous medical 'quack' was John Taylor (*c*.1703–*c*.1771), the British eye doctor, whose attempts at improving the eyesight

Aberdeen's St Paul's chapel had an organ built by John Donaldson of Newcastle. The piano-maker Stephen Moore was given permission to repair this instrument in 1798. A dispute later broke out over the quality of Moore's efforts, made public through a series of letters that appeared in the *Aberdeen Journal*. A pamphlet produced by Alexander Anderson, a 'Manager' of the chapel, was published in 1800 as *A Detail of the Facts Respecting the Late Attempt, made by Mr. Stephen Moore, to Tune and Repair the Organ of St. Paul's Chapel, Aberdeen.*[5]

With a focus on the Aberdeen case-study, this chapter explores the murkier side of the trade in pianos, organs and their maintenance in mid eighteenth-century Britain, where individuals with little or no experience would attempt to take advantage of widespread demand. Ultimately, this study sheds light on the issues some churches, situated far from London, had in maintaining their organs and the damage to these precious instruments that such quackery could cause.

Stephen Moore and London Piano Manufacture

London, in the second half of the eighteenth century, had become not only the centre of piano manufacture in Britain, but also in Europe.[6] The first British-crafted pianos were made there by German immigrants, one of the most significant of whom, Johannes Zumpe, set up his shop in 1761.[7] Zumpe is credited with the creation of the 'English Piano Forte', a 'low-cost practical instrument for domestic use within the reach of ordinary musicians and aspiring Amateurs'.[8] His square pianos were a favourite of Johann Christian Bach, Queen Charlotte's music master from 1763, which gave a boost to their fashionability.[9] Another early piano maker and 'creator of the first English grand pianoforte' was Americus Backers. He was active in London from at least 1763.[10] Native-born manufacturers were hardly unknown and one of the first was John Broadwood. He was apprenticed to the Swiss harpsichord maker, Burkat

---

of both J.S. Bach and Handel apparently had the opposite effect. See Roy Porter, 'Hospitals and Surgery', in Roy Porter (ed.), *The Cambridge Illustrated History of Medicine* (Cambridge, 1996, rpt 2006), 202–45, at 220.

[5] This pamphlet was published in Aberdeen by W. Rettie. While Anderson's document is an important source, and includes the testimony of several prominent musicians, it is, nevertheless, impossible to rule out any prejudice on behalf of the compiler. While every effort has been made to locate supporting evidence elsewhere, there is a notable absence of extant material.

[6] Cyril Ehrlich, *The Piano: A History Revised Edition* (Oxford, 2002), 20.

[7] David Carew, *The Companion to The Mechanical Muse: The Piano, Pianism and Piano Music, c.1760–1850* (Aldershot, 2007), 293–4.

[8] Margaret Debenham and Michael Cole, 'Pioneer Piano Makers in London, 1737–74: Newly Discovered Documentary Sources', *Royal Musical Association Research Chronicle*, 44/1 (2013), 55–86, at 55.

[9] Katalin Komlós, *Fortepianos and their Music: Germany, Austria, and England, 1760–1800* (Oxford, 1995), 6; Carew, *The Companion to The Mechanical Muse*, 15 and 294.

[10] Komlós, *Fortepianos and their Music*, 8.

Shudi, in 1761; eight years later he married Shudi's daughter, through which a partnership developed. Broadwood ultimately became head of the firm in 1771.[11] The demand for pianos increased dramatically over the coming decades, and while the fortepiano or square piano was the most popular, the grand piano became increasingly desirable.[12] Broadwood, for instance, sold more than 200 square pianos in a single year between 1784 and 1785, which increased to an average of 250 per annum in the 1790s. In that same decade, Broadwood was averaging around 140 grand pianos per annum.[13] By the year 1800 Broadwood's firm would become the largest piano manufacturer in Europe,[14] and, in the early nineteenth century, all the leading musicians used his pianos.[15] It was into this booming industry that the young Stephen Moore hoped to make his mark.

Stephen, the son of William, a tailor, and Elizabeth, was baptised on 20 December 1772 at Collier's Rents Independent Congregation, Southwark.[16] While we know nothing about his childhood, he was to allege that he had received piano lessons from Joseph Mazzinghi and Muzio Clementi, only for Clementi to deny all knowledge of him.[17] On 12 March 1787, aged fourteen, Moore was apprenticed to Francis Fane Broderip, of Longman and Broderip, whose business revolved around the manufacture of musical instruments and the printing of music books.[18] An apprenticeship was expected to last seven years, during which time an apprentice was expected to remain celibate, live within a stranger's household, and work for little or no pay.[19] In Moore's case,

[11] Ibid., 6.
[12] Ibid., 9.
[13] Ibid., 9–10.
[14] Ehrlich, *The Piano: A History*, 16.
[15] Carew, *The Companion to The Mechanical Muse*, 45.
[16] London, The National Archives (TNA), RG4/4145: Collier's Rents, White Street, Southwark, London: Baptisms 1751–1836; George S. Bozarth and Margaret Debenham in collaboration with David Cripps, 'Piano Wars: The Legal Machinations of London Pianoforte Makers, 1795–1806', *Royal Musical Association Research Chronicle*, 42 (2009), 45–108, at 88. Much of the details regarding Moore's birth, marriage and death were sourced from Margaret Debenham, *William Southwell (1736/7–1825): Musical Instrument Inventor and Maker*, at www.debenham.org.uk. I am grateful for the support of Margaret Debenham, with whom I have discussed both Moore's and John Watlen's piano businesses.
[17] Anderson, *A Detail of the Facts Respecting the Late Attempt, made by Mr. Stephen Moore, to Tune and Repair the Organ of St. Paul's Chapel, Aberdeen* (Aberdeen, [1800]), 7–8.
[18] TNA IR1/33: City (Town) Registers: February 1786–August 1788. In this document, Broderip is described as a 'Citizen & Spectacle Maker'. Instrument makers did not have their own guild, so anyone working in this profession needed to be a member of a different livery company. In this case, Broderip was a member of the Worshipful Company of Spectacle Makers. Jenny Nex, 'Longman and Broderip', in Michael Kassler (ed.), *The Music Trade in Georgian England* (London, 2016), 9–93, at 12.
[19] Christopher Brooks, 'Apprenticeship, Social Mobility and the Middling Sort, 1550–1800', in Jonathan Barry and Christopher Brooks (eds), *The Middling Sort of People: Culture, Society and Politics in England, 1550–1800* (Basingstoke, 1994), 52–83, at 74.

the apprenticeship apparently ended after only three years.[20] Such a situation was not unusual, as Christopher Brooks observed that between 'one-third to one-half of apprenticeships … ended prematurely'.[21] One possible cause for its early termination was Moore's marriage: on 11 January 1791 at St James, Westminster, he wed Elizabeth Beake.[22] While Brooks also observed that, by the late eighteenth century, it was not unusual for apprentices to wed before their period of indenture was complete, the absence of a salary or the possibility of pregnancy might have been enough motivation for an apprentice to quit.[23]

Whatever Moore's reason, he clearly felt sufficiently skilled in the art of piano making to enter into this profession. While details of the early part of Moore's career are lacking – at this stage Moore did not advertise his trade in the newspapers – the sole surviving example of his work dates from this period. This instrument, a square piano, was auctioned at Sotheby's in 1982, and now resides in the Geelvinck Music Museum, in Amsterdam.[24] Dated 1796, the instrument records Moore's address as 'Panton Square, Haymarket'. As his father resided at Panton Street, it seems likely that Stephen ran his fledgling business from the family home.[25] Nevertheless, there might have been issues with his business acumen, even at this young age. In a letter, the Longman and Broderip employee, Frederick Augustus Hyde, thought that 'Moore's unfortunate situation in life obliged him … to leave this country [England]'.[26] Hyde's cryptic statement gives no details as to the cause of Moore's 'unfortunate situation'. Nevertheless, soon after he had made the 'Geelvinck' piano, he moved northward to Edinburgh to establish himself there in the piano-making industry.

❧ Stephen Moore and the Music Trade in Edinburgh

At the time of Moore's arrival in Edinburgh, the music trade in the Scottish capital was booming. There had been a significant increase in the number of new businesses publishing music there during the last three decades of the century. Frank Kidson identified 36 music publishers based in Edinburgh, six of which were established in the 1770s; at least another thirteen had appeared before 1800.[27] The increase in the number of music businesses mirrors, in many ways, the changing economic situation of that city. While there had been a steady

---

[20] Anderson, *A Detail of the Facts*, 7.
[21] Brooks, 'Apprenticeship, Social Mobility and the Middling Sort', 74.
[22] London, Westminster Archives, Westminster Church of England Parish Registers, STJ/PR/6/7.
[23] Brooks, 'Apprenticeship, Social Mobility and the Middling Sort', 68.
[24] Nex, 'Longman and Broderip', 35; Museum Geelvinck, at www.geelvinck.nl/nieuwe-aanwinst-tafelpiano-moore-1796.
[25] Bozarth and Debenham, 'Piano Wars', 88.
[26] Anderson, *A Detail of the Facts*, 7. For more on Hyde, see Nex, 'Longman and Broderip', 55.
[27] Frank Kidson, *British Music Publishers, Printers and Engravers: London, Provincial, Scottish, and Irish* (New York, 1900, repr. 1967), 177–201.

growth in the population of Edinburgh over the eighteenth century, rising from 50,000 in the seventeenth century to 81,000 in 1801, much of this expansion took place in the third quarter of the eighteenth century.[28] By the 1790s Edinburgh's population was second only to London.[29] This precipitated, according to Christopher Smout, 'a great growth in facilities for private education by private tutors and in schools and academies of many kinds, bringing wealthy families into the town for the education of their children'.[30] This burgeoning of the populace coincided with the construction of the new town, proposals for which were first published in 1752.[31] Edinburgh's intellectual life similarly grew, and this helped draw into the city members of the gentry and nobility. Smout attributed much of this growth to the 'attraction of the clubs [which] had an economic as well as a social effect, in bringing visitors into the town to spend as well as to attend'.[32] Nevertheless, club culture had existed in Edinburgh much earlier in the century. One of the most influential of these early groups, the 'Easy Club', had been founded in 1712 by the poet Allan Ramsay and five friends. By the following decade, Edinburgh, like many other towns and cities in Britain, had its own musical society, a group that was formally established in 1728.[33] By 1779 the society, then at its peak, was described by Hugo Arnot as 'one of the most elegant and genteel entertainments … of any in Britain'.[34]

Into this cultural development, the piano became a favoured instrument in Scotland,[35] although most instruments and music sold in Edinburgh at that time were imported from London.[36] Nevertheless, from 1786 advertisements for locally-made pianos began to appear in the local press.[37] The city's piano makers tended to work from their homes, and instruments could either be purchased directly from their workshops, or through a music retailer.[38] Pianos

---

[28] John Langton, 'Urban Growth and Economic Change: From the Late Seventeenth Century to 1841', in Peter Clark (ed.), *The Cambridge Urban History of Britain, Volume II: 1540–1840* (Cambridge, 2000), 453–90, at 473.
[29] John Leonard Cranmer, 'Concert Life and the Music Trade in Edinburgh c.1780–c.1830' (PhD dissertation, University of Edinburgh, 1991), 376.
[30] T.C. Smout, 'Where had the Scottish Economy got to by the Third Quarter of the Eighteenth Century?', in Istvan Hont and Michael Ignatieff (eds), *Wealth and Virtue: The Shaping of Political Economy in the Scottish Enlightenment* (Cambridge, 1983), 45–72, at 58.
[31] Ibid.
[32] Ibid.
[33] Jennifer Macleod, 'The Edinburgh Musical Society: Its Membership and Repertoire 1728–1797' (PhD dissertation, University of Edinburgh, 2001), 11.
[34] Ibid., 1; Hugo Arnot, *The History of Edinburgh* (Edinburgh, 1779), 381.
[35] Ehrlich, *The Piano: A History*, 17.
[36] Cranmer, 'Concert Life and the Music Trade in Edinburgh', 252. In some cases, Edinburgh music sellers would use an agent to procure merchandise from London for their shop. Muzio Clementi was, in 1792, engaged by Neil and Malcolm Stewart to select some Broadwood pianos on their behalf. See Cranmer, 'Concert Life and the Music Trade in Edinburgh', 255.
[37] Cranmer, 'Concert Life and the Music Trade in Edinburgh', 380.
[38] Ibid., 377 and 382.

by Moore had been imported into Edinburgh from at least December 1795, at which time they were available for purchase from the shop of Neil Stewart and Co.[39] It may have been the demand for his pianos in Scotland that led to Moore's decision to relocate there.

Soon after his arrival in Edinburgh, Moore went into partnership with John Watlen, a music seller and former clerk to the Edinburgh-based music business of Corri and Co.[40] In the first instance, Watlen appears to have acted as an agent for Moore. In an advertisement in April 1796 Watlen informed the public that he sold Moore's 'PATENT SPRING FRAME for GRAND and SQUARE PIANO FORTES, HARPSICHORDS &c'.[41] The concept of placing a piano on springs was a relatively new development, having been first patented by George Buttery in 1792.[42] Moore's own account of the spring frame, and its benefits, was published in the *Edinburgh Advertiser* on 10 March 1797:

> The effects of the Spring Frame on the Grand Forte Piano and the finished elegance and lightness of its appearance, are at once striking and beautiful. The great bearing and density of the Grand Forte Piano on its common Frame has a tendency to check the vibration, similar to a mute on a violin. On the Spring Frame, the tone produced is clear and brilliant; and, while it rivals the powers of the Organ, it possesses the enchanting and delightful tones of the sweetest Flute. The beautiful *TOUT ENSEMBLE* can only be conceived by being heard.
>
> A most striking advantage of the Spring Frame is the length of time which the instrument so suspended will stand in tune.
>
> A Forte Piano, belonging to an officer on board one of her late Imperial Majesty's ships, when lying at the Nore, was put most completely out of tune by firing the guns; – by way of experiment, it was affixed to a Spring Frame, and although one gun, which run in within three feet of the Instrument, was repeatedly fired, yet not a note of the Forte Piano was the least altered. The reason is obvious, the shock was lost in the springs; and when it is admitted that the least jar has a tendency to put a Forte Piano out of tune, the advantage of the Spring Frame must be striking indeed.

By May 1796 two other businesses, one managed by Pietro Urbani and Edward Liston,[43] and a second by James Muir, were also selling Moore's pianos.[44] Watlen, perhaps sensing an opportunity for profit, entered into a partnership with

---

[39] Ibid., 287.

[40] Simon D.I. Fleming, 'Publishing Music by Subscription in Eighteenth-Century Edinburgh: John Watlen and his Collections of Circus Tunes', in Simon D.I. Fleming and Martin Perkins (eds), *Music by Subscription: Composers and their Networks in the British Music-Publishing Trade, 1676–1820* (Abingdon, 2022), 73–92, at 79.

[41] *Edinburgh Advertiser*, 19 April 1796.

[42] Cranmer, 'Concert Life and the Music Trade in Edinburgh', 397; B. Woodcroft (ed.), *Patents for Inventions: Abridgments of Specifications Relating to Music and Musical Instruments. A.D. 1694–1866* (London, 1871), 25–6.

[43] *Caledonian Mercury*, 16 May 1796.

[44] *Edinburgh Advertiser*, 31 May 1796.

Moore.⁴⁵ Nevertheless, the Watlen-Moore arrangement was short-lived and after six months, on 16 November, it was dissolved by mutual consent.⁴⁶ It may have been the poor quality of Moore's work that led to the partnership's failure. John Hamilton, an employee of Watlen, thought that 'none [...of Moore's pianos were] good, and of course he broke deep in debt'.⁴⁷ Watlen, after the dissolution of their partnership, initiated legal action against Moore over an unpaid bill of £14 14s. Moore was ordered to pay the outstanding amount, with interest, but he disputed his liability and successfully applied for a bill of suspension, granted in August 1797.⁴⁸ It is unknown whether Moore ever settled this debt, but he subsequently set up his own business on the fashionable shopping parade of South Bridge.⁴⁹

As part of the same 1797 advertisement in which he espoused the benefits of the spring frame, Moore made public his own credentials. He publicised his apprenticeship with Longman and Broderip (omitting to mention its premature termination) and claimed that pianos 'made under [his] direction' could 'find at this time the readiest sale in London'.⁵⁰ Given what we have so far learnt about Moore's London-based business, this appears to have been a distortion of the truth. Moore was not alone in making misrepresentations for personal benefit, as his former partner, Watlen, could be equally underhanded. Watlen had been selling discounted Broadwood pianos without the company's permission. When the matter became public, Watlen's business suffered and he rapidly fell into bankruptcy.⁵¹ As for Moore, his new business venture also failed and, having burnt all his bridges in Edinburgh, he set out from the city in 1798, at which time he reinvented himself as an organ builder.⁵²

❧ Stephen Moore, Organs and the Case of St Paul's Chapel, Aberdeen

Moore's advertisements in the Edinburgh press, while few in number, never mention any organ tuning services. However, he did work as a piano tuner, although apparently 'with *little satisfaction*'.⁵³ Neil Stewart gave an account of a piano belonging to 'Mrs. Allan of Arrol', which Moore 'repaired' at a cost of 22 guineas, but 'which was never in condition to be performed upon, till such

---

⁴⁵ GB-Enr CS271/15736: Moore vs Watlen (1797).
⁴⁶ Anderson, *A Detail of the Facts*, 9–10; *Edinburgh Advertiser*, 22 November 1796.
⁴⁷ Anderson, *A Detail of the Facts*, 8.
⁴⁸ GB-Enr CS271/15736: Moore vs Watlen (1797).
⁴⁹ Cranmer, 'Concert Life and the Music Trade in Edinburgh', 384; *Edinburgh Advertiser*, 10 March 1797.
⁵⁰ *Edinburgh Advertiser*, 10 March 1797.
⁵¹ Fleming, 'Publishing Music by Subscription in Eighteenth-Century Edinburgh', 85–7.
⁵² Cranmer, 'Concert Life and the Music Trade in Edinburgh', 398.
⁵³ Anderson, *A Detail of the Facts*, 8.

time as another person put it in order'.[54] Anderson, in preparing his pamphlet on Moore, wrote to several Edinburgh-based organists to enquire if Moore had any experience tuning their organs. All of the replies were negative, with Adam Christie, organist of St Peter's Chapel, attesting that:

> Mr. Stephen Moore never tuned a single note of the Organ upon which I perform – and I was always of opinion, that he was utterly incapable of tuning Organs.[55]

Christie's statement suggests an unsuccessful attempt by Moore at organ tuning in Edinburgh, or at least that he was known among some of the city's organists. Moore does not appear to have received any organ tuning experience during his apprenticeship either, since Francis Broderip asserted that Moore 'never had anything to do with Organ work; it being a particular branch of our business that he could not receive any information from'.[56] Moore appears to have lost access to a workshop for manufacturing pianos with the failure of his Edinburgh business and, at that point, reinvented himself as a professional organ tuner. From Edinburgh he made his way northwards, along the east coast of Scotland, visiting Dundee and Montrose in 1798. Moore stopped to repair organs at both places, where his efforts were, according to Anderson, not well received. Anderson reported that at Dundee, the 'Organ was not improved by Mr. Moore's operations, but the very reverse'. Nevertheless, Moore was apparently presented with a letter of recommendation, perhaps as an encouragement to leave.[57] That same letter helped him get access to the organ at Montrose. The chapel's treasurer, Colin Alison, provided Anderson with a long and detailed account of Moore's arrival and his efforts on their organ:

> On coming to this town, he [Moore] called on me; and shewing an open letter, from the Parson or Organist at Dundee, to a Gentleman in Aberdeen, I listened, and introduced him to the managers here, to whom he proposed making a vast deal of improvements on the Chapel Organ, as well as to tune her. After allowing him to go to work, he took her down, trifled much with us, and brought on a vast expense; but neither I nor any person else thought she was in the smallest degree improved. And Mr. Moore himself left the town in a very abrupt manner, after getting the *Cash* from me, without being able to tune the instrument properly, which he engaged to do to the managers' satisfaction. He attempted this week after week, but he could never put her in so good a tune as she was before he touched her; from hence … I was led to think he had not a thorough knowledge of the business, he professed being so much master of.[58]

George Anderson, the organist at Montrose, similarly thought that Moore had 'made the Organ much worse', bringing 'about £30 [in] expenses', but they still

---

[54] Charles Humphries and William C. Smith, *Music Publishing in the British Isles from the Beginning until the Middle of the Nineteenth Century* (Oxford, 1970), 301; Anderson, *A Detail of the Facts*, 8–9.
[55] Anderson, *A Detail of the Facts*, 9.
[56] Ibid., 6–7.
[57] Ibid., 12.
[58] Ibid., 12.

paid Moore thirteen guineas for his work.[59] The payment may even have been made to encourage Moore to move on. From Montrose, Moore made his way to Aberdeen where he offered his services on the organ at St Paul's Chapel, asserting that his employment at the chapels in Dundee and Montrose had, in his opinion, 'given satisfaction'.[60]

St Paul's Chapel, Aberdeen, had been erected in 1721 and, by the following year, an organ had been installed.[61] While the builder of the original instrument is unknown, William Bristow was paid £120 for repairs in 1726–7.[62] This instrument was largely replaced in 1783 by one built by John Donaldson,[63] but he retained the 'two sound-boards of the great Organ, and the pipes of the open Diapason'.[64]

From Anderson's pamphlet, we know that it was Moore who approached the managers of the chapel with an offer to 'tune and repair the Organ'.[65] Anderson was against Moore's engagement, feeling that he 'was not qualified to tune the Organ'.[66] Moore wrote a letter to the chapel clerk on 2 November 1798, in which he listed his proposed work, for which he would charge thirty guineas, and stipulated that 'I shall not consider myself entitled to receive one shilling, till the Organ is completed; and till you are convinced … that I have done the Organ substantial justice'.[67] Anderson gave his opinion to the chapel's managers, at which point Moore's application was rejected. However, Moore was not about to lose such a lucrative opportunity, so he called on the chapel managers individually and persuaded them to hold another meeting a few days later, on which occasion their decision was reversed.[68]

---

[59] Ibid., 13. It has been impossible to independently verify Moore's visits to Dundee or Montrose, and there are no records of any payments to him in the kirks' records, held by the National Records of Scotland in Edinburgh.

[60] Anderson, *A Detail of the Facts*, 24.

[61] David Welch, 'Further Notes on Pre-1820 Organs in N.E. Scotland', *Bios Reporter*, 29/2 (2005), 16–21, at 16. I am grateful to David Shuker for providing me with copies of Welch's articles.

[62] Ibid. Bristow was active in the North-East during the 1720s and 30s. Based in Newcastle, he built and sold organs, and was paid eight guineas in 1734 for repairing the 'little organ' at Durham Cathedral. See Roz Southey, *Music-Making in North-East England during the Eighteenth Century* (Aldershot, 2006), 108–9 and 181; Simon D.I. Fleming, 'A Century of Music Production in Durham City 1711–1811: A Documentary Study' (PhD dissertation, University of Durham, 2009), 34.

[63] Anderson, *A Detail of the Facts*, 2. In 1783 Donaldson also repaired the organ at St Nicholas' Church, Whitehaven after its vandalisation. See Simon D.I. Fleming, 'New Research into the Snetzler Organ of St Nicholas' Church, Whitehaven, during the Time of the Howgill Family', *Bios Reporter* 34/4 (2010), 19–22, at 21–2.

[64] Anderson, *A Detail of the Facts*, 3.

[65] Ibid., 1.

[66] Ibid.

[67] Ibid., 25–6.

[68] Ibid., 26–7.

Having secured permission to repair the organ, Moore placed an advertisement in the *Aberdeen Journal* promoting his services. Moore again referred to his apprenticeship and this time described his experience tuning harpsichords:

> MR. S. MOORE, Organ Builder, and grand and square Piano Forte Manufacturer, who served a regular apprenticeship with Messrs. Longman and Broderip, London, Musical Instrument Makers extraordinary to their Majesties, respectfully in[t]imates, that having occasion to remain some time in Aberdeen (being engaged in repairing the organ of St. Paul's Chapel and other organs,) he begs leave to offer his abilities to the service of the nobility and gentry.
>
> As he constantly tuned the harpsichord at the Opera House, and for the most eminent professors in London, he flatters himself, it will not be thought vanity in him to presume, he will give satisfaction to those ladies and gentlemen, who honour him with their commands.[69]

Moore appears to have begun his repairs to the Chapel organ but Anderson, doubting Moore's claims, set out to contact all those with some prior association with the organ tuner. This correspondence was ultimately published in his 1800 pamphlet, but the first time that dispute appeared in print was in September 1799 when Moore published a lengthy letter in the *Aberdeen Journal*. Moore asserted that:

> In consequence of the report that has been so industriously circulated, M[oore]. has found, to his great loss, that prejudices in other parts of the country are still entertained against him, from the story of the organ being imperfectly known. It is in Aberdeen, where the business has undergone a strict and full examination, and where malice can no more be called into action to his disadvantage.[70]

What is perhaps most interesting is that Moore here admits that there had been issues, or 'prejudices' as he called them, with his work at other places, giving credence to the accounts of his work at Edinburgh, Dundee and Montrose. In the same notice, Moore quoted from written testimony given by the music seller and publisher, Pietro Urbani (1749–1816), and the violinist Girolamo Stabilini (d.1815).[71] This is one of the only known positive reports of Moore's piano making abilities:

---

[69] *Aberdeen Journal*, 26 November 1798, repeated 14 January 1799. One suspects that Moore's claim that he 'constantly tuned the harpsichord at the Opera House' was a fabrication. It has certainly not been possible to locate any record of Moore's work there. I am grateful to Stephanie Rolt, Archivist of the Royal Opera House, Covent Garden, for her assistance in this regard. Moore later advertised his services as a piano teacher. See *Aberdeen Journal*, 28 January 1799.

[70] *Aberdeen Journal*, 2 September 1799, repeated 9 September 1799. Moore's statement that there were 'prejudices in other parts of the country' indicates that there had been issues with his previous work.

[71] Humphries and Smith, *Music Publishing in the British Isles*, 316. Both Urbani and Stabilini had previously been employed by the Edinburgh Musical Society. See Macleod, 'The Edinburgh Musical Society', 257.

> Having been requested by many respectable Gentlemen, to give our opinion, in writing, respecting the professional abilities of Mr STEPHEN MOORE, we do this with the more confidence, as we have had every opportunity of knowing and examining them. Mr Moore resided constantly in Edinburgh for three years, and was esteemed by all judges as the best tuner of Keyed Instruments that ever was in Scotland. It would not be doing justice to Mr Moore to consider him in the light of a tuner *only*, we were witnesses of his founding a very extensive manufactory of Instruments in Edinburgh; the workmen of which, near twenty in number, were taught the mechanical part of the musical business, personally by Mr Moore, as they were all common Cabinet Makers, till so employed.
>
> To our knowledge, Mr Moore has repaired and tuned several Organs, and, so far from his abilities in that line being depreciated, we never heard them mentioned, but with the highest respect, before we came to Aberdeen. As professional men, we should not discharge our consciences were we not to add that, there is not a person in Great Britain, whom we could recommend *sooner*, or, who is, in our opinion, more capable of tuning and repairing all Keyed Instruments whatever than Mr Stephen Moore, as witness our hands.[72]

Anderson, taking into account his own experiences with Moore and the testimonies provided by others, doubted the letter's fidelity so he wrote to Urbani and Stabilini, from whom he received the following reply:

> We hereby declare, that we never knew or heard of any Organ tuned by Mr. Moore, previous to his tuning the Aberdeen one; and that the last paragraph of our attestation in his favour is misrepresented.[73]

John Ross, organist at St Paul's Chapel since 1783 and harpsichordist to the Aberdeen Musical Society, appears to have been one of Moore's key targets.[74] Indeed, Moore threatened to publish a letter written by Ross that he thought would 'open the eyes of the public, and … place in a striking point of view this gentleman's real character'.[75] While Moore, in his threat, did not reveal much of the letter's content, it had apparently been 'invidiously circulated to M[oore].'s disadvantage'.[76] One wonders if it was due to this dispute that a rumour spread that Ross had considered leaving Aberdeen, a move he later refuted.[77] Ross, however, felt the need to address Moore's insinuations by writing to the *Aberdeen Journal* himself:

> MY character having been attacked by Mr Stephen Moore repeatedly in this paper, I feel it a duty which I owe to myself and to the public, to offer a brief review of the facts that have exposed me to the malevolent and unjust aspersions of that gentleman.

---

[72] *Aberdeen Journal*, 2 September 1799.
[73] Anderson, *A Detail of the Facts*, 11.
[74] Henry George Farmer, *Music Making in the Olden Days: The Story of the Aberdeen Concerts 1748–1801* (London, 1950), 69.
[75] *Aberdeen Journal*, 2 September 1799.
[76] Ibid.
[77] *Aberdeen Journal*, 20 May 1799.

> Mr Moore was engaged by the Managers of St. Paul's Chapel to tune the Organ, and make certain repairs on it; and his letter on the subject, which is addressed to me, concludes as follows, "I shall not consider myself entitled to receive one shilling, till the organ is completed, and till you are convinced (as Organist) that I have done the organ substantial justice."
>
> Here a trust was committed to, and confidence reposed in me by the Managers, which I felt conscientiously bound to discharge.
>
> When Mr Moore had finished his operations on the Organ, I was called upon of course by the Managers to inspect it, and report my opinion of its state – and I felt exceedingly sorry in being obliged to report, inter alia, "that I found all the stops much out of tune, and in some respects worse than formerly." And that my opinion might not stand alone, I referred the Managers to several gentlemen of the first character and respectability in Aberdeen, and known to be amongst the best judges of music in it, and whose unanimous opinion on the subject coincided with my own.
>
> I do not feel myself called on to enter upon the general point of Mr Moore's professional abilities, or to take any notice of the attestation of Messrs Urbani and Stabilini brought in support of them; my business is confined to the Organ of St. Paul's Chapel; and as I was satisfied that Mr Moore's operations on that instrument, instead of improving its effect, had rendered it much worse, I should have esteemed myself undeserving of the trust that had been reposed in me, and unworthy of the character of an honest man, had I returned a report contrary to my own conviction.[78]

This letter appeared in September, but the issues with Moore's work had by that time been rumbling for over seven months. In January Moore had claimed 'his operations [to the organ] were finished'.[79] Moore published a letter in the *Journal*, dated 26 January and attributed to a John Smith, in response to those critical of his efforts:

> In consequence of my having heard the Chapel Organ, and having heard a harpsichord in very fine order by Mr Moore, I find he does not only know fine tone, but perfectly understands how to pen a harpsichord; for these reasons I have employed him to put my own harpsichord in order, and Mr Moore is the only person, I have ever yet met with, who perfectly understands this business, or into whole hands I ever trusted it. All the common dabblers in this work, pen their instruments for noise, leaving fine expressive tone out of the question.[80]

Ross, however, on inspecting the organ:

> found all the stops much out of tune, and in some respects worse than formerly. One of the pipes of the Principal is wanting, which Mr. Moore acknowledges was broken by him, while he was tuning it. Some of the reeded pipes in the swell intermit now, and at times do not speak at all … I beg leave to observe here,

---

[78] *Aberdeen Journal*, 16 September 1799, repeated 23 September 1799.
[79] Anderson, *A Detail of the Facts*, 27.
[80] *Aberdeen Journal*, 28 January 1799.

that Mr. Moore positively refused to do any thing more to the Organ, although I entreated him repeatedly to re-touch and tune the whole.[81]

Moore, unwilling to accept the blame for the poor tuning of the instrument, circulated a report that Ross had been pressured into giving 'an unfavourable report'.[82] He then blamed Ross for its poor state, arguing that 'he [Ross] played on it in such a manner, as to make it appear out of tune'.[83] Moore nonsensically alleged that the poor sound quality was due to Ross playing 'upon discordant stops', and that he was causing the organ to cipher by 'putting leads on the keys'.[84] Moore continued his attack on Ross through the production of what appears to been a printed handbill.[85] The organist again decided to respond through the newspaper, making reference to Anderson's upcoming pamphlet, with which Ross clearly had close involvement:

> I Have seen a publication, bearing to be signed by Mr Stephen Moore, without any date, and intitled [sic] as a letter to me, chiefly in regard to the Organ of St. Paul's Chapel; in which he has taken occasion to load me with the most gross abuse, merely for the conscientious discharge of my duty.
>
> In regard to the tuning of the Organ of St Paul's Chapel, my opinion remains unaltered.
>
> When Mr Moore comes forward with his long threatened Appeal, there will be laid before the public, a short history of Mr Moore's professional career, supported by unquestionable documents, which will fully satisfy them that Mr Moore is by no means skilled in Organ-work; and it will afterwards remain no matter of surprise that he has injured the Organ of St. Paul's Chapel, which formerly was an excellent instrument, altho' Mr Moore now wishes to ruin its character.[86]

As far as the newspaper is concerned, the ongoing argument was brought to an abrupt end by the editors. Tired of the dispute, they advised that they would 'decline inserting any thing more on the subject'.[87]

It is apparent, however, that the matter became a topic of local conversation. In a letter sent to the Revd Patrick Torry, Incumbent at Peterhead,[88] the Bishop of Aberdeen, John Skinner,[89] made reference to a 'musical Stranger we have had here for some time'.[90] Skinner did not hold Moore in high esteem and refused

---

[81] Anderson, *A Detail of the Facts*, 28.
[82] Ibid., 28.
[83] Ibid., 18.
[84] Ibid., 18.
[85] *Aberdeen Journal*, 2 September 1799.
[86] *Aberdeen Journal*, 14 October 1799.
[87] Ibid.
[88] A.F. Pollard and Rowan Strong, 'Torry, Patrick (1763–1852)', *Oxford Dictionary of National Biography*.
[89] Nigel Aston, 'Skinner, John (1744–1816)', *Oxford Dictionary of National Biography*.
[90] GB-Enr CH12112/2318. Quoted with permission of the Scottish Episcopal Church.

his offer of work on the organ at St Andrew's Chapel, now Aberdeen Cathedral. He wrote that Moore:

> would have almost made the public believe that nothing was too difficult for him in the way of his profession, & therefore no Reward too great for his Merits. Although I am perfectly ignorant of the business he pretended to be Master of, I did not much like his boasting Outset, & therefore determined to wait for the wonderful Proof of his Abilities which was to be exhibited on the Gallowgate [St Paul's Chapel] Organ, before I would allow him to lay a hand upon ours, for the mere tuning of which, for he acknowledged it wanted nothing else, his very modest Demand was only 20 Guineas! From this Circumstance & what has happened since we plainly see that there are Quacks in the Musical, as well as Medical Science, pretending only to a great deal of Knowledge, but actually possessing a great deal of Greed. The Consequence has been a boisterous War & Conflict of Opinion respecting the present State of the Organ in question, one party insisting that it is much worse since Moore meddled with it, & another maintaining that the fault is in the Performer, who out of Envy or fear of Rivalship, makes the poor Organ speak the Language of discordant passions. Thus divided by such jarring Sentiments, & unable to say who is right or wrong, I cannot think of trusting our Instrument, pleased & happy as we are with it, to the Uncertainty of a dangerous Operation, whose Chance is equal either to kill or cure.[91]

St Paul's Chapel's managers met on 7 February to debate as to whether Moore should be paid for his efforts. At this meeting Moore made an attempt to place the blame for his bungled work at St Paul's Chapel on John Donaldson himself, presenting three pipes from the organ which, he argued, 'had been robbed of their metal' and were 'a mere botch, and a mass of corruption'.[92] This was despite the fact that two of these pipes, which were much lighter than the third pipe, had originated from the old instrument.[93] Fortuitously, Donaldson was passing through Aberdeen in 1799, on his way to install a new chamber organ for 'Colonel [Alexander Penrose] Cumming of Altyre'.[94] Anderson took advantage of this opportunity to request Donaldson to report on the state of the Chapel organ:

> The touch of the Great Organ is rendered, by improper management of the pallets and springs, irregular and difficult to play upon. The open Diapason, most part of which stands in the front, that was, when I left it, smooth and ready in its articulation, is now, from improper treatment, become poor, unequal, and in many of the notes, slow of speech.
>
> The Principal is injured in its tone, from causes that appear to be the effect of ignorance in the person who last attempted to tune it. The 12th, 15th, Sesquialtra

---

[91] Ibid.
[92] Anderson, *A Detail of the Facts*, 4 and 37.
[93] Ibid., 38.
[94] Ibid., 13; Bernard B. Edmonds, 'Yorkshire Organ Builders: the Earlier Years', *Bios Journal*, 9 (1985), 42–50, at 48; David Griffiths, *A Musical Place of the First Quality: A History of Institutional Music Making in York c.1550–1990* (York, [1994]), 230. Altyre is situated midway between Inverness and Elgin.

and Cornet, have all suffered in their turns, from a similar mode of treatment; and are indeed so deranged in their voicing, as to render any radical tuning impossible, without first restoring the pipes in each stop to their original firmness, and solidity of tone. And so far is the instrument from being in tune, that at present there is not almost a single Octave in the Organ that does not offend the ear.

The Trumpet has, from its appearance, received a part of its injury by having been blown into by the mouth; which has, from the humidity proceeding from it, corroded the Reeds, Tongues, and Springs, and thereby drawn on a general derangement in that stop, which an unskilful person may attempt to remedy, but cannot cure. This last stop is more than half of it slow in speaking, and many of the notes quite silent: of course it should not be used in its present state.

The same, or similar defects, appear in many notes of the Hautboy, which is in the swell; but otherwise, that part of the instrument seems to have suffered less violence, in proportion, than the great Organ; which I am almost unable to know, by its tone, to be the same I left, more than 15 years ago, in good tune, and sound harmony.[95]

Robert Boston, Donaldson's foreman, gave a similarly negative view of the organ's current state, writing that the instrument had been 'very ignorantly and improperly treated'.[96] Moore, feeling threatened by Donaldson's presence, apparently accosted him during a walk from the town's pier. Donaldson provided Anderson with a report, dated 7 November, of this encounter:

I told him [Moore], I was sorry to say, he had done the Organ so much damage, from an apparent inexperience in the business; and lamented that, besides this, (which his knowledge could not remedy) he had also (through a wandering stranger only) contrived to set at variance some of the most respected Gentlemen in the town. He saw clearly my desire to be rid of his company; which I did not however effect, till we came to Mr. Joseph Simpson's shop; where, he said, if I were not prejudiced, he would shew me, by walking in there, that he had been ill-treated by Bourtie [Alexander Anderson] and Mr. Ross, and that it was they who had done the injury to the Organ; which he owned was now much out of tune. As I had, during the time we were building the Organ, received many civilities from Mr. Simpson, I said I would most cheerfully go in and pay my respect to the Gentleman, for whom I had the most cordial esteem. On our entering the shop ... Mr. Moore opened up with a long list of grievances, and various reproaches against Mr. Anderson and Mr. Ross, which I observed were irrelevant and foreign to the intention of my report [on the organ], *in which I alone seemed to be concerned*. I said, that certainly the Organ was much out of order, from injudicious management; but that if (as an honest man should do) he would go to the Chapel, with his friends, and restore a single stop or two to their pristine state of fulness, and sweetness of tone, I would be ready to believe him to be

---

[95] Anderson, *A Detail of the Facts*, 14.
[96] Ibid., 15; Griffiths, *A Musical Place*, 213. Boston mentioned that he had worked for Donaldson since c.1778, which suggests that Donaldson's organ-building business was already well established by the late 1770s.

no imposter in the business; but that if *he* could not do this, which any man of experience could do with ease, it remained for me to be put to the trial; and if I restored each note to a roundness and smoothness, and equality of tone, which I would engage to do, I hoped his friends would have the candour to give their opinion freely … This offer I made in the presence of Mr. Joseph Simpson … and which offer Mr. Moore artfully parried, and wisely did not accept.[97]

While a local man, a Mr Corbet, was engaged to do some repairs, particularly in regard to the ciphering,[98] one suspects Donaldson may have been engaged to do further work on the St Paul's Chapel organ. Certainly this instrument appears to have been restored and did not require another overhaul until 1818; it was then moved to a new chapel in 1865 and rebuilt in 1881.[99] In terms of Moore, he, against the protests of Anderson and Ross, was paid for his work.[100] While in one notice Moore announced his intention to take up 'constant residence in Aberdeen', probably more a threat than a serious proposal, Moore did eventually move on.[101] From Aberdeen, he continued his journey northwards, and was employed to repair the organ at the Episcopal Chapel at Banff, although there are no details of his efforts in that place; while in the area, he also examined a chamber organ at Duff House for James Duff, 2nd Earl of Fife.[102]

Conclusion

In late 1800 or early 1801, Moore, perhaps finding increased hostility to his organ tuning endeavours, made his way back to London. Unfortunately for Moore, his return led to a period of time incarcerated in debtors' jail.[103] While it is impossible to ascertain whether this was for an old or new debt, he was committed to The Fleet Prison on 24 January 1801, owing £36 15s to Archdale Wilson Taylor, and £15 to William Moore.[104] In response to his imprisonment,

---

[97] Anderson, *A Detail of the Facts*, 16–17.

[98] Ibid., 39–42.

[99] *The National Pipe Organ Register*; David Welch, 'Organs Prior to 1820 in North-East Scotland', *Bios Reporter*, 28/3 (2004), 14–19, at 15. The Aberdeen Musical Society also owned an organ, built by John Snetzler. One suspects, given Moore's work on the organ at St Paul's, that he was not allowed near it. See Farmer, *Music Making in the Olden Days*, 38–9.

[100] Anderson, *A Detail of the Facts*, 5.

[101] *Aberdeen Journal*, 2 September 1799. Despite the issues with Moore's repairs, the managers wanted to pay him for his work. Anderson alleged that it was due to his unwillingness to pay Moore, who he thought had 'forfeited all title to any payment', that Moore launched his series of attacks in the *Aberdeen Journal*. Anderson, *A Detail of the Facts*, 1–2.

[102] GB-A MS 3175/919/1: Letter from Stephen Moore to the Earl of Fife, dated 6 February 1801. I am grateful to the University of Aberdeen for providing a copy of the letter.

[103] *London Gazette*, 4 July 1801, repeated 7 July 1801 and 14 July 1801.

[104] TNA PRIS10, King's (Queen's) Bench, Fleet, Marshalsea and Queen's Prisons: Miscellanea, no. 156. It has not been possible to ascertain if William Moore, to whom Stephen owed money, was a relative.

Stephen sent a letter, dated 6 February 1801, to the Earl of Fife requesting financial help. He wrote that:

> Unavoidable and accumulated Misfortunes having reduced me to the very uncomfortable Situation of a Prisoner for Debt in the Fleet Prison, I take the Liberty of humbly requesting your Lordship to realize your kind Intentions [of subscribing to Moore's repairs to the organ at Banff Episcopal Chapel].
>
> The Subscription I received was far short of the regular Price usually Charged for repairing and tuning Organs of that description and as I am confident your Lordship would wish every Tradesman to be paid for his Labor I run no hazard of your Lordship's displeasure in troubling you with this.[105]

While we do not know whether the Earl forwarded any payment to Moore, this was presumably one of several begging requests he sent. It appears that Moore had some success in raising the necessary funds, since he was released from prison on 6 August 1801.[106] He continued in the music business after his incarceration; his will, dated 20 December 1802, records that he was a 'piano forte maker in Upper James Street Golden Square'.[107] One suspects that Moore must have been ill at the time, since he died less than three months later, on 11 March 1803, aged 30.[108]

When one considers the music trade in eighteenth-century Britain, we tend to focus on those professionals whose businesses had a marked and often widespread impact. Evidence of their activities can be ascertained through their

---

[105] GB-A MS 3175/919/1. I am grateful to the University of Aberdeen for allowing the publication of this excerpt.

[106] TNA PRIS10: King's (Queen's) Bench, Fleet, Marshalsea and Queen's Prisons: Miscellanea, no. 156.

[107] TNA PROB 11/1400/174: Will of Stephen Moore, Pianoforte Maker of Saint James Westminster, Middlesex.

[108] Moore was buried on 17 March at St James' Church, Westminster. The burial record gives his address as St James Street (see TNA, RG 4/4181, Collier's Rents, White Street, Southwark, London: Burials 1767–1805). Margaret Debenham wondered if Moore may have been married twice. She discovered a burial record for Elizabeth Moore on 2 October 1795 at the Spa Field Burial Ground. A Stephen Moore then married Elizabeth Stacey at St Leonards, Shoreditch, Hackney on 27 September 1801, although this Stephen Moore, in the record of his marriage, is recorded as a 'bachelor' rather than a 'widower' (see www.debenham.org.uk [accessed 21st November 2024]). In his will, Moore left everything to his wife, Elizabeth, once his funeral expenses and debts were settled. It is doubtful that there was much, if anything, left for her, any young children, and what appears to have been an unborn daughter. Indeed, Elizabeth may have been pregnant at the time of Stephen's death as Sarah Moore, born on 18 September 1803, was baptised at St Leonard's, Shoreditch on 16 October. An earlier child, named Elizabeth, was born on 16 August 1802 and baptised at St Leonards on 5 September. She sadly died on 14 October 1802. Curiously, John Moore, born on 26 December 1798, was baptised at the same church on 6 February 1799. While Elizabeth is recorded as John's mother there is no mention of the father in the online record. Moore was resident in Aberdeen at that time. *International Genealogical Index*, at www.familysearch.org/search/collection/igi.

published editions of music, advertisements in the local or national press, or handwritten records such as diaries, accounts books and ecclesiastical documents. However, there were a number of other persons involved with the trade, whose activities are often missing from the archive record, but who would have offered their services as tutors, repairers and tuners of musical instruments. Indeed, for a musician who fell on hard times, it was a way through which they might earn a living while working from their own homes, and avoid the cost of renting a business premises. However, some who operated in this side of the profession clearly did not have the experience required and could, instead of repairing an instrument, cause considerable damage.

Stephen Moore was a piano maker who fell on hard times and saw organ tuning as an opportunity to make a living, even though he had little or no experience in this profession. He may even have felt confident in himself that he could do the work, but the end result was nothing short of disastrous. Visiting at least four churches, he apparently damaged no less than three of their precious organs and caused the church authorities further expense since these instruments would have required costly repairs.

While the accounts of Moore's activities in the press reveal that individuals would make false or inaccurate claims for financial gain, in the case of Moore it went much further as he sought to undermine the standing of two of Aberdeen's citizens. So acrimonious did the dispute become that Anderson and Ross saw fit to contact a large number of people who had previously been in contact with Moore, so as to mitigate his accusations against them. These letters were collated and published in a pamphlet and, while we cannot rule out any prejudice on behalf of the compilers, this document is a rich source of information. Stephen Moore might only have had a small role in the history of the music trade in Britain, but the reports of his activities in Aberdeen greatly add to our understanding of what was a shadowy and occasionally disreputable part of the British music trade.

Select Bibliography

In compiling this bibliography, it has been necessary to concentrate on key items cited in the chapters above. Regrettably, this has led to the omission of a great deal of interesting materials, which can nevertheless be found cited in the footnotes.

An, Yu Lee, 'Music Publishing in London from 1780 to 1837 as reflected in Music Publishers' Catalogues of Music for Sale: A Bibliography and Commentary' (PhD dissertation, University of Canterbury, 2008).
Banfield, Stephen, *Music in the West Country: Social and Cultural History across an English Region* (Woodbridge, 2018).
Barker, Nicolas, 'Sir Daniel Fleming, 1633–1701: Magistrate, Antiquary and Book-Collector', *The Library*, 23/2 (2022), 191–205.
Barnard, John, and Maureen Bell, *The Early Seventeenth-Century York Book Trade and John Foster's Inventory of 1616* (Leeds, 1994).
Bewick, Thomas, *A Memoir of Thomas Bewick, written by himself* (Newcastle, 1862).
Boalch, Donald H., *Makers of the Harpsichord and Clavichord, 1440–1840* (3rd edn, Oxford, 1995).
Bozarth, George S., and Margaret Debenham in collaboration with David Cripps, 'Piano Wars: The Legal Machinations of London Pianoforte Makers, 1795–1806', *Royal Musical Association Research Chronicle*, 42 (2009), 45–108.
Carter, Stephanie, 'Music Publishing and Compositional Activity in England, 1650–1700' (PhD dissertation, University of Manchester, 2011).
Carter, Stephanie, '"yong beginners, who live in the Countrey": John Playford and the Printed Music Market in Seventeenth-Century England', *Early Music History*, 35 (2016), 95–129.
Carter, Stephanie, 'Thomas Mace's *Musick's Monument* (1676) and his Subscribers in Late Seventeenth-Century England', in Simon D.I. Fleming and Martin Perkins (eds), *Music by Subscription: Composers and their Networks in the British Music-Publishing Trade* (Abingdon, 2022), 21–38.
Carter, Stephanie, and Kirsten Gibson, 'Printed Music in the Provinces: Musical Circulation in Seventeenth-Century England and the Case of Newcastle upon Tyne Bookseller William London', *The Library*, 18 (2017), 428–73.
Carter, Stephanie, and Kirsten Gibson, 'Amateur Music Making Amongst the Mercantile Community of Newcastle upon Tyne from the 1690s to the 1750s', in Stephanie Carter, Kirsten Gibson and Roz Southey (eds), *Music in North-East England, 1500–1800* (Woodbridge, 2020), 192–215.
Chapman, R.W., 'An Inventory of Paper, 1674', *The Library*, 7 (1927), 402–8.
Chartres, J.A., 'Road Carrying in England in the Seventeenth Century: Myth and Reality', *The Economic History Review*, 30 (1977), 73–94.
Cranmer, John Leonard, 'Concert Life and the Music Trade in Edinburgh c.1780–c.1830' (PhD dissertation, University of Edinburgh, 1991).
Crosby, Brian, *A Catalogue of Durham Cathedral Music Manuscripts* (Oxford, 1989).

Cullen, L.M., *Anglo-Irish Trade 1660–1800* (Manchester, 1968).
Davies, Robert, *A Memoir of the York Press, with Notices of Authors, Printers, and Stationers, in the Sixteenth, Seventeenth, and Eighteenth Centuries* (Westminster, 1868).
Day, Cyrus Lawrence, and Eleanore Boswell Murrie, 'Playford *versus* Pearson', *The Library*, 17 (1937), 427–47.
Day, Cyrus Lawrence, and Eleanore Boswell Murrie, *English Song-Books 1651–1702* (London, 1940).
Debenham, Margaret, and Michael Cole, 'Pioneer Piano Makers in London, 1737–74: Newly Discovered Documentary Sources', *Royal Musical Association Research Chronicle*, 44/1 (2013), 55–86.
Edmonds, Bernard B., 'Yorkshire Organ Builders: the Earlier Years', *Bios Journal*, 9 (1985), 42–50.
Fawcett, Trevor, *Bath Entertain'd, Amusements, Recreations and Gambling at the 18th Century Spa* (Bath, 1998).
Fawcett, Trevor, *Bath Commercialis'd, Shops, Trades and Market at the 18th-Century Spa* (Bath, 2002).
Fawcett, Trevor, 'Eighteenth-Century Shops and the Luxury Trade', *Bath History Journal*, 3 (2003), 49–75.
Fawcett, Trevor, *Georgian Imprints: Printing and Publishing at Bath, 1729–1815* (Bath, 2008).
Feather, John, *The Provincial Book Trade in Eighteenth-Century England* (Cambridge, 1985).
Feather, John, *Publishing, Piracy and Politics. An Historical Study of Copyright in Britain* (London, 1994).
Fenlon, Iain, and John Milsom, '"Ruled Paper Imprinted": Music Paper and Patents in Sixteenth-Century England', *Journal of the American Musicological Society*, 37 (1984), 139–63.
Fleming, Michael, and John Bryan, *Early English Viols: Instruments, Makers and Music* (London, 2016).
Fleming, Simon D.I., 'The patterns of music subscription in English, Welsh and Irish cathedrals during the Georgian era', *Early Music*, 48/2 (2020), 205–23.
Fleming, Simon D.I., 'Avison and his Subscribers: Musical Networking in Eighteenth-Century Britain', *Royal Musical Association Research Chronicle*, 49/1 (2018), 21–49.
Fleming, Simon D.I., 'The Gender of Subscribers to Eighteenth-Century Music Publications', *Royal Musical Association Research Chronicle*, 50/1 (2019), 94–152.
Fleming, Simon D.I., 'Foreign Composers, the Subscription Market, and the Popularity of Continental Music in Eighteenth-Century Britain', in Simon D.I. Fleming and Martin Perkins (eds), *Music by Subscription: Composers and their Networks in the British Music-Publishing Trade, 1676–1820* (Abingdon, 2022), 221–41.
Fleming, Simon D.I., and Martin Perkins (eds), *Music by Subscription: Composers and their Networks in the British Music-Publishing Trade, 1676–1820* (Abingdon, 2022).
Gerhold, D., 'Packhorses and Wheeled Vehicles in England, 1550–1800', *The Journal of Transport History*, 14 (1993), 1–26.
Gerhold, D., *Carriers and Coachmasters: Trade and Travel before the Turnpikes* (Chichester, 2005).

Gray, Sarah, 'William Flackton, 1709–1798, Canterbury Bookseller and Musician', in Peter Isaac and Barry McKay (eds), *The Mighty Engine: The Printing Press and its Impact* (Winchester, 2000), 121–30.

Greer, David, 'Manuscript Additions in Early Printed Music', *Music & Letters*, 72 (1991), 523–35.

Greer, David, 'Manuscript Additions in "Parthenia" and other Early English Printed Music in America', *Music & Letters*, 77 (1996), 169–82.

Greer, David, *Manuscript Inscriptions in Early English Printed Music* (Farnham, 2015).

Grieves, Kevin, 'Spreading the News: The Distribution of Bath Newspapers in the Eighteenth Century', *Bath History Journal*, 15 (2017), 58–73.

Griffiths, David, *A Musical Place of the First Quality: A History of Institutional Music Making in York c.1550–1990* (York, [1994]).

Griffiths, David, 'Music in the Minster Close: Edward Finch, Valentine Nalson, and William Knight in Early Eighteenth-Century York', in Rachel Cowgill and Peter Holman (eds), *Music in the British Provinces, 1690–1914* (Aldershot, 2007), 45–59.

Griffiths, David, 'Preston of York: A Restoration Organ-builder and his Family Connections', *The British Institute of Organ Studies Journal*, 46 (2022), 38–44.

Haggerty, Sheryllynne, 'The structure of the trading community in Liverpool, 1760–1810', *Transactions of the Historic Society of Lancashire and Cheshire*, 151 (2002), 97–125.

Hawkins, John, *A General History of the Science and Practice of Music*, 5 vols (London, 1776).

Haxby, David, and John Malden, 'Thomas Haxby of York (1729–1796) – an Extraordinary Musician and Musical Instrument Maker', *York Historian*, 2 (1978), 43–55.

Haxby, David, and John Malden, 'Thomas Haxby – a Note', *York Historian*, 3 (1980), 31–55.

Herissone, Rebecca, 'Playford, Purcell and the Functions of Music Publishing in Restoration England', *Journal of the American Musicological Society*, 63 (2010), 243–90.

Herissone, Rebecca, *Musical Creativity in Restoration England* (Cambridge, 2013).

Howard, Alan, 'Manuscript Publishing in the Commonwealth Period: A Neglected Source of Consort Music by Golding and Locke', *Music & Letters*, 90 (2009), 35–67.

Hulse, Lynn Mary, 'The Musical Patronage of the English Aristocracy, c. 1590–1640' (PhD dissertation, King's College, London, 1992).

Hume, Robert D., 'The Economics of Culture in London, 1660–1740', *Huntington Library Quarterly*, 69 (2006), 487–533.

Humphries, Charles, and William C. Smith, *A Bibliography of the Musical Works Published by the Firm of John Walsh During the Years 1721–1766* (London, 1968).

Hunter, David, 'English Country Psalmodists and Their Publications, 1700–1760', *Journal of the Royal Musical Association*, 115/2 (1990), 220–39.

Hunter, David, 'The Publishing of Opera and Song Books in England, 1703–1726', *Notes*, 47 (1991), 647–85.

Hunter, David, and Rose M. Mason, 'Supporting Handel through Subscription to Publications', *Notes*, 56/1 (1999), 27–93.

James, Kenneth Edward, 'Concert Life in Eighteenth-Century Bath', 2 vols (PhD dissertation, Royal Holloway, London, 1987).
Johnstone, Harry D., 'Instruments, Strings, Wire and other Musical Miscellanea in the Account Books of Claver Morris (1659–1727)', *Galpin Society Journal*, 60 (2007), 29–35.
Johnstone, Harry D., 'Claver Morris, an Early Eighteenth-Century English Physician and Amateur Musician Extraordinaire', *Journal of the Royal Musical Association*, 133/1 (2008), 93–127.
Kassler, Michael (ed.), *The Music Trade in Georgian England* (Farnham, 2011).
Kidson, Frank, *British Music Publishers, Printers and Engravers: London, Provincial, Scottish, and Irish* (New York, 1900, repr. 1967).
Kidson, Frank, 'The Petition of Eleanor Playford', *The Library*, 7 (1916), 346–52.
King, Alec Hyatt, 'Music Circulating Libraries in Britain', *The Musical Times*, 119/1620 (1978), 134–8.
Komlós, Katalin, *Fortepianos and their Music: Germany, Austria, and England, 1760–1800* (Oxford, 1995).
Krummel, D.W., *English Music Printing, 1553–1700* (London, 1975).
Krummel, D.W., 'Venetian Baroque Music in a London Bookshop: The Robert Martin Catalogues, 1633–50', in O. Neighbour (ed.), *Music and Bibliography: Essays in Honour of Alex Hyatt King* (New York, 1980), 1–27.
Luckett, Richard, 'The Playfords and the Purcells', in Robin Myers, Michael Harris and Giles Mandelbrote (eds), *Music and the Book Trade from the Sixteenth to the Twentieth Century* (London, 2008), 45–67.
Mace, Nancy A., 'Charles Rennett and the London Music Sellers in the 1780s: Testing the Ownership of Reversionary Copyrights', *Journal of the Royal Musical Association*, 129 (2004), 1–23.
Mace, Nancy A., 'The Market for Music in the Late Eighteenth Century and the Entry Books of the Stationers' Company', *The Library*, 10/2 (2009), 157–87.
Macleod, Jennifer, 'The Edinburgh Musical Society: Its Membership and Repertoire 1728–1797' (PhD dissertation, University of Edinburgh, 2001).
Magrath, J.R., *The Flemings in Oxford*, 3 vols (Oxford, 1902–24).
Marsh, Christopher, *Music and Society in Early Modern England* (Cambridge, 2010).
Maxted, Ian, 'A Common Culture?: The Inventory of Michael Harte, Bookseller of Exeter, 1615', in Todd Gray (ed.), *Devon Documents in Honour of Margery Rowe* (Tiverton, 1996), 119–28.
McKerrow, R.B. (ed.), *A Dictionary of Printers and Booksellers in England and Ireland and of Foreign Printers of English Books, 1557–1640* (London, 1910).
Money, John, *Experience and Identity: Birmingham and the West Midlands, 1760–1800* (Manchester, 1977).
Murray, Teresa Ann, 'Thomas Morley and the Business of Music in Elizabethan England' (PhD dissertation, University of Birmingham, 2010).
Nex, Jenny, 'Longman & Broderip', in Michael Kassler (ed.), *The Music Trade in Georgian England* (Farnham, 2011), 9–93.
Pearson, David, *Book Trade Bills and Vouchers from Durham Cathedral Library 1634–1740* (Wylam, 1986).
Perkin, M.R. (ed.), *The Book Trade in Liverpool to 1805: A Directory*, Liverpool Bibliographical Society Occasional Publications, 1 (Liverpool, 1981; repr. 1987).

Plomer, Henry R., *A Dictionary of Booksellers and Printers who were at Work in England, Scotland and Irland from 1641 to 1667* (London, 1907).

Pollard, Mary, *Dublin's Trade in Books, 1550–1800* (Oxford, 1989).

Roberts, Christopher, '"I esteem my lot fortunate, in residing in this happy country": Edward Miller, Social Networking and Music Making in Eighteenth-Century Doncaster', in Stephanie Carter, Kirsten Gibson and Roz Southey (eds), *Music in North-East England, 1500–1800* (Woodbridge, 2020), 89–108.

Roger, Alexander, 'Roger Ward's Shrewsbury Stock', *The Library*, 13 (1958), 247–68.

Rose, Stephen, 'Music in the market-place', in Tim Carter and John Butt (eds), *The Cambridge History of Seventeenth-Century Music* (Cambridge, 2008), 55–87.

Rowland, David, 'Clementi's Music Business' in Michael Kassler (ed.), *The Music Trade in Georgian England* (Farnham, 2011), 125–57.

Rylands, W.H., 'Booksellers and Stationers in Warrington, 1639 to 1657, with the Full List of the Contents of a Stationer's Shop There in 1647', *Transactions of the Historic Society of Lancashire and Cheshire*, 37 (1888), 67–115.

Seares, Margaret, 'The Composer and the Subscriber: A case study from the 18th century', *Early Music*, 39/1 (2011), 65–78.

Shay, Robert, and Robert Thompson, *Purcell Manuscripts: The Principal Musical Sources* (Cambridge, 2006).

Simpson, Adrienne, 'A short-title list of printed English instrumental tutors up to 1800, held in British libraries', *Royal Musical Association Research Chronicle*, 6 (1966), 24–50.

Smith, William C., *A Bibliography of the Musical Works Published by the Firm of John Walsh During the Years 1695–1720* (London, 1948).

Smith, William C., and Charles Humphries, *Handel: A Descriptive Catalogue of the Early Editions* (2nd edn, Oxford, 1970).

Southey, Roz, *Music-Making in North-East England during the Eighteenth Century* (Aldershot, 2006).

Southey, Roz, 'Managing a musical career in the eighteenth century: the interweaving of patronage and commercialisation in the careers of Charles Avison and Edward Meredith', in Roz Southey and Eric Cross (eds), *Charles Avison in Context: National and International Musical Links in Eighteenth-Century North-East England* (Abingdon, 2018), 179–213.

Southey, Roz, 'John Hawthorn's shop at the Head of the Side, near the Post Office', in Colin Coleman and Katharine Hogg (eds), *A Handbook for Studies in 18th-Century English Music*, 24 (2020), 1–43.

Sowerby, Scott, and Noah McCormack (eds), *The Memoirs of Sir Daniel Fleming of Rydal Hall from 1633 to 1688* (Carlisle, 2021).

Spring, Matthew, 'Benjamin Milgrove, the Musical "Toy man", and the "guittar" in Bath, 1757–1790', *Early Music*, 4/2 (2013), 317–29.

Spring, Matthew, 'Music Shops and the Music Trade in Eighteenth-Century Bath', *Brio* 50/1 (2013), 3–16.

Spring, Matthew, 'The Musical Life of Bath, 1800-1850', in Nicholas Temperley (ed.), *Musicians of Bath and Beyond, Edward Loder (1809-1865) and his Family* (Woodbridge, 2016), 2–41.

Spring, Matthew, 'Vauxhall Gardens: the provision of music in Bath's pleasure gardens and walks, and the development of Grand Gala Concerts, a

combination of pleasures "after the manner of Vauxhall"', *Bath History Journal*, 15 (2019), 74–92.
Stoker, David, 'The Norwich Book Trades Before 1800', *Transactions of the Cambridge Bibliographical Society*, 8/1 (1981), 79–125.
Stoker, David, '"To all booksellers, country chapmen and others": How the rural population of East Anglia obtained its printed materials (1570–1800)', in Giles Mandelbrote, Robin Myers and Michael Harris (eds), *Fairs, Markets and the Itinerant Book Trade* (London, 2007), 107–36.
Stoker, David, 'The Berry family of Norwich: The rise and fall of a book trade dynasty', *Publishing History*, 74 (2014), 67–95.
Thompson, Robert, 'English Music Manuscripts and the Fine Paper Trade, 1648–1688', 2 vols (PhD dissertation, King's College, London, 1988).
Thompson, Robert, 'Manuscript Music in Purcell's London', *Early Music*, 23 (1995), 605–18.
Thompson, Robert, 'Paper in English Music Manuscripts: 1620–1645', in Andrew Ashbee (ed.), *William Lawes (1602–1645): Essays on his Life, Times and Work* (London, 1998), 143–54.
Thompson, Robert, 'Sources and Transmission', in Rebecca Herissone (ed.), *The Ashgate Research Companion to Henry Purcell* (Farnham, 2012), 13–64.
Thompson, Robert, 'The Elusive Identity of John Playford', in John Cunningham and Bryan White (eds), *Musical Exchange Between Britain and Europe, 1500–1800* (Woodbridge, 2020), 344–56.
Tyson, Blake (ed.), *The Estate and Household Accounts of Sir Daniel Fleming of Rydal Hall, Westmorland* (Carlisle, 2001).
Weber, William, *The Musician as Entrepreneur, 1700–1914: Managers, Charlatans, and Idealists* (Bloomington, 2004).
Willan, T.S., *The English Coasting Trade 1600–1750* (Manchester, 1938).
Williams, N.J., *The Maritime Trade of the East Anglian Ports 1550–1590* (Oxford, 1988).
Wilson, John (ed.), *Roger North on Music* (London, 1959).
Winters, Jennifer, 'The English Provincial Book Trade: Booksellers Stock-lists, c.1520–1640', 2 vols (PhD dissertation, University of St Andrews, 2012).
Wolf, J.K., and E.K. Wolf, 'Rastrology and its Use in Eighteenth-Century Manuscript Studies', in E.K. Wolf and E.H. Roesner (eds), *Studies in Musical Sources and Style: Essays in Honor of Jan LaRue* (Madison, WI, 1990), 232–92.
Woolley, Andrew, 'Manuscript Additions to a Copy of John Playford's *Select Musicall Ayres and Dialogues* in the Dolmetsch Library: A Little-known Source of 17th-century English Music', *The Consort*, 66 (2010), 35–53.

Index

Please note that the page numbers that appear in italics refer to figures and tables.

Abel, Carl Friedrich   95
Aberdeenshire
   Aberdeen   11, 16, 17, 89, 208, 214–20, 222–24
      St Andrew's chapel   220
      St Paul's chapel   208–09, 213–22
Act of Anne   99–100
Alcock, John   80, 88, 93, 197–98
Aldrich, Henry   42, 48
Anderson, Alexander   208–10, 213–22, 224
apprentices   21, 67, 90, 103, 135, 153–54, 156, 159, 161, 168, 194, 208–10, 213–14, 216
Arne, Thomas   *57*, 66, 204
Austria   14
Avison, Charles jnr   *170*, 178, 182, 185–87
Avison, Charles snr   8, 12, 52, *53*, 67, 76, 78, *79*, 80, *80*, 83–87, 89, 93, 95–96, 132–34, 178

Bach, Johann Christian   66, 135, 205, 208
Beilby, Ralph   168, 173, 176
Berkshire
   Reading   12
Bewick, Thomas   16, 168–70, *170–72*, 172–88, *177*
Birmingham   15, 78, *83*, 89, 133, *140*, 146, 190–93, 196–202, 204–06
   Duddeston Gardens   191, 197
   St Bartholomew's chapel   197
   St Martin's church   191, 197, 205
   St Philip's church   191, 196–97
Blow, John   39, *57*, 90
Boccherini, Luigi   135
Bookbinders   10, 25, 27, 173, 202
   Dolliff, Mr.   10
   Foster, Anthony   10, 49
Bookbinding   102
   tools for   25
books
   chapbooks   6
   exchanging of   6, 29, 162
   loaning of   6, 29
   music books   1, 4–5, 7–13, 16–17, 19–21, 23–31, 33, 41, 46, 49–50, 53–62, 75–76, 143, 146, 151, 166, 203, 205, 209
   poetry   6, 28

psalms   4, 7–8, 11, 16, 22, 28, 32, 49, 51, 59–60, 66–67, 72, 78, *83*, 89, 129, *131*, 132–33, 135–38, *138*, 143–47, 197, 199
tracts   6
booksellers   3, 7, 10–11, 15–17, 19–20, 25–29, 31, 33, 47, 73, 75–76, 78, 84, 87–91, 93–94, 96–97, *97–98*, 99, 102, 130, 133, 136, 138, *138–142*, 143–46, 151, 161, 166, 195, 202
   Barley, William   7
   Bassadyne, Thomas   11
   Booth, Robert   27
   Brome, Henry   7
   Bryson, Martin   8
   Bynneman, Henry   7
   Burgess, Edward   90
   Cocke, James   26–27, 29, 31
   Corbett, William   28
   Cotton, Thomas   33
   Davis, Richard   47
   Freeman, William   47
   Hammond, Henry   151, 166
   Hutchinson, Hugh   47
   Langford, Toby   47
   Leake, James   93–94, *97*, 151, 161, 166
   London, William   27–28, 47
   Jordan, Toby   47
   Moseley, Humphrey   7, *57*
   Rackham, John   133, *138*, 145
   Scott, Richard   25–26, 28–29
   Smart, William   195, 203
   Story, John   11
   Tooke, Benjamin   11
   Werdon, William   47
Bookshops   7, 23, 25, 27, 29–30, 49, 145, 151, 170
Boruwlaski, Joseph   163
Boulton, Matthew   205
Bowman, Henry   42–43, 47
Boyce, William   58, 67–68, 78, *81*, 92, 95, *97*, 129
Braithwaite, Richard   30
Bristol   9, 87, 91, 133, 138, *140*, 152–53, 159–60, 166
Burney, Charles   92, 95, 204

Cambridgeshire   133, *142*, 145
   Brampton   24

232 INDEX

Cambridge   2, 11, 24–25, 27, 64, 88, 90, 93, *142*
  Ely   64
  Peterborough   9, 63
Camidge, John   69, 143
catalogues   2, 10, 19, 28–29, 32, 47, 51–52, *53–62*, 63, 90, 114, 116, *122*, *127–28*, 135–36, 144, 146, 164, 204
cathedral singing men   7, 27, 43, 50, 65, 77, 87, 90, 180, 182, 191–92, 195–96
  see also music sellers
Cavendish family   24, 45–46
Chapel Royal   45, 92, *97–98*, 134
Cheshire
  Warrington   27
circulating libraries   9, 12, 88, 93, 133, 135, 145–46, 151–52, 161, 175
Clark, Jeremiah   146, 198–99, 203
Clementi, Muzio   9, 164, 205, 209, 211
clubs and societies   2, 51, 77, 190, 211
  Aberdeen Musical Society   217, 222
  Canterbury catch club   91
  Edinburgh Musical Society   174, 183, 216
  Freemasons   170, *172*, 186–87
  Gentlemen of the Forest Hunt   170, *172*, 187
  Newcastle Musical Society   *172*, 177, 182
  Newcastle Volunteer Band   170, *172*
  Sunderland Musical Society   *172*, 175
  York Musical Society   67, 71–72
concerts   2–3, 66, 68, 71, 73, 86, 137, 149, 155, 157, 161, *165*, 170, 177–83, 186–91, 195–99, 201
  benefit concerts   66, 84, 87, 160–61, 170, 175, 181–82, 187, 191, 195
  promotor of   164, 170, *170–72*, 173–74, 178, 186–87, 190
  tickets for   9, 16, 86–87, 91, 137, 144, 161, 165, 170, 174, 176, *177*, 177–78, 180, 182, 185–87, 203
copyright   99–101, 105, 111–17, *120*
Copyright Act (1801), The   99
Corelli, Arcangelo   53–54, 62, 63, *131*, 151
County Durham   *141*
  Durham (city)   27–28, 84, 87, 100, *141*, 170, *171*, 182
    Cathedral   31, 47–48, 87, 168, 170, 176, 178, 180, 182, 187, 196, 215
  Gateshead   48, 64, 170, *171*
  Stockton   87, *141*
  Sunderland   87, 170, *172*, 175
Croft, William   36, 50, 91–93, 129
Cumberland   26
  Carlisle   25–26, 28, 64
    Cathedral   64

Eden valley   18
  Whitehaven   8, 133, *142*, 215
cutlery   176, 188

dancing masters   5, 170, *171*, 176, 191–92, 201
  Farlo, James   192, 201–03, 206
  Kinlock, Adam   *171*, 173–74, 183, *184–85*, 185
  Kinlock, Alexander   *171*, 173–74, 176, 183, *184–85*, 185
  Picken, Andrew   *172*, 172
Dawes, Sir D'Arcy   50–51, 64–65
Defoe, Daniel   18, 33
Denmark   14
Derbyshire   45, 133, *141*
  Mansfield   46
Devon   88, *142*
  Exeter   9, 27, 63, 94, *142*
Dibdin, Charles   100–01, 145, 166
distribution   3, 10, 16, 19–20, 23, 25, 27, 31, 33, 45
Durham *see* County Durham

Ebdon, Thomas   67, 89, 130, 168, *171*, 176, 180
Edinburgh   11, 14–15, 25, 87, 89, 94, *97*, 137, 152, 167, 210–14, 216–17
Essex   10, 133, *140*, 145

Falle, Philip   41
Farbeck, John   28
festivals   68, 179–80, 187–88, 191
Fiennes, Celia   26
Fleming, Barbara   31–32
  music lessons   32
Fleming, Sir Daniel   18–21, 26–33
  archive of   18
  buying books   19, 26–29, 32
  commonplace book   32
  daughters of   30–31
  library of   18, 28, 32
  Rydal Hall   18, 31
  son of   32
Fletcher, Barbara *see* Fleming, Barbara
Fletcher, Lady Mary   30
Forfarshire
  Dundee   214–16
  Montrose   214–16
France   14, 23, 35, 135, 182
Fraser, Peter   50, *82*
Fydell, Thomas   45

Gamble, John   *7, 57*
Garth, John   52, 67, *83*, 100, 135
George, James   154

Germany   14, 135
Giardini, Felice   103, 198
Gloucestershire   133
　Gloucester   43–44, 46, 103, 191
　　Cathedral   47
Gostling, John   45
Gostling, William   90

Hampshire
　Southampton   138
Handel, George Frideric   36, 53, 56–58, 63, 67, 134, 136, 144–45, 182, 198, 208
　Messiah   159, 179
Harwood, Edward   103, *104*, 105, *107–10*
Hatton family *see also* Jeffreys, George
Hawdon, Matthias   170, *171*, 174–83, *184*, 185–88
hawkers   153
　see also pedlars; newsmen
Hawkins, John   63
Hayes, Philip   90, 192
Hayes, William   82, 95–96, 130, 192
Hellier, Sir Samuel   193–94, 205
Henstridge, Daniel   44–46, 90
Herschel, William   157–58
Hook, James   101, 111–15, 117, *118–28*
Howgill, William   8, 72

India   14
instrument accessories   3, 134, 152, 157, 164, 190, 206
　bridges   1, 66, 152, 203
　reeds   1, 134, 152, 154, 200, 203, 221
　rosin   1, 152
　strings   1, 4, 6, 51, 65–66, 69, 71, 134, 152–54, 193, 200, 203
instrument makers   6, 9–10, 19, 31, 65–66, 73–74, *97–98*, 134, 152–53, 156–58, 164, 192, 194, 196–97, 199, 206, 209, 216
　Agutter, Ralph   12
　Banks, Benjamin   12, *142*
　Broadwood, John   14, 70, 208–09, 211, 213
　Fairbridge, Mr.   12
　Moore, Stephen   16, 207–10, 212–24
　Norman, Barak   6
　Pamphilon family   10
　Preston, John   9, 112, *131*, 136–37, *139*
　Tomlinson, Edward   73
　Tomlinson, Thomas Haxby   73
　Vesey, Richard   65, 74
　Watson, John   69, 74
　Zumpe, Johannes   154, 208
　see also music sellers; organ builders; piano manufacture; virginal makers
instrument making   2, 32, 152–53, 190, 192

see also instrument makers; music sellers; piano manufacture
instrument tuning   1, 7, 51, 64–68, 175, 192–93, 195–96, 198, 200, 203, 206, 213–14, 216–24
instruments   1–3, 6, 8–9, 12, 14–15, 21, 24, 27, 29–31, 51, *55–56*, *61*, 66, 68, 71–72, 88, 102, *106*, *108–10*, 115–16, 134, 137, 143–44, 149, 152–61, 164, 166–67, 175–76, 190, 192–95, 199, 201–02, 206–07, 217, 224
　bassoon   1, 71, 82, 135, 154, 201, 203, 205
　cittern   69, 135, 154
　clavichord   30, 193
　flute   1, 17, 51, *53–55*, *57–59*, *61–62*, 71, *81–82*, 85, 88, *106–10*, 115–16, *127–28*, *130–31*, 132, 134–36, 143, 151, 154, 158, 160, 201–03
　guittar   1, 669, *106–07*, 132, 143, 154, 156–57, 159–60, 163, 200, 202
　harp   4, 69, 135, 152, 163, 200
　harpsichord   30, 51, *61–62*, 65, 69, *70*, *80–83*, *109–10*, *121*, *124*, *126–27*, *130–31*, 132, 135, 144, 159, 162–63, 192–96, 198–99, 206, 208, 216, 218
　hautboy   1, *54*, 71, *81*, 132, 134, 154, 203, 205, 221
　lute   6, 11, 32, 39, 69, 153
　organ   9, 15, 25, 32, 39, 45, 47, 52, *53–55*, 62, 63–72, 74, 78, *80–81*, *83*, 91, *131*, 162, 188, 191–92, 194–96, 198–200, 202, 207–08, 212, 213–24
　piano   14, 66, 69–71, 73, *109–110*, 112–13, *121*, *124*, *126–127*, *131*, 135, 152, 159–60, 162, 165–66, 195, 198–200, 202–03, 207–14, 216
　pipes   1, 154, 156, 169
　spinet   51, 65, 68–69, 72–73, *97*, 134, 144, 195, 198, 200
　violin   1, 5–6, 9, 51–52, *53–56*, *58–62*, 69, 71–72, 78, *80–82*, 84, 86, 88, 91–92, 105, *106–07*, *110*, *126*, *130–31*, 132, 134–36, 143, 151–54, 156, 160, 198, 200–03, 212
　virginal   3–4, 9, 21, 25, 28, 31
internet shopping   2
Ireland   10, 99, 101–03, 111, 116
　Dublin   84, 99–102, 111–12, 115–17, *118–28*, 154
Italy   14, 94
　Cremona   9, 202

Jackson, Edward   44, 46
Jeffreys, George   44
Jenkins, John   46

Kent   25, 92, *142*
    Canterbury   16, 65, 75–76, 89–93, *98*, *142*
        Cathedral   45–46, 90, *97–98*
        Maidstone   9, 91, 93, *97–98*
        Margate   12, 91
    Rochester   44, 46, 90–91, 93, *97–98*
King, William   44

Lake District   18
Lancashire   133, *142*, 179–80
    Liverpool   13, 16, 94, 99–100, 102–03, *104*, 105, *106–10*, 111, 117, *141*, 187
Lauderdale, Earl of   25
Lawes, Henry   7
Leicestershire   *141*, 199
    Leicester   9, *141*
leisure, commercialisation of   14–16, 148–49, 167, 190
Licensing Act (1662), The   11
Lincolnshire   25, 133, 137–38, *140*
    Boston   137, *140*
    Horncastle   137, *140*
    Lincoln   27, 137, *140*
        Cathedral   64
    Louth   68–69, 137, *140*
    Melton Mowbray   137, *141*
    Retford   137, *141*
    Spalding   137, *140*
    Stamford   137, *140*
Locke, Matthew   39, 41, 47
London   1–4, 6–19, 21, 23–29, 32, 41, 44–46, 48, 51–52, 63–64, 67–68, 70–72, 74, 76, 78, *80–83*, 83–91, 93–97, *97–98*, 99–100, 102–03, 105, *106*, *108–110*, 111–12, 114–17, *118*, *120–21*, 127, 129, *130–31*, 132–38, *139*, 143–44, 146–47, 152, 154–55, 158, 160–61, 163–64, 166–67, 190–206, 208, 211, 213, 216, 222
    Fleet Street   5, 10, *97*
    London Bridge   10, 93
    St Paul's churchyard   5, 11, *98*
    Temple   5, 10, 32, *98*
    Westminster Abbey   41, *97*, 198
Lowe, Edward   32

Mace, Thomas   24, 32, 50, 76, 145
manuscript paper *see* music paper
Master of Ceremonies *see* Nash, Richard 'Beau'
mathematical instruments   12, 17
Méguin, A.B.   37–40, 45
Meredith, Edward   *106*, *110*, *171*, 180, 182, 187

Miller, Edward   16, 67, 72, 129, *130–31*, 131–38, *138–42*, 143–47, 199
    The Psalms of David   16, 67, 72, 129, *131*, 132–33, 135–38, *138–42*, 143–47, 199
Morris, Claver   151
music books *see* books, music books
music copying   3–5, 7, 10, 15, 19, 22, 41, 43–45, 47–48, 51, 67, 74, 159, 196, 203
music copyists   38–39, 41–44, 46–48, 51, 67, 195–96, 203, 206
    Benson, Thomas   51
    Cooper, John   51
    Greggs, William   47
    Harrison, Nicholas   48
    Husbands, Charles   42
    Merro, John   43–44
    Owen, Matthew   47
    Smith, Francis   42
    Strogers, Nicholas   4
music engravers   14–15, 22, 42, 78, 85–86, 89, 102, 116, 130, *139*, 146, 154, 196–97
music making   1, 3, 15–16, 18–19, 21, 31, 33, 178, 190
    recreational (domestic, amateur)   18, 21, 31, 33, 50–51, 67, 77, 88–89, 134, 143, 146–47, 190, 193, 208
    see also clubs and societies; festivals
music paper   1, 3–5, 10, 16, 22–23, 27, 34–50, 66–67, 71, 73, 112, 116, 134, 153, 199, 203
    compound rastra   34–36, 39–42, 45, 48
music patents   5, 13, 36–37, 69, 202, 212
    Abell, John   13
    Allde, Edward   37
    Byrd, William   4, 11, 37
    Hardanville, Susan   37
    Morley, Thomas   5, 37
    Tallis, Thomas   4, 11, 37
music printers   4, 7, 19, 40, *80–83*, 89, 91, 93, 95–96, 99, 103, *110*, 111–13, 115–16, 129–30, *130–31*, 133, 146, 154
    Barber, Joseph   16, 52, *53*, 75–76, 80, *80*, 83–91, 93, 96, *171*, 175
    Broome, Michael   78, 196–97
    Davis, Richard   47
    Day, John   4
    Cooper, Richard   14
    East, Thomas   4, 22
    Forbes, John   11
    Godbid, William   22
    Harper, Thomas   22
    Lekprevik, Robert   11
    Pearson, William   40–41, *59*–60
    Playford, Anne   22
    Playford, John jnr   22–23

Rastell, John   4
Vautrollier, Thomas   11
see also music sellers
music printing   4–6, 8, 10–11, 13, 22–23, 36–37, 40–41, 72, 76–77, 85, 89, 96, 101, 111, 116, 132–33, 167, 190, 209
   unauthorised reprints   12, 16, 99–102, 105, 111, 114,
music publishers *see* music sellers
music publishing   2, 5–6, 9–11, 13–15 19, 72, 75–76, 95–96, 105, 129, 132, 134–36, 143, 146, 160, 164, 210
   interrelated trades with   4–7
music sellers
   Angus, Alexander   17
   Ashley, John   *150*, 152, 163–64, 166
   Atkinson, John   1
   Atkinson, Joseph   17
   Babb, Samuel   9, 114
   Banks, Henry   2, 49
   Barber, Abraham   11
   Binns, John   137, *139*, 143–44
   Birchall, Robert   9, 116–17
   Bland, Anne   100–03, 105, 111–17, *118–28*
   Bremner, Robert   15, *80*, 130, 133, 136, 204–05
   Broderip, Francis Fane   *130–31*, 135–36, 209, 214
   Brooks, John   *150*, 153, 155–56, 159
   Carr, John   1, 5–6, 8, 23, 29, 75
   Carr, Robert   5
   Chew, James   192–96, 204, 206
   Cooke, Benjamin   58, *81*, 83–86, 96, 115, *119–20, 123, 125*
   Corri, Domenico   15, 72
   Dale, Joseph   9, 102
   Flackton, William   16, 65, 67, 75–76, *82*, 89–96, *97–98*
   Fletcher, William   192, 197–98
   Foster, John   27, 49–50
   Gawler, William   9, 164
   Hall, William   198
   Hare, John   6, *53*, *56–58*, *61–62*
   Hawthorn, John   12, *171*, 175
   Haxby, Thomas   49, 64–69, *70*, 70–74, 132–33, *139*, 143
   Hildyard, Francis   11, 50–51
   Hildyard, John   50–52, *53–62*, 63, 67
   Hime, Maurice   101–02, 111–12, 115–17, *118–25, 127, 141*
   Holl, John   202–03, 206
   Holl, Thomas   192, 202–03, 206
   Hudgebut, John   5–6
   Hunt, Richard   11, *59*
   Johnson, John   9, 78, *80–81*, *83*, 86, 95, *97*, *130*, 132, 134–35, 161,
   Knapton, Samuel   66, 71–74, *138*, 143
   Lintern, James   *150*, 152, 160–61, *162*, 162–64, 166–67
   Livingstone, Alexander   6
   Longman, James   *130*, 135, 161
   Longman and Broderip   8–9, 12, 14, 101–02, 105, 113–15, 117, 129, *130–31*, 135, 160, 209–10, 213, 216
   Mathews, James (or Matthews)   *150*, 164, *165*, 165–67
   Meares, Richard   6
   Milgrove, Benjamin   *150*, 152–53, 155–57, 159–60, 166–67
   Miller, Thomas   132–33, 145
   Miller, William Richard Beckford   *131*, 133
   Playford, Henry   6, 10, 35, 40, *57*, 75
      A General Catalogue   10
   Playford, John   5–8, 13, 16, 19, 21–23, 26, 29, 31–35, 45–46, 48, *59*, 76
      Introduction to the Skill of Music   34, *59*
      Musick's Hand-maid   16, 18–23, 26–27, 29, 31, 33
   Preston, John   9, 112, *131*, 136–37, *139*
   Prior, William   11–12
   Pye, John Bridge   16, 99–103, *104*, 105, *106–110*, 111–12, 114–15, 117, *118–28*
   Rhames, Elizabeth   111, 115, *118–19*, *123–24*
   Roger, Estienne   14
   Salter, Humphrey   11, *59*
   Scott, Samuel   5
   Shaw, Joseph   72–73
   Swinney, Myles   133, *140*, 146
   Tylee, Henry Dixon   159
   Tylee, Joseph   *150*, 156–59, 166–67
   Underwood, Thomas   148, *150*, 152–56, 158–59, 162, 166–67
   Urbani, Pietro   212, 216–18
   Walsh, John jnr   76, 78, *80–83*, 87, 89, 93, 95, 96, *98*, 136
   Walsh, John snr   8, 14, *53–62*, *63*, 76, 78, 80, *80–83*, 87
   Ward, Roger   27
   Watlen, John   212–13
   Welcker, Peter   9, 52, 112, *130*, 135, 204
   Weller, Edward   100–03, 105, 111–17, *118–28*
   Whitaker, John   111–12
   Whitehead, Thomas   *150*, 156, 159–60
   Wilkinson, Charles   129, *131*, 136
   Woodward, Michael   192, 199–201, 206

236   INDEX

see also dancing masters; instrument makers; organ builders; music printers; virginal makers
music selling   1, 4, 6, 8, 10, 12, 18–19, 23–24, 27, 33, 49–51, 63, 66–69, 71–74, 78, 84, 87–88, 96–97, 99–101, 134, 144–46, 151–54, 158, 161–63, 167, 175, 190, 194, 198, 200, 202–03, 206
  auctions   8, 29, 84–86, 160, 203, 210
  exchange   6, 161–62, 178, 202–03
  hire   12, 149, 152, 157–59, 161, 163–64, 167, 202–3
  second-hand market   8, 22, 29–30, 49, 51, 63, 84, 90, 161, 203
music shops   2, 5–8, 10–12, 15, 23, 26, 32, 49–50, 66–67, 70–73, 75–76, 86–87, 89, 91–92, 103, *110*, 111–12, 130, 132, 134–35, 137, 143–44, 148–49, *150*, 152–67, 170, *172*, 197–99, 201–04, 206, 208, 211–12, 221
  performances within   5, 7, 155
  see also music warehouses
music teachers   1, 6–8, 15, 21, 24, 30–31, 48, 51, 88–89, 95, 103, *108*, 152, 157–59, 162, 165–69, *172*, 175, 181, 185–88, 190, 192–93, 195, 197–99, 201, 203–06, 216
  Geminiani, Francesco   54, *56*, *61*, 95, *97*
  Moss, John   24
  Harris, Joseph   192, 205
  Hutchinson, William   31, 47
  Peacock, John   169, *172*
  Radcliffe, James   192, 195–96, 206
  Thompson, William   89
music warehouses   2, 8, 12, 16, 26, 66, 72–73, *106–10*, 149, 161–65, 167, 199, 201, 203–04, 206
  see also music shops

Nares, James   *61*, 64, 66, *79*, *83*, 135
Nash, Richard 'Beau'   148, 154
Newsmen   153
  see also hawkers; pedlars
Nine Years' War   35
Noble, William   42–43
Norfolk   88, 133, 138, *141*, 144–45
  King's Lynn   25, 88
  Norwich   9, 27, 45, 84, 88, 133, *141*, 144–45
North, Roger   46
North America   13, 157
Northamptonshire   44, 133, *141*, 207
Northumberland   133, *141*
  Alnwick   87
  Berwick upon Tweed   133, *141*

Newcastle upon Tyne   1, 10–12, 16–17, 25–28, 46–47, 52, *53*, 70, 75–76, 80, *80*, 84–89, 94, 133, *140*, 168–70, *170–72*, 173–77, *177*, 178–83, 185–88, 208, 215
  All Saints' church   182
  St Andrew's church   170, 188
  St John's church   175
  St Nicholas's church   174–75, *177–78*, 181–82
  Theatre Royal   174
  North Shields   87, 172, *172*
Nottinghamshire   133, 137, *141*
  Newark   137, *141*
  Southwell   64

organ builders   9, 63–65, 68, 70, 152, 196, 199, 213, 216
  Adam of Darlington   9
  Adcock, Abraham   194–95
  Brownless (or Brownlace), Ambrose   64
  Caddick, Thomas   194–95
  Dallam, Marc-Antoine   64
  Dallam, Robert   64
  Donaldson, John   70, 74, *171*, 208, 215, 220–22
  Gray, William   192, 195–96, 203
  Laycock, Henry   192, 200–01, 206
  Loosemore, John   9, 63
  Preston family   63–64
  Smith, Christopher   194
  Swarbrick, Thomas   191
  Thamar, Thomas   9, 63
  Woodward, Michael see music sellers
organ building   63, 68–69, 74, 206, 207
organists   *53*, *61*, 64, 89–90, 92, 97–98, 100, 105, 112, 129, 132–33, 138, *139*, 143, 157–58, 162, 168, 170, *170–72*, 174–78, 181–82, 186, 188, 193, 197, 199, 205, 207, 214, 217, 218–19
  mending organs   207, 216–19
  tuning organs   157, 193, 207, 214, 218–19
Oxfordshire   *140*
  Oxford   2, 10–11, 27, 32, 38–42, 47, 64, 90, 93, 95, *107*, 133, 137, *140*, 199

Partridge, George   194
pedlars   24
  see also hawkers; newsmen
Pepys, Samuel   21, 24
Petty, William   31
piano manufacture   208
Pierrepoint, Evelyn (2nd Duke of Kingston)   159

Pixell, John   78, *83*, 197
Playford family *see* music printers; music sellers
Pleyel, Ignace Joseph   205
Portugal   14
provincial printing   2, 10–11
psalmody   133
Purcell, Henry   23, 39, 43–44, *53*, 75, 90

Radcliffe, James   192, 195–96, 206
Raylton, William   90
royalty
  Anne   148
  Charlotte   208
  James II   87, 148
  Mary of Moderna   148
ruled paper *see* music paper
Russia   14
  St Petersburg   185

Shropshire   133, *142*
  Shrewsbury   7, 27, *142*
Simpson, Christopher   7, 42
Simpson, John   82–83, 86, 92–93, 98, *172*, 175
Somerset   133, *142*
  Bath   14–15, *81*, 93–94, *97*, 138, *142*, 148–49, *150*, 151–61, *161*, 162–64, *165*, 165–67
    Abbey   149, 157, 161, 163, 167
    Lady Huntingdon's Chapel   156–57
    market-place   165
    New Assembly Rooms   157, 163–64
    Royal Theatre   159
    Spring Gardens   157, 165
    Villa Gardens   157
Stabilini, Girolamo   216–18
Staffordshire   133, *142*, 193–94
  Wombourne   193–94
Stationers' Company   11, 59, 100–03, 105, *106–10*, 111, 113–15, 117, *118–28*
stationery   4–5, 9, 17, 23, 27, 29, 33, 50, 202–03
Storace, Stephen   72, 101, 144, 205
Stuart, George   11
subscribers   50, *61*, 67–68, 74–78, 86, 89, 92–95, *97–98*, 129, 131–33, 135–38, 143, 145, 147, 168, 170, 179–80
  traders as   10, 67, 71–72, 74–76, 80, *80–83*, 84–89, 91, 93–94, *97–98*, 130, 133, 136–37, *138–42*, 143–44, 146, 192, 197, 199
subscription   7, 16, 24, 67, 72, 75–78, 86–87, 91–93, 95–96, 129, 131–33, 136–37, 143, 145–46, 161, 168, 174, 176, 178–82, *184*, 188, 203, 223
  collecting of   1, 7, 29, 50, 75, 88, 138, 145, 154, 203
Suffolk   132–33, 138, *138*, 145
  Beccles   133, *138*
  Bungay   132–33, *138*, 145
  Bury St Edmunds   88, 133, 145
Sussex
  Brighton   12

Thackray, Thomas   66, 69, 143
Thompson, Thomas (of Newcastle)   *172*, 175, 182, 187
Three Choirs Festival   191, 203
toyshops   12, 149, *150*, 157, 167
transport   2, 40, 84, 99
  coastal shipping   13, 25, 29
  pack-horse   26, 46
  ports   13, 25–26, 102, 133
  postal service   13, 28, 46
  river navigation   25, 193–94
  roads   13, 25–26, 137
  stagecoach   13
  turnpike roads   13
  wagoners   26, 46

Vernon family   193, 204
  Hanbury Hall   193–94
virginal makers   3, 9
  Marsam, Andrew   9
  Treasorer, William   3
  Tyves, Lodeuyke   3

Wainwright, Richard   103, 105, *109*
Waits   71–72, 169–70, *170*–72, 175
Wass, Robert   98, 134
West Indies   14
Westmorland   16, 18, 26
  Ambleside   18, 30
    Rydal Hall   18, 31
  Appleby   30
  Kendal   26–27, 29, 33
  Kirkby Stephen   30
  Milnthorpe   26
  Warcop   30
  Windermere   18
Wilson, John   32
Wilton, Charles Henry   103, 105, *109–10*
Wiltshire   *142*
  Salisbury   9, 12, 64, *142*, 153, 164
Withy, John   43, 45
Withy, Richard   45
Wood, Anthony   47
Worcestershire   192–93, 201, 204

Bromsgrove   201–03
Worcester   15, 43, 45, 190–96, 201–04, 206
   Cathedral   191–95, 203
Wright, Thomas   67, 170, *172*, 174, 182, 188

Yorkshire   25, 50, 68, 133–34, 137–38, *138*, 143, 170, 175–76, 178–79
   Aston   68
   Beverley   68, *139*, 170, *171*, 178
   Doncaster   16, 129, 132–33, 136, 138, *139*, 146
   Halifax   68, 133, *139*
   Hull   25, 68, *139*, 170, *172*, 178, 181, 186
   Leeds   50, 68, 72, 137, *139*, 143–44, 180
   Ripon   64
   Scarborough   68
   Wakefield   11, *139*, 170
   Whitby   133, *139*,
   York   2, 9–11, 15, 25, 27, 49–51, 63–66, 68–69, 71–74, 87, 89, 93–94, *98*, 132–33, *138*–39, 143–45
      Assembly Rooms   66
      Minster   9, 49–51, *61*, 64–65, 67–68, 74, 143
      St Michael-le-Belfrey   64–65, 68
Young, Elizabeth   94–95
Young, Sir William   94

Music in Britain, 1600–2000

Titles originally published under the series title Music in Britain, 1600–1900 can be found on our website.

New titles published under the series title Music in Britain, 1600–2000
ISSN 2053-3217

Hamilton Harty: Musical Polymath
Jeremy Dibble

Thomas Morley: Elizabethan Music Publisher
Tessa Murray

*The Advancement of Music in Enlightenment England:
Benjamin Cooke and the Academy of Ancient Music*
Tim Eggington

George Smart and Nineteenth-Century London Concert Life
John Carnelley

The Lives of George Frideric Handel
David Hunter

Musicians of Bath and Beyond: Edward Loder (1809–1865) and his Family
edited by Nicholas Temperley

*Conductors in Britain, 1870–1914:
Wielding the Baton at the Height of Empire*
Fiona M. Palmer

Ernest Newman: A Critical Biography
Paul Watt

*The Well-Travelled Musician:
John Sigismond Cousser and Musical Exchange in Baroque Europe*
Samantha Owens

Music in the West Country: Social and Cultural History Across an English Region
Stephen Banfield

British Musical Criticism and Intellectual Thought, 1850–1950
edited by Jeremy Dibble and Julian Horton

*Composing History: National Identities
and the English Masque Revival, 1860–1920*
Deborah Heckert

With Mornefull Musique: Funeral Elegies in Early Modern England
K. Dawn Grapes

Music for St Cecilia's Day: From Purcell to Handel
Bryan White

*Before the Baton: Musical Direction and
Conducting in Stuart and Georgian Britain*
Peter Holman

*Organ-building in Georgian and Victorian England:
The Work of Gray & Davison, 1772–1890*
Nicholas Thistlethwaite

*Musical Exchange between Britain and Europe, 1500–1800:
Essays in Honour of Peter Holman*
edited by John Cunningham and Bryan White

The Symphonic Poem in Britain, 1850–1950
edited by Michael Allis and Paul Watt

Music in North-East England, 1500–1800
edited by Stephanie Carter, Kirsten Gibson, Roz Southey

*British Music, Musicians and Institutions, c. 1630–1800:
Essays in Honour of Harry Diack Johnstone*
Edited by Peter Lynan and Julian Rushton

John Gunn: Musician Scholar in Enlightenment Britain
George Kennaway

Exhibitions, Music and the British Empire
Sarah Kirby

Opera and Politics in Queen Anne's Britain, 1705–1714
Thomas McGeary

The Life and Music of Elizabeth Maconchy
Erica Siegel

Music in Edwardian London
Simon McVeigh

*The Cultural Politics of Opera, 1720–1742:
The Era of Walpole, Pope, and Handel*
Thomas McGeary

The Royal Musical Association: Creating Scholars, Advancing Research
Leanne Langley

Printed in the United States
by Baker & Taylor Publisher Services